Tourism, Leisure and Recreation Series

Series Editors
Gareth Shaw and Allan Williams

Tourism and Sex

Tourism and Sex

Culture, Commerce and Coercion

Edited by Stephen Clift and Simon Carter

PINTER
London and New York

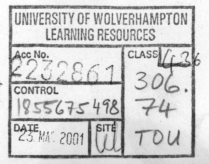

First published 2000 by Pinter
A Continuum imprint

Wellington House, 125 Strand, London WC2R 0BB, England
370 Lexington Avenue, New York, NY 10017–6550, USA

British Library Cataloguing-in-Publication Data

A catalogue record for this book is available from the British Library.

ISBN 1-85567-549-8 (hardback)
1-85567-636-2 (paperback)

Library of Congress Cataloging-in-Publication Data

Tourism and sex: culture, commerce and coercion/
edited by Stephen Clift and Simon Carter.
    p. cm. — (Tourism, leisure and recreation series)
    Includes bibliographical references (p.   ) and index.
ISBN 1-85567-549-8 (hb) — 1-85567-636-2 (pb)
1. Sex tourism.   2. Travelers—Sexual behavior.
I. Clift, Stephen, 1952–.   II. Carter, Simon, 1960–.   III. Series.
HQ117.T68   1999
306.74—dc21   99–25151
                                                               CIP

Typeset by Textype Typesetters, Cambridge
Printed and bound in Great Britain by Biddles Ltd, Guildford & King's Lynn

Contents

List of figures

List of tables

The contributors

Damiano Abeni, MD, MPH and specialist in infectious diseases, is a senior epidemiologist with the clinical Epidemiology Unit of the Istituto Dermopatico dell'Immacolata–IRCCS in Rome. His recent publications focused on surveillence and modelling of the HIV epidemic and on risk behaviours for HIV infection, and include chapters in the book *Drug Injecting and HIV Infection: Global Dimensions and Local Responses* (Taylor and Francis, London, 1998). He is now active in the field of dermatoepidemiology and evidence-based dermatology.

Paula Black is a lecturer in sociology at the University of Manchester. She has also lectured at the University of Derby. Her previous research has included work around HIV and sexuality; auto/biographical research; and an investigation of the sexual experiences of British tourists abroad. She is currently undertaking research into beauty therapy.

Michael Bloor has a personal chair in medical sociology in the School of Social Sciences at Cardiff University. His recent publications include *The Sociology of HIV Transmission* (published by Sage) and *Selected Writing in Medical Sociological Research* (1997) for Avebury.

Hannah Bradby has a BA (Hons) in human sciences from Oxford, an MSc in medical sociology from Royal Holloway College and a PhD from the University of Glasgow. She is currently employed at the Medical Research Council Medical Sociology Unit in Glasgow on the 'Ethnicity religion and health' programme and has published on the sociology of ethnic identity and its expression through food, language and social networks.

Simon Carter completed his first degree and doctorate at the University of Lancaster as a mature student, after working for several years in industry. He is currently a Research Fellow at the MRC Medical Sociology Unit, University of Glasgow. His research interests are in the areas of the sociology of risk, the sociology of tourism, and science and technology studies. In recent research he has examined the health aspects of international travel and tourism with particular reference to sexual risk.

Stephen Clift is Professor of Health Education at the Centre for Health Education and Research, Canterbury Christ Church University College. He is particularly interested in the health dimensions of international travel and tourism, and his most recent research projects have focused on the sexual behaviours and risks of gay men on holiday and the application of social cognitive theory to malaria prophylaxis adherence among tourists visiting malarious areas. He is currently working as a consultant to the World Health Organization's 'Healthy Travel and Tourism Initiative', and is providing training/evaluation support to the 'Living for Tomorrow' project, based at the Nordic Institute for Women's Studies and Gender Research at the University of Oslo.

Jason Ditton is currently Director of the Scottish Centre for Criminology in Glasgow and Professor of Criminology in the Faculty and Department of Law at the University of Sheffield. He was previously at the University of Glasgow. His current research interests include the use of 'ecstasy' by young people, the fear of crime and the effectiveness of city-centre CCTV.

Lawrence Elliott is currently Director of Health Services Research in the School of Nursing and Midwifery, University of Dundee. He has also held research posts within Glasgow University and the Greater Glasgow Health Board. His current research interests include the long-term impact of needle exchanges, methadone and benzodiazepine prescribing, peer interventions for drug injectors and young sexually active people.

Stephen Farrall is currently Research Officer at the Centre for Criminological Research, University of Oxford. He previously worked at the Scottish Centre for Criminology. His current research interests include the work of the probation service, the fear of crime, ethnic-minority attitudes to crime and why people cease offending.

Kathleen Ford received her PhD from Brown University in Providence, Rhode Island, in 1976 in population studies. She has held positions at the National Center for Health Statistics and at Johns Hopkins University before moving to the University of Michigan in 1985. She has been involved in research related to HIV prevention in the USA and in Indonesia since about 1990.

Simon Forrest is currently Research Fellow in the Department of Sexually Transmitted Diseases, University College London. He has been involved in studies of the sexual attitudes and lifestyles of injecting drug users, gay men and young people. He has also contributed to the development of sex education teaching materials and resources for young people.

Catherine Goujon is in charge of the Department of Immunizations and Advice for Travellers at the Hospital of the Pasteur Institute in Paris. Since 1995, she has been General Secretary of the Société de Médecine des Voyages; she has collaborated on the *Guide d'Information et de Conseils Pratiques* published by the Society. She was recently involved in the sixth ESCMID postgraduate education course in Montpellier, organized by the European Society of Clinical Microbiology and Infectious Diseases, the subject of which was travel medicine.

Laurence Gruer is currently Director of the Addictions, Mental and Sexual Health Team, Greater Glasgow Health Board. He has published widely on addictions and sexual health, and has also advised government through the Advisory Council on the Misuse of Drugs and the Scottish Advisory Committee on Drug Misuses. His current research interests include methadone prescribing, injecting prevalence and evaluating drug and sexual health services.

Graham Hart is Associate Director of the MRC Social and Public Health Services Unit, Head of the Unit's Sexual and Reproductive Health Programme and Professor in the Faculty of Medicine at the University of Glasgow. He has published widely on risk behaviour for HIV infection, the sociology of sexual health and on sexual risk associated with travel

Dominique Hausser is a physician with a doctorate in public health and prevention. He is currently Senior Researcher at the Swiss Federal Institute of Technology and a consultant at the International Centre for Migration and Health. He has been working in the HIV/AIDS field since 1985 and is the editor of a series on psychological and cultural aspects of HIV/AIDS, published by Stampfli Verlage. He has recently co-edited *Sexual Interactions and HIV Risk: New Conceptual Perspectives on European Research*, published by Taylor and Francis.

Sarah Hawkes is based in the Clinical Research Unit at the London School of Hygiene and Tropical Medicine. In 1998 she returned from three years in Bangladesh where she had worked as principal investigator on a sexual health research programme. Prior to working outside the UK (in Asia and West Africa) she collaborated with Graham Hart on two research projects investigating clinical and behavioural aspects of travel and sex among clients at both travel and sexual health clinics in central London.

Jayne Hoose was formerly a Senior Lecturer in the Department of Geography at Canterbury Christ Church University College and now works in overseas development education. She has an MA in Christian Ethics from King's College London and now concentrates her research on tourism in developing countries, tourism ethics and development ethics. She has worked as a Tourism Adviser to ECPAT(UK) and has recently been appointed to their management committee.

Michel Hubert is a sociologist and professor at the Facultés Universitaires Saint-Louis in Brussels. He was the Project Leader of the Concerted Action on Sexual Behaviour and Risks of HIV Infection and co-edited the resultant reader *Sexual Behaviour and HIV/AIDS in Europe: Comparisons of National Surveys*, published by UCL Press. He is now co-ordinating a European project on the study of HIV risk in new relationships.

Furzana Khan is currently a Consultant Researcher working in Glasgow. She previously worked at the University of Glasgow, the Triumph Health Project at Greater Glasgow Health Board and the Scottish Centre for Criminology. Her current research interests include ethnic-minority use of illegal drugs, the use of 'ecstasy' by young people and the use of cocaine in Scotland.

Dieter Kleiber is Professor of Psychology at the Free University of Berlin, where he is Director of the Institute for Prevention and Health Promotion and Co-Director of the Institute of Clinical Psychology, Community Psychology and Psychological Diagnostics. Among his recent publications is *AIDS, Sex und Tourismus* (with Martin Wilke), published by Nomos Verlagegesellschaft, Baden-Baden.

Michael Luongo has a Master's degree in city and regional planning from the Bloustein School of Planning and Public Policy at Rutgers University. He has worked extensively in AIDS intervention research, and previously held the position of Recruitment Director for the Sero-Positive Urban Men's Study, the largest federally funded project in the United States focusing on the sex lives of HIV-positive gay men and men who have sex with men. He also worked in the Centre for Health Education and Research in Canterbury, UK, on work to help the Terrence Higgins Trust develop a travel HIV prevention campaign for gay men.

Anita Morrison is a Research Officer in the Pediatric Epidemiology and Community Health Unit at the University of Glasgow. Her current research interests include injury epidemiology, European public health surveillance and socio-economic variations in health.

Jose Antonio Nieto is Professor of Social Anthropology and Director of the Master's degree in human sexuality at the Universidad Nacional de Educacion a Distancia (UNED). His last publication was *Transexualidad, Transgenerismo y Cultura: Anthropologia, Identidad y Genero*, published by Talasa, Madrid. He has also contributed with his colleagues to the *International Encyclopedia of Sexuality*, published by Continuum, New York.

Julia O'Connell Davidson is a Reader in sociology at Leicester University. She has been involved in research on prostitution and sex tourism since 1993, and has been particularly concerned to interrogate prostitute use and the motivations of clients and sex tourists. She is author of *Prostitution, Power and Freedom* (Polity, 1998).

Chris Ryan is Professor of Tourism, a member of the International Academy for the Study of Tourism, editor of the academic journal *Tourism Management* and the author of over 70 papers. His six books include *Recreational Tourism – A Social Science Perspective*, *Researching Tourist Satisfaction* and *The Tourist Experience*.

Jacqueline Sánchez Taylor has an MSc from Leicester University in social science research and is currently registered for a PhD in sociology at Leicester on 'hustling' and the commodification of 'Blackness' within tourism. She has conducted research with Julia O'Connell Davidson for ECPAT (End Child Prostitution in Asian Tourism) into the motivation, attitudes and identities of tourists who sexually exploit children in Cuba, the Dominican Republic, Costa Rica, Venezuela, Goa and South Africa. Recent projects include research on sex tourism in Jamaica. Her interests include sex tourism and prostitution, the informal economic sector around tourism, the gendered, racialized and sexualized body.

Emma Short was a Research Fellow at the Scottish Centre for Criminology where, until September 1996, she was working on an evaluation of CCTV in Glasgow and Airdrie, funded by the Scottish Office. After over a year travelling around the world, she is now buying a house in France.

Michelle Thomas is a Research Fellow at Cardiff University and the Health Promotion Division of the Welsh Office. Her research interests include the sociology of food and the sociology of health and illness, in particular gender issues in sexuality.

Dewa Nyoman Wirawan received a medical degree from Udayana University in Bali, Indonesia, and an MPH from the University of Hawaii. He is now Professor of Medicine at Udayana University and Director of the Kerti Praja Foundation, which is dedicated to improving public health in Bali and, in particular, the prevention of HIV infection.

Preface

The sexual activity of tourists and the phenomenon of 'sex tourism' have raised considerable concerns during the 1990s. Issues of sexual imagery in tourist marketing, the sexual behaviour of young people on holiday, risks of sexually transmitted diseases (including HIV infection), the contribution of tourism to the commercialization of sex in Third World destinations and the need to introduce extra-territorial legislation against the sexual exploitation of children by tourists are just some of the significant issues which have exercised intergovernmental organizations, national governments, public health and tourism authorities, and the tourism industry itself.

This is the first British academic publication which brings together important contemporary contributions by social scientists on tourism and sex, in a readily accessible volume. In the first part, chapters address issues related to commercial sex in such locations as the Caribbean, Bali, Amsterdam, Prague and New York; in the second, the contributions focus on broader questions of the sexual behaviour of tourists in the context of mainstream tourism.

The book explores a variety of theoretical perspectives on sexuality in the context of tourism, presents findings from some of the most recent and significant empirical investigations, explores serious issues of exploitation and human rights in relation to sex tourism and addresses important public health implications of tourist sexual activity – not least, the potential contribution of tourism to the continued international diffusion of HIV infection (both in relation to the indigenous populations of tourist destinations and to the tourists themselves).

This book will be of interest to researchers in the social sciences concerned with sexuality in social and cultural contexts and students on advanced courses in sociology, psychology and tourism with a focus on sexuality. It is of relevance to tourism specialists, policy-makers and all involved in the tourism industry, and outside, who are concerned with the social and cultural dimensions and impacts of contemporary tourism. And finally, it will be of interest to those researchers and professionals in sexual health services and health promotion who are concerned with the health dimensions of sexual risk behaviours in the context of tourism.

The editors are particularly indebted to Mrs Gillian Shaw for her invaluable help in preparing the manuscript for publication.

1

Tourism, international travel and sex: themes and research

Simon Carter and Stephen Clift

Prelude: mariners, microbes and other travellers

In the closing years of the fifteenth century a new and terrible disease appeared and subsequently spread over all of Europe with the rapidity of a fire burning in a field of wheat stubble.[1] The sickness was characterized by skin eruptions, a widespread rash, sores and ulcers. The victim was tortured with agonizing muscle pain, a general physical deterioration and, frequently, at least in the first years of the epidemic, an early death. Initially, long before the development of modern ideas about contagion and infectious disease, little was known about this new health problem and the medicine of the time had no effective remedies for it. Be this as it may, it was soon popularly believed that the illness was spread through sexual contact. Within thirty years of the first documented cases of this new malady something else also appeared – the longest-running controversy related to travel, sex and health that the world has seen. Namely, did Columbus, as well as bringing potatoes, chillies, peanuts and tobacco from the New World, also bring the disease we today know as *syphilis*?

The history of the disease syphilis, and the controversies surrounding its origins, illuminates several important points about travel and sex that are still pertinent today. Columbus made his first journey to the New World in 1492, after finally gaining patronage from the Spanish Court (and after many years of failing to generate any interest in his expedition). This was a period of significant change in Europe: it marked the closing of the Middle Ages and the zenith of the Renaissance in Italy; European trade routes to Asia had recently been cut by the Turkish capture of Constantinople, giving an impetus to new exploration; the first modern printing press had been constructed in the mid-fifteenth century; and the beginnings of modern national consciousness can be traced to this era. In short, it was a time when people, ideas and things began to flow in novel ways that had not been seen before.

The first recorded epidemic of syphilis was itself associated with the movement of a large number of men. In 1494, two years after Columbus's original journey to the New World, Charles VIII of France laid claim to the kingdom of Naples and despatched an army of between 30,000 and 50,000 men across the Alps. The army, consisting of French troops and mercenaries from Germany, Italy and Switzerland, made its way south via Rome and entered Naples in February 1495, without any full-scale battles being fought. By the early spring of 1495 many of Charles VIII's men were becoming gravely ill and displaying symptoms such as fever, chancroids, gummy tumours in the groin area and sores on other parts of the skin. The large numbers afflicted, together with the severity of the symptoms, probably contributed to the decision by Charles VIII for a tactical withdrawal from Naples. By October the army had reached Lyons and was demobilized, with mercenaries returning to their country of origin. Between the years of 1495 and 1496 similar diseases were recorded as appearing in France, Germany, Switzerland, Holland, England and, by the turn of the century, in Hungary and Russia (Pusey, 1933).

From its very outset the epidemic shared an important characteristic with modern debates about sexually transmitted illness in general, and travel and sex in particular. This was the desire to make 'others' accountable for the misfortune. This is most clearly expressed in the naming of the new illness, which from the beginning marked it as an import from faraway lands and different peoples – it was the classic disease of the 'other' (Brandt, 1993). The extent and variety of names for this new disease is well summed up by Crosby:

> Italians called it the French disease, which proved to be the most popular title; the French called it the disease of Naples; the English called it the French disease, the Bordeaux disease, the Spanish disease; the Poles called it the German disease; Russians called it the Polish disease; and so on. Middle Easterners called it European pustules; Indians called it the disease of the Franks (Western Europeans). Chinese called it the disease of Canton, that port being their chief point of contact with the West. The Japanese called it Tang sore, Tang referring to China; or, more to the point the disease of the Portuguese. A full list of the early names of syphilis covers several pages, and it was not until the nineteenth century that Girolamo Fracastoro's word, 'syphilis', minted in the 1520s, became standard throughout the world.
>
> (Crosby, 1972: 125)

The frequency with which the new illness was named after neighbouring lands is no doubt a reflection of a new nationalistic movement (the period in which Machiavelli's *The Prince* was written). As Tempkin says, 'these names express a national hatred unthinkable in a time without national consciousness' (Temkin, 1977). However, the link with Columbus and the New World was not made for another thirty years, until Ruy Diaz de Isla published *Tradado sobre el mal serpentino que vulgarmente en España se llama buvas* in 1539. This work claimed that the disease came from Española (Haiti), its first appearance in Europe was at Barcelona and that Columbus's crew brought it there. For the next 400 years the origins of syphilis were intensely debated and contested. Three hypotheses emerged: the Columbian theory, as outlined by Ruy Diaz de Isla, was that syphilis was brought to Europe by Columbus's crew in the 1490s; the misrecognition hypothesis held that, rather than this being a new epidemic, syphilis was a disease that had always been present but had been mistaken for something else (e.g. leprosy), and the circulation of medical texts (via the new technology of printing) allowed it to be recognized as a separate condition. According to the Unitarian theory – that infectious diseases do not exist in isolation but are the product of complex interactions between host, parasite and environment (both physical and social) – a non-venereal form of syphilis existed in both the New and Old Worlds but widespread changes in living conditions in the fifteenth century caused a mutated venereal form of syphilis to appear, and be recognized, for the first time.

The controversy over the origins of syphilis will probably never be fully resolved, but recent examination of skeletal evidence strongly suggests that something arrived in Europe from the New World in the late fifteenth century (Baker and Armelagos, 1988). Probably a non-venereal form of syphilis, carried by the seamen on Columbus's first voyage, this quickly adapted to new conditions in Europe and then spread sexually. Travel and movement play an obvious role in the Columbian theory, but the importance of travel is also present in the opposing explanations either through the movement of books and information or via an increased mobility that allowed the newly mutated venereal disease to spread and establish a viable ecology for itself. Whatever else syphilis was, its history shows that it is a disease associated with travel.

Its history also shows that it has had a profound effect on Western health and culture. In the immediate years following the first epidemic cities throughout Europe passed edicts in an unsuccessful attempt to prevent the spread, many of which imposed severe sanctions on the mobility of those thought to be infected (Naranjo, 1995). Its spread through all levels of society had a direct effect on the church, politics (several European dynasties may have died out because of the disease) and literature (Erasmus and Shakespeare both write of 'the Pox'). But perhaps the most significant consequences were in everyday life: public baths went out of fashion; common drinking vessels became less common; the kiss as a form of greeting came under suspicion; attitudes towards prostitution and sex outside marriage hardened considerably (Temkin, 1977); and the 'fear of infection tended to erode the bonds of respect and trust that bound men and women together' (Crosby, 1972: 158).

Almost five hundred years later another unknown infection appeared and, in many respects, it was similar to the early epidemic of syphilis. Between the years 1981 and 1982 a serious and life-threatening set of symptoms were marked out and classified as Acquired Immune Deficiency Syndrome (AIDS). Shortly after, a virus was identified as a possible cause of this illness – Human Immunodeficiency Virus (HIV). In the first years of its emergence little was known about this new health problem and medicine had no effective remedies for it. However, it was soon believed that sexual contact was the most important route of transmission and, although first observed in gay men, it was obvious that world-wide HIV was predominantly a disease of heterosexual contact.

The history of the HIV epidemic is much shorter than that for syphilis, but already there are at least as many diverse and eclectic theories about its origin. As with the theories associated with the spread of syphilis the roles played by travel and sex are a frequent part of these histories. Perhaps the most widely known and popular is that put forward by Randy Shilts in *And the Band Played On* (later made into a TV movie). In a series of ironic reversals of the Colombian hypothesis, Shilts's account of the early epidemic claimed that the infection was brought from the core of the Old World (Paris) to the heart of the New World (San Francisco). The vector of transmission, which in the Columbian theory had been seafarers, now became, in keeping with the post-industrial times, a single promiscuous gay flight attendant, working for a Canadian airline – the infamous 'Patient Zero'. While epidemiologists and medical historians can provide little evidence to support the flight attendant theory, the mainstream media focused on Shilts's 'Patient Zero' and did much to popularize the idea that AIDS originated with a single gay, sexually active, worker in the travel industry.

Other, more credible, theories of origin share aspects of the Unitarian thesis and suggest that human and/or non-human forms of the HIV virus may have long existed in either isolated human or, more likely, in animal populations. Changes in the world-wide physical and social environments led to the virus 'breaking out' and spreading around the globe. One of the key changes, it has been suggested, is the growth of mass transportation, travel and tourism since the end of the Second World War. As former director of the WHO's Global Program on AIDS, Jonathan Mann writes:

> The dramatic increase in world-wide movement of people, goods, and ideas is the driving force behind the globalisation of disease. For not only do people travel increasingly, but they travel much more rapidly, and go to many more places than ever before . . . Few inhabitants on the globe remain truly isolated or untouched, as tourists and other travellers penetrate into the most remote and previously inaccessible areas in their search for new vistas, business, or recreation.
>
> (Mann, 1995: xiii)

Some have even pointed to a specific development of the transport infrastructure as touching off the HIV epidemic. Richard Preston claims that the paving, in the 1970s, of the road connecting the east and west coasts of Africa – the Kinshasa highway – 'affected every person on earth, and turned out to be one of the most important events of the twentieth century' (Preston, 1995). The surfacing of the highway opened the route up for long-distance trucks and allowed HIV to begin its slow progress out of central Africa, and from there to be distributed globally. Perhaps this, too, is an oversimplification, as there is now good evidence to suppose that a Norwegian sailor (who died of AIDS in 1976) was infected in West Africa in 1961 – which implies that HIV-type infections had been circulating in this region for at least 35 years (Hooper, 1997), long before the Kinshasa highway was little more than a dirt track.

As with the history of syphilis, it is doubtful that debates about the origin of HIV will ever be fully resolved. One thing is, however, clear – if people did not travel in large numbers, and have sex while on their journeys, the world today would probably be unaware of the existence of HIV-type infections. The different accounts of the emergence of both syphilis and HIV should demonstrate that the subjects of tourism, travel and sex are far from trivial. Indeed, the recent resurgence of syphilis in Western Europe, after dramatic decreases since the early 1980s, has been linked to increased travel to and from the former Soviet republics (Deayton and French, 1997; Smacchia *et al.*, 1998). Currently, GUM physicians in the UK are likely to suspect international travel if they find cases of syphilis or penicillin-resistant gonorrhoea in their clinic. This may well be an assumption throughout Western European countries.

Defining, theorizing and researching tourism and sex

The advent of the HIV epidemic in the 1980s was one factor in an increasing research, and policy, interest in tourism, travel and sex. Over the last few years a relatively stable pattern has emerged indicating that the large majority of heterosexual cases of HIV in the UK are associated with sexual activity abroad. Many of these may be due to foreign nationals seeking treatment in the UK. But there is also evidence of HIV infections among indigenous UK nationals associated with travel and tourism, especially to sub-Saharan Africa. The available statistics have led some epidemiologists to claim that the risks associated with sex abroad for heterosexuals are several hundred times greater than the risks at home. The basic process at work is relatively straightforward and is as applicable to the soldiers involved in the syphilis epidemic of 1495 as it is to the modern traveller or tourist. The incidence of sexually transmitted infections varies within the populations of different global regions and is dependent on a range of local ecological, social and cultural factors. Visitors to a new region who are sexually active may come from populations characterized by a lower incidence, may acquire an infection and return home with it (and once there, carry on spreading it). In short, tourism and travel allows the rapid mixing of sexual networks that would otherwise never come into direct contact. The establishment of the AIDS and Mobility Project some years ago expressed concerns within the European Union about the links between HIV and travel (immigration, business and leisure travel). This was followed by the Europe Against AIDS – Summer Campaign, which ran for two years in 1994–5 across the whole of Europe and attempted to target young people travelling during the summer months.

Even though research into the sexual health risks associated with travel are of great importance, they are by no means the only issues that need to be considered when examining travel, tourism and sex. Indeed, in many respects the advent of the HIV epidemic served to focus attention on a whole range of issues connected with tourism and sex that pre-existed the current concerns of policy-makers: namely, that elevated levels of HIV, found in many developing countries, may be spread to Western hetero-sexuals. Any examination of sex, travel and tourism crystallizes a number of issues, such as: the configurations of power at local, national and transna-tional levels; sexual identity and representations of ethnicity; issues around gender, labour and leisure; and the economic inequalities often found between tourist-sending and host nations.

The single issue that captures all these tensions in this area, in addition to being 'one of the most emotive and sensational issues', is the subject of 'sex tourism' (Hall, 1996). As we shall see, attempts at defining 'sex tourism' rapidly become problematic, but a normal working definition is taken as travel for which the main motivation is to engage in commercial sexual relations. Just as in the early years of the first syphilis epidemic, no one wishes to claim responsibility for sex tourism – it is a problem of 'other' distant nations such as Thailand or the Philippines. It is often depicted in the Western media, and tourist guidebooks, in highly racialized tones as part of an Oriental and alien culture. Tourist destination states, and Asian women, are 'aligned with nature, receptivity, and sexual allure and danger', images that resonate with former colonial representations (Pettman, 1997: 97). As Hall has written, it is impossible to fully understand sex tourism unless it is examined within a 'framework which addresses the varieties of structural inequality that occur within the South-east Asian region' (Hall, 1996).

However, to rigidly separate 'sex tourism' from other forms of travel and tourism involving sex is to oversimplify a complex set of interrelations and interactions. One of the most obvious, but also one of the most overlooked, is the way in which erotic images and the allure of sexual activity are used by commercial organizations to promote many different forms of tourism and business travel. From the marketing of business seats on international airlines, to the use of 'red light' districts as tourist attractions (without necessarily implying participation), the line between commercial sex and tourism becomes blurred. Hence, it is vital to be more precise in proposing categories and dimensions that can help us conceptualize the various manifestations of the relations between travel, sex and tourism. For instance, Herold and van Kerkwijk (1992: 1) distinguish between narrow forms of tourism prostitution where sexual gratification is the '*main motivation*' for international travel from more subtle forms of sex tourism, in which tourists 'may not consciously focus on attaining certain sexual goals as the main objective, but may nevertheless be open to and possibly even desirous of a sexual adventure while travelling'.

It is notable that the principal criterion used in definitions such as these is the behavioural intent of the traveller. Such an approach may generate important insights into the phenomenon of travel and sex but it is also clearly limited, as definitions based on intent cannot easily admit the many structural, social and power inequalities that may also inform this issue. In this volume Ryan has sought to problematize many of the naïve definitions and conceptualizations of sex and tourism by providing a framework for positioning the varied forms of connection involved. Three interrelated but distinct dimensions are used to examine tourism and sex: non-commercial vs. commercial; voluntary vs. non-voluntary; and confirmation of identity vs. an assault on identity.

Many attempts have been made to quantify the incidence of 'sex tourism', as narrowly defined, and its associated health problems. For example, in Thailand, the country most popularly associated with 'sex tourism', the numbers of prostitutes are thought to have risen from 20,000 in 1957 to between 500,000 and a million in the early 1980s, with perhaps 200,000 working in Bangkok alone (Hall, 1996; Lea, 1988). In the late 1980s the rates of HIV infection for Thai prostitutes increased dramatically. Nation-wide, the number of HIV-positive prostitutes represented 3.5 per cent in June 1989; one year later this figure had become 9.6 per cent. By late 1990 18 per cent of Bangkok prostitutes were thought to be HIV-positive (Garrett, 1995: 698). Yet the role that international tourism has played in these inflations is not clear, because statistics cannot easily distinguish between prostitutes whose clients are tourists from those whose clients are locals.

Others have sought to represent the dimensions of sex tourism spatially by collating various forms of evidence into maps. Thus, Herold and van Kerkwijk (1992) provide a map that highlights the major sex tourism desti-nations and also gives an indication of the countries from which sex tourists mainly originate in each destination. At best, such representations can be thought of as semi-rigorous presentations of anecdotal evidence. The problem is that 'sex tourism', even when using a narrow definition, is a highly dynamic phenomenon that exhibits rapid changes in only a short space of time. For example, much research has focused on the underlying economic factors that structure prostitution, such as relative poverty. As capital ebbs and flows in the world economic system, so too do levels of prostitution. After the fall of the former Soviet Union, border controls were relaxed and female prostitutes began operating along cross-border roads between East and West Europe. In the newly 'liberated' populations, prostitution was one method women could use to earn money against a background of rapidly rising levels of unemployment, which often disproportionately affected the female workforce. It also allowed men, in Western Europe, to purchase sex at far cheaper rates than in their own home countries. It should also be remembered that 'sex tourism', like other types of tourism, is often motivated by a desire to find new experiences and 'unspoilt' new destinations.

Having looked at some of the problems in defining and conceptualizing the subject of travel, tourism and sex, it is also important to consider the formidable problems involved in researching sex and tourism. Hall (1996) outlines some of the major difficulties in studying 'sex tourism', the first and the last of which apply equally to research on non-commercial sex in tourist settings:

1. The seeming blindness of many tourism researchers to actually acknowledge that a link exists between sex and the tourism industry, particularly in respect of sex as a motivating factor for travel . . .
2. The extreme difficulties to be had in conducting research on tourism prostitution, which is typically an illegal informal activity, often with substantial crime connections . . .
3. The lack of common methodological and philosophical frameworks with which to explain the complex web of gender, productive, reproductive and social relations which surround sex tourism.

(Hall, 1996: 266)

Despite these difficulties a number of studies both of tourism prostitution and of sex in tourist settings have been undertaken over the last decade. A variety of different methodologies and approaches is distinguishable. The more sophisticated studies of tourism prostitution have used a multi-disciplinary approach to the subject in which historical, cultural, political, religious and economic factors are taken into account to explain the rise of a sex industry infrastructure. Often the way in which these factors intersect synergistically with international tourism and travel is also stressed. Analyses of this kind may be supported by the gathering of information from a diverse variety of sources, including: television and media representations; tourist industry publications; government health statistics; material from campaigning and pressure groups; and original ethnographic observations (see Truong, 1990).

The more general study of sexual activity among tourists, either in sex tourism resorts or quasi-touristic contexts (such as business travel), frequently focuses on more narrow issues, usually characterized by a concern with sexual health risks. Here one finds research that typically falls into two categories. First, research which utilizes a grounded approach employing qualitative methodologies, such as ethnographic fieldwork in tourism destinations, or semi-structured retrospective interviews. In such work, explanatory frameworks arise out of a close analysis of observations and accounts of sexual behaviour provided by tourists. Second, research which adopts a broadly quantitative approach to explore connections between sex and travel and a variety of contextual, social and psychological factors. Such work may be guided by a general conceptual model or may focus on specific factors considered to be significant.

An issue of particular interest is whether we have any reason to regard the nature and processes of sexual relations in tourist contexts as a special case. In other words, do we need to understand the sexual relations of travellers and tourists differently from the way we would regard the same people having sex at home? As Pettman genuinely asks, 'what is the difference between sex purchased by an Australian man in Bangkok and sex purchased by him from a Thai sex worker in Sydney?' (Pettman, 1997: 105). Or are the issues involved in considering tourism and sex basically the same as those for examining sexual relations at home – it may just be that the values of a number of key parameters shift, and simply produce change in the incidence and frequency of sexual activity.

Studies of 'sex tourism' and 'sex in tourism'

To illustrate some of these different approaches we will now focus on a number of writers who have examined the convergence of tourism and sex by analysing the phenomenon of 'sex tourism' or the broader issue of 'sex in tourism'. Feminist analysts have provided a number of significant analyses of 'sex tourism'. Many of these have concentrated on the structural position of women as the providers of sexual services and their relationship to the tourist industry. Enloe (1989), for example, approaches the issue of sex tourism from within a broad critique of the gendered character of the international tourism industry. Throughout history, she claims, travel has been primarily masculine:

> From the Roman Empire to the eighteenth century European grand tour, the rise of Cooks tours and Club Med, travel for pleasure and adventure has been profoundly gendered. Without ideas about masculinity and femininity and the enforcement of both – in the societies of departure and the societies of destination, it would be impossible to sustain the tourism industry and its political agenda in their current form.
>
> (Enloe, 1989: 40–1)

From this perspective, she claims that sex tourism 'is not an anomaly; it is one strand of the gendered tourism industry' with its central emphasis on the provision of services. In order for sex tourism to operate successfully it requires several things: a labour market in which women are economically desperate enough to enter prostitution; male travellers from affluent countries who are able to draw on a racialized ideology in which foreign women are imagined to be more available and submissive than women in their own countries; and an alliance between local governments, in search of foreign exchanges, and travellers willing to buy sexualized travel. Once this is in place, commercial interests and a variety of social and psychological factors conspire to facilitate and maintain patterns of commodified sexual relationships, in which women can be exploited and are at heightened risk of abuse or ill health.

In their analysis of 'sex tourism' Herold and Kerkwijk (1992) outline a number of factors that allow an articulation between commercial sex and travel to develop. A variety of media, such as guidebooks, travel literature and programmes, portray tourist settings as both romantic and as a different cultural environment in which different social norms apply. This can facilitate a sense of freedom from constraints for the traveller that is reinforced by a reduction of normal inhibitions as a result of factors such as loneliness and boredom. This can be further reinforced if like-minded acquaintances travel together or meet up in tourist areas. In addition, it is pointed out that analysis can be complicated if the dividing line between paid and unpaid sex is blurred (for example, through the exchange of gifts rather than cash).

Due to its standing as a 'sex tourism' destination, both in the mainstream media and in the epidemiological literature, much research has focused on Thailand's sex industry, especially that part of it geared towards the foreign traveller. Detailed multidisciplinary analyses of the historical, economic and cultural factors contributing to the development of Thailand's sex industry have been provided by commentators such as Truong (1990), Hall (1996) and Leheny (1995). Many of these writers identify similar underlying structures as helping to explain Thailand's development as the world's premier 'sex tourist' destination. In many respects Truong's (1990) *Sex, Money and Morality* is still one of the most far-reaching examinations of the international sex industry. Truong draws connections between the sex industry in Thailand and the international political economy of labour (particularly women's labour), local commoditization of sexual services and the needs of a global travel industry. Particular local conditions (such as a culture and religion that are patriarchal in the extreme) may have initially allowed prostitution to develop, but it is a series of international relations that have allowed it to thrive. Women providing sexual services in Thailand are part of an international division of labour producing wealth for international businesses, state agents and states: 'The emergence of tourism and sex-related entertainment is an articulation of a series of unequal social relations including: North–South relations, relations between capital and labour, male and female, production and reproduction' (Truong, 1990: 129).

The scale and character of Thai prostitution changed markedly with the appearance of a US military presence in the region during the 1960s and 1970s. Thailand served as a 'rest and relaxation' area for American servicemen, and in addition to the 50,000 men stationed in the country, some 70,000 men were flown in each year to recover from the stresses of the Vietnam War. It is estimated that 700,000 American servicemen visited Thailand between 1962 and 1976, and their spending in restaurants, bars and brothels over this period exceeded 40 per cent of Thailand's export earnings. In 1970 alone it is judged that the spending of US military personnel on leave in Thailand came to around US$ 20 million. The demand by military personnel for entertainment, including sexual services, led to a dramatic growth of investment in entertainment facilities, including hotels, brothels, bars, massage parlours and 'go-go' bars. Much of this investment came from outside Thailand and involved individuals who were closely associated with both the Thai and US military. The fact that many of those who controlled the investment, production and management of these enter-tainment facilities were non-Thai nationals led to the introduction of new Western methods of operation. Hence, the social relations of Thai prosti-tution were transformed with the arrival of practices associated with the Western traditions of commercialized sexual services, such as 'sex floor-shows' and 'go-go' bars. The expansion of prostitution, entertainment and 'personal services' led to a high demand for a sex- and age-specific labour force to meet these needs. The high turnover of female labour demanded a corresponding increase in spatial mobility, with women, either through choice or coercion, moving from rural areas to work in centres of commercialized prostitution. As Truong points out, the issue of power is central here:

> Power in production in the entertainment industry [that] provides prostitutes' services is in the hands of an influential group which controls the means of production as well as the enforcement of law. Law is enforced in such a way that the supply and control of prostitutes is ensured.
>
> (Truong, 1990: 184)

The use of Thailand as a place of 'rest and relaxation' during the Vietnam War led to the development of an infrastructure geared towards capital accumulation through the provision of entertainment services, including prostitution. However, the end of American involvement in the Vietnam War led to a rapid decline in the market for 'rest and relaxation' tourism. For the entertainment infrastructure to maintain its returns on investment alternative markets needed to be found. However, the decline of 'rest and relaxation' tourism occurred in a period when the disposable income of those in industrialized countries was increasing and, because of package tours and charter flights, mass leisure travel was becoming much cheaper. Thus, businessmen and tourists became a second important market for the provision of sexual services, as Thailand developed its international tourism market: 'The combination of shared vested interests led firms to incorporate diverse sexual services into a highly organised production process with diverse points of distribution on an international level' (Truong, 1990: 199).

Truong is, however, careful to point out that prostitution in Thailand operates under a multiplicity of social relations, with relations of power and production working in diverse ways. Hence, it is argued, those working in the sex industry cannot be thought of as a 'homogeneous group with common interests and a common understanding of the nature of power relations which surround them' (Truong, 1990: 189). Be this as it may, those who sell their labour in the sexual economy of labour do so under ideological and legal conditions where exploitation, coercion and abuse are, in differing degrees, common. As Truong concludes:

> The traffic in women and children as a means to supply labour in prostitution cannot be treated as a separate issue from the plurality of sexual choices of which prostitution is one. The border of sexual ethics extends beyond the question of individual choices regarding practice, or consumption. It concerns the process of sexual domination which precedes the availability of such sexual choices. In other words, for the market to avail itself of sexual choices, sex as a source of life (emotions, vitality) of some people must first be appropriated. It is therefore important to keep in mind that to stop judging prostitution is one thing, but to cease imposing ethical boundaries on the use of sexual labour is quite another.
>
> (Truong, 1990: 202)

An account such as Truong's demonstrates that the phenomenon of 'sex tourism' cannot be understood as a deviant and bounded activity that is somehow separate from the cultures that produce it. As we saw, the history and development of 'sex tourism' in Thailand was closely connected with a range of diverse issues, such as: a violent international conflict involving the transportation of hundreds of thousands of men; the local and international division of gendered labour; social and technological changes in world tourism markets; international trade and investment; and a series of intersecting ideologies and discourses around sexuality, gender and race. Many similar issues are of importance when considering the broader topic of 'sex in tourism' rather than tourism prostitution. In the early 1970s social, economic and technical innovation (namely the package holiday, charter flights and the mass production of jet aircraft) allowed increasing numbers of people to travel internationally for leisure purposes. This produced new opportunities for tourists to engage in sexual activity both with other tourists and with the locals who live in the new tourist-receiving regions.

When considering tourists who engage in sexual relations with locals, even where no explicit monetary transaction has occurred, it is crucial also to examine the way in which sexual activity may connect with broader cultural, ideological and economic issues. In the early 1970s some of the countries first to undergo development as mass tourist destinations for the 'package' traveller were those European nations with regions bordering on the Mediterranean, particularly Spain, Italy and Greece. Many of these regions were characterized by peasant family structures and economies based on traditional farming or fishing. The consequences of interactions between travellers, the tourist industry and local communities has been the subject of some debate between those who stress ideological effects (tourists as transmitters and 'carriers' of 'Western' values) and those who instead emphasize economic forces (such as changes in local labour markets). While not primarily concerned with sexual activity many writers on this subject do acknowledge the importance of tourist/local sexual interaction. Studies in the late 1970s, such as Boissevain's (1978) research in Malta and Costa del Sol, found that it was common for local young males to mimic tourist behaviour and engage in serial sexual activities with women from North European countries. For those who favour the ideological-effect explanations of social change these interactions are thought to have partially contributed to the breakdown of traditional peasant family structures. What was once 'functional' becomes 'dysfunctional', both as a result of families losing control of their children's courtship and marriage and because young men become subjected to opprobrium for their sexual behaviour with female tourists (Stott, 1978).

Other commentators have pointed out that economic, rather than ideological, factors often act as agents of social change in tourist regions (Kousis, 1996). The new economic activity of tourism in 'traditional' communities can lead to significant changes in patterns of wealth, the labour market and land ownership. It is argued that such changes have a more profound effect than the arrival of new ideological codes of sexual permissiveness, brought by tourists. However, even those who stress the economic determinants of social change also acknowledge the importance of sexual activity in understanding change in tourist-receiving communities. Thus, Kousis, in a study of rural Cretan tourism, points out that until the early 1960s young men and women were subject to severe restrictions on their sexual behaviour. Once tourism came to dominate the economy of the region, sexual moral codes were revised dramatically. Single female tourists made up a significant proportion of the new visitors to this region and during the seven-month tourist season female visitors outnumbered local males by a ratio of 10:1. The majority of local males aged between 16 and 30 (known as *kamakia* or 'harpoons') were reported to systematically 'date' foreign women, and around 9 per cent of all marriages in the 1970s and 1980s resulted from female tourists marrying local men. However, the strict moral codes governing the behaviour of local women did not undergo any relaxation in this period: 'Thus, the persistence of strict sexual conduct of local females, vis-à-vis the relaxed relationships between local males and foreign women, has widened the gap of sexual code behaviour for men and women' (Kousis, 1996: 231).

Research suggests, however, that the most common sexual interaction in leisure travel is probably that between the tourists themselves (Carter *et al.*, 1997). Most tourists, if they engage in new sexual activity at all, do so with other tourists who are remarkably similar to them. Indeed, the marketing of mass tourism is often characterized by three predominant advertising images:

> These are the 'family holiday', that is a couple with two or three healthy school-age children; the 'romantic holiday', that is a heterosexual couple on their own gazing at the sunset (indeed the sunset is a signifier for romance); and the 'fun holiday', that is same-sex groups each looking for other-sex partners for 'fun'.
>
> (Urry, 1996: 121)

Research that focuses on the 'fun holiday' (young single tourists' wish to have new sexual contacts with other travellers) often considers the issue from a public health standpoint. One concern is that some practices (such as drinking or taking drugs) on the 'fun holiday' may interact with sexual behaviour to make 'unsafe sex' more likely for young tourists. Eiser and Ford (1995) have explored some of these concerns in their study of single young people (aged 16 to 29) on holiday in south-west England. Eiser and Ford found that one-third of these tourists reported some form of sexual activity with a new partner, and one-quarter experienced intercourse with at least one new partner (with higher rates among men). Condom use among this group was inconsistent, with around three-quarters of men and half of the women reporting that intercourse occurred without the use of a condom. This study also explored the relationship between sexual activity and what the authors describe as 'situational disinhibition' – the feeling of being a 'different person' while on holiday. When this was explored an interesting gender difference in the beliefs and behaviour of travellers emerged. Sexual activity among women was found to be strongly related to 'situational disinhibiting' factors, and women were more likely to believe that condoms may reduce their sexual pleasure.

Organization of the book

Given the complexity and diverse nature of the issues that need to be addressed when considering 'sex tourism' or 'sex in tourism' it should be no surprise that no book has attempted comprehensively to explore sex and travel in its many dimensions. Over the past decade various researchers have separately examined sex and tourism from a variety of perspectives and have highlighted many different issues. However, to date, research reports and relevant literature on the connections between tourism and sexual behaviour have been widely scattered in conference proceedings, academic journals and the publications of organizations. These have not necessarily been available to a wider audience. It is the intent of this edited collection of papers to begin to fill a gap in the literature by collecting together, in one volume, some of the research that has recently been undertaken in sex and tourism.

Part I – tourism and commercial sex

This edited collection has been divided into two sections. Part I looks at the work of various researchers who have considered the place of commercial sex in tourism. In particular, the first part of the book will concentrate on the differing forms of commercial transactions involved in tourist prostitution and the social and health implications for those who work in the sex industry and for the communities that host these activities.

One of the problems, noted earlier, in examining 'sex tourism' or tourist prostitution is that anything more than a superficial examination of the issue finds that the phenomenon cannot be neatly separated from either tourism in general or from the cultures that produce it. Chris Ryan's contribution is valuable here for the way that it questions naïve definitions of 'sex tourism'. While the common conception of 'sex tourism' as involving red-light districts, prostitution and exploitation is true, it is only a partial truth. For Ryan 'there is no single paradigm of sex tourism, but many', and to understand these paradigms we must not lose sight of the wider context in which they are embedded. One of these wider contexts is the way in which tourism produces specific environments and peoples for the consumption of travellers. Jacqueline Sánchez Taylor considers this by examining ways that male and female sex tourists in the Caribbean seek experiences that are fictionalized, idealized or exaggerated models of more widespread social relations of power. Of particular importance is the articulation between discourses of 'race' and gender formed during colonialism. In this context tourism sustains particular racialized identities for locals working in tourist areas and also allows visitors to produce identities of 'whiteness' or 'Westernness'. The chapter by Julia O'Connell Davidson also considers the attitudes, identities and motivations of the clients of tourist-related prostitutes in the context of sex tourism involving children. This is a highly emotive topic that has recently been the subject of several high-profile cases in the media. O'Connell Davidson's research demonstrates that while the stereotypes in the media are not entirely without basis, the problem of child sexual exploitation by tourists is far more complex than they imply and is inseparable from the more general practice of sex tourism and prostitute use. Child sex tourism is, in addition, an issue which in recent years has been a focus of action by intergovernmental organizations, national governments and non-governmental agencies. Jayne Hoose, Stephen Clift and Simon Carter review some of these initiatives, focusing in particular on the work of ECPAT (End Child Prostitution, Pornography and Trafficking), the European Commission, the World Tourism Organization and the commercial tourism sector.

Continuous efforts are required to combat tourist sexual exploitation of children, and research is needed to evaluate the effectiveness of the various international initiatives currently under way.

In addition to the social and political implications of sex tourism it is also important to consider the often non-trivial health risks that tourism prostitution imposes on local communities and groups and tourists themselves. Chapters 6 and 7 consider the risks taken by sex workers and tourists in two very different places – Bali and New York. Kathleen Ford and Dewa Nyoman Wirawan look at the beliefs of male sex workers in Bali concerning their attitudes to HIV and STD infection. The results of their study show that significant groups of sex workers who serve tourist clients in Bali are vulnerable to sexual infection, specifically men who come from rural areas, men who were unaware of the asymptomatic nature of HIV infection and men who provide receptive anal intercourse. Michael Luongo's chapter considers the use travellers to New York make of the city's large gay commercial infrastructure, including sexual services (such as sex clubs and escort services). Luongo argues that in cities such as New York tourists are significant and visible users of the commercial sexual services aimed at gay men. Yet many may never have been exposed to safer-sex messages before they arrive in tourist destinations. One aspect of the provision of commercial sexual services for the traveller that is often ignored is the spatial organization of prostitution in the tourist city. The chapter by Simon Carter looks at the place of commercialized sex as part of the overall provision of tourist services in the Western City. Using Amsterdam and Prague as case studies, Carter argues that the spatial organization of sexual services has implications for the health and safety of sex workers.

Part II – tourism, sexual activity and risks

Part II of the book examines some of the implications of non-commercial sexual activity by travellers. This part of the book will focus more on the sexual interactions between travellers themselves, the different meanings they may bring to these interactions and the risks that such activities may expose them to.

One of the central questions in considering the health effects of sex in tourism is whether there are specific groups of travellers who are at particular risk of sexually transmitted infection. Chapters 9, 10 and 11 consider the issue of sexual risk behaviour among different groups of travellers. The chapter by Michael Bloor *et al.* reports the results of a telephone survey on a representative sample of international travellers. Their findings indicate that safer-sex practices among tourists are part of broader patterns of risk exposure. In other words, behaviour with regard to condom use at home is a good predictor of condom use while travelling. Bloor *et al.* also find that there are particular types of travel associated with risk behaviour (long and very short trips, and non-holidaymaking travel). The chapter by Graham Hart and Sarah Hawkes reviews studies of international travellers attending sexual health clinics. While these populations of travellers may not be 'representative' of the general public as a whole, it is argued that it is appropriate to study this group because they are likely to be precisely the travellers most at risk of sexually transmitted infections. Gay men are today a significant and important group of tourist consumers, and Stephen Clift and Simon Forrest report the results of research undertaken among gay tourists. A large sample of gay men resident in southern England were surveyed by means of a self-completed questionnaire that sought information on a range of tourist behaviours (including sexual behaviour while travelling). The evidence from this survey suggests that holidays are an important focus for HIV prevention initiatives (both before departure and while on holiday). However, it is also pointed out that only a third of those men surveyed regarded opportunities for sex as 'very important' in planning a holiday.

Chapters 12 and 13 take a broader approach by situating sexual risks within the overall context of tourism and holidaymaking. Using in-depth interviews and focus groups, Michelle Thomas's chapter explores the meanings women attach to new sexual activity while on holiday. Thomas finds that women who enter into new sexual relations while travelling have to negotiate multiple factors that may make sex unsafe (as broadly defined to include not only risks of sexual infection but also of coerced sex and emotional damage). These factors include both structural constraints placed on them by tourism and ideological constraints governing women's sexual behaviour. The chapter by Furzana Khan *et al.* reports the results of research examining the behaviours of young people travelling in groups to a Mediterranean island resort famous for its 'acid-house' music scene. Their research shows that 'package tour ravers', contrary to the stereotype, were less likely to have sex on holiday than at home. By examining the broad range of activities that these tourists engaged in Khan *et al.* argue that no single holiday activity is particularly hazardous, but that the various combinations of activity pose threats to health that future health messages should attend to.

The chapter by Hannah Bradby considers a group of travellers who are often ignored by tourist researchers. These are people whose identities are both defined by their relationship to distant places, from where they or their families have migrated in the recent past, and their ongoing relationship to their place of settlement. Bradby's research considers the role of travel in the lives of young Punjabi women living in Scotland. The traditional marriage system of rural Punjabis is patrilocal, which means that a bride moves from her parents' home to her husband's locality and therefore womanhood implies travel. This chapter shows the important role that international travel plays in the maintenance of marriage and sexual relations in a community with bicultural loyalties. Chapter 15 by Paula Black undertakes an important review of the extent to which sociological social theory, relating to tourism analysis, can inform empirical research into tourism and sexuality. By looking at the works of those theorists contributing to the debate in the social sciences about consumption, leisure and tourism and her own empirical research, Black argues for a multiplicity of approaches. Social theory into modern patterns of tourism and empirical research examining international travel and sexuality often deal with remarkably similar issues. Rather than the two almost operating as separate disciplines they should learn to inform and ground themselves in each other's insights. In the last chapter, Stephen Clift and Simon Carter reflect on the issues addressed by contributors to this volume, placing them in a broader context and identifying issues which need to be addressed in developing theoretical perspectives and empirical research, on tourism, travel and sex.

Tourism and Sex: Culture, Commerce and Coercion is aimed at any reader interested in exploring the role of different forms of sexual relations in tourism and their effects on both the international traveller and the local communities who serve tourists. It is hoped that this book will be useful both to those who are involved in ongoing inquiries into this field and those who may be new to research or study in this area. In addition, it should be of interest to the many professionals who are today involved either directly or indirectly in the travel industry.

Note

1. This was how the medical poet Girolamo Fracastoro described the initial spread of this disease.

References

Baker, B. J. and Armelagos, G. J. (1988) The origin and antiquity of syphilis – paleopathological diagnosis and interpretation. *Current Anthropology* **29** (5), 703–37.

Boissevain, J. (1978) Tourism and the European periphery: the case of the Mediterranean. In D. E. A. Seers (ed.), *Underdeveloped Europe: Studies in Core Periphery Relations*. London: Harvester Press.

Brandt, A. (1993) Sexually transmitted diseases. In W. F. Bynum and R. Porter (eds), *Companion Encyclopedia of the History of Medicine*. London: Routledge.

Carter, S., Horn, K., Hart, G., Dunbar, M., Scoular, A. and MacIntyre, S. (1997) The sexual behaviour of international travellers at two Glasgow GUM clinics. *International Journal of STD and AIDS* **8**, 336–8.

Crosby, A. W. (1972) *The Columbian Exchange: Biological and Cultural Consequences of 1492*. Westport, CT: Greenwood.

Deayton, J. and French, P. (1997) Incidence of early syphilis acquired in former Soviet Union is increasing. *British Medical Journal* **315**, 1018–19.

Eiser, J. R. and Ford, N. (1995) Sexual relationships on holiday – a case of situational disinhibition. *Journal of Social and Personal Relationships* **12** (3), 323–9.

Enloe, C. (1989) *Bananas, Beaches and Bases: Making Feminist Sense of International Politics*. London: Pandora.

Garrett, L. (1995) *The Coming Plague: Newly Emerging Diseases in a World out of Balance*. London: Virago.

Hall, C. (1996) Gender and economic interests in tourism prostitution: the nature, development and implications of sex tourism in South-East Asia. In Y. Apostolopoulos, S. Leivadi and A. Yianakis (eds), *The Sociology of Tourism: Theoretical and Empirical Investigations*. New York: Routledge.

Herold, E. S. and van Kerkwijk, C. (1992) AIDS and sex tourism. *AIDS and Society: International Research and Policy Bulletin* **4**(1), 1, 8–9.

Hooper, E. (1997) Sailors and star-bursts, and the arrival of HIV. *British Medical Journal* **315**, 1689–91.

Kousis, M. (1996) Tourism and the family in a rural Cretan community. In Y. Apostolopoulos, S. Leivadi and A. Yianakis (eds), *The Sociology of Tourism: Theoretical and Empirical Investigations*. New York: Routledge.

Lea, J. (1988) *Tourism and Development in the Third World*. London: Routledge.

Leheny, D. (1995) A political economy of Asian sex tourism. *Annals of Tourism Research* **22** (2), 287–304.

Mann, J. (1995) Preface. In L. Garrett, *The Coming Plague: Newly Emerging Infections in a World out of Balance*. London: Virago.

Naranjo, P. (1995) On the American Indian origin of syphilis: fallacies and errors. In G. Settipane (ed.), *Columbus and the New World: Medical Implications*. Providence, RI: Ocean Side Publications.

Pettman, J. J. (1997) Body politics: international sex tourism. *Third World Quarterly* **18** (1), 93–108.

Preston, R. (1995) *The Hot Zone*. London: Corgi.

Pusey, W. A. (1933) *The History and Epidemiology of Syphilis*. Springfield, IL: Charles C. Thomas.

Smacchia, C., Parolin, A., Di Perri, G., Vento, S. and Concia, E. (1998) Syphilis in prostitutes from Eastern Europe. *The Lancet* **351**, 572.

Stott, M. (1978) Tourism in Mykonos: some social and cultural responses. *Mediterranean Studies* **1** (2), 122–33.

Temkin, O. (1977) *The Double Face of Janus and Other Essays in the History of Medicine*. Baltimore: Johns Hopkins University Press.

Truong, T. D. (1990) *Sex, Money and Morality: Prostitution and Tourism in Southeast Asia*. London: Zed Books.

Urry, J. (1996) Tourism, culture and social inequality. In Y. Apostolopoulos, S. Leivadi and A. Yianakis (eds), *The Sociology of Tourism: Theoretical and Empirical Investigations*. New York: Routledge.

Part I

Tourism and commercial sex

2

Sex tourism: paradigms of confusion?

Chris Ryan

'Sex' and 'tourism'. Two words which together, for many people, conjure up images of red-light districts, prostitution and exploitation. This chapter argues that, while such a view of sex tourism is true, it is but a partial truth. To understand the social significance of 'sex tourism' requires looking past the bodies of gyrating strippers and their male audience to the people who fulfil those roles, what those roles actually are and why those roles emerge. Additionally, the view of sex tourism as solely occupying the bars of Patpong, Manila, Amsterdam or elsewhere is, again, an incomplete truth.

It can be observed that the tourism industry has long maintained an ambiguous relationship with 'sex'. It is not slow to use sexual imagery in its promotional materials, as illustrated by Heatwole (1989), Oppermann and McKinley (1996), among others, who have analysed tourism advertising. What is learnt about industry attitudes when the World Tourism Organization conducts a campaign to condemn child sex tourism (WTO, 1997, 1998)? Is sex with those other than children condoned? Are not women at risk too? Or does the WTO recognize the complexity of sex tourism and for pragmatic reasons chooses not to become involved in a debate about such complexities?

This chapter argues from definitions of 'sex' and 'tourism' that 'sex tourism' is a search for identity as well as exploitation. Also, while it is true that much of the exploitation is socially determined and reflects a wider degradation of women's role in society, this too is only part of the picture. For many women the display and use of their sexuality is a confirmation of their 'sexual beingness'; an enaction of the power of being female and the exercise of that power both to challenge and support males. Feminist descriptions of prostitution are not uniform, and like many other conceptualizations, are changing as writers struggle to encapsulate the paradoxes of the relationship between most men and most prostitutes and the environments within which those relationships occur. In short, there is no single paradigm of sex tourism, but many.

The preceding paragraph is also based upon an assumption of heterosexual relationships that are primarily commercial in their nature. Certainly, as Clift and Page (1996) and Clift and Grabowski (1997) have illustrated, such relationships have implications for both health and touristic authorities. But other relationships also exist between men and women that are not commercial in nature, but which occur within touristic settings. It is argued that these encounters are also part of sex tourism. For example, a significant body of research indicates that young people exhibit higher levels of sexual activity with those other than their normal partner while on holiday than at other times (Ford and Eiser, 1996; Ryan and Robertson, 1997; Josiam *et al.*, 1998). Additionally, loving, casual and commercial relationships occur at tourist destinations between lesbian and homosexual couples, as pink pounds and dollars become more important as a source of tourist expenditure. Thus, an increasing number of products are becoming available for this market. Interestingly enough, given a post-modernistic flux of symbols and their consumption, as gay events like Sydney's Mardi Gras, Auckland's Heroes Parade or San Francisco's Lesbian Gay Bisexual Transgender Pride Parade become more popular, so too do they attract increasing numbers of 'straight' visitors. It may be argued that to the lists of 'authentic' experiences sought by tourists (the 'real' Greek village, the 'real' Australian outback) has been added the 'real' homosexual community event – yet another product to be consumed by the ludic tourist (Urry, 1990, 1995; Urry and Rojek, 1997). This has given rise to concerns about the degaying of such events and areas, as described by Hughes (1997) in his assessment of Manchester's Gay Area. The parades mentioned, and other similar events, are, to this author's mind, part of sex tourism. They are certainly about senses of identity and images. But they too are confused. While Hughes argues that these events are confirmation of being homosexual and/or lesbian, to a commentator of the political right, the images are those that exploit women. Goldsmith (1996: 78) notes of Sydney's Mardi Gras:

> Some drag queens are an undisguised and vicious parody of woman-hood: their grotesque make-up and clothing and their grossly exaggerated breasts and mannerisms turn women into a joke . . . Again, some of the bondage in the Mardi Gras is a worry, when it displays, for example, men leading women along by chokers around their necks. In a society where women are demonstrably less than equal and are subject to domestic and sexual violence, such images reinforce negative stereotypes and show violence against women as acceptable.

Thus, Goldsmith turns the criticisms often made against heterosexual pornography, strip clubs and bondage massage parlours into a complaint about gay and lesbian portrayal of femininity. Sex tourism is about these issues, but in analysing sex tourism the conventional critiques of exploitation of sexuality and feelings of 'self-worth' are often overturned in the paradoxes that emerge.

So what of sex? While gender is a determinant of sex, sex in turn is a contributing factor to a sense of individuality. Yet sexual identity is a result of interaction between gender, personal feelings about oneself and social norms of what constitute the socially acceptable modes of behaviour, feelings and relationships between people (for a discussion of this, see Hirschman, 1984). To a large extent, sexual identity is socially learnt behaviour. The twentieth century has a history of challenge to what have been the norms of acceptable social sexual roles. From the suffragettes seeking a political voice for women, to the feminist writers of the 1960s, and the Gay Pride movements of the last two decades, gender, sex and identity has become a major issue in the western world. Arguably, the contemporary cult of individualism in the west has reinforced the importance of sex and gender as an inherent part of self-identity. From this perspective the claims made by the homosexual community are but part of this process. Tourism reinforces the claim by, paradoxically, making a commodity of the events held to claim a sense of homosexual community, and in doing so legitimizes and makes 'safe' the challenge to mainstream society. In the case of heterosexual sex tourism in a country such as Thailand, sex tourism juxtaposes two senses of identity – the west's individualism seeking confirmation of self through sex, and a Thai sense of identity through membership of a family, as women use prostitution with *farangs* (foreigners) to discharge familial duty of support for parents, children and siblings (Odzer, 1994; Seabrooke, 1997).

Within the feminist movement itself the role of the prostitute has opened up a division of opinion. For some writers, prostitution, along with pornography, represents the epitome of male commodification of the woman as sex object, a sex object which exists to pander to the sexual desires of men. For writers like Dworkin:

> the sexuality of women has been stolen outright, appropriated by men – conquered, possessed, taken, violated; women have been systematically and absolutely denied the right to sexual self-determination and to sexual identity; and because the sexuality of women has been stolen, this sexuality itself, it – as distinguished from an individual woman as a sentient being – it can be sold.
>
> (Dworkin, 1988: 229)

Whelehan (1995) comments that the radical feminism of the 1970s and its talk of a sexual revolution quickly led to disillusionment as it became confused with concepts of permissive society and men getting a free screw, as demonstrated by comments cited by Hite in her 'report' of 1977 (Hite, 1977: 456–7). The view emerged that the sexual revolution of the 1970s, based on the emancipation from pregnancy due to 'the pill', went awry. It was not a case of women exercising control, but men saying 'why not?' One result of the confusion was the redefinition of lesbianism as an expression of the sexuality of women untainted by the needs of heterosexuality. Whelehan (1995: 162) notes the slogan reputedly coined by Ti-Grace Atkinson that 'Feminism is the theory; lesbianism is the practice', while Rich (1980) explicitly argued that heterosexuality was a compulsory practice which arose from male expression of power, inhibiting women's sexual relationships with each other. In short, the dominance of a male-led heterosexuality deprived women of the comfort of each other and their bodies.

By extension, such views imply that the prostitute is a victim, subject to male whims and unable to properly define their own sexual relationships, a view that is still expressed today. Burrell (1997), reporting on a conference held in the UK, describes how many prostitutes were angered and dismayed at what they felt were simplistic feminist arguments portraying them as victims. However, newer themes have emerged, one of which is the inadequacy of men. Miles (1992) cites the encounters of Georges Simenon, the creator of Inspector Maigret, and his claim to have made love to 10,000 women:

> The root of his compulsion . . . was a sense of inferiority to women, a consequent fear of them, and a rage at that fear: he was convinced that all women were laughing at him, and he could only take his revenge and kill the fear by dissolving the imagined sneer on every female face into a real-life expression of sexual ecstasy.
>
> (Miles, 1992: 230)

This theme of the male as inadequate, unsure of their relationships not only with women but also with each other is one that emerges from social commentary, research within the field of prostitution and popular social psychology. Dexter-Horn Productions (1997), in the promotional video of Thailand aimed at male sex tourists, makes an explicit appeal to men who are disillusioned with demanding, liberated North American women. Thai women are 'real' women because they are submissive. O'Connell Davidson (1995) traces similar attitudes exhibited by British sex tourists in Thailand. Schlessinger (1997), a popular and controversial American media personality, notes that men have what she terms a 'stupid strength': uncomfortable with feeling weak, useless or rejected, they react with intimidation and the use of force. Maleness is measured by sexual conquest. But others, while viewing males as possessing weaknesses, argue that such weakness is also in part socially determined. Thus, there is a role for the prostitute to help males find themselves. In her research, Kruhse-Mount Burton, a working prostitute, specifically asked the question, can clienthood be explained as a manifestation of male power and dominance in wider society? She argues that the feminist tradition of writers like Dworkin is reductionist. For Kruhse-Mount Burton (1996: 14) masculinity is an evolving experience for men, a relational concept which stands with and complements the feminine: 'Men hold most of the power in society and yet they are the sexual and emotional supplicants who depend upon women's bodies for nurture and reproduction'. The prostitute's voice is one which, in the west, claims back the position of the priestess of ancient days as 'worker, healer, sexual surrogate, teacher, therapist, educator, sexual minority and political activist' (Bell, 1994: 103). For Sprinkle and Gates (1997) whores are heroes. They heal, help people explore sexual desire, are playful and tough. For these writers, based in the practice of prostitution, prostitutes have their own voice; rather than victims, they serve as positive members of society secure in their own identity and confident in their own integrity. One of the ironies of such a position is that in some senses it parallels a male demand to discover the sense of maleness described by writers like Bly (1990) and Moore and Gillette (1991). The latter argue that, through the roles of king, warrior, magician and lover, masculinity becomes a generative, creative and empowering process.

If, on the one hand, sex is partially about play and fantasy, with, on the other hand, exploitation and victimization as an alternative hypothesis, nonetheless both paradigms contribute to a sense of identity, whether positive or negative. The same is true of tourism. It has been observed that tourism is a socially sanctioned escape route for adults into play, fantasy and sexual adventure. Ryan (1991), Cohen (1982a, 1982b) and Crompton (1979) have made this point about tourism in general, while Ryan and Kinder (1995) have specifically argued that strong parallels exist between the demands for tourism and commercial sex motivations. They argue that needs for relaxation, company, sex, escape, fantasy and family bonding are common to both, and that given these parallels it is not surprising that sex and tourism have been closely associated. Just how closely associated has perhaps only recently become evident. Among young people casual sexual encounters are not uncommon. Ford (1991), in a study of 1000 young people on holiday in Devon, found 25 per cent had had sex with at least one new partner. In a New Zealand study of student-tourists, Ryan and Robertson (1997) questioned what 'having sex' means for young people, and found much lower levels of sexual intercourse with other than a normal partner for student holidaymakers (about 8.6 per cent). This is distinctly lower than the 66 per cent of French 15- to 18-year-olds who reported having inter-course in a study by Lagrande and Lhomond (1995), but is akin to the findings of the Clark and Clift (1994) study of British students that 6 per cent had had sexual intercourse with a new partner while on holiday.

Among adults there are a number of studies that have been based upon surveys and samples of patients in genito-urinary clinics. Daniels *et al.* (1992) found that 51 per cent of heterosexual men, 36 per cent of homosexual men and 20 per cent of women attending the clinics of Westminster and Charing Cross hospitals reported having sex with a local contact while abroad. Mendelsohn *et al.* (1996) report from a study under-taken at a Birmingham genito-urinary clinic that 30 per cent of trips made abroad included sex with a new partner. Of their sample almost 9 per cent

28   Chris Ryan

had had multiple partners. Carter *et al*. (1997), from studies carried out in Glasgow, report similar proportions. Black (1997), however, points out some problems with clinic-based studies, one of which is the nature of the sample itself – in view of the nature of the complaints requiring attendance at such clinics it is necessarily a self-selected sample. She reports findings derived from in-depth interviews, and remarks on the much-drawn distinction between travellers and tourists. She also comments on the role of fun in tourism, which 'centres around "going out" which often means to bars, clubs and restaurants or to other places where the main purpose of the activities is "to meet people". Fun also involves a high level of body awareness which contributes to feelings of pleasure' (Black, 1997: 171).

This is confirmed by Wickens's (1997) conceptualization of the 'Raver'. For 'Ravers', seeking sun, sand, cheap prices and drink, sex makes the holiday. Wickens's 'Ravers' are akin to Ryan and Robertson's (1997) 'Vibrant Voyagers' – both sets party hard and have high rates of sexual intercourse while on holiday. Wickens, building on her earlier research (Wickens, 1994), also emphasizes the role of women as pursuers of sexual adventure – it might be observed that both genders are voyeurs and participants. The findings of Black (1997) and Wickens (1994, 1997) also support the observation made by Ryan and Robertson (1997) that the activity of pub and club-going on holiday is an extension of normal weekend activities for some at least. In short, the holiday presents a new milieu for familiar behaviours, but ones within which sexual pursuit may become more explicit, as described by Wickens (1997). On the other hand, in some cases, while explicit it may be deemed 'safe'. Based on research undertaken in the dance clubs of Ibiza, Sellars (1998) comments that where the use of the drug ecstasy is common, females will flirt more in the knowledge that the drug is linked with impotency in males.

It is appreciated that this discussion of sex on holiday is removed from the conventional images of 'sex tourism', generally undefined as that term is. Equally, it is not denied that there are other aspects of sex, travel and tourism. Prostitutes travel and are drawn to holiday areas. Netzelmann (1995) and Bröring (1995) report on the international mobility of sex workers. There is also the linkage between travel, tourist and resident demand and the trafficking of women. And there is the much-researched issue of sex tourism in places like Thailand, Indonesia and the Philippines. No discussion of sex tourism can ignore these issues, but equally the view that such tourism is solely one of exploitation must be queried. The precise extent of prostitution in Asian countries is not known, but it is considerable. In Indonesia, in 1994, the official number of prostitutes was 71,281 (Indonesian Ministry of Social Affairs, 1994), but it is well recognized that this is an underestimate (Dorling, 1998). Based upon those working in official *lokalisasi* (brothel complexes), it does not include those working in massage parlours or bars. Indonesia also provides a clear example of the construction of a sex tourist development to cater for the needs of overseas tourists. The island of Batam is located about 30 kilometres south of Singapore and meets the needs of clients who travel from Malaysia and Singapore where tight controls on the sex industry exist. Batam attracted approximately 500,000 tourists in 1995 and was growing rapidly until the collapse of the ASEAN currencies in late 1997. In the small island of Babi a *kampong* of prostitutes was established, while on Batam island itself, in 1993, there were 348 prostitutes operating in official *lokalisasi*. It is carefully controlled, but outside of this area Hull estimated a further 1800 prostitutes were also working, but without health checks.

It might be argued that Thailand is Batam writ large. A variety of estimates exist of the numbers of prostitutes in Thailand. A commonly cited number is 1 million (Phongpaichit, 1982; Taylor, 1984), but more recent estimates are more conservative. For example, Seabrooke (1997) cites a figure of 200,000. However, Hall (1996) points out that while sex tourism has brought several millions of overseas earnings to Thailand, the cost of combating AIDS is rising to about US$3.5 billion per annum. Other parts of Asia have witnessed a growth in prostitution. In spite of its communist regime, within China women are still regarded as second-rate citizens. With a growth in prosperity has come a growth in pornography, prostitution and the trafficking of women. The *South China Morning Post* reported how the police rescued 10,000 women from slavery in Hunan Province (31 August 1991, cited by Jaschok and Miers, 1994: 264). The *Herald International Tribune* of 7 September 1991 revealed that Vietnamese women were being lured into prostitution in China (Jaschok and Miers, 1994: 265). Many writers explain the attitude towards women in Asian countries by reference to economic conditions, the discrepancy between rich and poor areas, and to cultural norms in part derived from the economic and politically powerful. Phongpaichit (1982: 3) refers to the Brahminical ideals of the Thai court thus:

> As in many aristocratic cultures, the women of the court were expected to function as decorative status symbols rather than productive workers, while the women of lower rank were often prey to some form of droit-de-seigneur. The result was a culture of male dominance in which polygamy and concubinage played a significant role.

Thitsa (1980) and Truong (1990) question whether the Asian view of women as 'lesser beings' is not due to some misogynistic theme within Buddhism. Jaschok and Miers (1994) also cite the culture of China and its attitudes towards sexual roles as a major determinant of the systems of concubinage, servant girls (*mui tsai*), *pipa tsai* (female musician working in a brothel) and similar roles. But they also point out that

> it is essential to note that the primary beneficiaries from their exploitation were usually other women. The *mui tsai* relieved the owning family women of household chores and agricultural labour. Even where the work was light and

the treatment humane, female owners depended on *mui tsai* for personal service, as allies in family disputes, or for emotional support. The lot of each girl depended largely on how her mistress treated her.

However, while true, it might be seen as the negotiation of space by women within a structure dictated by the hegemony of males. Given these attitudes and the social structures of Asian societies, it is clear why women turn to prostitution as a means of securing economic support for themselves and their families. Throughout the western and Asiatic worlds the economic truth is that for many females prostitution pays, and can pay well. Phongpaichit (1982: 19) compares the earnings of masseuses in Bangkok with those of other female occupations. Whereas a clerical worker could earn 1000 baht per month at the time of the study, all 50 masseuses were earning more, while 'over half of the girls fell into the range of B3000–6000 a month with another 28 per cent earning rather more than that'. It is also noted that 'Most of the girls found Bangkok expensive, but clearly also enjoyed the prospect of living well', although having little time for recreation. Yet as Phongpaichit implies there is a hierarchy of earning based on the roles women perform. Seabrooke (1997) describes that hierarchy and draws attention to the diminishing asset of the body as the women age – an ultimate view it might be said of the commodification of female sexuality.

Similar stories can be documented in the western world. In 1997, a stripper working in a Darwin hotel could easily earn, without prostitution, A$30,000 per annum through tips acquired through lap dancing (A$30), a strip in the 'fantasy room' (A$50 per session), removal of a top (A$5) and bikini bottom (A$10). However, many such women work part time earning enough for their needs but leaving plenty of free time rather than seeking to maximize their earnings. Also, a form of legalized pimping may be said to exist, with the employer paying no direct wage, superannuation or sick pay even though the working week could be 48 hours. Nonetheless, this income was more than most young women could earn in clerical posts, or as bar tenders or seamstresses, while the job offered company and the opportunity for travel and fun. Some working women are careful with their money – one Darwin sex worker has been able to invest in properties, and rents out rooms to other prostitutes for their business purposes. In the UK Matthews (1997) provides evidence of a hierarchy of earnings in London, with street workers at the bottom and those working for upmarket escort agencies at the top of the income level; and Carter (personal communication, 1997) observed a ten-fold difference in earnings between prostitutes working off the streets in Prague and those working in sex clubs. Whole economic structures, sometimes with national implications, have been known to be constructed upon sex tourism, Thailand again being one of the foremost examples (Bishop and Robinson, 1997).

Most of the prostitution that exists within Asia is for domestic clients, and thus falls outside the purview of this chapter. For the overseas tourist the bright lights of such places as Patpong have become well-known attractions. For most of the women working in these resorts' bars, overseas tourists represent good sources of income. They also intrude upon the lives of the women just as many males intrude upon the lives of many women. Some are a nuisance and mean with their money, others are fun, and many are caring. The relationships between the *farangs* (foreigners) and the bar girls of Patpong is often seen as one of male domination. Hall (1996: 182) notes that 'Most fundamentally, however, the motivations for sex tourism are an outcome of a desire on the part of the tourist for self-gratifying erotic power through the control of another's body', but goes on to write in the next sentence:

> sex tourism is not simply about sex, but is a response to the complex interaction of gender, class, cultural, sexual and power relations in both the tourist's and the sex worker's society which sanctions the commodification of certain human relationships.

While there is commodification – the very travel brochures that feature Patpong, the videos or the Internet pages that offer visitors guided tours of exotic pleasure are sufficient examples of this – the complexity of human relationships and the sexual roles, the fantasies and self-delusions – the essence of being human – make for a complicated and many-threaded theme. Consider Cohen's description of the letters written by the men who visit Patpong. In particular, Cohen notes the emotional letter of one young German writing in limited English which ends 'All my love only you. I waiting you! I love you! I want you!' (Cohen, 1986: 119–20). The emotional attachment is clear in these letters, as is the self-delusion exhibited by some males that they, and they alone, are the answers to the predicament they imagine the Thai girls to be in. Odzer also notes the 'white knight' syndrome that many western *farangs* adopt:

> Poor Thais didn't go to doctors or buy medicine easily. Farangs told me stories of dragging their Patpong girlfriends to the clinic when they were sick and then buying their medication. One farang visited a girl for months after he had her tuberculosis diagnosed. Though no longer with her, he knew if he didn't buy the medicine, she wouldn't take it.
>
> (Odzer, 1994: 184)

Odzer's account of her time spent in Patpong clearly shows the complexities of the relationships that existed between the women and their lovers. It reveals a positive side of the sex business in Thailand, but just how positive depended upon the level at which a woman worked within the hierarchy:

> A hierarchy of jobs existed on Patpong. Working in a blow job bar ... or performing in Fucking Shows was at the bottom. Next came dancing nude and performing trick shows in rip-off bars ... then dancing nude and trick shows in non-rip-off bars ... Bikini dancing in ground-floor establishments was high status, but working in evening clothes without having to dance ... was higher. A distinction existed, however, between pretty women

in dresses, who were brought out often, and less ravishing, perhaps fat, older women who served as hostesses only. Hostess-only types were pitied. Attractiveness and sex appeal were major elements of Patpong prestige ... At the top of the status hierarchy were the beauties who didn't work for a bar at all but came and went on their own time.

(Odzer, 1994: 65)

Yet, for many Thai women the advantages were mixed. Odzer notes the poise and confidence many women acquired from mixing with foreign males. This was partly due to economic independence, but other reasons also existed. For many males, particularly western males, the trip to Patpong is motivated by a desire not just for sex, but an illusion of femininity, which, while compliant to male demands, nonetheless recognizes the woman as an individual. The paradox is that those Dworkin accuses of wanting sexual commodification are the very males who recognize their (temporary) partner as sentient beings. Possibly escaping from a society within which they may have problems dealing with the 'independent woman', they nonetheless bring with them that society's cultural norm of respect for the individual. In doing so, however, they reinforce the marginalization of the Thai women they patronize. To cite Odzer again:

Even without their fashionable clothes and healthy bodies, Thai prostitutes could be immediately recognised. Long after a woman stopped working in a bar, she was labelled a bar girl, almost on sight. Having jumped to this conclusion myself, I tried to isolate the characteristics that were so identifiable. It seemed to involve the way they interacted with others – more forthright and confident, more demanding and outgoing. Thai culture viewed these as marks of dishonour for a woman, a symptom of prostitution. A proper woman was supposed to be shy and reserved, nonassertive and pliant.

(Odzer, 1994: 78)

Odzer is not alone in her views. Robertson (personal communication, 1998) also remarked upon the independence of the women who work in the bars, and how western they are in many of their attitudes. Seabrooke (1997) also describes the relationships that occur within the *soi* (lanes) of Patpong. However, whether the Thai woman feels 'empowered' will depend in part upon the type of client. Seabrooke comments on the young macho males who are simply seeking as many women as possible. O'Connell Davidson (1995) divides the clientele into three: 'Macho Men', 'Mr Averages' and 'Cosmopolitan Males'. However, while these categories are instantly recognizable, the boundaries between them are not fixed and can be crossed. 'Macho Men' are such arguably by reason of inadequacies, and as they grow older may seek affection they cannot find in their own countries; while 'Cosmopolitan Males' may become repeat customers, forging either imagined or real relationships with individual women. Incidentally, much of the research in the English-based literature is on European, Australasian and North American clients; and whether these typologies are valid for

Japanese clients is not well documented. Nor is it known whether these analyses of roles are applicable in the context of Asian male clientele.

In part therefore, the western voice of the prostitute as evidenced by groups like COYOTE (Call Off Your Old Tired Ethics: see Jenness, 1990; Delacosta and Alexander, 1987) finds an echo in an area seen as the epitome of sex tourism. But equally this positive aspect of sex tourism is accompanied by a darker side. The campaign group, End Child Prostitution, Pornography and Trafficking (ECPAT), which is also based in Bangkok, notes that 'The commercial sexual exploitation of children has paralleled the growth of tourism in many parts of the world' (ECPAT, nd: 25). ECPAT estimates there are between 60,000 and 100,000 children involved in the sex industry in the Philippines, that 20 per cent of Vietnam's growing commercial sex industry is comprised of children under 18 years of age, and that in Phnom Penh in Cambodia 31 per cent of sex workers were between the ages of 13 and 17. Trafficking in young women is also reported in Bangladesh, Burma and India. The sexual exploitation of children is part of a wider exploitation, as young children are forced to work in factories and on building sites. Muntarbhorn (1996) notes that 'there can be no more delusions – no-one can deny that the problem of children being sold for sex exists, here and now, in almost every country in the world'. These realities pose questions for the perception of Patpong women as free agents. At what age did these 'independent' women commence their careers? Are western concepts of childhood applicable to Asian societies? Is the imposition of western concepts a form of neo-colonialism? Yet, even if it were, it should not be supposed that Asian societies see child prostitution as a desirable thing – it may represent a submission to fate, offer an end to economic dependence or be something they simply become accustomed to, but desirable? And, if one is to write of neo-colonialism, is not a worse form of such colonialism the continuation of a sex slave trade? For example, Miranda (1998) notes an unpublished report by the Australian Federal Police and Immigration Department into the 'export' of bonded foreign female workers (mainly Thai) to brothels in Sydney.

Brief though it is, this review of perspectives on prostitution and tourism shows that any relationship between the two is subsumed by the wider context. First, any demand by tourists is, in most cases, but part of a demand that arises from the nationals who live in the tourist destination. Second, any relationship is subsumed by the wider social context of both the tourist's country of origin and the place within which the sexual act takes place. Staebler (1996), writing of the motives of men visiting Thailand, comments that 'With the traditional privileges of patriarchal society being closed off in many Western countries some men feel inadequate to cope with the change'. Hence, part of the context includes the role of women (and children). In the west this is undergoing a significant change, and, as discussed in the first part of this chapter, part of that role is the reclaiming of positive roles for prostitutes. Thus, without having discussed different forms of prostitution, it is clear that many paradigms already exist for the relationship between commercial sex and tourism, even before the non-commercial context of tourism and sex is considered. A third factor is the importance of poverty: the lack of well-paid alternative occupations and the brutal fact that for many women and their dependants their body is their only social security asset. Nor is this restricted to 'Third World countries'. Ryan, Murphy and Kinder (1998) highlight the relationship between low income and prostitution in New Zealand.

How then to make sense of this complex pattern of demands? Arguably, three key factors have emerged within this discussion. The first is whether the sexual relationship is voluntary or exploitative. In the cliché of western prostitution, if the sexual bargain is struck between two consenting adults, it is no one else's business. A second issue is whether the bargain being struck is a commercial or non-commercial transaction. As Ford (1991) has shown, much sexual holiday behaviour is non-commercial. The third dimension is that of self-image and the maintenance of self-integrity. The first two aspects, together with the different types of sexual relationships engendered within the matrix they form, is illustrated in Figure 2.1. It should be noted that these locations are subjective and the model is not empirically determined. The vertical axis represents a continuum from voluntary behaviour to that controlled by others (exploited behaviour), and argues that degrees of negotiation exist and the relationship is not dichoto-mous. The horizontal axis represents a continuum between commercial and non-commercial sex. Again, it is assumed that the realities of the relationships between client and prostitute are such that, particularly for 'long-term' clients, they need not be dichotomous, that indeed there can be affection between the two. Furthermore, in a work that is otherwise generally dismissive of the prostitute as being anything but a woman exploited by a male-dominated society (even by uncertain, psychologically and sexually immature males), Hoigard and Finstad (1992) recognize that pimps can also be boyfriends. Given the resultant matrix the question arises, where does one locate various examples of sex tourism? Thus, sex slavery and the trafficking of women occupies the lower side of the bottom right-hand cell. A rekindling of romance between a couple who use their holiday to reinforce their relationship lies in the opposite top left-hand cell. It is, however, difficult to precisely locate other aspects of sex on holiday. But the purpose is not to offer a precise definition of each of the other activities, rather to illustrate their complexity. Prostitution, for example, has the potential for being a statement of female sexuality, for offering a means to economic independence or simply reflecting a lifestyle of drugs dependency – in short, there are different classifications and relationships, and to speak of prostitution as being one thing is simplistic, unhelpful and confusing.

It is perhaps here that the third dimension of self-identity and integrity

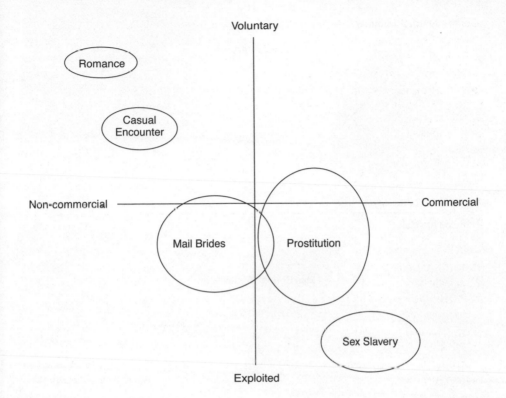

Figure 2.1 Sex tourism paradigms

comes into play. If, as shown in Figure 2.2, a diagonal line is drawn from the top left-hand cell to the bottom right-hand cell, it might be said that progression along this line from top to bottom represents an increasing assault upon the integrity of the person and their ability to assure a positive self-image. This, again, would be a misrepresentation of the prostitute view as expressed by Bell (1994), Leigh (1994) and others. Leigh, as her alter ego Scarlot Harlot, writing of her first experiences of prostitution, recalls: 'The silence of prostitutes becomes overwhelmingly loud. Suddenly I was surrounded by mute and righteous women.' Speaking at a seminar, she commented that prostitutes prostitute their bodies, academics their minds – and asks which is worse? However, as academics seek creativity in thinking, so too should prostitutes be able to seek a fulfilment of their identities, bodies and sexuality if they so wish. They are, indeed, righteous women. In Figure 2.1 it is possible to locate prostitution as a voluntary activity. That this is not the case for many women in practice is due to the social structures which have problems in recognizing women and their bodies. If, for example, in 1997, the Victoria Casino found it necessary to ask a woman to stop breast-feeding her baby in a public area, how then can society deal

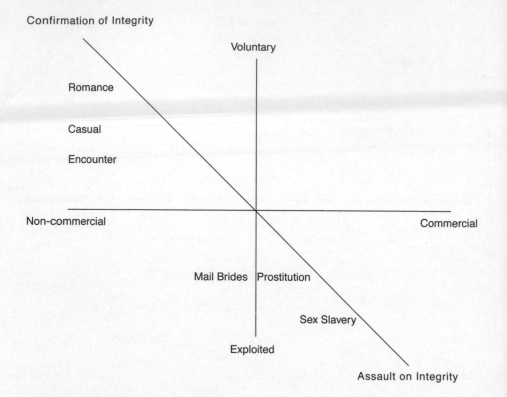

Figure 2.2 Confirmation vs. assault on integrity

with women's sexuality (*The Age*, 1998)? There seems to be a perversity that a gambling house has a problem with a simple fact of life.

How to define sex tourism? It may be simply described as sexual intercourse while away from home – an all-inclusive term, but one which permits a discussion of different paradigms. To restrict definitions of sex tourism, as is often done, to the red-light districts of places like Amsterdam and Bangkok is to limit our understanding of the phenomenon, and to artificially separate the location from the social context. To place sex tourism in Amsterdam, for example, is to draw a circle around it, to place it safely 'over there' and to escape the challenges and insights into our society that it provides. As 'circled entities' destinations like Patpong and Amsterdam are marked out in guidebooks, are viewed and consumed as sex theme parks, and by this very act of signing are reinforced as 'other' places. It is this 'otherness' that makes research difficult. As Douglas (1994: 308) comments:

> Communicating with anyone whomsoever is fraught with all the same difficulties as communicating with the Other designated by fieldwork. Anthropologists are not privileged by a special difficulty of their own. The wonder is that we can communicate with each other at all, and sometimes we have to be content with something less than perfection.

The 'otherness' of sex tourism can be, as ECPAT demonstrates, a location of exploitation and degradation where young women are shackled at night to beds, but it is also the place where a positive statement of femininity is being made. Both are challenges to our society, the one to be condemned and fought against, the other to be embraced. Any examination of sex tourism that discusses the one but not the other remains, by definition, incomplete. Additionally, to place sex tourism within a purely heterosexual context, or solely a commercial situation, is also incomplete. Both the world and its inhabitants are far more complex than that. Finally, to discuss sex tourism as separate from the prostitution, the heterosexual and homosexual relationships that occur in our homes and the backstreets of our own locales is also incomplete. The issues that arise from sex tourism – the needs for pair bonding, sexual adventure, fantasy, sexual exploration – and exploitation, do not start in the 'over there' – they begin here, in our places of home and work, and in ourselves.

References

The Age (Melbourne) (1998) Prudery sucks: nursing mothers – their place is where they want to be. Editorial, 10 January, p.9. Also see letters page.

Bell, S. (1994) *Reading, Writing and Rewriting the Prostitute Body*. Bloomington and Indianapolis: Indiana University Press.

Bishop, R. and Robinson, L. S., (1997) *Night Markets, Sexual Culture and the Thai Economic Miracle*. London: Routledge.

Black, P. (1997) Sexual behaviour and travel: quantitative and qualitative perspectives on the behaviour of genito-urinary medicine clinic attenders. In S. Clift and P. Grabowski (eds), *Tourism and Health: Risks, Research and Responses*. London: Pinter.

Bly, R. (1990) *Iron John: A Book about Men*. New York: Addison Wesley.

Bröring, G. (1995) *AIDS Prevention for Mobile Populations in the Black Sea Region: Report of a Bilateral Project between Sochi (Russia) and Trabzon (Turkey)*. Utrecht: Dutch Centre for Health Promotion and Health Education.

Burrell, I. (1997) Happy hookers declare war on feminist writers. *The Independent International*, 17–23 December, p.20.

Carter, S., Horn, K., Hart, G., Dunbar, M., Scoular, A. and Macintyre, S. (1997) The sexual behaviour of international travellers at two Glasgow GUM clinics. *International Journal of STD and AIDS* 8, 336–8.

Clark, N. and Clift, S. (1994) A survey of student health and risk behaviour on holiday abroad. *Travel, Lifestyles and Health Working Paper No. 3*. Canterbury: Canterbury Christ Church College.

Clift, S. and Grabowski, P. (eds) (1997) *Tourism and Health: Risks, Research and Responses*. London: Pinter.

Clift, S. and Page, S. J. (eds) (1996) *Health and the International Tourist*. London: Routledge.

Cohen, E. (1982a) Marginal paradises. *Annals of Tourism Research* **9**, 190–227.

Cohen, E. (1982b) Thai girls and farang men: the edge of ambiguity. *Annals of Tourism Research* **9**, 403–28.

Cohen, E. (1986) Lovelorn farangs: the correspondence between foreign men and Thai girls. *Anthropological Quarterly* **59** (3), 115–27.

Daniels, D. G., Kell, P., Nelson, M. R. and Barton, S. E. (1992) Sexual behaviour among travellers: a study of genito-urinary medicine clinic attendees. *International Journal of STD and AIDS* **3**, 437–8.

Delacosta, F. and Alexander, P. (1987) *Sex Work: Writings by Women in the Sex Industry*. Pittsburgh: Cleiss Press.

Dexter-Horn Productions (1997) *The Erotic Women of Thailand*. Video. Chau Bui, Santa Monica, CA.

Dorling, M. (1998) *A Study of Liminalities in Indonesian Sex Tourism*. Unpublished paper based on PhD research, Australian National University, Canberra, Australia.

Douglas, M. (1994) *Risk and Blame: Essays in Cultural Theory*. London: Routledge.

Dworkin, A. (1988) *Letters from a War Zone: Writings 1976–1987*. London: Martin Secker and Warburg.

ECPAT (nd) *End Child Prostitution, Pornography and Trafficking – An ECPAT Resource*. GPO Box 2593, Melbourne, ECPAT Australia.

Ford, N. (1991) *Sex on Holiday: The HIV-Related Sexual Interaction of Young Tourists Visiting Torquay*. Exeter: Institute of Population Studies, University of Exeter (unpublished report).

Ford, N. and Eiser, J. R. (1996) Risk and liminality: the HIV-related socio-sexual interaction of young tourists. In S. Clift and S. J. Page (eds) *Health and the International Tourist*. London: Routledge.

Goldsmith, M. (1996) *Political Incorrectness – Defying the Thought Police*. Rydalemere, NSW: Hodder and Stoughton.

Hall, C. M. (1996) Tourism prostitution: the control and health implications of sex tourism in South-East Asia and Australia. In S. Clift and S. J. Page (eds), *Health and the International Tourist*. London: Routledge.

Heatwole, C. A. (1989) Body shots: women in tourism related advertisements. *Focus* **39** (4), 7–11.

Hirschman, E. C. (1984) Leisure motives and sex roles. *Journal of Leisure Research* **16** (3), 209–23.

Hite, S. (1977) *The Hite Report: A Nationwide Study of Female Sexuality*. London: Summit Books.

Hoigard, C. and Finstad, L. (1992) *Backstreets – Prostitution, Money and Life*. Cambridge: Polity Press.

Hughes, H. (1997) Holidays and homosexual identity. *Tourism Management* **18** (1), 3–8.

Hull, T. H. (nd) *Preventing AIDS in Batam: Challenges and Responses in the Indonesian Health System*. Mimeo.

Indonesian Ministry of Social Affairs (1994) *Buku Putih: Rehabilitasi Sosial Tuna Susila* [*White Book: The Social Rehabilitation of the Immoral*]. Jakarta: Directorate General, Bina Rehabilitasi Sosial.

Jaschok, M. and Miers, S. (1994) *Women and Chinese Patriarchy: Submission, Servitude and Escape*. London: Zed Books.

Jenness, V. (1990) From sex as sin to sex as work: COYOTE and the reorganization of prostitution as a social problem. *Social Problems* **37**, 403–20.

Josiam, B. M., Hobson, J. S. P., Dietrich, U. C. and Smeaton, G. (1998) An analysis of the sexual, alcohol and drug-related behavioural patterns of students on Spring Break. *Tourism Management* (in press).

Kruhse-Mount Burton, S. (1996) *The Contemporary Client of Prostitution in Darwin, Australia*. Unpublished PhD thesis, Griffith University, Nathan, Queensland.

Lagrande, H. and Lhomand, B. (1995) *Le Comportement sexual de jeunes de 15 à 18 ans*. Enquete de L'Agence Nationale de Recherche sur le SIDA, Paris.

Leigh, C. (aka Scarlot Harlot) (1994) *Uncontrollable Bodies – Testimonies of Identity and Culture*. Seattle, WA: Bay Press.
   (See also: http://www.bayswan.org.thanskma.html)

Matthews, R. (1997) *Prostitution in London – An Audit*. London: Department of Social Science, Middlesex University.

Mendelsohn, R., Astle, L., Mann, M. and Shamanesh, M. (1996) Sexual behaviour in travellers abroad attending an inner-city genito-urinary medicine clinic. *Genitourinary Medicine* **72** (1), 43–6.

Miles, R. (1992) *The Rites of Man – Love, Sex and Death in the Making of the Male*. London: Palladin.

Miranda, C. (1998) 'Sex slave' rings net $1m a week. *Northern Territory News*, 24 February, p.10.

Moore, R. L. and Gillette, D. (1991) *King, Warrior, Magician, Lover: Rediscovering the Archetypes of the Mature Masculine*. San Francisco: HarperCollins.

Muntarbhorn, V. (1996) Rapporteur's report. World Congress against Commercial Sexual Exploitation of Children, Stockholm, Sweden, 27–31 August.

Netzelmann, R. (1995) *Patterns of Prostitution in Border Areas: A Short-Term Assessment of the Situation in the Border Region of the Czech Republic*. Copenhagen: WHO Regional Office for Europe.

O'Connell Davidson, J. (1995) British sex tourists in Thailand. In M. Maynard and J. Purvis (eds), *(Hetero)Sexual Politics*. London: Taylor and Francis.

Odzer, C. (1994) *Patpong Sisters – an American Woman's View of the Bangkok Sex World*. New York: Arcade Publishing.

Oppermann, M. and McKinley, S. (1996) Sex and image: marketing of tourism destinations. In M. Oppermann (ed.), *Pacific Rim Tourism 2000: Issues, Interrelations, Inhibitors*. Conference Proceedings, Centre for Tourism Studies, Waiariki Polytechnic, Rotorua, New Zealand.

Phongpaichit, P. (1982) *From Peasant Girls to Bangkok Masseuses*. Geneva: International Labour Office.

Rich, A. (1980) *Compulsory Heterosexuality and Lesbian Existence*. London: Virago.

Ryan, C. (1991) *Recreational Tourism: A Social Science Perspective*. London: Routledge.

Ryan, C. and Kinder, R. (1995) The deviant tourist and the crimagenic place. In A. Pizam and Y. Mansfield (eds), *Tourism, Crime and International Security Issues*.

Ryan, C. and Kinder, R. (1996) Sex, tourism and sex tourism: fulfilling similar needs? *Tourism Management* **17** (7), 507–18.

Ryan, C. and Robertson, E. (1997) New Zealand student-tourists: risk behaviour and health. In S. Clift and P. Grabowski (eds), *Tourism and Health: Risks, Research and Responses*. London: Pinter.

Ryan, C., Murphy, H. and Kinder, R. (1998) Tourist demand and the New Zealand sex industry. In M. Oppermann (ed.), *Sex Tourism*. New York: Cognizant Communications.

Schlessinger, L. (1997) *Ten Stupid Things Men Do to Mess up Their Lives*. New York: HarperCollins.

Seabrooke, J. (1997) *Travels in the Skin Trade: Tourism and the Sex Industry*. London: Pluto Press.

Sellars, A. (1998) The influence of dance music on the UK youth tourist market. Paper presented at the conference on 'Progress in Tourism and Hospitality Research', the Eighth Australian Tourism and Hospitality Research Conference, Griffith University, Gold Coast, Queensland, Australia.

Sprinkle, A. M. and Gates, K. (1997) Forty reasons why whores are my heroes, from Volume 1, XXX000. New York: Gates of Heck. (See also: http://www.heck.com/annie/40reasons.htm)

Staebler, M. (1996) Tourism and children in prostitution. Paper presented at the World Congress against Commercial Sexual Exploitation of Children, Stockholm, Sweden, 27–31 August.

Taylor, D. (1984) Cheap thrills. *New Internationalist* 142, p.14.

Thitsa, K. (1980) *Providence and Prostitution: Image and Reality for Women in Buddhist Thailand*. London: Change International Reports.

Truong, T. D. (1990) *Sex, Money and Morality: Prostitution and Tourism in Southeast Asia*. London: Zed Books.

Urry, J. (1990) *The Tourist Gaze: Leisure and Travel in Contemporary Societies*. London: Sage.

Urry, J. (1995) *Consuming Places*. London: Routledge.

Urry, J. and Rojek, C. (1997) *Touring Cultures: Transformations of Travel and Theory*. London: Routledge.

Whelehan, I. (1995) *Modern Feminist Thought: From the Second Wave to 'Post-Feminism'*. Edinburgh: Edinburgh University Press.

Wickens, E. (1994) Consumption of the authentic: the hedonistic tourist in Greece. In A. Seaton (ed.), *Tourism: The State of the Art*. Chichester: John Wiley and Sons.

Wickens, E. (1997) Licensed for thrills: risk-taking and tourism. In S. Clift and P. Grabowski (eds), *Tourism and Health: Risks, Research and Responses*. London: Pinter.

World Tourism Organization (1997) Campaign launched against child sex tourism. *WTO News*, May, 1–2.

World Tourism Organization (1998) New actions against child sex tourism. *WTO News*, January/February, 7.

3

Tourism and 'embodied' commodities: sex tourism in the Caribbean

Jacqueline Sánchez Taylor

Introduction

Jamaica, the Dominican Republic and Cuba, like other economically underdeveloped holiday destinations, are marketed as culturally *different* places (Momsen, 1994; Marshment, 1997), and all tourists are encouraged to view this 'difference' as a part of what they have a right to consume on their holiday. The construction of difference takes place around ideas such as 'natural' vs. 'civilized', leisure vs. work and exotic vs. mundane, rich vs. poor, sexual vs. repressive, powerful vs. powerless. So what is being commodified by tourism? MacCannell (1976: 23) has argued that to understand tourism, one has to analyse what he calls 'cultural experiences': 'The data of cultural experiences are somewhat fictionalised, idealised or exaggerated models of social life that are in the public domain, in film, fiction, political rhetoric, small talk, comic strips ... All tourist attractions are cultural experiences.'

Tourism is a medium through which people can purchase and consume such 'cultural experiences'. Film and fiction provides Westerners with a model of the life led by the rich and famous, and Third World tourism provides the vehicle through which they can momentarily 'own' this cultural experience. The obscene disparity of wealth between rich and poor nations means that even relatively low-paid workers from affluent countries can 'live like kings/playboys' in the Third World countries they visit, and enjoy the kind of economic power they cannot hope to enjoy at home. But it is also the case that many tourists to the Caribbean are using their economic power to obtain sexual experiences. This chapter will look at the buyers and sellers of this 'tourist experience' and, in particular, at the exchanges which involve sex. The informal sex industry that has developed in many Caribbean resorts means that sexual transactions also have this quality of 'difference', allowing tourists and some sex workers to convince themselves that what is happening is not like straightforward prostitution.

Restoring and reversing order

Western, white, male sex tourists have been travelling to Third World countries for many years and there is nothing new about the sexual exploitation of local women in this context. Indeed, there is a long history of sexual exploitation of women under colonial rule and Western men have long projected racist fantasies onto the 'primitive'/natural Other (see hooks, 1992; Collins, 1991; Gilman, 1985). But the long-haul tourist industry is turning this kind of lived colonial fantasy into an item of mass consumption. Sex guides written by white Western men, such as *Travel and the Single Male* (Cassirer, 1994) tap into the idea of 'difference' to justify the sexual exploitation of Black women in these countries. They tell tourists that prostitution does not have the same meaning in the Caribbean as it does in the West. The sex guides say that Caribbean women are not really prostitutes but 'nice' girls who like to have a good time. A key component of sex tourism is the objectification of a sexualized, racialized 'Other': 'You think of those incredible . . . women, ranging in colour from white chocolate to dark chocolate, available to you at the subtle nod of your head or touch-of-your-hat' (Cassirer, 1994: 2). This quote, from a self-confessed sex tourist, illustrates how important racism is in constructing a sexualized 'Other' for consumption, and how the body is a key signifier of availability. Lee (1991: 91) identifies racism as an important element in the South Asian sex tourist trade, arguing that 'Tourism often has the effect of turning people into objects, seen merely as part of the scenery or as servants existing only to make life more comfortable for the visitor.' The racist stereotype of the exotic and erotic Black woman is also an image that is used to sell sex tourism in countries like the Dominican Republic and Cuba. 'Blackness' and the ideology which constructs it are part of the commodity that sex tourists are buying.

Sex tourists are not a homogeneous group in terms of their economic, social, 'racialized', gender or age identities: they may be women or men, Black, Asian or white, homosexual or heterosexual, middle class or working class. Numerically, the foremost group of sex tourists are Western, white, heterosexual men, but it is important to recognize that even among this group there is a diversity in terms of sexual interests and attitudes towards prostitute use (see O'Connell Davidson, this volume, and 1995). Although it is necessary to recognize differences between sex tourists in their sexual practices, I want to tentatively suggest that sex tourism offers all of them opportunities to affirm a particular 'racialized' and gendered identity. So far as white male sex tourists are concerned, it is not just cheap sex they pursue. They also like travelling to 'Third World' countries, where they feel that somehow the proper order between genders and 'races' has been restored. Women and girls are at their command, Blacks, Hispanics and Asians are serving them, shining their shoes, cleaning their rooms and so on. All is as it should be. Western masculinity is constructed in relation to both an 'Other' gender and an 'Other' racialized identity (see Guillaumin, 1994; McClintock, 1995; Stoler, 1995). Back home, Black political activism and feminist politics have challenged and undermined the unquestioned power which gave some white men a sense of self from their gender and racialized identity. In this sense, sex tourists find that their masculinity and racialized power is affirmed in ways that it is not at home.

For example, sex tourists described how they loved the Dominican Republic, because, as white Westerners, they were placed at the apex of the social, economic and racial hierarchy. Two Canadians explained that in Canada, the welfare system penalized hard-working individuals like themselves and rewarded the idle and 'lazy' Blacks who lived off the state. As we talked, two shoeshine boys, aged 8 and 10, approached offering to shine their shoes. We were in a bar and it had gone midnight, yet these children were walking around barefoot looking for tourist shoes to shine in order to earn money for their families. In the words of one of these sex tourists:

> In Canada, those kids would be sat in front of cable TV. Their parents'd be on welfare, and the whole family would be just watching TV. I know. I'm a real-estate dealer, I see those people, how they live. They don't want to work. They just get their welfare, and it's the tax-payer who gets the bill.

Like many other sex tourists, these men were resentful of Blacks having even basic rights in Canada and preferred to see women and children prostituting themselves instead of 'sponging' off the state. 'At least they do something in return', they remarked.

Sex tourists can also give expression to more subtle forms of racism. Some choose to believe that they are inverting the hostile 'race relations' in their own country by mixing with Blacks in Cuba and the Dominican Republic. Their sexual relations with prostitutes become part and parcel of learning about the 'real culture', promoting racial harmony and reversing fears about 'race' conflict. While in their own countries they feel unable to approach Black men and women, when they travel they 'get close' to 'Others' and *really* bridge differences. A photographer from London complained that in London, 'coloured people keep to themselves' and that Black girls 'won't go out' with him. However, in Cuba his economic power meant that he was approached by Black people, something which he took to imply that in 'Cuba there is no racism'. Many tourists practising sex tourism feel that in the USA or Europe they are denied access to Black women because of racism, and that their sex tourism reverses this.

It is not only anxieties about racialized power that are calmed but also anxieties about gender. Sex tourists are often very resentful of women's perceived power in the West. They fear Western women's ability to reject their sexual advances and are alarmed by their demands for equality. A 37-year-old market trader in Cuba argued that British women demand too much from men:

> It's funny, but in England, the girls I fancy don't fancy me and the ones that do fancy me, I don't fancy. They tend to be sort of fatter and older, you know, 35, but their faces, they look 40. But in Cuba, really beautiful girls fancy me. They're all over me. They treat me like a star. My girlfriend's jet black, she's beautiful. She's a ballerina. She's so fit it puts me to shame really. I don't get much exercise . . . Women in England want too much nowadays . . . I'm a market trader, but I've done quite well for myself. I bought a house on the Isle of Dogs before the property boom, and I made a lot of money on that. So I'm residing in Wimbledon now. But English girls, they want someone with a good job as well as money. They don't want someone like me. They want a lawyer or a doctor or something, they want to move up in the world, and I can't blame them . . . Cuban girls don't expect so much. If you take a Cuban girl out for dinner, she's grateful, whereas an English girl, she's grateful but she wants more really.

Prostituted women in the Hispanic Caribbean, by contrast, neither challenge nor demand anything very much from male sex tourists. Another sex tourist, a policeman from the USA, told me he liked going to the Dominican Republic because there he became a desirable object much in demand. 'In the States,' he said, 'there are 20 men for every girl, here there are 20 girls for every man, and all of them eager to please.' A couple of Yorkshire miners also enthused about how the girls they were with had not only fucked them but also washed their feet on the beach, put sun-tan lotion on their backs, cleaned their rooms and fought over them, all for a mere US$25. Kruhse-Mount Burton (1995) notes that sex tourism can be understood as an endeavour to sustain a male identity; however, sex tourism is not just about masculinity, but about gender, and this becomes clear when the phenomenon of female sex tourism is explained.

Girl Power

The gendered body has largely been absent from general studies of tourism (Veijola and Jokinen, 1994). While the phenomenon of male sex tourism is increasingly well documented at an empirical level, at a theoretical level, debates on sex tourism are largely centred upon questions of patriarchy and male domination, and there is a tendency to assume that it is only men who travel to sexually exploit women. For instance, Enloe (1989: 36) argues that 'Sex tourism is not an anomaly; it is one strand of the gendered tourism industry' which she later notes '*needs* partriarchy to survive' (*ibid*.: 41, emphasis in the original). One problem with such analyses is that while female sex tourists are a numerically much smaller group than male sex tourists, some women do also practise sex tourism.

Social researchers have not been blind to the phenomenon of female sex tourism, yet they have tended to treat it as qualitatively different from male sex tourism. Both Meisch (1995) and Pruitt and LaFont (1995), who have undertaken research on sex tourism, use the term 'romance tourism' to refer to female sex tourism and imply that it could hold possibilities for positive changes. As Pruitt and LaFont note (1995: 423):

> Whereas sex tourism serves to perpetuate gender roles and reinforce power relations of male dominance and female subordination, romance tourism in Jamaica provides an arena for change. By drawing on their respective traditional gender models as well as their imaginings and idealisations of each other and new possibilities the partners in these relationships explore new avenues for negotiating femaleness and maleness.

Female sex tourists are sometimes sympathetically construed as 'lonely women' whose 'economic and social ability to travel alone is being exploited by Caribbean tourism' and the 'beach boys' who either offer the possibility of a 'holiday romance' or sexual harassment (Momsen, 1994: 116). The tendency to de-sexualize female sex tourism by labelling it as 'romance' hides the complexities involved in the social interaction between affluent, Western women and poor Black men. My research suggests that differences between male and female sex tourism may not always be so great as has often been assumed.

Prostitution is a contentious area for feminist theorists (Shrage, 1994). It is viewed by some as a form of male violence and by others as a form of work, albeit a stigmatized one. Male prostitution in the context of sex tourism further challenges and complicates many of these debates. Local men's commercial sexual activity can neither be understood as a form of male violence nor as a form of straightforward employment, as some do not rely solely on encounters with tourists for an income. Usually placed at the top of the hierarchy in the informal sex industry around tourism, these men are not controlled by a pimp or any other third party, nor is their status affected by their sexual behaviour in the same way that a female prostitute's status is affected (Sánchez Taylor, 1997). Female prostitutes are seen as vulnerable, male prostitutes are not. Yet both are motivated to enter into sexual exchanges not through personal desire but in order implicitly or explicitly to obtain money or goods. It would be wrong to assume that male prostitutes are therefore more powerful in relation to their clients, even though they may be more powerful in relation to female prostitutes.

Having conducted interview research with male sex workers in Cuba, the Dominican Republic and Venezuela in August 1997, I conducted preliminary research on female sex tourism in Negril, Jamaica. Semi-structured interviews were conducted with 45 individuals involved in the informal sex industry and female sex tourists. Data were also gathered from a

questionnaire administered to an opportunistic sample of 86 tourists.[1] The
survey found that almost half of single women had entered into one or
more sexual relationships with Jamaican men while on holiday. Although
this was a non-random sample, and generalized conclusions cannot be
drawn on the basis of it, one can conclude that some women travel for sex
in much the same way that some men do. Moreover, it seems that female
sex tourists are very similar to male sex tourists in terms of their attitudes
and motivations and the narratives they use to justify their behaviour. The
women questioned, interviewed and observed who had specifically chosen
Negril as a holiday destination for sexual purposes were not a
homogeneous group but differed in terms of their age, economic status,
social and racialized identities and their sexual interests. Furthermore,
female sex tourists could also be subdivided into various 'types' according
to their sexual practices and attitudes, and just as male sex tourism can be
understood as an attempt to affirm a given racialized and gendered identity,
so female sex tourism appears to reflect a concern to reverse and restore a
particular order and to ensure their own position and power within that
order.

Women have traditionally used travelling as a way of masculinizing their
identities rather than as a way of affirming their femininity (Enloe, 1989;
Kinnaird and Hall, 1994). Today, some female sex tourists are travelling to
cross traditional male domains using traditional male powers to reaffirm
their femininity. It is important for many female sex tourists to reaffirm their
sense of 'womanliness' by being sexually desired by men. In Western
culture part of a woman's engendered power and honour comes from being
a sexually desirable object for others (see Bartky, 1990). Women who feel
rejected by men in the West for being 'sort of fatter and older, you know, 35,
but their faces, they look 40' find that in Jamaica all this is reversed, as they
are chased and 'romanced', sweet-talked and 'loved' by men and once again
find that they exist as sexual objects. Sex tourism allows some Western
women to sexualize their bodies in ways that would be difficult to achieve
back home.

Who women found they are desired by is also an issue, however, as it is
important for these women to attract men who are desirable and sexually
valued by others in order to demonstrate their own attractiveness. Female
sex tourists, like their male counterparts, tap into existing frameworks of
racism to consume racist fantasies about Black Jamaican men as being
hypersexual. The fact that they are publicly seen as able to 'tame' a man
who is reputed to be the raw, highly sexed 'Other', a 'real' man with a
'primitive manhood', further affirms them as 'real' women. For instance,
when asked to describe 'boyfriends' in the questionnaire most of the female
sex tourists emphasized how for them Black Jamaican men possessed
bodies of great sexual value. One woman described her lover as 'sweet,
friendly, gorgeous-great body'; another woman summed up her boyfriend

in this short sentence: 'dark skin-younger-small frame'; and another as 'Handsome, physically fit, 27-year-old, honest, proud, serious, family man, excellent lover'. These comments objectify the men in much the same way that Black women are sexually objectified as 'Other' by male sex tourists. Black bodies become commodities which allow affluent Western women (both Black and white women) to experience an alternative form of embodied power. Masculine narratives, differentiated by 'race' and sexualized (Frankenberg, 1993; Mercer, 1993), underpin female sex tourism and allow some women to act out certain fantasies. In this case, they are allowed to be in control of masculinities which are 'Black', hypersexual and 'dangerous'. This type of female sex tourist does not want to establish a loving relationship with a Jamaican man and take him back to meet her parents, nor does she challenge racism back home but rather accepts the racial hierarchy and her position in it. It is not just sex these women are seeking but sexual experiences with the 'embodiment' of their racialized fantasies, and tourist destinations become a safe environment where female sex tourists can enact control over an imagined masculinity which is stereotypically constructed as aggressive and violent.

Even Western women who live up to Western ideals of beauty participate in sex tourism, because they can use their greater economic resources and/ or racialized identities to exercise power and control over the relationships into which they enter with Jamaican men. One Jamaican in his twenties, who sold tour-boat rides to tourists and also approached tourist women for 'friendships', told me of one relationship he had had with an older, attractive white American divorcee in her forties:

> Well, she tell me straight up front she start that she have three kids and she don't want to get involved. We could do this, we could do that. She don't want no personal relationship. One day you don't hear from me, things happen, you must take it just like that because it's not a long-term relationship, ya know.

The controls exerted by women mean that they can limit their risks of being rejected or humiliated. As one woman remarked about the end of one relationship, 'I got more out of him than he got out of me'. They can also transgress sexual, gendered, racialized and age boundaries without the consequences of becoming a social outcast. While at home they are stigmatized by having legitimate or casual relations with Black men, younger men, 'womanizers' or by having many sexual partners, in holiday resorts such as Negril they are permitted to 'consume' the Black male, the younger boy, the playboy or as many men as they desire, while maintaining their honour and reputation back home. A young Black woman from Florida also felt free to do 'things' in Jamaica she would never do at home and justified her behaviour by saying 'when in Jamaica you have to experience what is on offer'. Another white North American woman, who was a frequent visitor to Negril, explained her excursions to Jamaica as 'a secret, it's time out, like a fantasy and then you go home', since in the United States interracial relationships were frowned upon, especially in her home town of Chicago. Women like these female sex tourists use traditional discourses around 'race' to feel empowered in relation to male 'Others' (see Bederman, 1995). Their sense of racialized superiority in Caribbean countries, together with their economic power, puts them on the same level as white men operating in tourist areas in the Caribbean, and for once they can experience feeling more powerful than a man.

Thus, the contours of female sex tourists' encounters with Jamaican men are dictated by the particular type of affirmation they wish to achieve. While some female sex tourists have the power to control a relationship as well as simultaneously affirming their sense of being a 'real' woman or feeling like a beautiful film star, others prefer to use the power to affirm their role as a kind and good carer. For example, one Canadian woman, a divorcee near retirement age, conducted a long-distance romance for a year and a half with a Jamaican 'countryman' who is 20 years younger than her. She described his simple life as a farmer in the mountains, where all he had was a hut and a small plot of land which he used to enable him to look after himself and his mother. She sends him money and brings things over from Canada, and he was always very grateful for her help. She is teaching him to read and write and to appreciate classical music. She does not want someone who will swamp her with his emotional demands and she likes having the power to arrange the relationship to suit her needs. When she visits every few months for a holiday, she spends her time buying him shorts and shirts and cooking him big pots of food, because when she goes back to Canada he eats very little. She has conquered a 'noble savage' and can teach and help him towards civilization. Tourist women seem to find the idea of caring for and taming a 'noble savage' romantic, and many of the 'gigolos' in Negril claim to be 'country' farmers who lead simple lives and only venture into Negril now and then to sell products they have grown or made. The real point is that this woman, like the others who want to be considered 'beautiful' or sexually desirable, uses her sex tourism to reconstruct her identity. The 'Others' become a mirror which reflects back the female sex tourist's chosen image of femininity.

Embodied hustling

The quality of 'difference' in sexual transactions with locals allows tourists and some sex workers to tell themselves that what is happening is not straightforward prostitution. Sellers of 'cultural experiences' have to reaffirm not only their client's gender but also their racialized identity, and to do this they have to be the bearers of very specific racialized and gendered identities. Employment opportunities in the informal tourist industry are shaped by 'race' and gender, and hustlers in the Caribbean are forced to sell themselves in ways which are bound up with conceptions of self and identity which relate to wider context ideologies, in particular, colonial ideologies of 'race' and gender (Sánchez Taylor, 1996).

For example, Juan was a 20-year-old young Black Cuban, with a debonair and charming manner, who sold sexual services to female tourists on a full-time basis. He touted for business during the day along the beaches of Varadero and roamed the discos at night searching for female tourists. His hard sell would start from the moment he lay down beside tourist women on the beach, in his brief trunks, giving them a full centrefold pose. This pose exposed his unique selling-point which played on and 'confirmed' the myth of Black male sexuality, and tapped into these women's 'racialized' sexual fantasies. His successful business thus relied on the fact that he lived up to the racist stereotype these tourist women held of the 'big black dick' (see Small, 1994, on sexual stereotypes). He bought into the racist mythology about Black sexuality that persists in Cuban society, packaging and selling it for a living. He believed the racist-sexualized stereotypes given to Black men (e.g. larger genitals and greater sexual stamina than white men: see Karch and Dann, 1981; Gilman, 1985; Mercer, 1993). He was proud of the 'fame' attached to Black male sexuality and told me: 'I would rather be "caliente" than be intelligent, the more fame you have, the more people want to fuck you. What use is being intelligent if no one wants to fuck you?' It became apparent when talking to Juan that his subjective identity was directly related to the oppressive historical and cultural ideology used by colonial white males to construct Black male identity (see Mama, 1995, for a discussion of the importance of these discourses in understanding an individual's social and political position). Juan's subjective identity is inextricably linked to his involvement in the informal economy. He has been unable to challenge the racist ideologies that legitimized the objectification of Black people as sexual creatures in Cuba, because although the state claims to have eradicated institutionalized racism the reality is very different for millions of Black Cubans (Sarduy and Stubbs, 1993). Not only is it difficult for Black Cubans to find employment in the formal tourist economy but they have also grown up in the shadow of sexualized racisms and the myths that have evolved from them. For Juan and others like him, these myths are often the only benefit they can derive from being Black. The myth thus becomes a self-fulfilling prophecy as the interplay of race and gender limit the opportunities for Blacks in the formal economy and shape their entry into the informal economy.

It is also important to note that sexualized racisms are gendered in content and as such have various effects and consequences. Unlike women involved in the sex trade, Juan did not experience any stigma through his activities. If anything, his masculinity was all the more validated and a certain kudos was awarded to him by other males, while at the same time sexist norms mean that it is the women tourists who are more likely to be branded as loose. As one man in Jamaica exclaimed about a tourist:

'Rassclat! That woman went with three different men last night. She act like a one woman Oxfam shop' (quoted in Noakes, 1995: 375).

At a theoretical level, the most interesting feature of sex tourism is how locals' involvement rests on using their 'Blackness' as part of the commodity that they are selling. For along with the actual services, whether it be acting as a guide, fruit-seller, artist or gigolo/prostitute, they are selling part of their personal self. It has been argued that in service industries, workers are often selling more than simply their capacity to perform physical labour (see Hochschild, 1983, on emotional labour). In the informal tourist sector in the Caribbean, informal service workers are also selling something 'inalienable' – their 'racially' marked bodies. If the worker were only selling 'labour power', then it would not matter how the body was marked, yet it is quite clear that in the informal sector that feeds off the tourist industry, how the body is marked is integral to the commodity exchanged.

Although Juan may be classed as an extreme example of the influence of sexualized racism in the construction of subjective identity, all the local men I interviewed who worked in the informal sex industry in other parts of the Caribbean also drew on discourses around the male sexualized 'Other' in order to sell sex. In Jamaica, gigolos refer to 'big bamboo' and myths about Jamaican male sexuality to explain why white women travel to Jamaica for sex, while Dominican *Sanky Pankies* argue that Dominicans are more sexually attentive and romantic than men in the West. All the narratives employed are bound by specific national identities which rest on a particular set of discourses on 'race' and masculinity formulated during colonialism, and interlinked racial, sexual and cultural characteristics to form a hierachy of power.[2] It is therefore important to note that sex tourism sustains a particular racialized identity for the local individuals working in tourist areas as well as a particular vision of whiteness or Westernness for the tourists.

Conclusion

Tourism is a useful lens through which to view questions about embodiment and embodied power. In this chapter I have tried to show that tourism allows both male and female sex tourists to seek experiences that are 'fictionalised, idealised or exaggerated models' not simply of social life, but of social relations of power. Both male and female sex tourists derive power from a framework of real racialized and gendered inequalities which are written on the body. The existence of female sex tourists who also use their greater economic, racialized and aged power in interactions with locals in the informal sex industry to feel engendered and powerful not only undermines notions of 'romance tourism' as something distinct from 'sex tourism' but also illustrates how central constructions of the body are to the individual's sense of social power. The commodification of 'difference' makes it possible for sex tourists to construct and consume 'Others/Otherness', while the commodification of 'Blackness' encourages locals to sell tourists different forms of 'embodied racisms'.

At a time when Caribbean nations face enormous economic problems and are under pressure from world financial institutions to use tourism as a means of economic 'development', it is especially disturbing to note just how heavily tourist demand rests on and reproduces racist images of sexual and servile 'Others' (Burns and Holden, 1995). Indeed, Western sex tourism to the Caribbean provides another example of what hooks (1992: 31) terms 'eating the Other':

> Currently, the commodification of difference promotes paradigms of consumption wherein whatever difference the Other inhabits is eradicated, via exchange, by a consumer cannibalism that not only displaces the Other but denies the significance of that Other's history through a process of decontextualisation.

So long as it remains acceptable to use 'difference' as the Caribbean's unique selling-point, the tourist industry will continue to provide a framework which permits (even encourages) sex tourism. This in turn serves to entrench not only inequalities between the West and the developing countries but also the very forms of racism and sexism which structure the patterns of exclusion and exploitation that have been described in this chapter.

Acknowledgements

I would like to gratefully acknowledge the support of ECPAT, which funded research in the Dominican Republic and Cuba, and the Economic and Social Research Council, which is currently funding ongoing research in the Dominican Republic and Jamaica (award number R000 23 7625). Above all, I would like to thank Julia O'Connell Davidson for her analytical insights, and moral and emotional support throughout the research process and the many drafts of this chapter.

Notes

1. Fifty-eight single women were questioned, of whom 25 had entered into at least one or more sexual encounters with a Jamaican man while on holiday. Out of the women who admitted to having a relationship, 21 identified themselves as white and 4 as Black.
2. Though the Dominican Republic is distinguished from Jamaica and Cuba by the fact that the country lacks a popular anti-racist rhetoric (Fennema and Loewenthal, 1987), in practice, sexualized racisms enjoy currency in all three countries.

52   *Jacqueline Sánchez Taylor*

References

Bartky, S. (1990) *Femininity and Domination: Studies in the Phenomenology of Oppression*. London: Routledge.

Bederman, G. (1995) *Manliness and Civilization: A Cultural History of Gender and Race in the US, 1880–1917*. London: University of Chicago Press.

Burns, P. and Holden, A. (1995) *Tourism: A New Perspective*. London: Prentice Hall.

Cassirer, B. (1994) *Travel and the Single Male*. Newsletter. CA: TSM Publishing.

Collins, P. H. (1991) *Black Feminist Thought: Knowledge, Consciousness, and the Politics of Empowerment*. London: Routledge.

Enloe, C. (1989) *Bananas, Beaches and Bases: Making Feminist Sense of International Politics*. London: Pandora.

Fennema, M. and Loewenthal, T. (1987) *Construccion de Raza y Nacion en Republic Dominicana*. Santo Domingo: Editoa Universitaria – UASD.

Frankenberg, R. (1993) *The Social Construction of Whiteness: White Women, Race Matters*. London: Routledge.

Gilman, S. L. (1985) Black bodies, white bodies: toward an iconography of female sexuality in late nineteenth century art, medicine and literature. *Critical Inquiry* **12** (1), 205–3.

Guillaumin, C. (1994) *Racism, Sexism, Power and Ideology*. London: Routledge.

Hall, D. (1994) Gender and economic interests in tourism prostitution: the nature, development and implications of sex tourism in south-east Asia. In V. Kinnaird and D. Hall (eds), *Tourism: A Gender Analysis*. Chichester, West Sussex: Wiley.

Hochschild, A. (1983) *The Managed Heart*. Berkeley: University of California Press.

hooks, b. (1992) *Black Looks: Race and Representation*. London: Turnaround.

Karch, C. and Dann, G. (1981) Close encounters of the Third World. *Human Relations* **34**, 249–68.

Kinnaird, V. and Hall, D. (eds) (1994) *Tourism: A Gender Analysis*. Chichester, West Sussex: Wiley.

Kruhse-Mount Burton, S. (1995) Sex tourism and traditional Australian male identity. In M. Lanfont, J. B. Allcock and E. M. Bruner (eds), *International Tourism: Identity and Change*. London: Sage.

Lee, W. (1991) Prostitution and tourism in South-East Asia. In N. Redclift and M. T. Sinclair (eds), *Working Women: International Perspectives on Labour and Gender Ideology*. London: Routledge.

MacCannell, D. (1976) *The Tourist: A New Theory of the Leisure Class*. New York: Schocken.

McClintock, A. (1995) *Imperial Leather*. London: Routledge.

Mama, A. (1995) *Beyond the Mask: Race, Gender and Subjectivity*. London: Routledge.

Marshment, M. (1997) Gender takes a holiday: representations in holiday brochures. In M. T. Sinclair (ed.), *Gender, Work and Tourism*. London: Routledge.

Meisch, L. (1995) Gringas and Otavalenos: changing tourist relations. *Annals of Tourism Research* **22** (2), 441–62.

Mercer, K. (1993) Just looking for trouble: Robert Mapplethorpe and fantasies of race. In L. Segal and M. McIntosh (eds), *Sex Exposed: Sexuality and the Pornography Debate*. New Brunswick, NJ: Rutgers University Press.

Momsen, J. (1994) Tourism, gender and development in the Caribbean. In V. Kinnaird and D. Hall. (eds), *Tourism: A Gender Analysis*. Chichester, West Sussex: Wiley.

Noakes, K. (1995) Ruff spots and rent a dreads. In N. Jansz and M. Davies (eds), *More Women Travel: A Rough Guide Special*. London: Rough Guides.

O'Connell Davidson, J. (1995) British sex tourists in Thailand. In M. Maynard and J. Purvis (eds), *(Hetero)Sexual Politics*. London: Taylor and Francis.

Pruitt, D. and LaFont, S. (1995) For love and money: romance tourism in Jamaica. *Annals of Tourism Research* **22** (2), 422–40.

Pryce, K. (1979) *Endless Pressure: A Study of West Indian Life-Styles in Bristol*. Bristol: Bristol Classical Press.

Sánchez Taylor, J. (1997) Marking the margins: research in the informal economy in Cuba and the Dominican Republic. *Discussion Papers in Sociology* No. S97/1. Department of Sociology, University of Leicester.

Sarduy, P. and Stubbs, J. (eds) (1993) *AfroCuba: An Anthology of Cuban Writing on Race, Politics and Culture*. Melbourne: Ocean Press.

Shrage, L. (1994) *Moral Dilemmas of Feminism: Prostitution, Adultery and Abortion*. London: Routledge.

Small, S. (1994) *Racialised Barriers*. London: Routledge.

Stoler, A. L. (1995) *Race and the Education of Desire: Foucault's History of Sexuality and the Colonial Order of Things*. London: Duke University Press.

Veijola, S. and Jokinen, E. (1994) The body in tourism. *Theory, Culture and Society* **11**, 125–51.

4

Sex tourism and child prostitution

Julia O'Connell Davidson

Introduction

Over the past two decades, child sexual abuse has increasingly been treated as a newsworthy topic in the West. Child pornography, child sex tourism, child sex 'rings' and a number of cases of extremely sadistic child sexual abuse and killing have received a great deal of media attention, coverage that almost invariably invokes the concept of paedophilia to explain these violations. So far as child sex tourism is concerned, it is widely assumed to involve paedophiles who travel to poor countries where pre-pubertal children are enslaved in brothels. Though shocking in itself, this stereotype is convenient, even comforting, for Western audiences. It implies that responsibility for the problem of 'child sex tourism' lies largely with the culture and/or government of the countries that host sex tourists (what kind of culture produces people who would sexually enslave children, and what kind of government would allow them to do so?). It also suggests that the clients of child prostitutes are almost unimaginably monstrous (what kind of man would go into a filthy, sordid brothel in order to have sex with an enslaved and brutalized 7-year-old?) In short, popular stereotypes present 'child sex tourism' as a phenomenon quite discrete from sex tourism or prostitute use more generally.

This chapter draws on a series of research projects undertaken by Jacqueline Sánchez Taylor and myself which involved interview work with some 230 sex tourists and other prostitute users and around 150 adult and child prostitutes, brothel-keepers, pimps, procurers and other third-party beneficiaries of prostitution in eight countries.[1] This research led us to conclude that, while the stereotypes are not entirely without basis, the problem of child sexual exploitation by tourists is far more complex than they imply and is inseparable from the more general practice of sex tourism.

I will begin by looking at those forms of child sexual abuse which approximate most closely to the stereotypical images, and then move on to consider 'ordinary' sex tourism and child prostitution.

Paedophiles who travel abroad

The term 'paedophile' is a clinical one, used to refer to an adult who has a personality disorder which involves a specific and focused sexual interest in pre-pubertal children. Though the majority of individuals diagnosed as paedophiles are male, female abusers are not unknown; though some have a focused interest in either female or male victims, others have no consistent gender preference (Browne, 1994). The term 'preferential child sex abuser' is sometimes used to refer to those individuals whose preferred sexual objects are children who have reached or passed puberty. Such abusers are usually, but not always, men, and their victims may be either male or female children. Again, psychiatry views their taste for immature sexual partners as the manifestation of a personality disorder (hebephilia).

In all known societies, there are rules and conventions which govern and constrain people's sexual interaction. The twilight and often illicit world of prostitution provides an arena within which the laws and rules which constrain sexual practice can be evaded, and, in this sense, the attraction of child prostitution to adults who have a focused sexual preference for children is obvious. Laws and social conventions make it very difficult and dangerous for such people to satisfy their sexual interests in non-commercial contexts, but prostitution potentially provides 'instant access', often to a selection of children. Since there are very few countries where large numbers of pre-pubertal children are prostituted, those which have a reputation for child prostitution attract child abusers, described by Ireland (1993) as 'paedophiles who travel abroad', from around the world (at least those who can afford to travel).

Some such individuals are known to limit their sexual activities in their own country to fantasy and/or non-contact abuse for fear of prosecution; others would appear to have a history of child sexual abuse at home as well as abroad. There are at least two known cases in which British paedophiles (Douglas Black and Brett Tyler) who have killed or taken part in the killing of children in Britain have planned visits or practised sex tourism in South-east Asia (Tate and Wyre, 1995; Duce, 1996).

Sometimes paedophiles obtain sexual access to local children through contacts with like-minded local or expatriate men, as illustrated by the case of Freddie Peats. Between 1984 and 1991, Peats ran a boarding house for children in Goa, but in 1996, he was found guilty of having sexually abused and prostituted children in his care. The prosecution showed that Peats had confined children in his flat in Fatorda:

Photographing them in unnatural and obscene postures . . . transmitting

obscene   photographs   abroad . . . having   sexual   intercourse . . . with   the
children . . . [procuring] children . . . for purposes of prostitution . . . sponsoring
the boys under his care and control with those who called on him, especially
foreigners, in order that they could abuse them sexually.

(Navhind Times, 1996)

The case of Andrew Mark Harvey, a US citizen arrested in the Philippines in
1988, provides another example of this type of abuse (Lee-Wright, 1990:
226–32), and similar cases of expatriate involvement in child prostitution for
tourists and other expatriates have been reported in Costa Rica (Aguilar,
1994). As one man who identifies himself as a paedophile who has travelled
widely and abused children in a number of countries told me, there is an
'old boy' network of what he terms 'Boy Lovers', men who have already
been to or are 'on site in various of the sex tour stops. And they seem to be
willing to make introductions and give advice to newcomers.'

Not all 'paedophiles who travel abroad' rely on others like themselves to
provide them with access to children. Some make use of 'facilities' that are
primarily geared towards the interests of 'ordinary' sex tourists. Thus, for
example, a group of American sex tourists in the Dominican Republic
whom Jacqueline Sánchez Taylor and I interviewed in March 1998 identified
one of their cronies as having 'an obsession with virgins'. The man
concerned boasted of having paid the families of eight Dominican girls aged
around 11 in order to rape them, and had shown pornographic photographs
of one of his victims to his sex tourist friends. All of these men, including
the serial child rapist, were friends with an expatriate American who uses
an Internet site which promotes sex tourism to drum up tourist trade for the
brothel his Dominican wife operates. The wife recruits labour for her
brothel from inland villages, and while this couple's core business serves
'normal' sex tourists (of whom more will be said below), they clearly have
the kind of 'connections' that would allow paedophiles and preferential
abusers to safely arrange the sexual abuse of local children.

Extracts from a letter written to me by the paedophile quoted above
perhaps give the best insights into why men like him elect to practise sex
tourism:

There are several motivations for the men I have known to travel for sex. I
think the main one for the men I know is the fact that they could have sex with
a person easily found and with low risk (legally more than medically). They
could not do this in their home country. In the Philippines, they would have
the opportunity to indulge in a no-risk or low-risk sexual encounter which
they could not do back in Boston or London or wherever . . . The second
reason for sex travel is a social one. It has much to do with the reason gays
flock to Castro Street in San Francisco or Greenwich Village in New York. The
travel allows a person from a prosecuted, persecuted, closeted – even sad and
lonely? – minority to socialize . . . share a drink, compare experiences and
share the smile of some passing youngster who might be working in the bar or
café . . . 'It's good to talk' and other than in some Third World bar, we don't
have much of a chance to talk with others . . . Probably on a par with the social

motivation of travel is the fantasy fulfilment one . . . it is very exciting to be in an environment where sex for sale, men and boys openly being together, perhaps some nudity at a beach . . . is there to be shared . . . The fourth motivation for sex tourism . . . is for the producing of pornography. Of the 50 men I can recall, only one refused to take any photos . . . Some travelled specifically to produce soft- or hard-core porn. Others wanted to remember a particular boy or boys . . . Everyone took pictures. I feel that it is part of our phantasy about boyhood. I know well that it is my driving force. The last motivation is an economic one. Most of the sex tourist destinations are economically possible.

The relative economic power of 'paedophiles who travel abroad' allows them to exploit the misfortunes of children who are made vulnerable not simply by poverty but also by other forms of social and political inequality and/or exclusionary practices based on notions of 'race', ethnicity, 'caste' or sexual 'Otherness', for, as a general rule, 'child prostitutes come from marginal families in the cities and destitute families in the country, or are the children of prostitutes' (Coalition on Child Prostitution and Tourism, 1995). The relatively low risk of prosecution associated with child abuse in the countries they visit is also a combined function of economics and various forms of exclusionary practice. 'Paedophiles who travel abroad' do not pose a threat to the children of middle-class, wealthy or politically powerful families and, in the destinations they favour, police forces are massively under-resourced and individual officers paid extremely low wages. The chances of detection are therefore low, and when foreign men are arrested, it is not usually difficult for them to find someone who will help them to skip the country in exchange for a bribe. Furthermore, as Roujanavong (1994: 6) notes, successful prosecution of foreign 'paedophiles' is hampered by the following climate:

> Most government officials are confused because of conflicts between the Government's tourism promotion policy and child sexual abuse suppression policy . . . some [law enforcement officers] have close personal relationships with procurers or owners of entertainment places who facilitate child sexual abuse . . . The staying periods in the host country of foreigners are usually short. Thus when offences become known the foreigner has already left the country. It is very difficult to locate the victimised children, who may be homeless or from broken homes and to persuade them to testify in court. They do not want to be witnesses because they believe that they are guilty too.

Although the governments of affluent countries which send sex tourists manage to arrange for drug-liaison officers to work abroad, they have to date been unwilling to invest much, if anything at all, in policing their own paedophiles on site (indeed, there are cases in which embassies are alleged to have helped their nationals to flee back home when facing charges of child sexual abuse: *Bangkok Post*, 1995: 3). Western governments' lack of interest in crimes against 'Other' children has led many sex tourist receiving countries to pursue a policy of deporting foreign nationals accused of child sexual offences rather than prosecuting them. This may be gradually changing as a result of campaigns against child sex tourism, but there are still many countries in the world where Westerners perceive child sexual abuse to be a relatively low-risk crime.

For obvious reasons, individuals who conform to the clinical definition of 'paedophile', especially those who perpetrate particularly sadistic acts of abuse, tend to command the lion's share of press coverage and public indignation. However, in the following section, I want to argue that the idea that child prostitution is sustained solely by demand from paedophiles is untenable.

Child prostitution, prostitution and sex tourism

Childhood is, as many authors have pointed out, a socially constructed condition rather than one which can be clearly defined through reference to biological fact or chronological age. Its perimeters vary cross-culturally and historically, and even within any one nation state, its boundaries are often indistinct (see Pilcher, 1995). For the international community to concern itself with the condition and experience of children around the globe, however, it must necessarily employ some universal definition of childhood, and the United Nations and many other international bodies define a child as a person under the age of 18. I follow this definition, though I am aware of the case made by those who hold such a definition to be Eurocentric (see, for example, Ennew, 1986).

Even when a definition of childhood is agreed, it is extremely difficult to obtain accurate information about the extent of child prostitution in the contemporary world (see Ennew, 1986, and Fyfe, 1989, for methodological critiques of research purporting to quantify the phenomenon). However, I would argue that the more general body of empirical evidence on prostitution around the world does provide enough reliable information to enable us to challenge popular myths and stereotypes about child sex tourism on a number of grounds. To begin with, academic and journalistic research suggests that the vast majority of child prostitutes in the contemporary world are post-pubertal, rather than pre-pubertal, children. This is, of course, irrelevant to questions about the harm caused by prostitution, but it does have implications for our understanding of the demand for child prostitutes. It means that not all of their clients can be technically defined as paedophiles. Moreover, the existing body of research evidence suggests that most child prostitutes of whatever age are actually integrated into the mainstream prostitution market serving *all* prostitute users, rather than working in some discrete 'market niche' that caters solely to the desires of paedophiles or child molesters. Thus, for example, girls between 10 and 14 years of age are variously reported to be prostituting alongside older teenagers and young women in mining encampments in

Brazil and Surinam (Sutton, 1994; Antonius-Smits and the Maxi Linder Association, 1998), in brothel districts in Bombay and Bangladesh (Rozario, 1988; INSAF, 1995; Radda Barnen, 1996), in tourist areas in the Dominican Republic (Silvestre *et al.*, 1994), in brothels in Thailand (O'Grady, 1994), as well as on the streets in red-light areas in affluent Western countries (Silbert and Pines, 1981; Kelly *et al.*, 1995; O'Kane, 1996).

The same research further suggests that, depending on the setting from which they work, child prostitutes 'service' between 2 and 30 clients per week, that is, somewhere between 100 and 1500 clients a year. Even if the lowest estimates on the numbers of child prostitutes are accepted, the number of *clients* of child prostitutes would still run into several millions annually. These millions of clients are a disparate group in terms of their nationalities and their socio-economic, cultural and religious backgrounds. To explain the behaviour of such a large and varied group through reference to two clinically defined personality disorders, paedophilia and hebephilia (diagnostic categories which are themselves based on research with a relatively small and atypical sample of Western men), would clearly be unsatisfactory. Indeed, it is more reasonable to assume that a majority of these people are first and foremost *prostitute users* who become child sexual abusers through their prostitute use, rather than first and foremost paedophiles or hebephiles using prostitution as a means of obtaining sexual access to children.

Groups that campaign against child sex tourism are sometimes accused of overplaying the relationship between child prostitution and tourism, ignoring the far greater demand from locals and other non-tourist groups and so failing to address many of the structural factors that underpin child prostitution. I am not sure that such criticisms are always justified, but I will reiterate the fact that child prostitution is rarely hived off from adult prostitution, and that the clients of child prostitutes are therefore usually drawn from those groups that supply the more general demand for prostitution in any given area, by no means always tourists. It should further be noted that children's invariably weak economic, political and social status makes them vulnerable to extremes of abuse and exploitation within prostitution (just as child labourers in other sectors are especially vulnerable: see Fyfe, 1989; Sawyer, 1986). As a result, children often represent the cheapest segment of the prostitution 'labour market' and probably the majority of them therefore serve demand from the poorest clients rather than working in settings geared to the tourist market.

Having said this, it is important to keep in mind the fact that tourist-related prostitution develops on a large scale in settings within which poverty is widespread and women and children are especially economically vulnerable (see Truong, 1990; Lee, 1991; Chant and McIlwaine, 1995), so that tourists' sexual access to children is still very much predicated upon those children's relatively weak economic, social and political status. So far as the association between child prostitution and sex tourism is concerned, it should further be noted that prostitution is not a homogeneous phenomenon. Its social organization varies enormously both within and between countries that receive sex tourists. In Thailand, for example, early tourist development in the 1960s and 1970s attempted to maximize profits by capitalizing on accommodation and 'entertainment' facilities which had been put in place to serve US military personnel on 'rest and recreation' (Truong, 1990), and this is characteristic of several South-east Asian countries where, as Hall (1994: 151) notes, a period of 'economic colonialism and militarisation in which prostitution is a formalised mechanism of dominance' has been a key stage in the development of sex tourism. But sex tourism does not always or only involve the maintenance and development of existing large-scale, highly commoditized sex industries serving foreign military personnel. It has also emerged in locations where no such sex industry existed – for instance, the Gambia (Morris-Jarra, 1996), Cuba (Sánchez Taylor, 1997) and Brazil (Perio and Thierry, 1996) – and even in countries like Thailand and the Philippines, tourist development has been associated with the emergence of an informal prostitution sector (in which adult and child prostitutes solicit in hotels, discos, bars, beaches, parks or streets, often entering into fairly protracted and diffuse transactions with clients) *as well as* the reproduction of an existing, formally organized sector (see, for example, Montgomery, 1998). In many places informally arranged prostitution spills over into apparently non-commercial encounters within which tourists who do not self-identify as prostitute-users can draw local/ migrant persons who do not self-identify as prostitutes into profoundly unequal and exploitative sexual relationships.

It follows from this that the image of children enslaved in brothels offers only a very partial view of the phenomenon of child prostitution. Though some are subject to what Truong (1990) has termed 'relations of confinement', wherein a third-party prevents exit from prostitution through the use of debt bondage and/or physical restraint, physical violence or the threat thereof, other child prostitutes have entered into some form of employment relation with a third-party employer, others are pimped in informal settings and still others prostitute independently on a self-employed basis. All of this has implications for our understanding of the demand side of sex tourism, including the demand for child prostitutes.

Prostitute use, sex tourism and child prostitution

Kruhse-Mount Burton (1995: 192) observes that to define sex tourism as a form of tourism motivated by the desire to engage in commercial sex 'masks the complex process by which individuals choose to seek sexual gratification, first within prostitution and secondly as a part of the tourist experience'. To this, I think we need to add that various forms of racism are pivotal to this complex process (see Sánchez Taylor, this volume; Kempadoo, 1995; O'Connell Davidson, 1998), and it is also important to recognize that sex tourism is not always subjectively perceived as a choice to use *prostitution* as a means to sexual gratification. Indeed, different sub-groups of sex tourists can be distinguished through reference to their attitudes towards prostitute use and their practices as prostitute users. This helps to explain both the extent and diversity of child sexual abuse by tourists to poor countries.

'Macho Lads' and commodified sex

In a number of otherwise very different societies, men are socialized into a gender ideology which equates masculinity with the successful exercise of control over women, over other men, over their own bodies and over material objects (Segal, 1990). They are also often fed a diet of pornography in which 'ideal' men exercise enormous power over sexually objectified women (or, in the case of much homosexual pornography, men). Many men's non-sexual daydreams as well as their masturbatory fantasies centre around the idea of becoming truly 'masculine' in the sense of having the power to command others, and, providing they have money, the institution of prostitution equips them with precisely this kind of power. Because prostitution constructs sexual licence as a 'commodity' to be bought and sold like any other, it simultaneously turns clients into 'sovereign consumers', and all over the world, there are some men who find prostitute use affirmative for this reason.

Not all prostitute users are motivated by an explicit and acknowledged desire to control and command sexually objectified human beings, but for those who are, locations which combine widespread poverty with a well-developed and highly commercialized sex industry are ideal. This is of particular relevance to understanding one type of sex tourist, the 'Macho Lads', who make repeated visits to cities or resorts which conform to this description. These men's annual or biannual trips to such places resemble passing through the looking glass into a world wherein all their mastur-batory fantasies are miraculously embodied and attainable. This is partly because sexual access to prostitutes is extremely cheap, partly because the array of different forms of commoditized sex on offer is so extensive that they are in a position to command 'anything and everything' and partly because their racism allows them to reduce 'Other' women to nothing more than their sex. Thus, whether in Thailand, the Philippines or the Dominican Republic, men like this often describe the women/girls they exploit as 'Little Brown Fucking Machines'.

The particular organization of the sex trade in some of the cities favoured by sex tourists objectifies and deindividualizes prostitutes to a quite extraordinary extent, and this too helps to disinhibit the Macho Lad. The seemingly endless numbers of go-go bars and brothels in Bangkok, for instance, present sex tourists with a sense of prostitutes not only as somehow 'mass produced' but also as highly standardized commodities (for example, large numbers of girls/women or boys/men of roughly similar physical proportions are displayed in matching costumes, and often have numbers pinned to their clothing). Meanwhile, the live sex shows which some exploiters frequent (generally featuring girls and women performing acts which involve expelling air or objects from their vaginas, or pulling long strands of cloth or strings of bells or razor blades from them) further reinforce the idea of these racialized 'Others' as nothing more than animated sexual organs. By no means all sex tourists like this kind of very explicit commoditization (see Wilson, 1995), but the pleasure that those who do derive from it appears to reflect a gender socialization which requires boys and men to repudiate their own feelings of need, emotionality and dependency, and so to value sexual relations within which there is no danger of intimacy (see Seidler, 1987; Hollway, 1996). To see women and girls lined up in a brothel, numbered and available to any man who picks them is to see them as both controlled and controllable. They are stripped of their humanity and individuality, and so of the power to 'incite' feelings of dependency.

Many of the 'Macho Lads' we have interviewed have abused child prostitutes, not because they have a focused sexual interest in children, but because they are morally and sexually indiscriminate. They do not really care whether the girl they take from a brothel or bar is 14 or 24, providing they 'fancy' the look of her, and furthermore, child sexual abuse becomes just one more sexual experience in the range that is on offer to them as 'consumers'. An anonymous contributor to a 'World Sex Guide' available on the Internet, for example, provides descriptions of six 'adventures' he had on his 'holiday', the last of which features a visit to a brothel where 12-year-old girls were on offer. The sexual acts he performed upon a physically small and immature child are recounted as neither more nor less than another new and exciting 'commodity/service' purchased during the course of his trip.

Women-Haters and powerless sexual objects

Many societies socialize their members to believe that the human male has a natural, biologically based *need* for penetrative sex with females, and for some men, this belief informs a profound, almost pathological, misogyny. Because they see themselves as victims of a biological compulsion to have sex with any 'beautiful' female they meet, women are imagined to control a resource (their female bodies) that is vital to men's physical well-being. Women are therefore resented for their power to 'withhold' sexual access and unconditional emotional support, while men are viewed as out of control and powerless. The work of psychoanalyst Robert Stoller (1986) provides an insight into the psychodynamics of these men's prostitute use and their propensity to sexually abuse children. Stoller argues that sexual 'perversion' is essentially a gender disorder constructed out of a triad of hostility (*rage* at giving up one's earliest bliss and identification with the mother, *fear* of not succeeding in escaping out of her orbit, and a need for *revenge* for her putting one in this predicament). For the subgroup of male sex tourists under discussion here, adult women who are their economic, social and/or legal equals are perceived as hugely threatening simply because they are in a position to control *themselves*, that is to say, to exercise choice over whether or not to meet a man's demands.

The distinction I am making between Macho Lads and Woman-Haters is not absolute or clear-cut, for as should be clear from the description of Macho Lads above, they too are deeply misogynist. However, the 'ideal-typical' Woman-Hater has a far more intense and driving rage against women than does the Macho Lad, as well as slightly different attitudes towards sexuality and prostitute use. Where Macho Lads happily use prostitution as a means of acquiring control over themselves and others as sexual beings, the Woman-Hater is far more ambivalent about prostitute use, especially when prostitute women are in a position to determine the limits of the contractual exchange, as many adult Western prostitutes are. Men like this view prostitute women as taking advantage of men's 'weakness' (their biological *need* for sex), and so are fearful that the experienced adult Western prostitute may be exploiting them rather than vice versa (see also Bishop and Robinson, 1998). An interview with a Canadian sex tourist who admitted to having abused prostitute girls as young as 13 years of age is revealing. He told us that he 'hated' prostitutes. He had used prostitutes all over the world, and he hated European and North American prostitutes in particular:

> It's all businesslike. It's by the hour, like a taxi service, like they've got the meter running . . . There's no feeling. If I wanted to fuck a rubber doll, I could buy one and inflate it . . . A prostitute in Europe will never kiss you. In Canada, it's ridiculous. You know, if you go with a prostitute and you don't pay her, you know what? They call it rape. You can be in court on a rape charge.

The children and women this man exploits in Cuba and the Dominican Republic by contrast are so desperate that, as he puts it, 'Here, they don't even ask for the money. It's up to you.' As an affluent tourist to countries where female prostitutes are not only economically vulnerable, but further disempowered by legal frameworks which penalize female prostitutes rather than their clients as well as by various other gender discriminatory social practices, this man enjoys the fact that 'if you don't pay a girl here, there's nothing she can do. She's not supposed to be with you anyway. It's just tough.' Sex tourists who fall into the 'Woman-Hater' category carefully assess the vulnerability of prostitutes in any given destination, seeking out inexperienced 'brand-new girls' and complaining when they feel that prostitutes in a particular location are becoming too 'commercial' (for which read 'too powerful in relation to their clients'). Thus, a British sex tourist in Pattaya told me:

> It's all changed here. You never saw a girl drink or smoke when I first came to Thailand. All the business with whisky and cigarettes is totally new. They were nice girls then. They were soft, very soft. Now it's all changed. It's commercialism. They're hard and they're after money.

In the following year, he intended to visit Vietnam or Cambodia instead, where the girls were reputed to be fresher and less commercial. The search for 'freshness' (i.e. powerlessness) often leads men of this type to favour child prostitutes, as the following quote from a German expatriate in South Africa shows:

> The little girls, 10 or 12 years old, I wouldn't describe them as innocent, they're not innocent, but they're fresh. They don't have the attitude of the older whores. The older whores have gone downhill. They use foul language. They drink. They're hardened. The little girls, they're not experienced. They're not hardened, they want to please you, they don't know what to expect, you get a better service from them.

Again, racism plays a significant role in disinhibiting the tourist and enabling him to rationalize his acts of abuse. Men like this have told us that the way in which 6-year-olds dance *proves* that they are more physical and sexual than Western children; that girls in 'these countries' are grown up and sexually experienced by the time they are 14; that 'They' are all 'at it' all of the time. This is often coupled with a horribly warped interpretation placed on knowledge about the prevalence of incest and/or child prostitution in the host countries. Child prostitute users will tell themselves that the harm from adult–child sexual contact has already been inflicted by someone else, and that their own acts of abuse are not, therefore, the real crime. To quote a particularly repellent sex tourist of the Woman-Hater variety:

> Sex is a natural thing [in the Dominican Republic]. Everyone's at it, fathers do it with their daughters, brothers do it with their sisters, they don't care. They'll do it with anyone, they do it with everyone, they don't care who it is or how old they are. They're like animals. That's the only way I can explain it to you . . . By the time a girl is 10 years old, she's had more experience than . . . well, an American woman or an Irish woman won't never have that much experience in her whole life . . . Girls learn it's the way to keep a man happy. It's natural to them, it's a natural way to please men.

Finally, because the sexual use of children is, in itself, a transgressive act, it represents a form of revenge against the authority figures who such men imagine are attempting to control them (see Brace and O'Connell Davidson, 1996). It seems reasonable to suppose that, taken to its most extreme form, the desire for this type of control and vengeance can lead individuals to find sexual pleasure in the infliction of pain and/or damage on another human being and so perhaps help to explain cases in which child prostitutes are sadistically abused and/or murdered.

'Situational' prostitute users

Another clearly identifiable subgroup of sex tourists is comprised of men and women who cannot properly be described as choosing to seek sexual gratification within prostitution because they do not subjectively perceive themselves as prostitute users. They are able to deceive themselves about the true nature of their sexual interaction with local people first because prostitution takes a number of different forms in the countries they visit and second because they too buy into highly sexualized forms of racism. It was noted above that as well as brothel-based prostitution, there exists an informal prostitution sector, comprised of adults and children either soliciting independently from beaches, parks and ordinary tourist bars, or supplementing their very low pay from, say, hotel or bar work with occasional prostitution. Equally significant, in most sex tourist destinations, prostitute–client exchanges, especially in the informal sector, have a different character from prostitute–client transactions in the West. In Western countries, prostitution is typically organized as a narrowly contractual commodity exchange – x sexual 'service' or amount of time with the prostitute in exchange for y sum of money. Moreover, experienced adult prostitutes in the West typically negotiate clear limits to the client's powers within the transaction so that the prostitution contract is not, in general, a *carte blanche* for the client to do as he pleases.[2]

In the cities and resorts that attract sex tourists, the prostitute–client exchange is often more open-ended and loosely specified. Prices and limits to the contract are not always negotiated in advance, prostitutes may provide anything from two hours to two weeks of full access to their persons, performing non-sexual labour for the client (shopping, tidying, washing, translation, and so on) as well as sexual labour. They will also often act in ways that their Western clients take to signify genuine affection, for instance by holding hands, kissing, walking arm in arm, sharing a bed, things that an experienced Western prostitute would *never* do with a client.

Research has consistently found that these differences are central to Western heterosexual men's demand for sex tourism in South-east Asia (Kruhse-Mount Burton, 1995; O'Connell Davidson, 1995; Seabrooke, 1997; Bishop and Robinson, 1998). Men who are prostitute users back home compare Western prostitutes extremely unfavourably against their counterparts in Thailand and Indonesia, for example, and those who do not engage in domestic prostitute use find that the informal and non-contractual nature of prostitution in sex tourist resorts allows them to delude themselves about the commercial basis of their sexual interactions. Instead of having to go into a brothel or to negotiate a 'deal' in advance (the two things which, to most Westerners, are viewed as integral to 'prostitution'), they can pick up a 'freelance' by using the same scripts that they use in non-commercial encounters ('Can I get you a drink?', 'Would you like to have dinner with me?', 'Do you want to come up to my room?'). The whole process can be interpreted as confirming a mutual attraction, and the client can then construct the act of giving money to the prostitute not as payment for services rendered, but as a gesture of friendship, generosity or compassion.

Such self-delusion is again shored up by racism. Rather than being confronted by what they understand and recognize as prostitution, the Western tourist sees local/migrant women, men and children dancing, drinking and smooching with tourists, and interprets this as validating racist fantasies of the hypersexual Other (Kempadoo, 1995). The scenes they witness in sex tourist resorts are taken as proof that different meanings attach to sexual behaviour in the host country, that sex is more 'natural' to local people than to Westerners. Awareness that local people are actually prostituting does not necessarily prompt the reappraisal of such ideas. Instead, sex tourists tell themselves that there are 'cultural' differences as regards prostitution, and/or that they are not paying for sex when they give money to a local sexual partner, but rather 'helping' her or him out. Take, for example, the following extract from a guidebook for gay male sex tourists to Thailand:

> Many Westerners are troubled about the idea of paying a young man for his time or sex, seeing it as pure prostitution, but this is an oversimplification. In Thailand, as in other less-developed countries, you will be considered a higher-status person . . . with obligations to those less fortunate than yourself.
> (Hammer, 1997: 18)

All this helps to explain the demand for male prostitutes by female tourists (see Sánchez Taylor, this volume), the vast majority of whom would not enter into explicit prostitution contracts, as well as the fact that men who do not and would not use prostitutes in the West can become prostitute users in sex tourist destinations. Consider the case of a mature student, a white British man aged 35, who came to see me following a lecture I had given on sex tourism. He told me how he had been backpacking in Thailand where he had entered into sexual relationships with two Thai women (one of whom was almost 15 years his junior), both of whom worked as prostitutes, but that he was not a sex tourist. He then explained that one of these women worked in a bar brothel, and that he had paid a 'bar fine' to the bar owner for every night he had spent with her. He had also had sex with her. But, he insisted, the sexual relationship they had was based on mutual attraction. He had also paid money to the other woman, but he was not paying her for sex, of course, since she too was *genuinely* attracted to him:

Basically the thing was, she basically said to me, 'I'm going to have to go and sleep with somebody because I need the money.' So we were left in this awful situation where . . . she was going to have to sleep with somebody unless I paid her money not to . . . So we talked about it and we agreed, I would give her money so that she didn't go off and sleep with somebody.

Sex tourists of this type tend to view their sexual encounters with local people as 'holiday romances' (even when they enter into five or six such relationships in the course of a two-week holiday and even when they consciously select a particular holiday destination because they know that they will be able to form such sexual relationships there). The fact that they do not self-identify as prostitute users does not make them any the less likely to become child sex abusers through their prostitute use, however. They find their 'girlfriends' or 'boyfriends' among the prostitutes who solicit in tourist bars, discos and other public spaces, selecting the one(s) they happen to find most physically appealing. Given that large numbers of freelance prostitutes working in sex tourist resorts are under the age of 18 (indeed, the bulk of child prostitution often takes place in this kind of informal prostitution sector), it is unsurprising to find that sex tourists of this type often do end up exploiting child prostitutes. These points are equally valid in relation to female sex tourists, and we have interviewed male prostitutes in Latin America and the Caribbean who report having been sexually used by tourist women when they were aged 17 or under. The women concerned ranged in age from 23 to 62, and claimed to be 'in love' with the boys.

Unlike 'preferential abusers' and 'Women-Haters', neither 'Situational Prostitute Users' nor 'Macho Lads' consistently or consciously seek out children as sexual partners. The 'fitness' of the prostitute ('girlfriend'/ 'boyfriend') is more important to them than her/his age. 'Situational' sex tourists generally deny to themselves that they have sex with under-18s. (On numerous occasions we have interviewed men in their thirties and forties who have 'girlfriends' aged 15, and asked them how old they think the girl at their side is. They have invariably replied '19'.) It does not seem helpful to describe such people as sexually 'perverse' (in the sense of deviating from culturally prescribed sexual norms), since the physical characteristics that they are attracted to often conform to cultural ideals of 'youthful' feminine or masculine beauty, and not to cultural ideals of *childlike* innocence. Children mature physically at very different rates, so that a 14- or 15-year-old, for example, can combine certain physical characteristics associated with adult women or men with attributes of youth that are much admired (good muscle tone, unlined, hairless skin). It is also worth noting here that many models used in the production of pornography aimed at 'normal' men are actually under the age of 18, and an adult who is sexually aroused by the sight of someone who is legally and chronologically a child, but physically 'mature' and/or close to cultural ideals of sexual beauty, cannot necessarily be understood as sexually or psychologically 'aberrant'.

Lastly, I should note that misconceptions about the transmission of STDs can encourage sex tourists from all subgroups to select younger prostitutes in the mistaken belief that they are less likely to be infected with HIV or AIDS.

Child sex tourism: some conclusions

The 'double standard' which most societies apply to male and female sexual behaviour encourages condemnation of female prostitutes but tolerance for, even acceptance of, their male clients. As McIntosh (1978: 63) notes, 'unchastity is much more evil in a woman than in a man. For a man, it is simply giving in to his sexual urge; for a woman, it is a betrayal of her husband or father and of her whole home and family life'. A man who uses prostitutes is often considered to be acting in a fashion consistent with the attributes associated with his gender (he is active and sexually predatory, impersonal and instrumental), and his sexual transgression is thus a minor infraction, since it does not compromise his gender identity. By contrast, a woman who works as a prostitute is viewed as acting in a way wholly inconsistent with her 'womanhood'. Thus, we find that prostitute women are not only vilified by religious zealots as 'unnatural' but also constructed as such in much of the 'scientific' and psychoanalytic literature on prostitution that has been produced this century.

The fact that prostitute women are viewed as somehow 'degendered' and 'unnatural' in itself places them outside the boundaries of the imaginary community of 'normal' gendered folk (and, of course, male prostitutes who accept male clients are outsiders by virtue of the 'unnatural' and 'unmanly' sexual acts they perform). But there is more to prostitutes' exclusion than this. Both male and female prostitutes are typically considered to be dishonoured by their transgression of codes and conventions pertaining to money-making as well as sexuality. Because they break strictures around gender and sexuality and because they trade in something which cannot honourably be traded, prostitutes are almost universally constructed as moral and sexual 'outsiders', a status that is often enshrined in law. Prostitutes (and prostitute women in particular) have historically been and still are frequently subject to controls which would not be imposed upon full, juridical citizens (required to register with the police, forced to undergo medical tests and examinations, their freedom of movement restricted) and refused the protection accorded to full citizens (Walkowitz, 1980; Smart, 1995).

Pilcher (1995: 35) observes that in the contemporary Western world, childhood is socially constructed and legally regulated through reference to 'notions of children as "separate", as innocent, happy, apolitical, asexual, vulnerable, as in need of protection and dependent, and of childhood as lived out in family settings, educational settings, and through leisure and play' (see also Ennew, 1986; Kitzinger, 1988). Given this stress on children as both asexual and innocent, the idea of a 'child prostitute' becomes almost a contradiction in terms. Thus, we find that children are often refused legal and social recognition as children if they prostitute. Until recently in Britain, for example, the criminal justice system has not differentiated between child and adult prostitutes (between 1989 and 1993, 3300 children under 18 were charged or convicted on prostitution offences: Kelly *et al.*, 1995), and some of the organizations and agencies around the world that work with children and/or child prostitutes are much preoccupied by the idea of the child prostitute's supposed lost 'innocence' and sexual agency.

All of this ambiguity is eliminated if children in prostitution are assumed to be the victims of paedophiles and the criminals who serve them by trafficking in and/or enslaving children in brothels, and this, I think, explains the appeal of the stereotypes about child prostitution mentioned at the start of this chapter. As Liz Kelly (1996: 45) has noted in relation to the debate on child sexual abuse more generally:

> Immediately the word *paedophile* appears we have moved away from recognition of abusers as 'ordinary men' – fathers, brothers, uncles, colleagues – and returned to the more comfortable view of them as 'other', a small minority who are fundamentally different from most men . . . Attention shifts immediately from the centrality of power and control to notions of sexual deviance, obsession and 'addiction'.

As I hope this chapter has shown, the reality is that while some children are prostituted by and/or specifically for paedophiles and preferential abusers, the majority of sex tourists who use child prostitutes are first and foremost *prostitute users* who become child sexual abusers through their prostitute use, rather than the other way about. Questions about child sex tourism are therefore very much questions about power, for the sex tourists who exploit both adult and child prostitutes are not only empowered to do so by economic, social and political inequalities (between rich and poor nations, between men and women, between adults and children, between non-prostitutes and prostitutes, between white and Black and ethnic majority and minority) but are also motivated and disinhibited by ideologies which reflect and reproduce those very same inequalities of power.

For this reason, I would argue that far from manifesting abnormality or any pathological condition, child prostitute use by tourists, including the small number of female tourists who sexually exploit children, often expresses attitudes and desires that are very ordinary and widely accepted. The kind of racisms espoused by sex tourists are not unusual, but routinely voiced in mainstream white Western culture. Male sex tourists' beliefs about their own sexuality and their attitudes towards prostitute women are not uncommon. If anything, it is unusual to find people who do *not* believe that men are possessed of almost uncontrollable, biologically determined sexual drives and who do *not* dehumanize prostitutes. Nor is the sexual value that male and female sex tourists attach to youth extraordinary. And when sex tourists justify their sexual exploitation of local people in, say, Thailand or the Dominican Republic, by explaining that the 'girls' (or boys) are economically desperate and that they are therefore 'helping' them out, it does not sound so very different from the rationalizations given by spokespersons for the Western-owned companies that generously create the staggeringly low-paid jobs in tourism and in Free Trade Zones in the same countries.

I have not yet interviewed a 'preferential child abuser' or an 'ordinary' sex tourist who feels morally responsible for child prostitution in the tourist destinations they visit. They reason that prostitution and child sexual exploitation exists without them, and, where they acknowledge that they have used or do use child prostitutes, they are quick to point out that it was not they who *forced* the child to prostitute. But then, they did not need to. They were not called upon to abduct or rape or starve children, or sever them and their families from subsistence land, or marginalize them on grounds of their ethnic or 'racialized' identity or their status as the children of a prostitute, or deny them educational opportunities, or prevent them from finding jobs that pay above subsistence wages, in order to obtain sexual access to them. Such things had already been done. In this sense, we can say that sex tourists are merely parasites exploiting the harm already inflicted by other persons and structures, and very often, they are beneficiaries of the structural adjustment programmes and tourist development policies foisted on poor and indebted countries by world financial institutions.

As moral agents, it seems to me that sex tourists must be deemed blameworthy for exploiting the misfortunes of others to satisfy their own ends. However, sex tourists also act within a given set of structural constraints and opportunities, and give meaning to their action through reference to ideologies that naturalize class inequalities, poverty, racism and sexism. Their power – as well as their desire – to sexually exploit 'Other' children, women and men can only be fully explained through reference to those broader systemic factors. Political campaigns against child sex tourism therefore need to be simultaneously campaigns against poverty, 'Third World' debt, sexism, racism and the gender and sexual ideologies which 'Otherize' prostitutes, as well as against legal frameworks and law-enforcement practice that criminalize female prostitutes and exonerate their clients.

Acknowledgements

My thanks are due to Jacqueline Sánchez Taylor. Since she co-researched almost all the material presented in this chapter, it is no exaggeration to say that without her, it would not exist. I would also like to gratefully acknowledge the support of the Social Science Research Board, Leicester

University, which funded fieldwork in Thailand and Cuba, ECPAT, which funded research in the Dominican Republic, Cuba, Costa Rica, Venezuela, South Africa and India, and the Economic and Social Research Council, which funded fieldwork in the Dominican Republic and Jamaica (award number R000 23 7625).

Notes

1. In 1994, I undertook a small study of British sex tourists to Thailand. In 1995 and 1996, Jacqueline Sánchez Taylor and I were commissioned by ECPAT (End Child Prostitution in Asian Tourism) to investigate the attitudes, identities and motivations of the clinets of children involved in tourist-related prostitution. We undertook fieldwork in the Dominican Republic, Cuba, Venezuela, Costa Rica, India and South Africa. Since February 1998, we have been working on an ESRC (Economic and Social Research Council)-funded research project examining tourist-related prostitution in Jamaica and the Dominican Republic.
2. It should be noted, however, that the Western prostitute's capacity to enforce such limits varies according to a range of factors (see O'Connell Davidson, 1998).

References

Aguilar, M. (1994) Alarma corrupcion de menores en Puntareas. *Sucesos*, San Jose, Costa Rica, 9 January.
Antonius-Smits, C. and the Maxi Linder Association (1998) Gold and commercial sex: exploring the link between small-scale gold mining and commercial sex in the rainforest of Surinam. Unpublished contribution to The Working Sex: Caribbean Development, Tourism, Sex and Work Conference, Kingston, Jamaica, 16–17 July.
Bangkok Post (1995) Child molester flees Thailand. *Bangkok Post*, 31 January.
Bishop, R. and Robinson, L. S. (1998) *Night Market: Sexual Cultures and the Thai Economic Miracle*. London: Routledge.
Brace, L. and O'Connell Davidson, J. (1996) Desperate debtors and counterfeit love: the Hobbesian world of the sex tourist. *Contemporary Politics* 2 (3), 55–77.
Browne, K. (1994) Child sexual abuse. In J. Archer (ed.), *Male Violence*. London: Routledge.
Chant, S. and McIlwaine, C. (1995) *Women of a Lesser Cost: Female Labour, Foreign Exchange and Philippine Development*. London: Pluto.
Coalition on Child Prostitution and Tourism (1995) *Factsheet*, 6. Unit 4, Stableyard, Broomgrove Road, London.
Duce, R. (1996) Psychiatrist tipped off police about Daniel's murderer. *The Times*, 9 May.
Enloe, C. (1993) *The Morning After: Sexual Politics at the End of the Cold War*. Berkeley: University of California Press.
Ennew, J. (1986) *The Sexual Exploitation of Children*. Cambridge: Polity.
Fyfe, A. (1989) *Child Labour*. Cambridge: Polity.
Hall, C. M. (1994) Gender and economic interests in tourism prostitution: the nature, development and implications of sex tourism in south-east Asia. In V. Kinnaird and D. Hall (eds), *Tourism: A Gender Perspective*. London: Routledge.

Hammer, D. (1997) *Thai Scene*. Swaffham, Norfolk: Gay Men's Press.

Hollway, W. (1996) Recognition and heterosexual desire. In D. Richardson (ed.), *Theorising Heterosexuality*. Buckingham, Bucks: Open University Press.

INSAF (1995) The needs of children in Goa: towards building an adequate response. *Interim Report*. Panjim: Indian National Social Action Forum.

Ireland, K. (1993) *'Wish You Weren't Here': The Sexual Exploitation of Children and the Connection with Tourism and International Travel*. Working Paper No. 7. London: Save the Children.

Kelly, L. (1996) Paedophiles and the cycle of abuse. *Trouble and Strife* 33, 44–9.

Kelly, L., Wingfield, R., Burton, S. and Regan, L. (1995) *Splintered Lives: Sexual Exploitation of Children in the Context of Children's Rights and Child Protection*. Ilford: Barnardo's.

Kempadoo, K. (1995) Prostitution, marginality and empowerment: Caribbean women in the sex trade. *Beyond Law* 5 (14), March.

Kitzinger, J. (1988) Defending innocence: ideologies of childhood. *Feminist Review* Spring (28).

Kruhse-Mount Burton, S. (1995) Sex tourism and traditional Australian male identity. In M. Lanfont, J. Allcock and E. M. Bruner (eds), *International Tourism: Identity and Change*. London: Sage.

Lee, W. (1991) Prostitution and tourism in South-East Asia. In N. Redclift and M. T. Sinclair (eds), *Working Women: International Perspectives on Labour and Gender Ideology*. London: Routledge.

Lee-Wright, P. (1990) *Child Slaves*. London: Earthscan.

McIntosh, M. (1978) Who needs prostitutes? The ideology of male sexual needs. In C. Smart and B. Smart (eds), *Women, Sexuality and Social Control*. London: Routledge and Kegan Paul.

Montgomery, H. (1998) Children, prostitution and identity: a case study from a tourist resort in Thailand. In K. Kempadoo and J. Doezema (eds), *Global Sex Workers*. London: Routledge.

Morris-Jarra, M. (1996) No such thing as a cheap holiday. *Tourism in Focus* 26, Autumn, 14–16.

Navhind Times (1996) Peats found guilty of child prostitution. *Navhind Times*, 34 (27), 27 (Saturday 16 March).

O'Connell Davidson, J. (1995) British sex tourists in Thailand. In M. Maynard and J. Purvis (eds), *(Hetero)Sexual Politics*. London: Taylor and Francis.

O'Connell Davidson, J. (1998) *Prostitution, Power and Freedom*. Cambridge: Polity.

O'Grady, R. (1994) *The Rape of the Innocent*. Bangkok: ECPAT.

O'Kane, M. (1996) Death of innocence. *Guardian*, 12 February.

Perio, G. and Thierry, D. (1996) Tourisme sexuel au Brésil et en Colombie. Rapport d'enquête. 53 rue de Tilleul, 59200 Tourcoing.

Pilcher, J. (1995) *Age and Generation in Modern Britain*. Oxford: Oxford University Press.

Radda Barnen (1996) Daughters are worth a fortune in the brothels of Bangladesh. *Barnen Och Vi*, Special feature issue. Stockholm: Radda Barnen, pp. 26–7.

Roujanavong, W. (1994) Thailand's image attracts the wrong people. *ECPAT Newsletter* 11, December.

Rozario, R. (1988) *Trafficking in Women and Children in India*. New Delhi: Uppal.

Sánchez Taylor, J. (1997) Marking the margins: research in the informal economy in

Cuba and the Dominican Republic. *Discussion Papers in Sociology* No. S97/1, Department of Sociology, University of Leicester.

Sawyer, R. (1986) *Slavery in the Twentieth Century.* London: Routledge and Kegan Paul.

Seabrooke, J. (1997) *Travels in the Skin Trade: Tourism and the Sex Industry.* London: Pluto Press.

Segal, L. (1990) *Slow Motion: Changing Masculinities, Changing Men.* London: Virago.

Seidler, V. (1987) Reason, desire and male sexuality. In P. Caplan (ed.), *The Cultural Construction of Sexuality.* London: Routledge.

Silbert, M. and Pines, A. (1981) Sexual abuse as an antecedent to prostitution. *Child Abuse and Neglect* **5**, 407–11.

Silvestre, E., Rijo, J. and Bogaert, H. (1994) *La Neo-prostitucion Infantil en Republica Dominicana.* Santo Domingo: UNICEF.

Smart, C. (1995) *Law, Crime and Sexuality.* London: Sage.

Stoller, R. (1986) *Perversion: The Erotic Form of Hatred.* New York: Karnac.

Sutton, A. (1994) *Slavery in Brazil.* London: Anti-Slavery International.

Tate, T. and Wyre, R. (1995) *Murder of Childhood.* Harmondsworth: Penguin.

Truong, T. D. (1990) *Sex, Money and Morality: Prostitution and Tourism in Southeast Asia.* London: Zed Books.

Walkowitz, J. (1980) *Prostitution and Victorian Society: Women, Class and the State.* Cambridge: Cambridge University Press.

Wilson, A. (1995) Commoditization and the nature of demand in the tourist sex trade in Bangkok. In C. Fink and J. Forshee (eds), *Travellers and Tourists in Southeast Asia.* Berkeley, CA: Center for South-east Asia Studies.

5

Combating tourist sexual exploitation of children

Jayne Hoose, Stephen Clift and Simon Carter

Introduction

Earlier in this volume, Ryan notes the complexities of the interconnections between tourism and sex, but suggests that these can be conceptualized along two primary dimensions: non-commercial vs. commercial, and autonomous vs. coerced. Sexual activity in tourism contexts which involves commercial transactions can arise 'informally' around the margins of the legitimate tourist industry, or it can to a greater or lesser extent be more formally organized, giving rise to well-known 'sex tourism' destinations. Many adults, and it appears children of both sexes, are forced to work within the informal and formal frameworks of 'sex tourism', either from economic necessity or as a result of being 'contracted' into a form of slave labour. Sex tourism appears to be a large-scale and growing global phenomenon, exhibiting a dynamic shifting pattern over time (Ireland, 1993; Burrell, 1998), and the commercial sexual exploitation of children and child prostitution is an extreme and particularly unpalatable dimension of this practice (International Labour Organization, 1998). This has led in recent years to considerable media attention and significant actions have been taken to combat sex tourism in general and child sex tourism in particular. Governments in tourist-receiving countries have passed legislation outlawing child prostitution and fixing severe penalties for anyone, including foreign nationals, involved in child sex. Governments in countries from which sex tourists originate have passed extra-territorial legislation to make it possible to prosecute child sex tourists 'at home' and have devised industry training and public information initiatives (Levy, 1998). A range of international governmental organizations (e.g. World Tourism Organization, International Labour Organization, European Commission) and non-governmental organizations (e.g. ECPAT, Save the Children) have recently gathered intelligence on the issue of sex tourism, supported basic research, convened conferences and organized or promoted active campaigns against child sex tourism. Commercial travel and tourism organizations have also formally supported such initiatives and established their own policies and guidelines to suppress sex tourism (e.g. International Association of Tour Operators). While most people in Europe are aware of the existence of child sex tourism, far fewer are, however, aware of such campaigns or initiatives to address the problem (INRA, 1998). The objectives of this chapter are, first, to address briefly some of the major questions raised by the existence of child sexual exploitation by tourists (see also the discussion by O'Connell Davidson in this volume) and, second, to discuss more fully some of the recent initiatives that have been launched to combat such exploitation.

Tourism and the sexual exploitation of children

Definitions of 'child sex tourism'

The principal international legal reference providing a definition of 'a child' is the United Nations Convention on the Rights of the Child (United Nations, 1991) whose Article 1 defines a child as: 'every human being below the age of 18 years unless, under the law applicable to the child, majority is attained earlier'. Majority is, however, attained in most countries by the age of 16 and it is the commercial sexual exploitation of minors which has drawn attention. The commercial sexual exploitation of children is defined by the World Congress against the Commercial Sexual Exploitation of Children (Stockholm, 27–31 August 1996) (United Nations, 1996) as: 'sexual abuse by the adult and remuneration in cash or kind to the child or to a third person or persons . . . it constitutes a form of coercion and violence against children and amounts to forced labour and a contemporary form of slavery'. The phrase 'commercial sexual exploitation of children' is increasingly used to describe the various practices that exploit children for their commercial value, such as prostitution, trafficking and pornography. The term implies that the child is not only sexually abused but also that there is a profit arising from the transaction where the child is considered a sexual and commercial object. ECPAT UK (1997: 7) have provided a number of definitions of aspects of the sexual exploitation of children which are of value in clarifying the nature of the phenomenon:

- Sale of children – refers to the transfer of a child from one party (including biological parents, guardians and institutions) to another, for whatever purpose, in exchange for financial or other reward or compensation.
- Child prostitution – refers to the sexual exploitation of a child for remuneration in cash or kind, usually but not always organised by an intermediary (parent, family member, procurer, teacher, etc.). Put another way, it is the act of engaging or offering the services of a child to perform sexual acts for money or other consideration (i.e. gifts, food) with that person or any person.

- Child pornography – refers to the visual or audio depiction of a child for the sexual gratification of the user, and involves the production, distribution and/or use of such material.
- Child trafficking – refers to the illegal moving and selling of a child across countries and continents in exchange for financial or other compensation.
- A street child – refers to any boy or girl for whom the street (in the widest sense of the word, including unoccupied dwellings, wasteland, etc.) has become their abode and/or source of livelihood, and who is inadequately protected, supervised or directed by responsible adults.

Categories of child sex exploiters in tourist contexts

The individuals who carry out sexual exploitation of children come from almost anywhere in the world and span all cultures, ages, social classes and occupations. Child sex offenders who are involved in sex tourism fall within three categories (ECPAT UK, 1997):

- Paedophile – an adult who has a personality disorder which involves a specific and focused sexual interest in pre-pubertal children.
- Preferential child sex abuser – those individuals whose preferred sexual objects are children who have reached or passed puberty.
- Situational child sex abuser – those who do not consistently or consciously seek out children as sexual partners, but who do on occasion have child sex.

The first two groups are characterized by long-term and persistent patterns of behaviour which often result in sophisticated criminal networks to provide access to child victims. Such abusers often deny any knowledge of the suffering caused to children by using a variety of rationalizations – e.g. 'A child who does not physically resist really wants sex' or 'Having sex with a child is a good way to show love or teach the child about sex.' They will often point to the gifts and inducements given to the child as evidence of their care for him or her. In contrast, situational child sex abusers have sex with a child either because

- they are morally and/or sexually indiscriminate and wish to 'experiment' with child sexual partners;
- they have entered into situations in which children who meet their ideals of physical attractiveness are sexually accessible to them;
- certain disinhibiting factors are present which allow them either to delude themselves about the child's true age or about the nature of the child's consent;

and/or

- they have the opportunity to delude themselves that such behaviour is acceptable in the country they are visiting.

(ECPAT UK, 1997; Hoose, 1997)

The scale of child prostitution in tourism

Due to the nature of child sex tourism it is very difficult to produce reliable statistics on the number of children involved world-wide. Estimates were,

Table 5.1 Estimated numbers of children in child prostitution

Country	ECPAT/NGO	UNICEF
China		200,000+
Dominican Rep.		25,500
India	300–400,000	
Pakistan	20,000	40,000
Sri Lanka	20,000	30,000
Taiwan	60,000	
Thailand	200–250,000	100,000
Venezuela		40,000

however, presented at the 1996 World Congress against the Commercial Sexual Exploitation of Children (see Table 5.1). In addition, Table 5.2 reports estimates for the increasing numbers of children involved in prostitution in Thailand during the 1990s. It is expected that an increase in the numbers of children involved in prostitution in recent years may well point to an expansion of child sex tourism.

Table 5.2 Estimated numbers of prostituted children in Thailand

Date	Prostituted children	Source
1991	20,000	ECPAT Thailand
1994	36,000	Report of Consultation held in Tapai
1994	80,000	Thai NGOs
1996	200,000	ECPAT
1996	250,000	World Congress against the Commercial Sexual Exploitation of Children

It should be recognized also, however, that international patterns of sex tourism may shift over time as local prevention or legal initiatives arise in one destination to suppress the industry, and new possibilities for sex emerge in alternative destinations elsewhere in the world. As a recent report in the *Independent* newspaper indicates:

> Exotic holiday destinations in the Caribbean and Africa have become the new destinations for British paedophiles after a clampdown on sex tourism by authorities in Thailand and the Philippines. Organisations fighting the sexual exploitation of children said yesterday that child abusers were heading to the Dominican Republic, Cuba, the Gambia and Kenya, where package tourism has led to the growth of local sex industries.
>
> (Quoted in Burrell, 1998: 10)

Types of child prostitution

The routes by which children come to be involved in prostitution vary from country to country and within countries. In some cases, children may be sold into prostitution by family members, while others may be forcibly abducted and held in a form of sex slavery. Some may be coerced by friends or family to engage in prostitution, and be tied to controlling pimps or venues, but many children prostitute themselves independently outside of commercial sex establishments (e.g. on beaches, around hotels), in order to make money to support themselves and family members. While some children may be regarded as child prostitutes it must be recognized that many are prostituted children. They do not choose this way of life but are forced into it. These children may service local clients or sex tourists from abroad, or both. For example, child prostitutes surveyed by ECPAT in the cities of the Dominican Republic reported that between 20 and 30 per cent of their customers are tourists. In tourist areas and resorts, this figure rose to 80 per cent (Silvesta *et al.*, 1994).

Combating tourist sexual exploitation of children

Legislation against child sex tourism

While in recent years much media attention has been given to the issue of extra-territorial legislation, which allows tourists to be prosecuted in their country of origin for sexual offences against children committed abroad, it is important to acknowledge the more important role of national legislation in combating sex tourism in general and sex tourism involving children in particular. This is a complex field which defies a simple summary, but the World Tourism Organization (WTO) have begun to compile details of national legislation which has relevance to the combating of child sex tourism (WTO, 1998; see also Hoose, 1997, for examples of national legislation to protect children). Currently, information is available on their website for 28 WTO member states, and it is clear that in most countries specific legislation exists relating to 'sex offences and crime against children in the country' which provides the basis for the prosecution of foreign nationals involved in sexual abuse of minors (as defined in law). In addition, prostitution *per se*, or profiting from the organization of prostitution, may be illegal. In the case of Brazil, for instance, details are given of penalties specified in law: for adults who sexually exploit children between 14 and 18; 'for the manager, controller, pimp or owner of a prostitution place' where sex occurs with a child under 18; and, 'for the procurer or trafficker who procures, seduces or traffics another person for prostitution' who is under 18. Laws and regulations may also exist on a national level which could be used specifically to prohibit organized sex tourism within the country. In the Philippines, for example, a Department of Tourism Administrative Order (No. 95-17):

prohibits hotels and other accommodation establishments to permit any person whom they know or have reason to believe to be either a prostitute, a paedophile or of questionable character to occupy a room or to enter the premises of the establishment.

National legislation may also exist which could be used to prevent the organization of sex tours and trips by their own nationals to other countries, either directly through the prohibiting of sex tours affecting children (as in Germany, for instance) or indirectly, through regulations pertaining, for example, to obscenity in advertising or pornography.

A number of recent convictions of tourists for child sex offences illustrate the use of national legislation in tourism-receiving countries in combating child sex tourism. For example, Michael Clarke, a 48-year-old Briton from Eastbourne was sentenced in October 1996, in the Philippines, to 16 years' imprisonment after being convicted of 'promoting and inducing child prostitution' in the context of organized sex tours. Another Briton, Gavin Scott, was convicted in October 1995 of the attempted rape of five boys in Cambodia. He received a two-year prison sentence, of which he served five months in jail in total (see Hoose, 1997, for examples of other convictions of British citizens for sexual offences against children overseas).

In recent years, increasing attention has been given to the establishment of 'extra-territorial' legislation. The international lead in establishing such legislation to combat sex tourism was taken by Australia in 1994.

> The Crimes (Child Sex Tourism) Amendment Act was passed in 1994 and makes sexual activity with a child under 16 years, committed in an overseas country by an Australian citizen or resident, a criminal offence punishable in Australia. The law applies to individuals, companies or corporations and provides for a term of imprisonment of up to 17 years and fines of up to A$500,000.
>
> (ECPAT Australia, 1998: 1)

The concern of the Australian government to address this issue reflects the extent to which Australian business interests became involved in sex tourism within South-east Asia, and especially the Philippines, following the abandonment of American military bases in 1991. As Jeffreys (1998: 9) notes in her description of the sex tourism business in Angeles City in the Philippines:

> When the Americans withdrew there was a hiatus in the sex industry in the city which was quickly filled by Australian entrepreneurs and Australian sex tourists. At least 80 per cent of the 153 nightclubs and other entertainment spots are owned and operated by Australians. There are no beaches or views in Angeles City, only prostitution, and almost all hotels and bars are dedicated to that end. Australians formed the largest number out of the 120,000 tourists who visited the area in 1994. Agencies in Australia arrange package tours for sex tourists to the city, amongst other destinations.

Similar extra-territorial legislation is now in place in 25 other 'tourist-sending' countries (Levy, 1998), including New Zealand, Germany, Sweden, Belgium and the UK.

In the UK, part of the Sex Offenders Act 1997 made it an offence under British law for UK citizens and residents to engage in underage sexual activity with a child in another country (where the activity is also illegal in the country concerned). If convicted, an individual would be liable to the same penalties that would be faced if the offence had been committed within the UK. Legislation also made it an offence for individuals, groups or organizations to conspire or incite others to engage in sexual activities with children. These offences now attract severe penalties, up to life imprisonment.

Some 70 child sex-abuse cases have so far been brought world-wide under the terms of extra-territorial legislation. Countries where prosecutions have taken place include Sweden, The Netherlands, Germany, Switzerland, France, Belgium and Australia. The first such prosecution involved a 66-year-old Swedish man 'convicted in Stockholm of the sexual abuse of a 13-year-old Thai boy at Pattaya' (Levy, 1998). Of the eight prosecutions pursued in Australia since the law changed in 1994, five were successful and involved offences against children in the Philippines, Cambodia, Thailand, India, Ghana and the USA (Levy, 1998).

The work of ECPAT

ECPAT has been particularly active in campaigning against the commercial sexual exploitation of children and for the establishment of extra-territorial legislation. ECPAT was established following a conference held in Chiang Mai (Thailand) in May 1990, at which the problem of Asian children in prostitution was explored and the extent of such involvement began to be fully appreciated. A community of concerned individuals and organizations from Asian countries decided to work together to end child prostitution in Asian tourism (ECPAT stood initially for 'End Child Prostitution in Asian Tourism').

The ECPAT campaign focused initially on political action, law reforms, education and media coverage and the link between prostitution of children and tourism. This work culminated in the World Congress against the Commercial Sexual Exploitation of Children, which was organized by ECPAT, UNICEF and the NGO Committee on the Rights of the Child and hosted by the Swedish government in August 1996. After the Congress, ECPAT broadened its scope to include all children exploited in the commercial sex industry. Correspondingly, the acronym ECPAT now stands for 'End Child Prostitution, Child Pornography and the Trafficking of Children for Sexual Purposes'. ECPAT's fundamental aim is

> to raise awareness and call for informed action to ensure children everywhere enjoy their fundamental rights free and secure from all forms of commercial sexual exploitation, namely child prostitution, child pornography and the trafficking of children for sexual purposes.

The international ECPAT movement has continued to grow and strengthen since its foundation, and currently there are over 250 groups in the coalition which forms the ECPAT network, in more than 30 countries world-wide (ECPAT UK, 1997).

At the Travel Trade Fair held in London in November 1997 Veitch (1997) provided an overview of work undertaken by national ECPAT organizations. In November 1997, for example, ECPAT UK in collaboration with HM Customs and Excise, the Foreign and Commonwealth Office, the Home Office and ABTA (Association of British Travel Agents) launched a leaflet aimed at raising British travellers' awareness of the recently established extra-territorial legislation within the UK. In conjunction with this ECPAT UK also produced an Industry Training Pack (Hoose, 1997) funded by ABTA and the Travel Training Company, which provides the travel industry with background information on the problem of child sex tourism and details of the extra-territorial legislation. Veitch also describes recent or ongoing initiatives in The Netherlands, Belgium, Spain, Sweden, Australia, Taiwan and Brazil, which illustrate the concerted attempts being made by this network to work closely with governments and commercial interests in tackling child sexual exploitation around the world.

International campaigns against child labour and in support of children's rights

International Labour Organization

Whatever the scale of sexual exploitation of children by tourists, it should be acknowledged that 'child sex tourism' is only one aspect of the wider problem of the sexual exploitation of children and, furthermore, this is but one facet of the more widespread phenomenon of child labour, particularly in the developing world. Any efforts to reduce child labour and its causes, including the reduction of the sexual exploitation of children *per se*, will clearly serve to challenge the sexual exploitation of children by tourists. The International Labour Organization (ILO) (Jankanish, 1998) has recently proposed new international labour standards on child labour aimed at abolishing its extreme manifestations as a matter of urgent priority in the fight against all forms of economic exploitation of children. As the ILO information pack points out:

> All over the world, children continue to work, putting at stake their education, their health, their normal development to adulthood, and even their lives. Millions are working in hazardous occupations, in prostitution and pornography, or are exploited as slaves and bonded labourers.

The ILO's International Programme on the Elimination of Child Labour (IPEC) has organized several programmes around the world to combat child prostitution. These initiatives, in Thailand, Nepal, Brazil and Kenya, have galvanized the involvement of local communities both to prevent children entering prostitution and to rescue and rehabilitate those who have already experienced sexual exploitation. In Thailand's Chiang Rai Province, for example:

> IPEC is assisting a local non-governmental organization (NGO) in its work to prevent young village girls from becoming trapped in prostitution. Together with community leaders, this group identifies girls involved in prostitution and visits them and their families to discuss other available options, including enrolment in basic education, skills training, and programmes to repair the children's self-esteem.
>
> (Jankanish, 1998)

The International Save the Children Alliance

While the problem of child labour and child prostitution is particularly serious in many developing countries, there are also serious issues regarding child labour, prostitution and children's rights to be addressed within a broad European context. The International Save the Children Alliance – Europe Group (Sutton *et al.*, 1998) have recently argued that the European Union should formally adopt the United Nations Convention on the Rights of the Child, so that 'the policies and programmes of the European Union can be assessed for their impact on children and checked against an internationally agreed set of minimum standards'. In the context of the present chapter the articles of most direct relevance are Article 19, which requires Member States to protect children from 'all forms of physical or mental violence' including sexual abuse, and Article 34, which specifically requires Member States to protect children against 'all forms of sexual exploitation and sexual abuse', including coercion to engage in sexual activity and the exploitative use of children in prostitution and pornography. The authors assert that these issues are of increased importance within the European Union, since

> the free movement of persons encouraged by the development of the Single Market has enabled abusers to move more freely around the Member States and has increased the potential for transnational crime, trafficking in children and the exchange of pornographic material. (Sutton *et al.*, 1998: 10)

Nordic–Baltic initiatives in preventing prostitution

Within Europe, following the collapse of the Soviet Union, greater freedom of movement has also extended beyond the borders of Western European countries, to include countries in Eastern Europe, the Baltic states and Russia. Concerns about links between such enhanced mobility and prostitution – both on the part of customers (mainly men) seeking sex and prostitutes (mainly women and girls, but also young men and boys) – have resulted in a number of European initiatives. While some of these have been motivated primarily by sexual health concerns and are focused on HIV/AIDS risk reduction (European Project AIDS and Mobility: Bröring, 1996), others are ideologically committed to the prevention of prostitution itself. For example, the Finnish Ministry of Social Affairs and Health has recently launched a five-year national Programme for the Prevention of Prostitution and Violence against Women (1998–2002), based at the National Research and Development Centre for Welfare and Health. As the project outline explains:

> The questions related to prostitution have notably gained prominence on the international agenda during the last decade. Due to the geopolitical location of Finland as a border country of the European Union, prostitution has aroused great concern in the other Scandinavian countries and in the EU. Finland is a country of origin of sex tourists who increasingly head for Baltic and Russian destinations. Finland is also a transit country and a country of destination of mobile prostitution. A crucial point is that the sex trade is increasing not only in terms of foreign prostitution and sex tourism, but that also domestic prostitution is growing in Finland.
>
> (STAKES, 1998: 2)

And as recent studies in Estonia (the nearest Baltic state to Finland) have shown (Kalikova *et al.*, 1995), prostitution, controlled in the main by the Russian Mafia, involves the widespread exploitation of underage girls or young women.

Initiatives sponsored by the European Commission to combat child sex tourism

In a recent detailed communication, the Commission of the European Communities (1996: 3–4) has acknowledged a special responsibility to address issues relating to child sex tourism:

> The Commission is fully aware both of the extent and seriousness of the problem and of the fact that European public opinion in general, and tourists and the tourist industry in particular, are becoming increasingly sensitive to this affliction . . . The Commission is aware that, although the tourist industry can contribute to combating child sex tourism, the means at its disposal are nevertheless limited. To be effective, measures taken by the industry must be part of a wider approach, combining increased action by the countries involved and by the relevant international organizations, and the many measures taken by civil society and non-governmental organizations with recognized experience in this area.

Co-ordinated action by the European Community is needed, the Commission argues, for several reasons. First, child sex tourism is a transnational phenomenon which cannot be effectively tackled by 'isolated reactions or piecemeal measures'. Second, those measures which have been taken so far may be 'spread too thinly' if efforts at co-ordination are not taken. And third, the Community has the infrastructural capacity to galvanize 'a greater political and financial commitment both within Europe and in its relations with third countries' towards tackling this problem. In taking matters forward, the Commission proposed that three lines of action are needed: to deter and punish child sex abusers; to address issues of supply and demand in relation to sex tourism; and to encourage Member States to adopt a consistent position in combating tourist sexual exploitation of children.

More recently, the European Commission (DGXXIII, Directorate-General 'Enterprise Policy, Distributive Trades, Tourism and Co-operatives') funded a 'Eurobarometer' survey throughout the European Union to assess public opinion on child sex tourism (INRA, 1998), the results of which were presented at a meeting organized by the Tourism Directorate at the 1998 Brussels Travel Fair (Carter, 1998). Over 16,000 respondents were interviewed across 15 European states to assess their knowledge of, and attitudes towards, this issue. Respondents were aged 15 and above and selected in order to achieve a broadly representative sample of each national population. While variations from one country to another were found in responses to the various questions asked, in general across Europe the following patterns were apparent:

- the vast majority of Europeans were aware of child sex tourism (88 per cent)
- over half believed it to be fairly or very common (63 per cent)
- the places most commonly associated with child sex tourism were Asia (83 per cent), South America (69 per cent), central and eastern Europe (68 per cent) and Africa (67 per cent)
- a majority of Europeans believe that child sex tourism is a growing problem (55 per cent)
- the perpetrators of child sex tourism are generally believed to be older men (68 per cent) and single men (51 per cent), with few respondents believing that women are involved
- large majorities of respondents believed that child sex tourism is not morally acceptable (94 per cent), that it is illegal (86 per cent) and that it can be avoided (63 per cent)
- with respect to national legislation, almost 90 per cent believed that child sex tourism is illegal within their own country, and just under 70 per cent of people believed that their national legislation made it an offence for nationals to engage in child sex tourism abroad
- a majority of Europeans were dissatisfied with measures taken so far by authorities to prevent child sex tourism (57 per cent), and were not aware of any information or awareness campaigns undertaken in their country (68 per cent), but over half believed that campaigns can be effective (54 per cent)
- a large majority were in favour of the European Union being involved in combating this problem (84 per cent)
- over half of respondents would not go on holiday to places where there is child sex tourism (54 per cent), and a large majority (69 per cent) would demand that services offered at their holiday destination are in no way connected with child sex tourism
- finally, only 4 per cent of respondents had been aware of the existence of child sex tourism in a place they had visited for a holiday

In a further analysis of the basic patterns reported by this survey, Carter (1998) has focused on those respondents who expressed 'uncertainty' in response to some of the questions asked. He argues that these people may represent an important subgroup who need to be targeted by future information and awareness campaigns. In addition, uncertainty about child sex tourism in general populations may be a factor which allows tourists who sexually abuse children to continue their activities unhindered. As Hoose (1997) points out, public awareness is vital in preventing the actions of the situational sex abuser and exposing those of the systematic abuser. A lack of awareness, for instance, of the illegality and the unacceptability of their actions may provide an essential element in the circumstances necessary for promoting situational abuse, and a similar lack of awareness may lead to the behaviour of the systematic abuser remaining unchallenged.

While a large majority of tourists were aware of the existence of child sex tourism, across Europe 12 per cent of respondents claimed not to have heard of it, with percentages varying from less than 1 per cent to 28 per cent. The lowest levels of uncertainty were found in northern Europe (Sweden, Denmark, The Netherlands and Finland) and the highest levels in Ireland, the UK, Spain and Greece. Similarly, in response to a question on how common child sex tourism is, over Europe 15 per cent of respondents did not know whether it was common or not (varying from 5 per cent to 32 per cent), with the lowest levels of uncertainty found in the same four northern European countries and the highest levels in the UK and Ireland. Substantial national differences were also found concerning uncertainty over whether child sex tourism is increasing or decreasing, whether it is morally acceptable and whether it is legal. Further analysis revealed that countries where the issue was least discussed were also the countries where there was most uncertainty about prevalence. In addition, for 11 of the 15 countries in the Union, respondents with a minimum level of education were significantly less likely to have heard of child sex tourism when compared with those who finished education at 20 or above. Awareness was also significantly related to age in 9 of the 15 countries, with respondents aged 15 to 24 and those over 55 less likely to have heard of child sex tourism, when compared with respondents aged 25 to 54 years. Carter (1998: 15) concludes that 'future information and awareness campaigns should be designed to encourage discussion and be targeted at the young, the old and those who have left education early'.

The European Commission is, however, aware of the need for such education campaigns and alongside the Eurobarometer survey also co-financed an awareness, education and training pilot project developed by ECPAT, Groupe Développement and ECTAA. This pilot project had two key objectives and was carried out in Germany, Belgium, France and The Netherlands with the intention of later expanding it to the other countries of Europe. The first part of the project was based on the distribution of a luggage tag accompanied by an information leaflet designed to inform travellers about child sex tourism and inviting them to show a commitment to the fight against the practice by displaying the tag on their luggage. The second part of the project was aimed at those working in the travel industry and the development of teaching tools for those involved in training in travel and tourism. The results of this project were reported at the ECPAT European seminar held at the 1998 Brussels Travel Fair (EC DGXXIII Tourism Directorate, 1998).

A combined luggage tag and flier had been produced and the pilot countries had implemented its distribution with the assistance of travel operators, with the exception of Germany where fliers had been produced and were ready for distribution early in 1999. Italy, while not a pilot country, had also taken up the luggage tag and combined fliers and were distributing 52,000 copies supported by the use of television commercials. All of the countries involved are to carry out an evaluation of the impact of this project and reports are expected in the near future, in particular from The Netherlands, which has been running a luggage-tag distribution scheme for over two and a half years.

The industry training and information aspect of the project had also already been implemented in varying degrees. The implementation of this section of the project was strongly based upon the use and adaptation of a training resources kit previously produced by France. The training for travel and tourism students in France has been incorporated into the already existing BTS vocational training followed by 70 per cent of all tourism students and is supported by the State Secretariat. In The Netherlands both higher (university disciplines and trade schools) and intermediate (vocational training) education levels have been involved with the production of a manual to help guest lecturers introduce the topic in higher education, and a resources kit to support teaching at intermediary level. Again, in Belgium and Germany vocational training is being supported by a resources kit for lecturers, and students have been heavily involved in designing campaign material to further disseminate the information within the industry. All of the pilot countries have found that teaching and training in this area is best approached through the incorporation of information in core subject courses – for example, marketing, geography, sales and communication and sustainability – as opposed to a specific course which concentrates on child sex tourism. (For further details see Groupe Développement *et al.*, 1998a and b.)

Tourist industry initiatives in combating child sex tourism

The WTO has been at the forefront of international efforts to combat child sex tourism for a number of years. At the eleventh meeting of the General Assembly in 1995, in Cairo, the WTO adopted a resolution on 'the prevention of organized sex tourism', which it defined as 'trips organized from within the tourism sector, or from outside this sector but using its structures and networks, with the primary purpose of effecting a commercial sexual relationship by the tourist with residents at the destination' (WTO, 1998). The WTO rejected such activity as 'exploitative and subversive to the fundamental objectives of tourism in promoting peace, human rights, mutual understanding, respect of all peoples and cultures, and sustainable development', and condemned child sex tourism, in particular, as a violation of Article 34 of the Convention on the Rights of the Child (United Nations, 1991) and as requiring 'strict legal action by tourist sending and receiving countries'. The statement also requested governments to undertake a wide range of actions, including gathering evidence of organized sex tourism; encouraging education on the adverse effects of sex tourism; issuing guidelines to the tourism sector; and, not least, establishing 'legal and administrative measures to prevent and eradicate child sex tourism, in particular through bilateral agreements to facilitate, *inter alia*, the prosecution of tourists engaged in any unlawful sexual activity involving children and juveniles'.

The WTO statement also appealed directly to the travel and tourism industries to co-operate with governments and non-governmental organizations in eliminating organized sex tourism, by educating staff and tourists about the harmful consequences of sex tourism; by developing professional codes of conduct and industry self-regulation against sex tourism; and by undertaking such measures as 'banning commercial sex services, in particular involving children, on the contracted tourism premises'.

In addition to this statement adopted by the WTO, a variety of international umbrella organizations within the travel and tourism industry, representing travel agents, tour operators, airlines and hotels, have also adopted policy positions which highlight the issues involved in sex tourism for their members throughout the world. For example, the International Federation of Tour Operators (IFTO), with 25 member organizations worldwide, has adopted a Code of Conduct against the Sexual Exploitation of Children, which recommends that all tour operators:

- Inform staff, suppliers and customers where appropriate about this problem and its unacceptability.
- Deter staff, suppliers and customers from taking part, encouraging or condoning the exploitation of children.
- Cease using any supplier who engages in or knowingly condones the sexual exploitation of children.
- Co-operate with the appropriate authorities of all countries to identify and investigate sexual abusers of children and those who seek to benefit from sexual abuse of children.

Similarly, the International Air Transport Association (IATA) has adopted a resolution condemning commercial sexual exploitation of children, in which it 'Endorses the practical measures being taken by the industry to educate staff, inform passengers, co-operate with government agencies, and establish guidelines covering advertising and doing business with tour operators and hotels.'

During the Stockholm Congress against the Commercial Sexual Exploitation of Children (August, 1996), the WTO proposed the establishment of a task force of tourism industry groups, governments and non-governmental organizations, Child Prostitution and Tourism Watch, which would mount an international campaign to 'prevent, uncover, isolate and eradicate the exploitation of children in sex tourism'. The work of the WTO in this area is co-ordinated with the activities of other intergovernmental organizations concerned with the welfare of children and protecting their rights, and with the activities of non-governmental organizations such as ECPAT. At a meeting of the task force in 1997, an international logo was adopted 'to help unite and highlight the tourism industry struggle against child prostitution'. The logo (see WTO, 1998) has three purposes:

- To identify organizations, companies and establishments actively working to prevent and eliminate child prostitution.
- To sensitize the staff concerned.
- To inform travellers, the users of tourism establishments and the public at large of the campaign.

Conclusion

There is no doubt that the sexual exploitation of children is a global problem, more widespread in impoverished developing countries, but increasingly an issue in Europe and the United States (ILO, 1998). In addition, over a relatively short period of time, a child sex industry has arisen in certain countries throughout the world, which ECPAT Australia (1998) has argued 'can be paralleled with the growth of tourism to many of these countries'. While ECPAT Australia is careful not to claim that tourism is 'responsible' for child sexual exploitation, it believes that it 'does provide an environment for easy access to vulnerable children' in particular destinations.

The fight against child sex tourism is a movement of the 1990s and reflects international recognition of the scale and seriousness of the problems involved in many different countries around the world. The lead has been provided by campaigning groups such as ECPAT and other non-governmental organizations, and the challenge has been picked up by national governments, supranational organizations (e.g. WTO, European Commission) and the tourism industry itself. There is a consensus that tackling this problem effectively requires concerted and co-ordinated actions to stem both the demand from tourism-sending countries and the supply within tourism-receiving countries. This surely requires legislation, but legislation is not sufficient, especially where there is a lack of political will to use such legislation once in place (Levy, 1998). There is, more importantly, a need for positive local action in many impoverished countries: to address the economic and cultural forces which render children vulnerable to exploitation; to provide resources to support alternatives to child labour; and to rescue and support the many young people who are subjected to the horrific abuses of child sex tourism. There is a need too, as Jeffreys (1998: 1) forcefully argues, to address the 'many forces at work in the normalisation of the international sex industry' and to recognize and challenge 'the extent to which the individual women and boys used in prostitution are now subject to the exploitation of international capitalism'. This, of course, broadens the focus of attention beyond the specific concerns of child sexual abuse in the context of tourism, and questions the acceptability of all forms of sex tourism and all forms of prostitution. Inevitably too, it renders problematic broader cultural assumptions regarding the interconnections between tourism and sexuality addressed elsewhere in this collection.

Given that the initiatives described in this chapter to address child sex tourism are so recent, and ongoing, it is not surprising that as yet no evidence is available on their tangible impact on the extent of tourist sexual exploitation of children. The major challenge for the future is to ensure that the high principles reflected in the United Nations Convention on the Rights of the Child, in legislation enacted around the world to protect children from sexual exploitation and in resolutions by the European Commission, the ILO, the WTO and many other parties – are translated into actions which actually succeed in eradicating child sex tourism.

References

Bröring, G. (1996) International tourists: a specific target group for AIDS prevention programmes. In S. Clift and S. Page (eds), *Health and the International Tourist*. London: Routledge.

Burrell, I. (1998) Sex tourists turn to the Caribbean. *The Independent*, 13 October, p.10.

Carter, S. (1998) Levels of uncertainty among Europeans about 'sex tourism' involving children: an analysis of the Eurobarometer Survey. First European Meeting of the Main Protagonists in the Fight against Child Sex Tourism, Brussels Travel Fair, 24–6 November, Brussels.

Commission of the European Communities (1996) *Communication from the Commission on Combating Child Sex Tourism*. COM(96) 547 final, Brussels, 27 November.

EC DGXXIII Tourism Directorate (1998) *European Union Communication: Actions to Combat Child Sex Tourism*. Information Leaflet, EC DGXXIII, Brussels.

ECPAT Australia (1998) *Childwise Tourism: Travel and Tourism Initiatives to Combat Child Sex Tourism*. Collingwood: ECPAT Australia.

ECPAT UK (1997) *Resource Pack*. London: ECPAT UK.

Groupe Développement in association with ECPAT and ECTAA (1998a) *Fight against Child Sex Tourism. Guidelines on Distributing the Luggage Tag: Experiences from*

Belgium, Germany, France and Netherlands. Report presented at the ECPAT European Project Seminar against Child Sex Tourism, Brussels Travel Fair, 26 November, Brussels.

Groupe Développement in association with ECPAT and ECTAA (1998b) *Tourism Teacher-Training against Child Sex Tourism: Experiences from Belgium, Germany, France and Netherlands*. Report presented at the ECPAT European Project Seminar against Child Sex Tourism, Brussels Travel Fair, 26 November, Brussels.

Hoose, J. (1997) *New UK Laws against Child Sex Tourism: Industry Training Pack*. London: ECPAT UK.

ILO (1998) *Combatting Extreme Forms of Child Labour*. Geneva: International Labour Organization.

INRA (1998) *Europeans and Their Views on Child Sex Tourism*. Brussels: European Commission Directorate-General XXIII.

Ireland, K. (1993) *'Wish You Weren't Here': The Sexual Exploitation of Children and the Connection with Tourism and International Travel*. Working Paper No. 7. London: Save the Children.

Jankanish, M. (1998) *Targeting the Intolerable: Towards the Adoption of New International Labour Standards on Extreme Forms of Child Labour*. Geneva: International Labour Organization.

Jeffreys, S. (1998) Globalising sexual exploitation: sex tourism and the traffic in women. Paper presented at the Fourth International Conference of the Leisure Studies Association, Leeds, UK, July.

Kalikova, N., Vessin, T., Melesko, L. and Kalikov, J. (1998) Prostitution in Estonia. Poster presented at the XIth International AIDS Conference, Geneva, July.

Levy, A. (1998) Punish the perverts. *Guardian*, 15 December, p. 37.

Silvesta, E., Rijo, J. and Bogaert, H. (1994) *La Neo-prostitucion Infantil en Republica Dominicana*. New York: UNICEF.

STAKES (1998) *Prevention of Prostitution 1998–2002*. Helsinki: National Research and Development Centre for Welfare and Health.

Sutton, D., Ek, S., Barnen, R. and Bell, B. (1998) *Towards an EU Human Rights Agenda for Children*. Brussels: International Save the Children Alliance Europe Group.

United Nations (1991) *Convention on the Rights of the Child*. New York: UNICEF.

United Nations (1996) *Report of the World Congress on the Commercial Sexual Exploitation of Children*. Stockholm: United Nations.

Veitch, H. (1997) ECPAT national initiatives on tourism. World Tourism Organization Task Force on Child Prostitution and Tourism, London Travel Trade Fair, November.

WTO (1998) website: http://www/word-tourism.org.

6

Tourism and commercial sex in Indonesia

Kathleen Ford and Dewa Nyoman Wirawan

Introduction

Studies of male prostitutes have been conducted in the USA, Canada, Europe, Asia and South America (e.g. Sittitrai, 1988; Sittitrai *et al.*, 1989; Pleak and Meyer-Bahlburg, 1990; Waldorf and Lauderback, 1991; Morse *et al.*, 1992; Elifson, 1993; Sittitrai *et al.*, 1993; Linharea-Carvalho *et al.*, 1996; Schlich, 1996; McCamish *et al.*, 1998; Schechter *et al.*, 1998). However, the volume of research on male sex workers remains small relative to that of female sex workers. Since there is a potential for the spread of HIV infection through male commercial sex, research is needed on the behaviours of these men to assess the size of these groups, the potential for disease transmission and the structure of appropriate interventions. We have already published data focused on the psycho-social factors related to condom use among male workers and their male tourist clients in Bali, Indonesia (Ford *et al.*, 1995). The objective of this chapter is to examine in more detail the life histories of the sex workers, their perceived vulnerability to HIV and other sexually transmitted diseases, and other health behaviours. Factors related to susceptibility to HIV and STD infection are also examined.

Study context

As of 1998, the documented number of AIDS cases and HIV-infected persons in Indonesia remained lower than many other countries in Southeast Asia (685 persons were reported to be HIV-positive or to have had AIDS, as of May 1998). At the time this study was conducted, the number of cases was smaller (in 1993, 188 persons had been reported HIV-positive or with AIDS). It is likely that this reported number of HIV infections underestimates the extent of the epidemic.

Homosexuality is generally not accepted in Indonesia and persons who reveal their identity may be subject to discrimination. A transvestite group known traditionally as *wadam*, but more recently as *waria*, is visible and officially recognized in Indonesian cities. The *waria* often work as entertainers, hairdressers, and sex workers. However, apart from this group only successful persons in the arts and the entertainment business tend to be open about their sexual orientation.

Commercial sex is illegal throughout Indonesia and the law is periodically enforced in Bali by means of token arrests and deportations of female sex workers to their homes in East Java. Male sex workers have generally not been subjected to such arrests. While the number of female commercial sex workers in Bali is estimated to be over one thousand, the total number of male sex workers in Bali is estimated at one to two hundred (Ford *et al.*, 1993).

Bali is an island characterized by mobility due to its popularity as a tourist destination as well as its role as a commercial centre for the garment, fishing and manufacturing industries. Furthermore, due to its relative wealth compared to nearby Java and other Indonesian islands, considerable migration to Bali occurs for employment in these industries.

In Bali, the commercial sex industry is concentrated in the provincial capital city of Denpasar and the nearby tourist centres of Kuta, Sanur and Nusa Dua. Both Sanur and Nusa Dua tend to cater to tourists of higher socio-economic levels staying in relatively expensive hotels. Kuta is the largest tourist centre and it attracts a wide variety of tourists, who stay in accommodation ranging from cheap 'homestays' to exclusive five-star hotels.

Samples of male commercial sex workers and their male tourist clients from the Kuta resort were interviewed for this study. These men tend to work independently without the supervision of a pimp. Several methods are used to meet customers. These include approaching potential customers in particular areas along the beach or on the street and meeting them in bars, nightclubs and discos. About 50 to 100 of this group may be working in Kuta at any time, and they tend to have mainly tourist clients, although Indonesian men are also among their clientele. The tourist clients of these workers include adult men from Australia, Europe and many other countries (Ford *et al.*, 1995). Many of these men were well educated and were well informed about AIDS and other STDs. Generally, they had considerable travel experience and often they had paid for sex in other countries.

Sexual activity may take place in the clients' hotel rooms, or in the rooms of cheap hotels rented specifically for the purpose. Sex encounters may also occur along the beach, in the bushes or small shacks made from palm fronds. Liaisons may be brief, but some become extended with the client providing room and board, clothes, jewellery, other presents and travel as well as direct payment to the worker. In some cases, the worker may conceal his identify as a sex worker from the client, while feigning genuine attraction. Payment in these cases may be mainly indirect through 'gifts' to the worker. The male Kuta workers reported an average of about three clients per week, charging US$18 for a full night for an Indonesian client and US$33 for a tourist client. A short time costs an average of US$9 for an Indonesian and US$16 for a tourist.

Methods

Sampling

The data for this paper are drawn from the Udayana-Michigan AIDS Behavioral Study, which conducted interviews with several groups of female and male sex workers and their clients. This paper focuses on the data collected from male workers. The main data-collection period ran from February 1992 to December 1993 in Bali. The sample discussed in this paper included one to two-hour face-to-face structured interviews with 80 male sex workers. Since the number of Kuta workers was relatively small and in view of their independent method of working, the study interviewed all available workers during the study period. The sample was limited in size due to the size of the Kuta group.

Survey instruments

The survey interview consisted mainly of closed-ended questions and assessed: 1) knowledge of AIDS, STDs, and condoms; 2) socio-economic and demographic characteristics and migration history; 3) sexual experience, including experience as a sex worker and experience with intimates and other unpaid partners; 4) attitudes and beliefs about condoms; and 5) other health practices.

The questionnaires were developed in a two-phase process. The first phase involved an initial set of interviews with 20 sex workers using mainly open-ended questions. This open-ended free response format has been recommended as a good means of identifying beliefs and social norms (Ajzen and Fishbein, 1980) and constructs most likely to influence behaviour (Higgins and King, 1981; Bargh, 1984). Results from this first phase were used to develop a closed-ended instrument for the main study. Significant findings from this first phase regarding the male workers and male clients were reported elsewhere (Ford *et al.*, 1993). The second phase of instrument development included pre-tests with small groups (10–15) of respondents before the start of the main fieldwork.

Interviewing procedure

The interviewing staff for the male workers consisted of two Balinese males. The Balinese interviewers were university graduates in anthropology who had previous experience working with sex worker communities. These interviewers conducted all of the interviews with the male commercial sex workers in the Indonesian language. Interviewer training included knowledge of AIDS and STDs, techniques for obtaining and conducting interviews, detailed study of the questionnaire and supervised field practice in conducting interviews. Interviews of sex workers from the Kuta area were conducted at locations throughout the resort area, including homes, beach areas, hotels and restaurants. Locations were chosen to ensure privacy during the interview.

Measures

Most of the data reported in this paper consists of simple means and percentages derived from survey data. Indices of AIDS knowledge were also computed by summing the number of correct answers to a series of questions about AIDS. An index of condom use, discussed in the chapter as the *per cent condom use*, was computed as follows: 'Number of acts of a specific type of intercourse using condoms in a given time period, multiplied by 100, divided by total number of acts of a specific type of intercourse in a given time period.' Factors related to perceived susceptibility to HIV and STD infection were evaluated using logistic regression analysis. This method was chosen due to the dichotomous nature of the dependent variables.

Results

Demographics

The demographic characteristics and sex work histories of the male sex workers are shown in Table 6.1. The men ranged in age from 15 to 36 with a mean age of 24.4. Education averaged about 13.3 years (range 8–15). Only a small proportion (7 per cent) grew up in Bali and most were from other parts of Indonesia.

Some of the men began their experiences with paid sex in their teenage years. The mean age at first sex with a man was 17.5 years. Thirty-six per cent of these encounters were paid. The majority of men (66 per cent) had had sex with a woman and the mean age for this experience was higher (18.2 years). The mean number of months since they had had sex with a female was 12 months.

The men were asked open-ended questions about how they became involved in sex work. The most common answer (71 per cent) was that the

Table 6.1 Demographic characteristics and sex work history of male sex workers, Kuta, Indonesia, 1992–3. (n = 80)

Item	Response(s)	%
Age	Range: 15–36 years Mean: 24.4 years	
Education	Range: 8–15 years Mean: 13.3 years	
Place grew up	Bali Jakarta Other Indonesia	7 29 64
Age at first sex with a man	Mean: 17.5 years	
First sex with a man paid	Yes	36
Ever had sex with a female?	Yes Mean: 18.2 years	66
Months since last sex with a female	Mean: 12 months	
How did you come to work like this?	Gay since young, use it to get money Introduced to this by my gay friends Expelled by my family, ran to Bali I'm not gay, I do it to find money	71 18 14 24
Time working as a commercial sex worker	12 months or less 13–24 months 25+ months	31 19 50
Other places worked as a commercial sex worker in last two years	Jakarta East Java Other Indonesia Outside Indonesia	19 32 19 10
Methods of obtaining clients	Wait on street Clients come to house Go to hotels Go to bars and discos Wait on beach Currently holding another job	48 43 28 89 81 36

man was aware of his gay sexuality from a young age and now uses sex with men to get money. Some others (18 per cent) reported that they were introduced to this job by their gay friends. Others revealed that they had been expelled by their families (14 per cent) or that they were not gay, but do it to get money (24 per cent). About half of the men had been working as sex workers for more than two years, while 31 per cent had been working a year or less. Many of the men had worked as sex workers in other parts of Indonesia, including Jakarta (19 per cent), East Java (32 per cent) and other parts of Indonesia (19 per cent). Ten per cent had also worked outside Indonesia.

The men use several methods for soliciting clients. They may wait on the street (48 per cent), have clients come to their house (43 per cent), go to hotels (28 per cent), go to bars and discos (89 per cent) or wait on the beach

(81 per cent). More than a third (36 per cent) of respondents were currently holding another job.

STD knowledge

The respondents were asked a series of questions on STD knowledge followed by a series of questions on AIDS knowledge. Almost all of the men had heard of STDs (Table 6.2). Syphilis and AIDS were most often named, and many had also heard of gonorrhoea. A number of men also mentioned symptoms such as painful abrasions on the genitals (34 per cent) and fever or hot and cold flushes (23 per cent) as STDs. The men were also asked to list

Table 6.2 STD knowledge of male sex workers (n = 80)

Item	Response(s)	%
Heard of STDs?	Yes	99
Diseases mentioned	Syphilis	93
	AIDS	99
	Gonorrhoea	29
	Urinary discharge	21
	Bleeding anus	14
STD symptoms	Painful urination	71
	Urinary discharge	83
	Red spots on body	24
	Painful abrasions on genitals	34
	Fever, hot/cold flushes	23
Infected person can be asymptomatic?	Yes	59
Worried or very worried about syphilis?	Yes	86
At risk of syphilis or gonorrhoea?	Yes	53
	No	29
	Maybe	16
	Don't know	1
If yes, why?	Sex with many people	65
	Clients have diseases	58
If no, why?	Take medicines regularly	33
	Choose clients carefully	50
	Always wear a condom	39
Have friends who work like you do caught these diseases?	Yes, many	11
	Yes, some	6
	Yes, a few	43
	No	11
	Don't know	28
How would you know if a client had one of these diseases?	Examine penis for discharge/lesions	72
	Dull pallor of client's face	29
	Bad odour from mouth/body	29
What would you do if a client had one of these diseases?	Refuse client	68
	Advise client to get medical treatment	20

symptoms of STDs. These included painful urination (71 per cent), urinary discharge (83 per cent), red spots on the body (24 per cent), painful abrasions on genitals (34 per cent) and fever and hot and cold flushes (23 per cent). More than half of the men reported that STDs can be asymptomatic (59 per cent).

Most workers felt susceptible to these diseases, with 86 per cent reporting that they were worried or very worried about catching syphilis or gonorrhoea. Many workers thought that they were at risk of being infected (53 per cent), the main reasons being that they have sex with many people (65 per cent) or that the clients have diseases (58 per cent). Among those who felt they were not at risk, the main reasons included taking medicine regularly (33 per cent), choosing their clients carefully (50 per cent) and always wearing a condom (39 per cent).

Most of the workers were aware that at least some of their co-workers had acquired STDs. They said that they would know if a client had one of these diseases by the presence of discharge or lesions on the penis (72 per cent), dull pallor of the client's face (29 per cent) or mouth or body odour (29 per cent). Many workers (68 per cent) said that they would refuse a client with one of these symptoms or characteristics.

AIDS knowledge

The interview included a number of questions concerning knowledge of AIDS (Table 6.3). During the interview, the men were asked to describe the symptoms of a person with AIDS. Common answers were that a person becomes thin (94 per cent), develops red spots on their body (90 per cent), experiences reduced stamina (96 per cent) and their hair falls out (67 per cent).

It is very important for a sex worker to understand that a person with AIDS can appear to be healthy, and most of the sex workers (73 per cent) were aware of this. However, some misconceptions about AIDS emerged, including that it can be transmitted by casual contact (exchange of clothing, eating from the same plate, shaking hands or urinating in the same place). Almost all (89 per cent) reported that a mother can pass the disease to her child and that there is no cure available (82 per cent).

The workers realized that disease could be spread by persons of many nationalities, including Western, Japanese or Singaporean tourists, and also by Indonesians. They were also aware of the vulnerability of gay men and sex workers who have sex with men and their clients. One hundred per cent were aware that the sex workers and clients could catch AIDS, and 91 per cent reported that gay men in general could catch AIDS.

In terms of preventative methods, most of the men (70 per cent) reported that AIDS could not be prevented by taking medicines or getting injections on a regular basis. They also reported that condoms provide protection

Table 6.3 AIDS knowledge of male sex workers (n = 80)

Item	Response(s)	%
Heard of AIDS?	Yes	99
A person with AIDS	Becomes thin	94
	Has red spots on body	90
	Has reduced stamina	96
	Hair falls out	67
Can a person with AIDS appear healthy?	Yes	73
Can a person with AIDS who appears healthy spread the disease?	Yes	71
Can individuals catch AIDS through exchange of clothing, eating from the same plate or shaking hands?	No	59
Can a person who is pregnant pass the disease on to her child?	Yes	89
Can we catch AIDS by urinating in the same place as someone with AIDS?	No	62
Can the AIDS virus be spread by kissing on the mouth?	No	30
Is the AIDS virus spread by Western tourists?	Yes	100
Can the AIDS virus be spread by Japanese or Singaporean tourists?	Yes	100
Can the AIDS virus be spread by Indonesians?	Yes	99
Can gay men who work like you catch the AIDS virus?	Yes	100
Can men who are gay but do not work like you catch this virus?	Yes	91
Can men who come as clients to gay sex workers also catch the virus?	Yes	100
Can this disease be prevented by taking medicines or getting injections on a regular basis?	No	70
Will using a condom when having sex, provided that it does not break, protect against the AIDS disease?	Yes	82
At this point in time, is there a medicine that cures this disease?	No	82
Which sexual practices are more likely to spread the disease if having sex with a person already infected? Oral sex? Anal sex?	Oral	9
	Anal	68
	Same	23
Who is more likely to catch the AIDS disease, the person who inserts his penis into his partner's anus or the person whose anus is entered?	Person who inserts	5
	Person who receives	57
	Same	38
Are there Indonesians here in Bali who have already caught the disease?	Yes, many	35
	Yes, a few	54
	No	5
	Don't know	5

against AIDS (82 per cent). Over half of the men (68 per cent) were aware that anal sex was more risky than oral sex, while almost a quarter of the men (23 per cent) believed that oral was riskier. Over half of the men reported that receptive anal sex was riskier than insertive anal sex.

Perceived susceptibility to HIV infection

Most of the workers (91 per cent) reported that they thought it was possible they might catch the AIDS virus and that they were worried about this (see Table 6.4). Responses to an open-ended question about reasons why it was possible for them to become infected included sex with tourists (66 per cent), sex with many people (78 per cent) and frequent anal sex (24 per cent). Only 4 per cent reported that is was because they often have sex without a condom.

The men were also asked an open-ended question about what they have done to protect themselves from this disease. Close to 70 per cent replied that they choose clients carefully. Use of a condom was the only other very common answer (60 per cent). Other responses included taking medicine (16 per cent), looking for healthy clients (16 per cent), reducing anal sex (16 per cent), seeing a doctor (12 per cent), and having sex quickly (4 per cent).

Condom beliefs and attitudes

Asked an open-ended question about reasons for using condoms (see Table 6.5), the male workers' replies included preventing diseases (80 per cent),

Table 6.4 Perceived susceptibility to HIV infection of male sex workers (n = 80)

Item	Response(s)	%
Are you worried that you might catch the AIDS virus?	Very worried	91
	Worried	7
	A little worried	1
Is it possible that you might catch this virus?	It is possible	91
	It is not possible	7
	Maybe yes, maybe no	1
Why might it be possible?	I have sex with tourists	66
	I have sex with many people	78
	I often have sex without a condom	4
	I often have anal sex	24
Have you ever done anything to protect yourself from catching the AIDS disease?	Choose clients selectively	70
	Use a condom	60
	Take medicine	16
	See a doctor	12
	Have sex quickly	4
	Look for healthy clients	16
	Reduce anal sex	16

Table 6.5 Condom beliefs and attitudes of male sex workers (n = 80)

Item	Response(s)	%
Why use a condom?	To prevent diseases	80
	To prevent AIDS	73
	To protect the genitals from being chafed	8
	For cleanliness, to catch the semen	24
	For family planning	71
What are the negative things about condoms?	Unpleasant to use	90
	Taste bitter	8
	Can break	13
Do you like clients to wear condoms for oral sex?	Yes	37
Why do you like it?	Prevents diseases	82
	Prevents AIDS	90
	Cleanliness	18
Why don't you like it?	Tastes bitter	46
	Unpleasant	65
	Oral sex is not dangerous	23
Do you like your clients to use condoms for anal sex?	Yes	67
Why do you like it?	Prevents diseases	93
	Prevents AIDS	90
	So anus is not injured	17
Why don't you like it?	Not pleasant/unsatisfying/slippery	92
	Painful	8
Supposing you want a client to wear a condom, how certain are you that they would be willing to wear one?	Very certain	61
	Not very certain	24
	Not at all certain	6
	Don't know	9

preventing AIDS (73 per cent), for family planning (71 per cent), for cleanliness (24 per cent) and to protect the genitals (8 per cent). When asked about the negative aspects of condoms they replied that they were unpleasant to use (90 per cent), they can break (13 per cent) and they taste bitter (7 per cent).

The men were also asked whether or not they liked clients to wear condoms for oral and anal sex, and their reasons. They reported that they liked the clients to use condoms to prevent AIDS and other diseases (80–90 per cent). They also liked them for reasons of cleanliness when engaged in oral sex and so that the penis is not injured in anal sex. Reasons for disliking condoms differed for oral and anal sex. For oral sex, the use of condoms was disliked because they taste bitter (46 per cent), they are unpleasant (65 per cent) and that oral sex is not dangerous (23 per cent). For anal sex, condoms were disliked because they are unpleasant, unsatisfying or slippery (92 per cent), or they could be painful (8 per cent).

Self-efficacy for condom use was measured with the question, 'Supposing you want a client to wear a condom, how certain are you that they would be willing to wear one?' The majority of the men said that they were very certain (61 per cent), although 24 per cent reported that they were not very certain, 6 per cent were not at all certain and 9 per cent did not know.

Sexual practices and condom use

All of the workers reported tourist clients, and many also reported Indonesian clients, (Table 6.6). The workers reported an average of 2.8 clients during the past week, and most of these were new customers. A small number of workers also reported unpaid partners 'in the past week'. Both oral and anal intercourse were common activities for sex workers and clients: anal receptive was reported by 47 per cent of workers and anal insertive by 41 per cent; oral receptive was reported by 61 per cent of workers and oral insertive by 57 per cent. Condom use was higher for anal intercourse (48 per cent receptive, 55 per cent insertive) than for oral intercourse (17 per cent receptive, 14 per cent insertive). Condom use with unpaid partners was much lower.

Table 6.6 Sexual experience and condom use of male sex workers with male clients and male unpaid partners in the last week (n = 80)

Item	Response(s)	
Clients include:	%	
Indonesians from outside Bali	56	
Indonesians from Bali	45	
Tourists	100	
In the past week clients include:	Range	Mean
New clients	0–12	2.45
Repeat clients	0–2	0.34
Intimate clients/boyfriends	0–4	0.41
No. of different clients	0–12	2.80
Intercourse with clients last week:	% of workers with one or more episodes	Mean % condom use[1]
Anal receptive	47	48
Anal insertive	41	55
Oral receptive	61	17
Oral insertive	57	14
Intercourse with unpaid partners last week:	% of workers with at least one episode	Mean % condom use[1]
Anal receptive	33	19
Anal insertive	19	33
Oral receptive	26	0
Oral insertive	29	0

[1] Condom use rates were computed only for persons who reported the indicated type of intercourse with the indicated type of partner.

Workers were asked about the sexual practices requested by clients, and whether or not they provide that particular service (Table 6.7). Almost all workers receive requests for oral insertive and oral receptive sex, and almost all provide these services. Anal sex is also requested by many clients, and the majority but not all of the workers report that they provide these services. Seventy-five per cent provide receptive anal sex and 79 per cent provide insertive anal sex.

Another reported sexual practice was 'rimming', or licking the anus. About 63 per cent reported requests that the client lick the sex worker's anus, while 70 per cent reported requests for the sex worker to lick the client's anus. However, only 55 per cent indicated that they allow clients to lick their anus, and only 11 per cent reported that they lick the client's anus.

Finally, requests to masturbate the client and to have the client masturbate the worker were reported by almost all workers. The vast majority of the workers also report providing these services.

STD infection and health practices

The majority of the male workers had had a health check-up in the last year (Table 6.8). Reasons cited for these checks include preventing diseases (28 per cent), illness (53 per cent) and general health (43 per cent). Only 38 per cent reveal to the doctor that they are commercial sex workers.

Use of traditional medicines, called *jamu*, is very common in Indonesia and more than half of the workers report using these medicines. About a quarter drink them daily. Reasons reported for their use include maintaining health (66 per cent), preventing STDs (4 per cent), treating illness (6 per cent) and appearing youthful and strong (66 per cent).

Symptoms of STDs reported by the men included pain and burning when urinating (21 per cent), abrasions of the genitals (15 per cent), and chafing or lesions around the anus (23 per cent).

Table 6.7 Services requested by clients and services provided by sex workers (n = 80)

Sexual Practice	% of sex workers who say:	
	clients request this service	they provide this service
Client performs oral sex on sex worker's penis	99	96
You perform oral sex on client's penis	100	90
Client inserts penis into sex worker's anus	83	75
Sex worker inserts penis into client's anus	99	79
Client licks sex worker's anus	63	55
Sex worker licks client's anus	70	11
Sex worker masturbates client	100	99
Client masturbates sex worker	99	98

Table 6.8 Medical care, use of medicines, and STD symptoms of male sex workers (n = 80)

Variables	Response(s)	%
Had a medical exam in the last year?	Yes	64
Reason for exam	Prevent diseases	28
	Had an illness	53
	General health check-up	43
Did you tell the doctor that you are a sex worker?	Yes	38
Do you normally take medicines (that you have bought on your own) such as tetracycline either before or after sex?	Yes	80
Do you drink jamu?	Yes	60
How often?	1–3 times a day	26
	1–6 times per week	28
	1–3 times per month	4
	Rarely	43
Why do you drink jamu?	Maintain health	66
	Prevent STDs	4
	Treat illness	6
	Appear youthful and strong	66
STD symptoms in the last six months	Pain and burning when urinating	21
	Abrasions/lesions on the genitals	15
	Chafing/scratches/lesions around the anus	23

Alcohol and drug use

Alcohol use with clients was very common (Table 6.9). Thirty per cent of the workers reported that they often use alcohol with clients, 58 per cent sometimes and 13 per cent never. Many workers also report that almost all of their clients drink alcohol and many of them drink until they are drunk.

Use of other substances was more limited. About 18 per cent of workers reported that they had used other drugs such as marijuana or morphine, and they reported that 29 per cent of their clients had also used these drugs. Only 7 per cent of workers reported that they had taken drugs with a needle, while they revealed that 29 per cent of clients use needles to inject drugs.

Factors related to perceived susceptibility

In Table 6.10, logistic regression models are shown for factors related to perceived susceptibility to STD and HIV infection. Table 6.11 shows the means for variables included in these models. Independent variables for the model were chosen to represent salient demographic characteristics, work history, knowledge of HIV/STD transmission and risk behaviours. Specific variables included are:

Table 6.9 Alcohol and other substance use of male sex workers (n = 80)

Item	Response(s)	%
Use alcohol with clients?	Often	30
	Sometimes	58
	Never	13
Use drugs such as marijuana, morphine, heroin with clients?	Yes	18
Ever taken drugs with a needle?	Yes	7
Clients use alcohol?	Yes	99
Clients drink until drunk?	Most drink until drunk	8
	About half drink until drunk	33
	Only a few drink until drunk	39
	None drink until drunk	20
Clients use drugs such as marijuana, morphine, heroin?	Yes	29
Clients use a needle to take drugs?	Yes	29
Drugs used (n = 23)	Marijuana	46
	Morphine	23
	Heroin	5
	Hallucinogens	5

- Age. Age is measured in single years.
- Rural origin. Rural origin is measured as 1 = rural, 0 = other.
- Time working. This variable is measured as number of years working as a sex worker in Bali.
- Knowledge of asymptomatic syphilis. This variable is coded 1 if the worker knew that syphilis can be asymptomatic, 0 otherwise.
- Knowledge of asymptomatic AIDS. This variable is coded 1 if the worker knew that a person with AIDS can appear healthy, 0 otherwise.
- Provide anal receptive. This variable is coded 1 if the worker provides anal receptive intercourse to clients, 0 otherwise.
- Used a condom. This variable is coded 1 if the respondent used a condom in the last month, 0 otherwise.
- Possible to get syphilis or gonorrhoea. This variable is coded 1 if the respondent thought that it was possible for him to become infected with gonorrhoea or syphilis, 0 otherwise.
- Possible to get AIDS. This variable was coded 1 if the respondent thought that it was possible for him to become infected with AIDS, 0 otherwise.

Variables that were significantly related to susceptibility to gonorrhoea and syphilis were rural origin, knowledge of asymptomatic AIDS and whether the worker provides anal intercourse to clients. The odds ratios for these variables were 7.39 for rural origin, 5.94 for knowledge of asymptomatic AIDS and 3.22 for receptive anal intercourse. Only one of these variables was related to susceptibility to AIDS infection – knowledge of asymptomatic AIDS – and its odds ratio was 4.93.

Table 6.10 Factors related to perceived susceptibility to HIV and STD infection (n = 71)

Independent variables	Dependent variables			
	Possible to get syphilis or gonorrhoea		Possible to get AIDS	
	Coefficient	Odds ratio	Coefficient	Odds ratio
Age	0.16	1.17	0.02	1.02
Rural origin	2.00	7.39**	0.09	1.10
Time working	−0.02	0.98	0.01	1.01
Knowledge of asymptomatic syphilis	−0.42	0.65	−0.82	0.44
Knowledge of asymptomatic AIDS	1.78	5.94**	1.69	4.93**
Provide anal receptive intercourse to clients	1.17	3.22*	0.49	1.64
Used a condom in the last month	−0.53	0.59	−1.06	0.34
Constant	−5.16		−0.45	
Model chi-square	14.48**		7.83	

* $p < 0.05$
** $p < 0.001$

Table 6.11 Mean of variables included in models in Table 6.10 (n = 71)

Variables	Means
Age (years)	24.41
Rural	0.20
Time working (months)	27.89
Knowledge of asymptomatic syphilis	0.59
Knowledge of asymptomatic AIDS	0.73
Provide anal receptive intercourse to clients	0.75
Used a condom in the last month	0.76
Possible for you to get syphilis or gonorrhoea	0.53
Possible for you to get AIDS	0.63

Discussion

Several limitations of this study must be kept in mind. The data come from convenience samples and, thus, generalizations to Bali and other areas of Indonesia are limited. Because of the difficulty of recruitment, the data may undercount long-term relationships. It should also be noted that the data are self-reports on sensitive topics that are not easily verified.

The results of this study have illustrated the vulnerability to HIV/STD infection of a group of male sex workers who serve tourist clients in Bali. The male workers come from a large number of different areas of Indonesia and many engaged in commercial sex work in other parts of Indonesia.

When asked about how they became involved in sex work, most of the men replied that they had been gay since they were young and that they use sex as a way to earn money. Others reported that they were expelled by their families or that they were not gay, but do sex work for money.

The male workers are aware of AIDS and STDs, although some misconceptions about transmission and the risks associated with different sexual practices remained. Most men felt vulnerable to STDs and AIDS. While some men reported that they use condoms to protect themselves from AIDS and STDs, others reported ineffective strategies such as choosing clients carefully and taking medicines. Both oral and anal intercourse with tourists were common and condom use was far from consistent.

An analysis of demographic, belief and behavioural factors related to the perceived susceptibility of these men to STD infection showed that men from rural areas, those who were aware of asymptomatic HIV infection and those who provide receptive anal intercourse to clients were more likely to report that they were at risk of STD infection. Men who were aware of asymptomatic HIV infection were more likely to think that they were at risk of HIV infection.

Interventions for these men should include educational programmes to correct their misconceptions about HIV infection and to promote safer-sex practices and condom use. Making the men aware of asymptomatic HIV infection may be particularly effective in developing an awareness of their vulnerability. Peer education may also be a useful approach for these men, in view of their concerns about discrimination from persons who are outside their group. In addition, due to the strong association between experience with STDs and HIV infection (Wasserheit, 1992; Grosskurth *et al.*, 1995), attention should also be paid to effective STD diagnosis and treatment for both sex workers and clients.

In summary, the results of this study have illustrated the vulnerability to HIV/STD infection of a group of male sex workers who serve tourist clients in Bali. Interventions with these men are needed because of the workers' low level of knowledge about AIDS, their experience with STDs and STD symptoms and the level of risky sexual behaviour. Interventions for tourist clients should include media that promote safer sex and use of condoms. Outreach workers could also be usefully employed at popular tourist bars and beach settings. The accessibility of condoms at tourist sites should also be improved.

Acknowledgements

This project, the Udayana-Michigan AIDS Behavioral Study, is a collaborative effort between the Faculty of Medicine of Udayana University in Bali and the School of Public Health of the University of Michigan, Ann Arbor. Dr Wirawan had overall responsibility for the administration of the survey in Bali, while Dr Peter Fajans also served as an investigator for the study and Lorna Thorpe acted as a behavioural research fellow. Many other persons have assisted with the project in Bali, including Dr Komang Gunung and Dr Made Sutarga of Udayana University as well as Dr Wayan Semendra of the Balinese Provincial Health Department. Financial support for this study was provided by Family Health International with funds from the United States Agency for International Development (AID).

References

Ajzen, I. and Fishbein, M. (1980) *Understanding Attitudes and Predicting Social Behavior*. Englewood Cliffs, NJ: Prentice Hall International.

Bargh, J. (1984) Automatic and conscious processing of social information. In R. Wyer and T. K. Skrull (eds), *Handbook of Social Cognition*, Volume 3. Hillsdale, NJ: Erlbaum.

Elifson, K. W., Boles, J. and Sweat, M. (1993) Risk factors associated with HIV infection among male prostitutes. *American Journal of Public Health* **83**, 79–83.

Ford, K., Wirawan, D. N. and Fajans, P. (1993) AIDS knowledge, condom attitudes, and sexual behavior among male sex workers and male tourist clients in Bali, Indonesia. *Health Transition Review* **3**, 191–204.

Ford, K., Wirawan, D. N., Fajans, P. and Thorpe, L. (1995) AIDS knowledge, risk behaviors, and factors related to condom use among male commercial sex workers and tourist clients in Bali, Indonesia. *AIDS* **9**, 751–9.

Grosskurth, H., Mosha, F., Todd, J. *et al.* (1995) Impact of improved treatment of sexually transmitted diseases on HIV infection in Tanzania: results of a randomized, controlled trial. *The Lancet* **346**, 530–6.

Higgins, E. T. and King, G. (1981) Accessibility of social constructs: information processing consequences of individual and contextual variability. In N. Cantor and J. F. Kilstrom (eds), *Personality, Cognition, and Social Interaction*. Hillsdale, NJ: Erlbaum.

Linharea-Carvalho, M. I., Galvao-Castro, B., Berro, O., Parseghian, M., Costa, S. R. and Castello-Branco, L. R. R. (1996) Prevalence of HIV infection amongst prostitutes attending an outpatient clinic for social outcasts in Rio de Janeiro, Brazil: 1985 to 1995. Paper presented at XIth International Conference on AIDS, Vancouver, Abstract Pub.C.1145.

McCamish, M., Storer, G., Greg, C. and Kenkanrua, K. (1998) Development of effective interventions for male sex workers in Thailand. Paper presented at XIIth International Conference on AIDS, Geneva (Abstract 43330).

Morse, E. V., Simon, P. M., Balson, P. M. and Osofsky, H. J. (1992) Sexual behavior patterns of customers of male street prostitutes. *Archives of Sexual Behavior* **21**, 347–57.

Pleak, R. and Meyer-Bahlburg, H. F. (1990) Sexual behavior and AIDS knowledge of young male prostitutes in Manhattan. *Journal of Sex Research* **27**, 557–87.

Schechter, M., Martindale, S., Miller, M. L., Strathdee, S., Corneliesse, P., Tetlock, E., Tigchelaar, J. and Schechter, M. T. (1998) Characteristics of male sex trade workers enrolled in a prospective study of HIV incidence. Paper presented at XIIth International Conference on AIDS, Geneva (Abstract 23525).

Schlich, H. P. (1996) HIV and STD intervention for male prostitutes and male street kids – 'Kiss'– a place for the homeless. Paper presented at XIth International Conference on AIDS, Vancouver (Abstract Pub. C. 1165).

Sittitrai, W. (1988) Qualitative research for development of IE and C materials for high-risk groups in Thailand. Paper presented at the First International Symposium on Information and Education on AIDS, Ixtapa, Mexico.

Sittitrai, W., Brown, T. and Sakondhavat, C. (1993) Levels of HIV risk behavior and AIDS knowledge in Thai men having sex with men. *AIDS Care* 5, 261–70.

Sittitrai, W., Phanuphak, P., Salivahan, N., Ehweera, E. W. and Rhoddy, R. E. (1989) Demographic and sexual practices of male bar workers in Bangkok. Paper presented at the Fifth International Conference on AIDS, Montreal, 4–9 June, Abstract MDP19, 714.

Waldorf, D. and Lauderback, D. (1991) Condom failure among male sex workers in San Francisco. Institute for Scientific Analysis (unpublished manuscript).

Wasserheit, J. N. (1992) Epidemiological synergy: interactions between Human Immunodeficiency Virus infection and other sexually transmitted diseases. *Sexually Transmitted Diseases* 19, 61–77.

7

The use of commercial sex venues and male escorts by gay tourists in New York City

Michael Luongo

Introduction

The link between gay men's travel and sexual behaviour was an important factor in the early spread of the Human Immunodeficiency Virus (HIV) throughout the gay male community of the United States. Sexual contact tracing in the early 1980s of the first men infected with the disease linked one man, a Canadian flight attendant who became known as Patient Zero, to at least 40 cases of transmission of the virus. Through his occupation, he was able to travel frequently to many of the gay urban centres in the United States. He and other highly mobile gay men like him may have been the reason for the acceleration of the disease's movement between New York City, San Francisco and Los Angeles, where enormous infrastructures of sex environments catered to men living in the cities, and to those who travelled to them (Shilts, 1987; Clift and Wilkins, 1995; Rotello, 1997).

American gay neighbourhoods have changed drastically since the early 1980s, with a marked reduction in many of the commercial sex venues. AIDS service organizations now work with those that remain. However, in spite of the link between gay tourism and the spread of HIV throughout the United States and eventually the world, little work has been done to focus specifically on sexual behaviour among gay tourists in the United States. Many discussions of commercial sex and tourism have focused on Third World destinations, particularly in Asian countries (Enloe, 1990; Ford and Koetswang, 1991; Herold and van Kerkwijk, 1992; Ford *et al.*, 1995). Perhaps few gay men will ever go to Asia for commercial sex, but the growth of gay tourism in the United States and Europe indicates that travel is an important component of gay life. US gays vacation 4.5 times more often than their straight counterparts (Holcomb and Luongo, 1996). What distinguishes this type of travel is that, unlike trips to the Far East, it may not be based solely on obtaining sex, but can place a gay man in situations where he will have sexual opportunities he would not ordinarily find at home (Clift and Forrest, 1998). Ignoring the sexual behaviour of gay men on vacation is to ignore sex in a context that is in certain ways a defining characteristic of gay men's lives.

This chapter will look at the ways in which gay male travellers access sex while in New York City, the largest city in the United States and one with numerous gay neighbourhoods and a large gay commercial infrastructure. New York is examined in the context of gay tourism in other important destinations in the United States. The chapter will examine the media tourists use to access commercial sex in these destinations, and how much of the current HIV prevention work aimed at men who have sex with men excludes travellers. Interviews with male escorts and sex club managers will provide information about the origins of many of these travellers, their motivations for obtaining sex, as well as the economic importance gay tourism has to New York City. This will be examined in the context of the current political framework in New York City where an ongoing battle is being waged between mainstream touristic enterprises and the availability of commercial sex. Though the size of New York City makes it a special case in certain ways, some of the findings may be relevant to other American cities with large gay infrastructures.

Growth of gay tourism

While gay tourism has only recently been studied, its roots go back much further. In the last century, the Mediterranean maintained a strong pull for homosexual men from Northern Europe keen to explore their sexuality. There, away from the constraints of their societies, they could form relationships with other men. In these exploits, such men felt an ideological connection to the Mediterranean's ancient past, where free expression of love between men was celebrated (Aldrich, 1993).

These men bear some similarities to today's gay men who still travel to particular destinations to seek out the companionship of other men. Unlike the Victorian era when such travel was clandestine, gay travel today has come out of the closet. A network of travel companies exists within the United States, Europe and Australia catering nearly exclusively to gay men. Guidebooks and a myriad of other aids facilitate gay men with their travels.

World-wide, the economic significance of gay travel has also recently been recognized. Sydney's Gay and Lesbian Mardi Gras is Australia's largest tourist event, and major cities, including London, now officially promote themselves as gay tourist destinations (Wieder, 1998). The combined impact of the 1994 Gay Games IV and Stonewall 25 produced more tourist dollars for New York City than the concurrent hosting of World Cup soccer, and in the United States overall, gay and lesbian travel is estimated to be worth more than US$10 billion (Holcomb and Luongo, 1996). Gay travel has even resulted in odd spillovers into other sections of the economy. For instance, international gay travel, and the subsequent exposure of gay American men to the penises of Europeans, has been cited as responsible for a trend towards expensive foreskin replacement therapies (Seomin, 1997).

While the scope and openness with which gay men travel has broadened in recent years, one thing remains the same: travel to destinations popular with other gay men remains strongly connected to a sense of gay identity (Hughes, 1997). Few places in the world are as firmly connected with gay history and identity as key urban areas in the United States. It was here, in 1969, that the modern gay rights movement was born, at the Stonewall Inn in New York City. As a placename, Stonewall is so closely associated with the gay civil rights movement that it has been adopted by the main gay civil rights group in the UK. The names of other US cities and places associated with gay men are also used around the world to signify gay identification, and one international gay tourist guide lists such diverse places and events as Key West Sauna in Paris, Christopher Street Day in Turkey or Castro's Bar in South Africa (Rauch, 1997).

This points to a few of the US cities with strong associations as destinations for gay travellers. Among these are the large cities of New York, Los Angeles and San Francisco, as well as smaller cities and seasonal resorts, such as Key West, West Hollywood, Miami Beach and Provincetown (Holcomb and Luongo, 1996; Hughes, 1997). US media strengthens these associations, and such cities are sometimes the locations for films on gay life. New York City was the site of *Jeffrey*, *Torch Song Trilogy* and various other films. Miami Beach was the location for the *Bird Cage*, the American remake of *La Cage aux Folles*. And certainly, West Hollywood and other locations throughout Los Angeles are embedded in the psyche of millions of gay men as the palm-treed backdrops in gay pornographic images distributed throughout the world.

It is with New York City that we primarily concern ourselves in this chapter. Ideologically, New York has perhaps the oldest associations with the homosexual subculture of any US city. Even in the Victorian era, at least one guidebook to the city made references to locations where homosexual men gathered (Averell and Company, 1877). Chauncey (1994) indicates the importance of both Greenwich Village and Harlem as places where gay men could openly express themselves since the beginning of this century. Today, the continuing importance of New York City as a gay tourist centre is epitomized by the words of one Christopher Street business owner: 'This is a "Gay Mecca". Sooner or later, every gay man in America will pass in front of my store' (Martin, 1993).

Size of gay populations

The importance of New York as a gay destination is not just ideological but is also rooted in the sheer enormity of the city and its gay population. The now-defunct New York Gay and Lesbian Visitor's Center estimated that gay men and lesbians represented 25 per cent of lower Manhattan's population. Such a density created the gay infrastructure that in turn fuelled gay tourism (Goldstein, 1993). Though there are no accurate estimates for the actual gay and lesbian population in the entire city, the number is very large. New York City contains more than 7.3 million people according to the 1990 census. Even at the commonly stated 10 per cent, the gay and lesbian population of New York City would be nearly 730,000 people, more than the total population of San Francisco (United States Department of Commerce, 1991).

Statistical research bears out some relationship between large gay populations and visible gay infrastructure. Laumann *et al.* (1994) found that same-gender sexuality among men was highest in the 12 largest US cities, falling between 9.2 per cent and 16.7 per cent of survey respondents. This was statistically significant when set against the 2.8 per cent to 7.7 per cent for all men throughout the United States. The researchers cite these higher numbers as related to the visibility of gay communities in such cities as New York, Los Angeles and Chicago. Other demographic studies have subsequently related this to HIV prevalence. One study of HIV incidence rates in the 96 largest metropolitan regions in the United States found that among men who have sex with men, New York, Los Angeles, Miami and San Francisco 'continue to have substantially higher HIV incidence than that observed in most other cities' (Holmberg, 1996).

These four cities – New York, Los Angeles, Miami and San Francisco – dominate the books written for gay travellers. *Fodor's Gay Guide to the USA* describes 29 separate cities, but these four represent nearly 25 per cent of the books pages (Collins, 1996). The *Damron Address Book*, a more comprehensive guide to thousands of US destinations, devotes almost one-sixth of its pages to these cities (Gatta, 1996). Internationally, *Spartacus 1997/98* also indicates the importance of these cities to gay tourism, dedicating more than 25 per cent of its US pages to them (Rauch, 1997). This highlights a crucial relationship and an irony of gay tourism. If it is true that gay travel is very specifically concentrated, much of it centring on locations with large year-round gay populations, it is also true that AIDS and HIV infections have concentrated in the same locations. Thus, the places in the United States that gay tourists most want to visit are the ones where they are most at risk from HIV infection.

How HIV research on gay men ignores the issue of travel

Some important gay writers have linked travel to the early spread of HIV throughout the gay community. Shilts (1987) in his book, *And the Band Played On*, discussed a French-Canadian flight attendant, Gaeten Dugas, who was linked to nearly 40 of the earliest cases of what we now know as AIDS. Rotello (1997: 84) also discusses Dugas and HIV's spread through travel and how 'researchers discovered clusters of gay men in New York, San Francisco and Los Angeles who were connected to each other through sexual relations'. Others have attempted to examine Dugas's behaviour in the context of the times (Chesnut, 1997).

However, in spite of the issue's discussion by some, the link between gay travel and HIV in the United States has not been fully explored by many researchers and prevention experts. This may be due to the structure of sexual behaviour research conducted in the United States, which does not simply ignore the traveller, but is specifically written to exclude him. Even the language in some HIV-prevention programmes, which use code words like 'community', 'friendship networks' and 'social group', may also exclude and isolate the travelling gay man. For instance, one paper discusses study design and the assessment of 'sexual communities', which assume that while people will move from one social group to another, they remain physically sedentary in the broader sense. The authors discuss the 'sexual geography' of a locale, and specific spaces within a city where men will seek sex, but fail to mention that men may move between cities to seek sexual opportunities (Parker and Carballo, 1990). Studies of the maintenance of safer-sex behaviour, such as that carried out by Ekstrand and Coates (1990), also exclude the traveller, looking soley at the behaviour changes of a fixed group of men in a given location.

Traditional recruitment methods can also exclude the traveller from participating in a study. For instance, one study described how it recruited men through 'a standard array of recruitment procedures, such as personal referral, advertising in mass and special media and formal presentations to targeted groups and organisations' (Fishbein *et al.*, 1993: 419). While the advertising methods could gain the attention of travellers, personal referrals and appeals to groups are unlikely to do so.

Yet, some of the research that excludes the traveller may also show how prevalent he is. One study conducted in several small American cities recruited men from gay bars for a community-based behavioural change programme based on friendship and leadership networks. The researchers excluded more than half of the men who completed the questionnaire because many were 'transients' (Kelly *et al.*, 1997). One of the co-authors of the study, Dr Sikkema (1998), explained that transients were any men who had not been to the bar more than five times in two months. She was unsure, though, how many tourists were in the excluded population group.

However, transients made up such a significant proportion of one wave of the study conducted over the summer months that all data from that period were excluded, at the very time one would expect the highest number of tourists.

One of the few American articles to look at HIV and travel (Lewis and Bailey, 1992–3) discusses the spread of HIV in the Pacific area, touching on Hawaii and various US possessions. Importantly, while travel may be a reason for the spread of the disease, the authors point to the dilemma destinations have in acknowledging HIV, frightened that it may scare visitors away. The authors also discuss how the Hawaiian government understands that its image as a 'paradise' reduces a traveller's inhibitions, and therefore creates opportunities for the spread of the disease.

Travel and HIV risk do appear in a qualitative study of 41 American gay men (Offir *et al.*, 1993) which found that some men in their study described vacations as an excuse to engage in risky behaviour, even if they usually practised safer sex. The authors state that 'another common situation leading to accidental AIDS risk behaviour occurred for men on vacation, especially during vacations in seaside locales'. A quote from one of their subjects described vacations as when 'you get back to the old "having a good time" sort of thing'. For these men, a vacation is a time out not just from work but from safer-sex practices as well.

While more information is needed to better understand gay men's sexual behaviour when they travel, such work does not necessarily require a major change in the structure of current research. Standard research studies can quite easily include questions on sexual behaviour in the context of travel along with questions about other behavioural patterns.

Guidebooks and other information sources

Whether as a tourist on vacation or a businessman at a convention, the travelling gay man has a variety of sources of information on accessing sex throughout the United States. These range from guidebooks, to local scene guides, to the Internet. Each of these provides different forms of information about sexual opportunities in a particular destination.

Guidebooks

One of the most important US guidebooks is the *Damron Address Book*, often abbreviated as *Damron's* (Gatta, 1996). The book has existed for 33 years and details thousands of US cities. Depending on the size of the city, it lists community and AIDS resources, bars and discos, hotels and other information. The book also describes sex clubs, which it describes as 'Men's Clubs', and public sex environments (PSEs), which are labelled 'Cruisy Areas'. It is not always accurate, however. For example, in New York City, the book lists five Men's Clubs, and no Cruisy Areas, underestimating both types of sex location.

Spartacus is an international guidebook published in Germany with details in five languages – English, German, Italian, Spanish and French. While it lists virtually every country in the world, none occupies more page space than the United States. In fact, in the introduction to the US in the 26th edition, the editor comments, 'Nowhere on the globe is there a gay scene bigger and more diverse than in the USA' (Rauch, 1997: 980). The book contains many types of listings for the different cities, including community and AIDS resources, bars, clubs, bookstores, restaurants, hotels and other forms of lodging and sex venues. Like *Damron's*, it is not always complete in its lists of sex locations. The 1997/8 version lists seven men's clubs or saunas, and only two cruising areas in New York City.

There are several other choices for gay travellers, some of which provide information for accessing sex on vacation. *Betty and Pansy's Severe Queer Guide* is a series of city-specific books for New York, Washington and San Francisco (Pearl and Pansy, 1997). The books humorously describe locations for accessing sex. *The Black Book* (Brent, 1994) lists sex and fetish venues, both gay and straight, in the United States. Additionally, there are travel magazines such as *Out and About*, published in New York City (Kolber-Stuart, 1992–8). Its focus is both international and domestic, and when describing a destination, sex venues are often mentioned casually along with other types of attractions.

An important gay tourism book is *Fodor's Gay Guide to the USA* (Collins, 1996), the first to be published by a mainstream publisher. However, as it is a mainstream publication, it contains virtually no information about accessing sex while on vacation. For instance, in the section on New York City, there is only one small reference to the Rambles, a Central Park public sex environment, and there are few references to commercial sex venues in any of the other cities it covers.

The *Columbia Fun Maps*, published in New York, is a series of individual maps of various US and European cities. The maps contain advertisements and listings of hotels, bars, discos and community and AIDS resources. Mainstream advertisements are often included, such as for airlines. Sexual advertisements may include saunas, phone lines and escort services. The 1997 Manhattan edition devotes nearly 25 per cent of its advertising to sex-oriented businesses (Beck, 1997).

Local scene guides

Virtually every major US city has a gay scene guide. Unlike travel books that are meant specifically for gay travellers, local scene guides provide regular updates for both the indigenous gay population and the traveller. They are highly accurate guides for the traveller to a particular city, but only once he has arrived in that destination. New York City has two primary local gay scene guides, both of which are published weekly. The older of the two is *HX*, formerly known as *Homo Xtra*, and the other scene guide is *NEXT*. Both contain articles on fashion, music and other issues, as well as listings for clubs, restaurants, community and AIDS resources and extensive coverage of New York City's gay sex scene.

The Internet

The Internet has connected the world in ways that virtually no other invention has been able to. For gay men and other men who have sex with men, it has created the opportunity to seek out the companionship of others in nearly complete privacy. At the same time, the Internet has enabled destinations around the world to provide information to people who are planning their next vacation. Sometimes, those two purposes collide, and some Internet sites enable men to plan a vacation that incorporates seeking sex with other men.

There are Internet sites run by sex venues that give details about a particular sex club, or a consortium of sex clubs that have branches in different cities. Escorts and escort agencies run their own sites, and these will be discussed further in the section on male escorts. Other sites may list public sex environments in a particular destination. Chat rooms also enable men to meet other men in different cities, with whom they may eventually have sex when they travel.

Perhaps the most comprehensive Internet sex site for men who travel within the United States is cruisingforsex.com. Though the bulk of information on the website concerns the United States, the listings cover more than a hundred countries. The site details cruising grounds and other public and commercial sex venues. Visitors to the website can look up locations by state or city, and in the case of very large cities, by neighbourhood. The site is run by Keith Griffith, formerly the Associate Publisher of *Steam* magazine, a now-defunct publication on bathhouses and saunas. In an interview with the author, Mr Griffith explained that when he began cruisingforsex.com in late 1995, he intended that it would be used by men in particular locations to find local men for sex, not for vacation planning. It seems, however, that travel is increasingly becoming an important aspect of the site, as Griffith explains:

> I knew that men travelled to places and always made a point of going to those places with a certain amount of knowledge about where to go to have sex when they got there. But I never realized that there were actually men who went to places solely to have sex in these places. But there are, and that's astonishing to me.

When Griffith began the site, he had a basic list of sex locations, which was then supplemented by input from site visitors. However, while travellers have provided input about experiences on vacation, this information is not usually about known sex tourism destinations. Instead, most write about sex locations they have discovered in a city, as Griffith explains: '[I have] rarely encountered any examples of people writing to me about places that people generally think of when they think of people going to a place to have sex, like a man going to Bangkok.'

Griffith tracks the number of visitors to his site, which has grown steadily since he began counting. In February 1997, he had only 2000 visitors per day. By December of that year, the number had grown to over 10,000. He is not sure what percentage of the men who visit the site are actually planning a vacation, but revealed that it is a common topic in e-mail conversations.

Men using his site to plan their vacations originate from a variety of locations, though most are domestic. His overseas visitors are usually from the UK, Japan, Australia, Canada and Germany. Griffith stated that this corresponds with his understanding of which nations are the highest users of the Internet, but only about 10 per cent of his e-mails come from overseas. Communications from New York and Los Angeles lead other US cities. Griffith is convinced that vacations are important times when men do choose to have sex with each other:

> I think a lot of men certainly have a great deal of the sex that they have in any given year . . . on their vacation. And a lot of men that are travelling as part of their business have a great deal of their sex when they are outside of their location that they live in. And I never quite understood why, but I know myself that it seems to be easier for me to meet men when I am in a strange environment.

As men have begun to adapt his site to their own travel purposes, Griffith has also begun to alter the site to accommodate their needs. For the other larger US cities, he includes hotel listings, general tourist-information contacts, as well as links to AIDS-information websites. Still, Griffith acknowledges that his site is not comprehensive enough to be the only resource men refer to for a vacation, and he recommends its use in conjunction with published guidebooks. However, unlike books that are updated only once per year, the people who use Griffith's site can instantaneously update it.

Commercial sex workers and advertising

Travel to the major gay urban centres of the United States places a tourist in close proximity not only to many commercial and public sex environments but also to large numbers of escorts and other commercial sex workers. A myriad of methods exists for the tourist and the escort to find each other before or during a visit. Some escorts use phone lines, bars or the streets of the city. Others may work with agencies or advertise in local and national gay publications, or on the Internet, providing them with an international market.

The most internationally accessible method of advertising for escorts is the Internet. People expecting to visit a specific destination can pull up various websites, often arranged by city. As an example, r e n t b o y . c o m highlights gay capitals such as New York, San Francisco, Amsterdam and Miami. A viewer clicks on a city, revealing pages of photographs with details on different escorts. Some ads include phrases such as 'will travel for extra cost', 'will travel world-wide' or 'new in New York'. Individual escorts also update their sites with their personal travel schedules, revealing intense mobility.

Unlike printed advertisements, almost anyone in the world who can afford an on-line computer may access web ads. A traveller seeking sex through printed matter must know first where to find such publications, and they are often only available in gay-identified venues in the very cities where he may be heading. With websites, one need know nothing more than how to use a search engine and spell 'gay male escort'. Websites are also ideally suited to people on tight schedules who need to make appointments ahead of time.

The politics of sex and tourism in New York City

In New York City, the concept of tourism and its relationship to the access of commercial sex appears ironic in light of the city's current conservative administration. Closing sex venues was one of Mayor Giuliani's major campaign promises and continues to be an integral component of his quality-of-life policy (Kolbert, 1997). The Mayor credits his zoning laws with removing 'the sick and the perverted' from Times Square, once New York's main red-light district, and now an area of family entertainment (Firestone, 1997a). Times Square is important to New York's tourist economy, as 20 million tourists visit the area every year (Holusha, 1996).

However, if there were no crackdowns on sex venues, would tourists still come to New York City? Have the policies affected gay tourism in the city? These are not merely hypothetical questions. The relationship between gay tourism specifically and access to sex venues was debated in the city's last mayoral election. Ruth Messinger, the Democratic candidate against Republican Giuliani, felt that sex businesses in gay neighbourhoods increased the number of gay tourists, and therefore were significant components of the city's economy. A letter she wrote explaining her position was quoted in the *New York Times* prior to the elections (Firestone, 1997a: B6). Here is an extract:

> The proposed adult establishment zoning text could well result in the closing of most of the gay adult-oriented businesses of Christopher Street, as well as those in other predominantly gay neighbourhoods of the city. This could have profoundly detrimental consequences for the gay community, not to mention an important part of our city's economic and tourism-industry base.

Ruth Messinger lost against Giuliani in the 1997 elections, and sex venues, both gay and straight, continue to close. It is important to note that the closing of the venues in Times Square did not begin under Giuliani, but rather was part of an earlier plan created by mainstream businesses in the area. Most Times Square sex businesses had already closed by 1989 (McNamara, 1995).

Redick of *Sex Panic*, a group challenging the closures, pointed to the connection between the crackdown on sex venues and the rise of family tourism: 'The zoning [out] of sex businesses and the massive influx of primarily tourist-oriented commerce under Mayor Giuliani's supervision are closely linked.' She continued on the touristic irony, adding: 'Times Square was already a source of tourism, patronised largely by heterosexual populations, presumably many of the same people who will now bring their families into the city' (Redick, 1997: 31).

While the arguments and the closing of the venues continue, the relationship between control over tourism and sexuality in the city has been strengthened in the Mayor's favour. In December 1997, Deputy Mayor Fran Reiter, one of Giuliani's most important advisers, was made president of the New York Convention and Visitor's Bureau. As a result, the Bureau will 'take on an expanded role as the chief marketer of New York City's shiny new image around the world, working much more closely with the Giuliani administration' (Firestone, 1997b).

Interviews with commercial sex providers

While the debate over tourism and the access to commercial and public sex in New York continues in print media, direct discussions with those who provide sexual services to tourists can provide more information on the subject. The author conducted interviews with three managers of New York City gay commercial sex venues and five gay male escorts based in Manhattan. For both sets of interviews, tourists were defined as men who were visiting from other countries, or from other parts of the United States itself, and excluded those from New York City or the surrounding metropolitan region. Such men might be on vacation, or merely visiting the city for conventions or other business purposes.

Sex venue managers

The author interviewed three contacts for five Manhattan sex venues in December 1997. The contacts were asked general questions about the history of their businesses as well as specific questions about men who frequent their venues as tourists. Due in part to the political climate in New York City, their names and that of their venues will not be directly discussed in this section. One contact, who will be called Charlie, managed three bathhouses: one in lower Manhattan, one in Chelsea and one in Midtown.

Another contact, who will be called Frank, dealt with management and health promotion in an uptown bathhouse, the oldest still operating in the United States. A third contact, who will be called Gary, managed a downtown sex club with a leather and fetish theme. The bathhouse interviews cover four of the five bathhouses in the city.

Listings and advertising

All three managers indicated a wide variety of methods for advertising and listings, ranging from guidebooks, listings in local publications and even cable television. Frank's venue used the fewest methods, and was not in many guides, preferring word of mouth to gain clients. Gary's leather venue used a website, gay media and *The Black Book*. Charlie explained that his company was planning a website, but did not have one running at the end of 1997.

When asked whether local or national media was more important in gaining clients who are tourists, both Gary and Charlie indicated that while tourists used both, local advertising media such as *HX* and *NEXT* often garnered those men who had never initially thought of coming to a sex venue when planning their trips. Charlie cited one example: 'For instance, I one time talked to a man from Canada. He came here [to New York] to shop. He never came to a gay place. He saw it in a magazine and then he decided to come. He was here for ten days and he came every day after that.'

Gary felt that New York's local gay guides were very explicit in describing what a venue offered, especially when compared to the yearly guidebooks/and or local guides available in other US cities: 'The travel guides that I have looked through tend not to even list sex establishments, and if they do, they don't list them specifically as sex-oriented.' He also felt that the pedestrian-friendly nature of New York City added to the ease with which a tourist can access such information.

Percentage of clients who are tourists

Based on his experiences with customers, Frank estimated the percentage of tourists in his bathhouse at about 35 per cent. He was unable to break the percentages down nationally and internationally, but revealed that most came from Germany and England, with many also coming from France, Australia and Japan. As the venue was in an African-American neighbourhood, one might expect a fairly large number of tourists from Africa, but Frank explained that this was not the case. Clients from the United States came from all over, but primarily from Philadelphia, Washington DC and California.

For all three of his venues, Charlie stated that tourists averaged approximately 25 per cent of the clientele. However, the bathhouse in

Chelsea attracted the most, with tourists making up 45 per cent of all clients. The neighbourhood played a major role in this, he explained: 'It's more central. It's in Chelsea, there's more gays.' Most foreign tourists were European, primarily from Germany, England and France. US clients were largely from the Midwest and California, but he was unable to give specific breakdowns.

Gary indicated that for his leather-oriented sex club, the percentage of tourists will vary depending on the time of year and on what particular event he is presenting. Usually, the range fell between 20 per cent and 30 per cent, but special events could peak at 50 per cent. Most of his tourists were European, with Germans standing out in particular: 'the Germans seem to be more interested in leather than most other Europeans, so they'll come to a place like this'. Domestic tourists tended to be from California or other north-eastern cities: 'there's almost a circuit between New York, Washington and Boston, because it's so easy to travel back and forth'.

All three managers concurred that there were specific touristic seasons – the summer, and the December to January holiday season. European tourists came at both times but peaked in summer. Americans tended to stand out more significantly during the December to January holiday season, the time when the interviews were conducted. Gary commented on some of the recent American tourists:

> People coming in from the Midwest and wherever, coming in to see the city in general for the holidays, and then getting a taste of gay life because they may not have as big of a gay life at home. And for many of them, a place like this is completely foreign. You know, the thought that you can go to a public place, get naked and then play with other men.

Tourist events and trends
Each of the managers was asked to comment on whether two factors had brought about a significant increase in the number of tourists visiting their venues. The first was if New York City's hosting of the Gay Games in the summer of 1994 had significantly impacted their business. The second concerned whether the recent increase in the number of visitors to New York City had also meant that more tourists were using their facilities.

Frank mentioned that as far as his venue was concerned, the Gay Games had increased business, but he could not state specifically to what degree. The venue had not made extra staffing preparations for the event, but did spend more on advertising during that period. Though the numbers of tourists may be increasing in New York City, Frank indicated that he had not seen his own numbers rising with it. Gary's leather venue was not open during the Gay Games, and he was not sure if the recent increases in business he was seeing had more to do with establishing a reputation over time.

Charlie explained that both factors had significantly impacted on the number of tourists using the three venues he managed. He described the impact of the Gay Games: 'It was major. Fifty per cent increase across all three venues. Extra staff at all three venues.' Recently, he had also seen an increase in tourists using the facilities as well: 'I think there's more than two years ago. I think that now when they're saying New York is a safer place for people to visit and do business.' He also commented on the irony of the increase in light of the precarious nature of sex businesses in the city: 'With this 'Quality of Life' they think that sex is not part of life, especially gay sex. There's gay people who must have sex.' And quite often, they come to New York City to do it.

Commentary

In view of the tremendous variety of sex venues in New York City, these interviews may not be representative of all types that exist. Moreover, even if the percentages of tourists are representative for New York City, the same may not hold true in other US cities. However, they are an indication of the mobility of the gay population, and the importance of gay tourism economically for New York City.

All three of the managers indicated that there were distinct tourist seasons – summer, when the tourists are noticeably European, and the December to January holiday season, when most of the tourists are American. Any attempt to gather information about tourists cannot be done at one time only, but must take these different periods into account.

Importantly, the managers discussed two types of tourists who frequented their venues, and this may be crucial for HIV intervention. The first are the tourists who make regular visits. Both Frank and Gary revealed that many of their clientele came from other north-eastern cities. More importantly, though, both Gary and Charlie mentioned tourists who had never been to a sex venue before. Such men came across the venues after seeing a local advertisement, having originally come to New York for other reasons. As these men are often completely unfamiliar with such venues, they may be entering a sexual ecology they are unable skilfully to negotiate (Rotello, 1997). At the same time, it also underscores the importance of such venues as distribution points for safer-sex information aimed specifically at tourists. Having come from areas with less gay infrastructure, such men may have been exposed to little or no safer-sex information.

Finally, the interviews also indicate an important finding – that men will travel considerable distances to have sex with other men. While no such survey has ever been undertaken of men in New York City, one London survey did find that specialized gay sex venues exerted a strong geographic pull (Kelley, 1996). There is reason to believe that this may also be true in New York City, but only direct work with the clientele will give us an indication of where these men are from, their motivations for coming to these venues and what their special needs are from the point of an HIV intervention campaign.

Interviews with male escorts

The author interviewed five gay male escorts based in Manhattan. Two were contacted through a key informant from a past research project who is himself involved in the field. The remainder were recruited by responding to advertisements placed in *HX* and *NEXT*. Approximately 30 escorts were contacted in this manner, but few chose to participate. The two men contacted through the key informant also advertised in these magazines. Two interviews were completed in person. Two were begun over the telephone and completed via e-mail. The fifth interview was conducted by phone, but the participant was unable to answer all of the questions as he was only currently building up his tourist clientele. The men were interviewed on the premise of anonymity, and each is given a pseudonym.

The escorts were asked various questions, including how tourists made contact with them, where the tourists were from, as well as whether the escorts had ever travelled with a client. Other questions centred on how the tourist clients differed from clients from the New York area in such areas as safer-sex knowledge. The men were asked if they discussed sex clubs and other gay venues with their clients.

Percentages of clients who are tourists

There was a broad range in the percentage of tourist clients for the five men, going from a low of 20 per cent to a high of 72 per cent. Joe explained that he fell into the low category, as he advertised only in local publications. Mark fell into the high category, at 72 per cent, and deliberately tracked these clients, as they were an important part of his business. The remaining three fell within this range.

Within the definition of tourist, most of the clients were visiting businessmen, as opposed to vacationers. For instance, Luke stated that 65 per cent of his clients who had travelled to New York were out-of-town businessmen. For John, the number was 80 per cent. For David, the split was even between businessmen and vacationers, and such men made up most of Mark's out-of-town clients.

The four men who had large percentages of tourist clients indicated that these clients came from many parts of the world, but that it differed depending on whether they were in New York on business or on vacation. In general, the businessmen were more likely to be from the United States, while those on vacation usually came from other parts of the world. For instance, John stated that 70 per cent of his business clients were from the United States, specifically the South and California. In contrast, 70 per cent of his vacationing clients hailed from Europe.

Like John, most of David's business travellers were from the United States. His vacationers, however, were more mixed. One-third originated from Europe, specifically the UK, Switzerland, the Czech Republic and France. Half came from the United States, and he listed Los Angeles, Chicago, Boston and Atlanta as some of their hometowns. The remainder of the vacationers came from South America, Russia or Korea. Most of Mark's clients were businessmen from the United States, though he mentioned a few Asian clients. While Joe had the lowest overall percentage of tourist clients, most were from other parts of the United States. Luke's experience differed in this respect from the other four escorts. His business clientele was more international, mostly Europeans, and his vacationers were primarily from the United States.

Indicative of the wealth of many of their clients, some of the men had periodically been retained for travel. Using the phrase 'will travel' in advertisements facilitated this. John said, 'I've gone to Puerto Rico for a week. I've gone to Spain for a week. And they pay good money.' David had travelled to various cities with clients, including Los Angeles, Dallas, Boston and abroad to Paris. Mark did not include the travel phrase in his ads, but would discuss it individually with clients. Luke used the phrase, but did not reveal where he had travelled to. As he was building this segment of his clientele, Joe could not properly answer the question.

Methods of obtaining clients
Each of the men indicated the advertising method they used to gain clients. It was clear from their answers that each knew specifically which methods would attract what types of clients. Two methods were considered essential for obtaining tourist clients – the national publication *Unzipped* and the Internet. Three of the men advertised in *Unzipped*, and Joe was about to do so, specifically to gain more tourist clients. Three of the men had websites, and Mark had recently hired someone to create one for him to increase business in this segment.

While these methods were the most successful, David indicated that they differed in terms of the types of tourist clients they produced: 'I tend to get more foreign clients from my web page, as well as travellers from other parts of the country, and these clients tend to plan well in advance.' His experience with men who saw his advertisement in *Unzipped* was slightly different, however: '*Unzipped* brings in many business travellers from other parts of the US.' Mark confirmed the importance of these two methods, but also found local methods useful, as they were more likely to produce clients who were on vacation and were calling on impulse. However, these calls tended to be problematic, for, as Mark explained, such men often change their mind at the last minute. Joe revealed that some vacationers who make contact through this method will also be shocked by what he called 'Manhattan prices'.

Locations for sex
Escort advertisements sometimes include the phrase 'in/out', indicating the location for the sexual exchange. 'In' means the home of the escort, 'out' that the escort will meet the client in another location. The men stated that most of the tourist transactions were 'out' calls, and that hotels were the main locations. However, two of the men indicated that the type of hotel affected the rates they charged their clients. John discussed specific hotels where he can charge very high rates. He explained how, after being paged by a potential client in one of these hotels:

> When I call [back], it goes through the switchboard and I find out what hotel they're at, which is another trick I learned working at Las Vegas, where you base the price according to the hotel . . . and the higher up they are in the hotel, that's the more they are paying for the hotel, so the more you could charge.

Mark used a similar method to evaluate his vacationing clients. While he preferred businessmen, who usually pay high rates, he stated: 'there are tourists for whom money is not an object. You also look at it from the point of view of what hotel they are staying in.' Still, not all tourists can be met in a hotel. Luke explained that this was often the case for men who were not travelling alone. Mark and David both indicated that they maintain more than one apartment to accommodate clients who prefer an 'in' call and are staying in different locations throughout the city.

Repeat clients
The escorts were asked about out-of-town clients who use their services more than once, or for periods longer than a single session, as well as if such clients call to make appointments before they arrive in the city. The significance of repeat clients is indicated by the precision with which the escorts knew how much of their business this type of client represented.

John explained: 'If they're staying for maybe two or three days, and they like me, they'll hire me everyday until they leave.' He revealed that men who hire him for long periods on their first visit often become repeat clients on subsequent visits. Such men represented approximately 30 per cent of his clients who were from out of town and they usually called him in advance to make sure that he is available. Mark, who maintained method-ical records of his clients, stated: 'I have approximately 26 individuals so far that when they are in New York, retain my services on a 24-hour basis.' He revealed that he sometimes had difficulty accommodating all of them. Perhaps for this same reason, David explained that clients 'almost always book in advance when they are out-of-towners'. Repeat clients make up about 25 per cent of his tourist business. Luke indicated that not all of his clients had the money to maintain him for long periods. However, repeat out-of-town clients who booked in advance were still very important: 'the mainstay of any business is repeat loyal customers, most of them call in advance to book'.

Safer-sex discussion

It was unclear whether there was a general pattern in differences between tourists and local clients in terms of safer-sex discussion. This was also the case with tourists from other countries. John commented that among 'the Europeans, I think there's such a lackadaisical attitude towards safe sex to begin with because sex is so much more open in Europe'. Among his American clients, however, he did not feel that safer-sex discussion differed between tourists and the clients who resided in the New York area. Mark revealed that he refused risky sex with all of his clients, but found that language difficulties in safer-sex discussions had arisen with three Asian clients. He also stated that some repeat clients will make requests for unsafe sex after initially engaging in safer activities. David explained that self-identification issues among his clients sometimes translated into requests for unprotected sex, especially for those clients from the smaller cities:

> I haven't found language to be a problem in understanding of safer sex, but perception of sexual identity is. Some people who identify as bi-curious or 'straight' tend to think that they can have unsafe sex as long as the person 'seems clean' or doesn't get fucked. Others assume that because I live in New York and have sex with men, the chances are much greater that I am sick.

Luke's discussion of safer-sex perceptions among his tourist clients was particularly poignant: 'I often initiate the discussion if I feel they could use the education or discussion. This is one of the greatest services and sources of personal satisfaction in this industry. I am often the first or only gay person they know.'

Commentary

The large majority of the tourist clients of these five escorts are out-of-town businessmen, and such men make ideal clients for several reasons. They are often alone and have a location for a sexual encounter, usually a hotel. Some of them also plan their appointments in advance and become repeat clients. Accessing such clients through national publications and websites, escorts can develop a guaranteed source of steady income with appointments that can be booked in advance. John and Mark also explained that many of their business clients are extremely wealthy men, and both mentioned that CEOs (chief executive officers) of companies were on their client lists.

However, an escort must do some work in order to develop this area of clientele. It requires advertising in media with circulation outside of New York, particularly the magazine *Unzipped*. Local advertising media is useful, but such transactions can be fraught with difficulty. The medium providing the escorts with the most exposure both nationally and internationally, however, was the Internet. For escorts who themselves travel frequently, the Internet advertisements may also be updated regularly, something not so easy to do with printed media.

Importantly, as the escorts are contact points for men from different parts of the country and the world who may come from places with less of an AIDS infrastructure, they may also serve as important dissemination points for safer-sex information. Luke, in particular, had even mentioned that he is sometimes the very first person some of his clients had ever spoken with on such issues.

These interviews serve as a point of reference for work on how tourists access escorts, where the tourists are from and HIV prevention issues relating to tourists. Ideally, a larger study could look at a broader section of commercial sex workers, from escorts like these men to street hustlers, who may have different range of experiences, including more unsafe sex acts with clients (Estep *et al.*, 1992). Such a study may also attempt to directly interview the clients themselves, understanding their motivations for accessing sex when travelling and asking whether they engage in similar behaviours at home. Ideally, the commercial sex workers involved in a study could recruit their clients.

Conclusions

Travel is an important characteristic of gay life, and Hughes (1997) goes so far as suggesting that 'tourism and being gay are inextricably linked'. The epidemiology of HIV in the Western world has also been closely tied to being gay. Yet, while both are features of gay life and identity, little is done to connect the two from the point of view of prevention. We have seen that many studies and prevention programmes exclude the traveller, whether by structure or by recruitment method. However, interviews with sex club managers and escorts, as well as observations of some public sex environments, indicate that tourists represent a significant and visible component of the commercial sexual infrastructure of New York City, and possibly other US cities. Many prevention agencies and research studies already do work in these locations with the local population. Thus, to structure a study or programme looking at the sexual behaviours and prevention needs of tourists should not prove difficult.

The high numbers of tourists in these venues also suggest additional HIV funding issues. If current HIV prevention funding is aimed solely at estimates of gay men living in these cities, the potential preventions aimed at men using these facilities are even further under-served. The need for additional funding aimed at tourists becomes paramount when one considers that in some venues up to 45 per cent of the men are tourists. Importantly, both the sex club managers and escorts explained that some of these tourists seemed completely unfamiliar with gay sex venues and may never have been exposed to gay safer-sex messages previously.

The geographical concentration of gay tourism in the United States creates both problems and opportunities for HIV prevention initiatives. On the one hand, travel to these destinations places gay men within close proximity to most of the gay commercial sexual opportunities in the cities with the highest HIV infection rates. At the same time, the concentration of gay men from all over the United States and the world means that increased HIV prevention efforts aimed at tourists would allow many of these men to access HIV information they would not be able to in their resident locations. This underscores the importance of continued co-operation among these venues, AIDS service organizations and municipal governments.

References

Aldrich, R. (1993) *The Seduction of the Mediterranean: Writing, Art and Homosexual Fantasy*. London: Routledge.

Averell and Company (1877) *Pictures of New York Life and Character*. New York: G. W. Averell and Company.

Beck, A. (1997) *Manhattan Columbia Fun Map*. New York: Columbia Fun Maps.

Brent, B. (1994) *The Black Book: Guide for the Erotic Explorer*. San Francisco: Amador Communications.

Chauncey, G. (1994) *Gay New York*. New York: HarperCollins.

Chesnut, M. (1997) Much ado about Gaetan. *Skyjack Magazine* 3, 4–7.

Clift, S. and Forrest, S. (1998) *Gay Men, Travel and HIV Risk*. Canterbury, Kent: Centre for Health Education and Research, Canterbury Christ Church College.

Clift, S. and Wilkins, J. (1995) Travel, sexual behaviour and gay men. In P. Aggleton, P. Davies and G. Hart (eds), *AIDS: Safety, Sexuality and Risk*. London: Taylor and Francis.

Collins, A. (1996) *Fodor's Gay Guide to the USA*. New York: Fodor's.

Ekstrand, M. L. and Coates, T. J. (1990) Maintenance of safer sexual behaviors and predictors of risky sex: the San Francisco Men's Health Study. *American Journal of Public Health* 80 (8), 973–7.

Enloe, C. (1990) *Bananas, Beaches, and Bases: Making Feminist Sense of International Politics*. Berkeley: University of California Press.

Estep, R., Waldorf, D. and Marotta, T. (1992) Sexual behaviour of male prostitutes. In J. Huber and B. Schneider (eds), *The Social Context of AIDS*. Newbury Park, CA: Sage.

Firestone, D. (1997a) Mayor removes the gloves and laces into Messinger. *New York Times*, 19 September, p.B6.

Firestone, D. (1997b) Longtime Giuliani assistant will lead Tourism Bureau. *New York Times*, 13 December, p.B3.

Fishbein, M., Chan, D. K. S., O'Reilly, K., Schnell, D., Wood, R., Beeker, C. and Cohn, D. (1993) Factors influencing gay men's attitudes, subjective norms, and intentions with respect to performing sexual behaviors. *Journal of Applied Social Psychology* **23** (6), 417–38.

Ford, K., Wirawan, D. N., Fajans, P. and Thorpe, L. (1995) AIDS knowledge, risk behaviors, and factors related to condom use among male commercial sex workers and male tourist clients in Bali, Indonesia. *AIDS* **9**, 751–9.

Ford, N. and Koetswang, S. (1991) The socio-cultural context of the transmission of HIV in Thailand. *Social Science Medicine* **33** (4), 405–14.

Gatta, G. M. (1996) *Damron Address Book*. San Francisco: Damron Company.

Goldstein, J. (1993) Co-Founder, The New York Gay and Lesbian Visitors' Center, New York. Personal communication.

Herold, E. S. and van Kerkwijk, C. (1992) AIDS and sex tourism. *AIDS and Society: International Research and Policy Bulletin* **4** (1), 1, 8–9.

Holcomb, B. and Luongo, M. (1996) Gay tourism in the United States. *Annals of Tourism Research* **23** (2), 711–13.

Holmberg, S. D. (1996) Estimated prevalence of and incidence of HIV in 96 large US metropolitan areas. *American Journal of Public Health* **86** (5) 642–54.

Holusha, J. (1996) For the great white way, more glitz. *New York Times*, 1 September, p.R9.

Hughes, H. (1997) Holidays and homosexual identity. *Tourism Management* **18** (1), 3–7.

Kelley, P. (1996) *How Far Will You Go? A Survey of London Gay Men's Migration and Mobility*. London: Gay Men Fighting AIDS.

Kelly, J. A., Murphy, D. A., Sikkema, K. J., McAuliffe, T. L., Roffman, R. A., Solomon, L. J., Winett, R. A., Kalichman, S. C. and the Commmunity HIV Prevention Research Collaborative (1997) Randomised, controlled, community-level HIV-prevention intervention for sexual-risk behaviour among homosexual men in US cities. *The Lancet* **350**, 1500–5.

Kolber-Stuart, B. (ed.) (1992–8) *Out and About*. New York: Out and About.

Kolbert, E. (1997) Not too adult to make issue of sex stores. *New York Times*, 29 September, p.B1.

Laumann, E. O., Gagnon, J. H., Michael, R. T. and Michaels, S. (eds) (1994) *The Social Organization of Sexuality: Sexual Practices in the United States*. Chicago: University of Chicago Press.

Lewis, N. D. and Bailey, J. (1992–3) HIV, international travel and tourism: global issues and Pacific perspectives. *Asia Pacific Journal of Public Health* **6** (3), 159–67.

Martin, D. (1993) Christopher St rebounds as thriving 'Gay Mecca'. *New York Times*, 21 June, p.B3.

McNamara, R. (1995) *Sex, Scams, and Street Life: The Sociology of New York City's Times Square*. Westport, CT: Praeger.

130   *Michael Luongo*

Offir, J. T., Fisher, J. D., Williams, S. S. and Fisher, W. A. (1993) Reasons for inconsistent AIDS-preventative behaviors among gay men. *Journal of Sex Research* **30** (1), 62–9.

Parker, R. G. and Carballo, M. (1990) Qualitative research on homosexual and bisexual behaviour relevant to HIV/AIDS. *Journal of Sex Research* **27** (4), 497–525.

Pearl, B. and Pansy (1997) *Betty and Pansy's Severe Queer Review of New York.* San Francisco: Cleiss Press.

Rauch, R. (1997) *Spartacus 97/98.* Berlin: Bruno Gmünder Verlag GMBH.

Redick, A. (1997) The mixed constituency of sexual commerce. In *Sex Panic!* New York: Sex Panic!

Rotello G. (1997) *Sexual Ecology: AIDS and the Destiny of Gay Men.* New York: Penguin.

Seomin, S. (1997) Skin game. *Genre Magazine* **54**, 62–5.

Shilts, R. (1987) *And the Band Played On: Politics, People and the AIDS Crisis.* New York: St Martin's Press.

Sikkema, K. (4 February 1998) Medical College of Wisconsin. Personal communication.

United States Department of Commerce (1991) *State and Metropolitan Area Data Book 1991: Metropolitan Areas, Central Cities, States.* Washington, DC: USDoC.

Wieder, J. (ed.) (1998) *The Advocate* **754**, 23.

8

Sex in the tourist city: the development of commercial sex as part of the provision of tourist services

Simon Carter

Introduction

For most of this century, there has been an interest in the city as a suitable topic for academic study and research. Over recent years, this has been manifest in a growing number of analyses of the city that focus on urban consumption – the use people make of goods and services within the city. These have used a variety of conceptual frameworks in order to examine the city and consumption. In the immediate post-war era much attention was given to 'mass' or 'collective consumption' and the processes of 'subur-banization', whereas in the period since the early 1970s writers have increasingly focused on concepts relating to 'gentrification' and the 'post-modern city' (see Mullins, 1991). This reflects a switch from concerns about the consumption of collective services, such as the state provision of welfare, to an interest in the mass consumption of goods and services associated with pleasure. The place of tourism services within the city has therefore become the subject of critical analysis within urban geography, sociology and tourism research (Mullins, 1991; Meethan, 1996; Lash and Urry, 1994). However, despite this interest in 'tourism urbanization' there is one aspect of consumption in the city that has rarely been examined, namely the provision of commercial sexual services and the use of these services by travellers or tourists.

There is also a growing literature about 'sex tourism' or 'tourism prostitution' and much of this literature has provided critical understandings of
the complex issues surrounding the provision of commercial sexual services
for tourists. However, this literature is separate from the studies of tourism
urbanization in that it does not use the idea of the city, or spatial relations
within urban economies, as an organizing principle of the analysis. This
oversight means that an important dimension in our understanding of
'tourism prostitution' is absent. For instance, most tourists who encounter
prostitution, or other commercial sexual services, do so while visiting urban
centres, and most tourist cities have definable 'red-light' areas where a
variety of sexual services are available for the exchange of cash and/or
goods. Indeed, such localities are a distinctive feature in the urban landscape of the tourist city and are mentioned in guidebooks and travel
literature. Even for those people who have never visited them, red-light
districts have become a familiar part of the cognitive map of many tourist
cities.

The intention in this chapter is to review the limited literature that exists
on the spatial organization of tourist urban prostitution. A theoretical
framework will be developed and applied to the analysis of two case
studies of European cities: Amsterdam and Prague. These two case studies
are based on original research conducted in these cities between 1994 and
1996.

Studies of prostitution in the city

It would appear then that gaps exist in the analysis of both the tourist city
and tourism prostitution. Yet, this has not always been the case. While not
specifically concerned with tourists, many commentators on city life, in the
first half of the twentieth century, wrote about prostitution in the context of
the modern urban environment. These writers were responding to general
concerns about the growth of major cities in Europe and America during the
late nineteenth and early twentieth centuries and the enormous impact they
may have 'not only on social structures but also on patterns of thought and
feeling' (Lees, 1991: 153).

Perhaps the most widely known academic study is the collection of
essays to emerge from the Chicago School, particularly those written by
Park and Burgess (Park *et al.*, 1967), which attempted to define an ecological
and functional model of city geography. The discussion of prostitution is
limited and somewhat coy – they only ever talk of an ill-defined and
amorphous 'vice'. But they were clear about where this 'vice' was to be
found in the city. In the map that was to become the emblem of the Chicago
School, vice was located in the 'zone of transition' – the area of economic
deterioration around the central business district. Here were found the 'so-
called "slums" and "bad lands", with their submerged regions of poverty,

degradation, and disease, and their underworlds of crime and vice' (Burgess, 1967b: 54). Burgess and Park even suggested a number of expla- nations for 'vice' being clustered in particular districts, foremost of which was individual and demographic mobility: 'the areas of greatest mobility in the city have the greatest concentration of poverty, vice, crime, juvenile delinquency, divorce, desertion, abandoned infants, murder and suicide' (Burgess, 1967a: 153).

They attributed the growth of 'vice' districts to a breaking down of local attachments experienced by those mobile individuals and groups coming under the influence of the urban environment. The account of urban ecology developed by the Chicago School, influenced as it was by plant biology, almost saw the 'vice' districts as an 'inevitable' outcome of the exposure of certain human populations to particular urban environments. This general approach of the Chicago School has been criticized as overly simplistic and deterministic (Castells, 1977). Similar points could be made about the way that the concept of 'vice' is left unexplored and simply lumped together with other 'deviant' and criminal activities. This is uncrit- ical of wider social structures, because the issue is only considered in terms of the internal conditions of a socially 'disorganized' area. Be this as it may, as Ashworth *et al.* (1988) point out in their critical review of the place of prostitution in urban geography, it is the works of Burgess which are remembered and often reproduced without comment.

However, not all research into prostitution conducted by the Chicago School was so simplistic. During the 1920s Walter Reckless researched and wrote his doctoral dissertation, which was later published as a book (Reckless, 1969), on prostitution in the city. Though often overlooked and rarely cited, Reckless's work is worthy of examination because, while still firmly within the 'ecological' tradition, it does problematize Burgess's original work on 'vice' in a variety of ways. The account Reckless provides of prostitution in Chicago includes limited original empirical research (a few statements from sex workers) and was mainly based on materials gathered by others (such as press reports, court records, police reports and the reports of various local and national governmental organizations). While this approach has its obvious limitations, Reckless did manage to build up a complex picture of a highly dynamic urban environment in which the provision of commercialized sexual services was not exclusively restricted to particular zones associated with crime. Indeed, he finds that the number of street prostitutes and brothels in the 'zone of transition', identified by Burgess, had been in decline since soon after the turn of the century and that new 'independent' forms of prostitution were emerging in the place of 'organized vice'. He found that prostitutes were increasingly working from flats in suburban and residential areas because

Easier and more refined working conditions and a higher type of patronage can be commanded as an independent in an apartment. The type of girl who

maintains the greatest independence and greatest anchorage with respectabil-
ity is the 'call girl'. She works when she pleases; she may have vocational and
domestic interests outside her small business of prostitution; she preserves
only a telephone connection with the place of resort and lives elsewhere.

(Reckless, 1969: 146)

Like other writers of this period, Reckless does not specifically mention
tourists or tourism. However, his account does hint that a significant
proportion of the clients of prostitutes in Chicago were travellers. The
statements taken from women working in the sex industry often mention
'out-of-town visitors', who were mostly business travellers. Also, the
'independent' prostitutes, working from flats and apartments, were noted to
have established contacts with hotel clerks, cabaret attachés, waiters and
cabbies who 'frequently acted as guides to visitors' (Reckless, 1969: 154). In
addition, he observed that those brothels (or 'vice resorts') that did still
exist, rather than being concentrated in crime areas, often shared activity
spaces with entertainment outlets and premises. Hence Reckless discusses
at length the emergence of a 'hitherto unrecognized institution' in city life at
around 1914 – the cabarets – and how these shared the same geographical
location as the 'vice resorts':

If the old saloon and bawdy house seemed tame alongside the cabaret, it was
mainly because the combination of saxophone music, fox-trotting, risqué
entertainment, open promiscuity, wholesale intoxication and cigarette smoking, prostitutes, shop girls and slumming society folk was new and unheard
of. Even the reporters were shocked.

(Reckless, 1969: 101)

The importance of Reckless's work is that, despite his ecological framework,
he shows the dynamic nature of commercialized sexual services in the city.
In response to economic, social, cultural and legal change, prostitution
adapted and in doing so its geography shifted. As the social forces of
control focused on the old 'vice districts' or red-light areas, new types of
prostitution emerged and these often relied on new forms of city technology, such as the telephone or the automobile. Reckless also demonstrated
that there is a relationship between prostitution and other city activities
such as entertainment and business. As we shall see, the integral relationship between business, entertainment and prostitution is still part of the
development of commercialized sex as part of the overall provision of
tourist services.

One final commentator on the city is also worthy of mention for its
analysis of urban prostitution. In the opening years of the twentieth century
Hans Ostwald compiled a series of 50 pamphlets on city life in turn-of-the-
century Berlin. About thirty writers contributed to the volumes, which were
published between 1905 and 1908 under the title of *Großstadt-Dokumente*.
Each of the pamphlets was about one hundred pages long and was part
sociological analysis and part guidebook to the labyrinth of the modern city.

The essays were varied and discussed many aspects of the urban experience (such as entertainment, work, transport, the criminal justice system, health and social welfare), but several discussed prostitution in the city. As Fritzsche writes, in his review of the *Großstadt-Dokumente*, Ostwald's analysis of prostitution in the city was innovative at this time in that it placed little emphasis on 'urban depravity' or social 'deformation'. Instead, in examining prostitution, 'Ostwald analysed the poor working conditions of maids and waitresses, the pressures on middle class girls to keep up appearances, the attractions of independence, and the pull of passion and love, even in the underworld' (Fritzsche, 1994: 390). Despite the *Großstadt-Dokumente's* enormous influence on the Chicago School (and thus on urban geography in general), the works remain almost completely unknown and ignored outside Germany.

A locational model of urban prostitution

In the second half of the twentieth century there has not been this level of academic interest into the geography of urban prostitution or the role of commercial sexual services in the tourist city. One of the few accounts that does explore this subject is the brief examination of European red-light districts by Ashworth *et al.* (1988), who develop a model of urban prostitution based on the spatial relationships between the activity areas used for prostitution and other functions. They also acknowledge the increasingly important role of international tourism in urban prostitution. Using major European cities as case studies they suggest that it may be useful to consider three related concepts: accessibility, opportunity and constraint. It will be useful to examine the insights that these three concepts provide.

Accessibility

In most Western countries the forces of legal and social control view prostitution with ambivalence and hence the activity becomes marginalized – it is made 'unacceptable while not entirely criminal' (Ashworth *et al.*, 1988). As prostitution is a commercial activity, this presents a problem of access for both the client and the sex worker. In short, how is the provision of sexual services marketed to its customers under conditions of illegality or quasi-illegality?

Historically, the problem of marketing the many different products and services in the city has often been overcome by vendors locating to particular areas. Potential customers do not need to know a specific building or address, just a particular street or general area (a process often reflected in street names). The existence and inertia of red-light areas, often over many centuries, in European cities suggest a similar function has occurred. For the international visitor or tourist, the existence of localities with an established reputation makes it 'relatively easy for the potential customer to know where to seek the service' (Ashworth *et al.*, 1988: 208). Once established, such a place-reputation becomes difficult to change and is 'also a valuable asset for the trade, not to be lightly discarded' (*ibid.*). In addition, areas of urban prostitution may have 'spatial affinities' with other commercial services used by visitors – especially entertainment facilities (bars, nightclubs, hotels and restaurants) and other commercialized sexual services (sex shops and video shows). By contrast, an area of prostitution with only a local clientele 'may have few or no spatial links with a wider entertainment industry' (*ibid.*).

However, urban prostitution, even that aimed at the visitor or tourist, does not necessarily have to be concentrated in particular zones and have links to the entertainment industry. The existence of the car, taxi, telephone and, more recently, the Internet facilitates a 'completely different locational relationship between customer and service' (Ashworth, 1988: 209). The sex worker can thus be some distance from the centres of tourism or entertainment and the potential client, especially if a visitor to the city, now has to obtain information via some form of advertising, third party or informant.

Opportunity

Even if sex workers have access to clients, they must still have the possibility of completing the transaction – including display, negotiation and sexual activity 'in conditions that confer some protection from law, from a disapproving society, and even the clients themselves' (Ashworth, 1988: 209). The particular spatial relation between display, negotiation and sexual activity depends on the form of prostitution in question. For the sex worker in a 'sex club' or brothel all three of these functions essentially take place in the same location. However, for street prostitutes the place of display and negotiation will typically be separate from the place of sexual activity – some may use a client's car, have access to 'hotel' rooms or use accessible but secluded outside areas.

If a locality is to persist as a red-light area, it must have a spatial geography that allows opportunity for all of these stages in the transaction. For instance, for street workers the local architecture must allow a balance to be struck between a display stage that is obvious to potential clients but does not leave the prostitute vulnerable to arrest or harassment. Some may use the doorways, alleys, courtyards and side-streets found in the older areas of cities. Where the local geography allows only modest security, prostitutes may gain limited protection from 'group solidarity' with a number of prostitutes working the 'street' together. The window prostitution found in some European cities is a hybrid involving an immediate and blatant display at ground level, where the negotiation and activity stages of transaction are controlled by the use of a room directly linked to the display space.

Constraints

While the geography of prostitution is associated with issues to do with accessibility and opportunity, these in turn are related to the exertion of a variety of constraints. These constraints can either be exercised through legal and police controls or may result from social and political pressure leading to informal action. In practice, Ashworth *et al.* (1998: 210) argue, the policing of prostitution, rather than attempting to eradicate the activity, seeks to restrict open displays of commercial sexual services to areas where they are either politically tolerated and/or socially controlled. 'The underlying structure of prostitution cannot be divorced from wider social power structures, and the spatial organisation of prostitution in the city reflects the mechanisms of these'. Hence, through a variety of mechanisms of social control, particular city zones become designated as localities where commercialized sexual services may be available. This can happen by default, as either police action or local political lobbying relocate commercialized sexual activity to areas without such pressures. On the other hand, it can be the result of decisions by city planners and legal agencies to tolerate a discrete district of activity, in which prostitution is contained and controlled.

Sex in the tourist city: Amsterdam and Prague

The remainder of this chapter uses the model of urban prostitution suggested by Ashworth *et al.* (1988) to analyse two case studies of European cities – Amsterdam and Prague – with particular attention being given to the provision of sexual services for visitors and tourists (see Figure 8.1). As well as considering the issues of accessibility, opportunity and constraint, the intention is also to examine the spatial dynamics of health and risk – in other words, are there facets of particular environments that are dangerous for sex workers? The use of Amsterdam and Prague as case studies allows an interesting comparison to be made between a city with a long-established, and internationally famous, red-light area and a city that has only relatively recently gained a reputation as a destination where tourists may purchase sex. As several behavioural studies of prostitution in Amsterdam have been undertaken (see De Graaf, 1995), I shall focus more closely on the emergence of urban prostitution in Prague. Empirical material was collected from interviews with local health officials and outreach workers (in both the public and voluntary sectors), from locally collected tourist paraphernalia, from limited non-participant observation and from published secondary sources.

Amsterdam: city of windows

Amsterdam is one of Europe's foremost city tourist locations. From 1990 to 1994 between 1.65 and 1.9 million tourists spent one or more nights in the

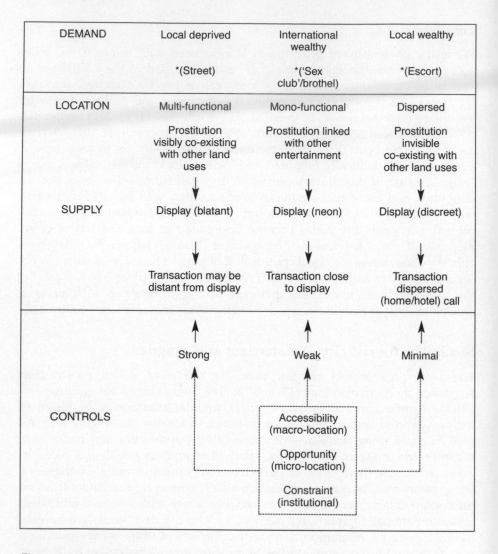

Figure 8.1 Locational model of urban prostitution areas (from Ashworth et al., 1988: 208)
*Words added to original table

city for each of these years. There are a far higher number of tourists visiting Amsterdam for day trips and, while figures for this form of tourism are not collected, estimates would suggest that up to 11.5 million people visit the city on short excursions each year. The majority of visitors, as well as being Dutch nationals, come from neighbouring countries such as the UK, Belgium and Germany (Amsterdam Tourist Office, 1992, 1994). As Dales (1998: 55–6) observes, two major themes dominate the image of Amsterdam as a tourist destination: first, as a city characterized 'by the urban design of the early modern period'; and second, an image formed in the late 1960s based 'upon a youth culture of sexual liberation and narcotic indulgence'.

Many different forms of prostitution exist in Amsterdam, but perhaps the most widely known is window prostitution. While not unique in this area of Europe, window prostitution is closely associated with Amsterdam. Part of the reason for this may be because the Baroque architecture found in the city centre has a very high density of windows. Alongside canals, there are narrow four-storey buildings whose fronts are covered with many paned windows. Before the age of electricity, a northern merchant city needed all the natural light that was available, especially as tightly packed narrow houses could only receive daylight through their forefronts.

The existence of window prostitution in Amsterdam is itself the result of constraints place on the activity at the beginning of this century. Following a widespread abolitionist movement, which argued that any government regulation of the activity was a tacit acknowledgement of the practice as inevitable, local and national authorities, in 1897 and 1901, made the organization of prostitution and brothels illegal. This resulted in the emergence of new and often individually organized forms of prostitution. In 1937 the head of the Amsterdam vice squad summed up the effects of this prohibition:

> At the time there was an initial 'panic' among proprietors of the brothels. However, they gradually changed their establishments into hotels, fashion-houses etc. The women who lived there were put in charge of 'domestic' activities . . . Furthermore, there was a large expansion of the number of bars with waitresses, which was even publicised by the handing out of cards on the street . . . Prostitutes promoted their trade by standing in the window or in front of the door of their houses – which became known as hustling on the street.
>
> (van Slobbe, quoted in De Graaf, 1995: 12–13)

After this period, the government moved away from a policy of eradication and adopted a pragmatic approach of containing, managing and tolerating urban prostitution.

The geography of Amsterdam's city centre is organized with concentric circles of tree-lined canals bordered by cobbled streets. These circles of street and water are criss-crossed by many smaller streets and alleyways. The red-light area occupies the nucleus of this centre in a rough triangle between Dam, Nieuwmarkt and Central Station. However, the zone where window prostitution predominates is much smaller than this and occupies the northern end of two canals that traverse this area and the alleyways that connect them (see Figure 8.2). Some streets are mono-functionally given over to window prostitution; however, in other areas space is shared with different forms of commercial entertainment. Many of these are related to the sex industry (such as massage parlours, sex shops, 'erotic' perfor-mances), but others are more general (such as cafés, coffee shops, bars and

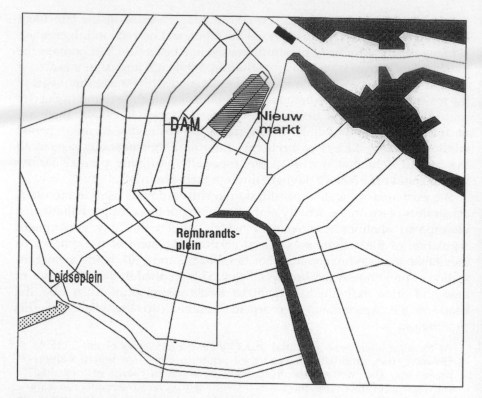

Figure 8.2 Amsterdam 'red-light' area (shaded)

even a few small hotels). As one moves away from this area the number of windows used by prostitutes declines rapidly. One city block to the west comprises the main commercial retail street (with banks, shops and department stores), and to the east, in the area around Nieuwmarkt, there are bars, restaurants, coffee shops and a busy street market. To the south lie the more traditionally tourist areas of Rembrandtsplein and Leidseplein with their bars, restaurants and nightclubs.

Hence, the red-light area of Amsterdam, while being relatively self-contained, is also spatially and functionally related to other entertainment facilities used by tourists. To gain access to this district one must pass on foot through areas where a variety of forms of tourist consumption take place. In addition, tourists passing between different city zones are likely to pass through the red-light area either by chance or intention. Indeed, the area is itself one of the city's spectator tourist attractions (it is mentioned in most guidebooks and has been allocated as a stop on guided tours of Amsterdam). In terms of access then, the red-light district of Amsterdam is spatially discrete. But it cannot be viewed as a purely mono-functional district, rather it is intimately related to a number of other tourist activities in the city.

Opportunities for the completion of the transaction are also well served by the spatial organization of window prostitution. The number of occupied windows increases throughout the day and reaches a peak in the evening. At this time many men, either alone or in groups, can be observed strolling along those streets used by prostitutes and sex workers engaged in displays to solicit clients from behind their windows. Many of these windows are at ground level and open directly on to the street – where this is not the case, a doorway will be immediately adjacent. The sex worker therefore can choose the clients who will be allowed access to the initial negotiations – which are conducted in the doorway. When negotiation has been completed success-fully, the sexual activity takes place in a 'work-room' immediately behind the display area. This allows a high turnover of clients, with each trans-action lasting an average of 17 minutes (9 of which are spent on sex) (De Graaf, 1995). Most of these display windows and work-rooms are rented (at around 100 guilders per evening or afternoon) from a proprietor who plays no further role in the business. The geography of Amsterdam's red-light area also affects the health and safety of prostitutes working there. Sex workers have a relatively large amount of control over their working environment, being able to refuse clients and not having to travel between the place of display and activity. The concentrated layout of the red-light area also has advantages for health and outreach workers, who can easily circulate around all prostitutes in the district. The small area means that it is possible for health and outreach workers to develop a limited relationship with the prostitutes so that, for example, new sex workers are quickly noticed, given safer-sex information and invited for a health check. Many of the windows used by prostitutes display 'safe sex' symbols that indicate condoms will be used during all sexual activity.

There are, of course, other types of prostitution present in Amsterdam. However, street prostitution (with sex workers actually walking the street) is rare in the city centre, with the activity confined to the evening use of an industrial estate just outside the central region. While it may be possible for a tourist to access this district, it would necessitate the use of a car and knowledge of the area. On the other hand, there are a number of 'sex clubs' that explicitly advertise in locally available guidebooks and 'what's on' magazines for tourists and visitors. Many of these clubs are situated away from the city centre but provide 'free pick-up' services. 'Sex clubs' normally have several prostitutes, who work less independently than those in windows (since the negotiation stage commonly takes place through an intermediary, such as a proprietor or *maître d'hôtel*, the sex worker therefore has little control over this stage of the transaction). The venue also com-monly includes a bar area where prostitutes and clients socialize before sexual contact takes place in private rooms. These establishments are aimed at a more affluent visitor, with a typical advertisement boasting:

> For fl. 400, you can spend a full hour with the lady of your choice, all drinks included. This may sound expensive at first, but the price is a reflection of the quality and satisfaction you can expect . . . All our ladies have received special training in a range of social skills such as etiquette and ballroom dancing. It goes without saying that all our ladies speak their foreign languages fluently . . . Credit cards and most foreign currency accepted.
>
> (Advertisement in *Amsterdam in One* guide, 1996)

Advertisements for 'escort' services also feature in guidebooks, magazines and on prominent city-centre lamppost placards. While some sex workers in this sector of the industry work independently, a tourist or visitor is more likely to discover advertisements for one of the 'escort' agencies that advertise in tourist literature. These agencies take telephone bookings and handle the negotiation/payment stages of the transaction (via credit cards), with the sex worker visiting the client in their hotel. One advantage for those sex workers associated with both 'escort' agencies and 'sex clubs' is that the geographical dispersion of the activity allows a relative degree of anonymity. However, this anonymity also presents problems for the delivery of health care, as the sex workers are unlikely to be known to health or outreach professionals.

The organizational infrastructure, of both 'sex clubs' and 'escort' services, allows them to operate in city locations that are remote from tourism centres. With window prostitution, its close relationship with other tourist activity spaces means that no further 'marketing' is needed – as access and opportunity both exist in the same well-known space. However, the 'sex clubs' and 'escort' services need to employ remote methods to make themselves accessible from their dispersed locations (see Figure 8.3).

Prague: living in 'freedom'

In recent years, Prague, like Amsterdam, has gained a reputation as a city location where tourists may purchase sexual services relatively easily. There are, however, important differences in the way that tourist prostitution is spatially organized in Prague. To understand these we must first examine some of the background to Prague's development as a tourist destination.

In November and early December 1989, in the aftermath of widespread public demonstration, a coalition of political groups forced the resignation of the communist Czechoslovakian government (the 'Velvet Revolution'). Immediately after this, new leaders introduced democratic elections and the general privatization of state enterprise and property. In the following years the Czechoslovakian state was split into the southern Slovakia and the more northerly Czech Republic (with Prague as its capital city). The new Czech Republic came under the leadership of playwright Václav Havel, as President, and right-of-centre politician Václav Klaus, as Prime Minister – two very contrasting figures:

	Prostitutes		
	Window 'red-light area'	Club	Escort
Tourist clients	Individuals/groups	Individuals/groups	Affluent — Solitary
Geographical/location	• Largely mono-functional (some shared tourist activities) • Close relation to other tourist activity spaces • City centre	• Dispersed • Venue mono-functional (built/adapted for purpose)	• Workers dispersed • Workers and agencies invisible, co-exist with other city activities
Geographical/access	Foot	Phone 'Limousine'	Phone Hotel call
Marketing/display	Blatant	Tourist guidebooks 'What's on guides'	Tourist guidebooks 'What's on guides' City-centre placards
Marketing/transaction	Immediate	In same venue	Dispersed
Controls, constraints and health — Institutional	Control, containment and toleration 'Health surveillance'	Minimal	Minimal
Controls, constraints and health — Risk, health, and safety	Defensible/controlled space Independent work Lack of anonymity	Anonymity Transaction controlled by owner Defensible space	Anonymity Controlled transaction

Figure 8.3 Spatial model of Amsterdam tourist prostitution

Where Havel is a subtle humanist with a self-effacing personality, Klaus is a blunt and arrogant free-marketeer. Where Havel is elliptical and absurdist, Klaus is all hard edges. He demands 'a market without adjectives' arguing (with characteristic certitude) that 'adjectives like "socially or environmentally conscious" are nothing other than attempts to restrain, limit, block, weaken, dissolve or make fuzzy the clear meaning of a market economy'.

(Sommer, 1994: xiv)

Some of the first changes to occur, in the years following the start of economic restructuring, were those in the labour market. With the newly privatized state enterprises having to compete in a no longer centrally planned economy, unemployment appeared for the first time in five decades. Though low by the standards of many western countries (about 3.5 per cent at the end of 1993), opinion polls show that citizens fear unemployment more than inflation. This unemployment was not evenly spread throughout the Czech Republic but disproportionately affected rural areas, the young and women (Janacek, 1995). Prague consistently had the lowest level of unemployment in the years after the 'Velvet Revolution' (about 0.4 per cent at the end of 1993). In addition, levels of unemployment benefit were cut in a general move to reduce state expenditure (Nesporova, 1995).

After the 'Velvet Revolution', Prague experienced a spectacular boom in tourism. While it was possible to visit Prague before 1989, in practice, few tourists travelled there. Today revenues from tourism-related industries are an invaluable source of foreign currency for the Czech economy ($2.5 billion in 1995 (Dorling Kindersley, 1996). The peak year was 1992, with an estimated 60 million tourists visiting Prague (Sommer, 1994). Since this time, there have been around 17 million tourists a year spending one or more nights in the Czech Republic each year (World Tourism Organization, 1998). Of these visitors 90 per cent will visit Prague during their stay. The large numbers of international tourists visiting Prague in the early years of the 1990s transformed the city centre into a location where a large variety of tourist services are available for consumption (such as museums, international shops, hotels, restaurants, cafés, bars and other entertainment). It is worth noting that for the residents of Prague most of these services would not be affordable on local wages, as in 1994 the average gross monthly wage was 6100 to 7800 Czech crowns (Kc) for a Czech citizen[1] (Trade Links, 1994).

Among the services that tourists may consume in Prague are various forms of prostitution. In terms of legal constraint prostitution ceased to be a criminal offence in 1990, with the repeal of two articles of the penal code (No. 203 on 'social parasitism' and intentional work avoidance, and No. 10 concerning 'unfair' ways of living). In the early 1990s, legislation was passed allowing city authorities to license premises offering sexual services and to control solicitation in public places. Yet in practice, police rarely intervene to limit the operation of prostitutes or their clients. The growth of tourism prostitution in Prague is then linked to both the relaxation of legal constraints and the high relative earnings that can be made by locals exchanging sexual services for cash. However, the different forms of prostitution available to tourists, as in Amsterdam, have distinct spatial organizations.

The most obvious manifestation of commercial sexual services for the visitor to Prague is the area of street prostitution in the city centre. This is concentrated to the northern end of Wenceslas Square and the surrounding side-streets and alleyways. This region also marks the beginning of the pedestrian area that extends to the north, through much of the Old Town (Staré Mesto). Sex workers are therefore present both on streets with foot access and on those with vehicle access. The activity space of street prostitution is shared with the other tourist services in Wenceslas Square – namely cafés, shops, nightclubs and hotels. Furthermore, this area is one of the gateways to the pedestrianized tourist districts of the Old Town and Prague Castle, with several important subway and tram intersections being in the immediate vicinity (see Figure 8.4).

Sex workers begin to appear in this location in mid- to late evening – a time when large numbers of tourists and visitors are also present or passing through Wenceslas Square. Prostitutes gather singly or in groups, accosting the male pedestrians and slow-moving cars that are moving through the district. Also present in this area are 'runners', who distribute flyers (in different languages) for 'sex clubs' and venues for 'erotic' performances. In this locality, a street-working prostitute therefore has a largely unrestricted

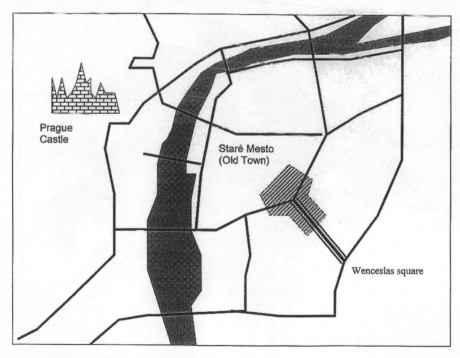

Figure 8.4 Prague city-centre street prostitution (shaded)

access to tourists, travellers and local clients. However, the client and prostitute must travel to some other location where the sexual activity will take place (either a local hotel room or the client's car) to complete the transaction. This is both time-consuming for the sex worker and, more seriously, places them in an environment over which they have little control – where the potential for violence or pressure to have unsafe sex are ever-present risks.

There are also a large number of 'sex clubs' in the Greater Prague area, along with several agencies which arrange escort services. These are typically dispersed from the central tourist districts (see Figure 8.5) and have little spatial relationship to other tourism services. The remote location from the centres of tourist activity presents the problem of accessibility. However, two tourist products are widely obtainable to allow potential clients to find information about commercial sexual services in Prague (see Figure 8.6). The first of these is the 'Erotischer Stadtplan' ('Erotic Street Map'), which is prominently displayed in city-centre news-stands and sales booths. This tourist map of Prague has been available, and updated, since the middle of the 1990s. The map uses a variety of garish cartoon icons to indicate the sexual services that are available in the different venues (such as 'sex clubs', 'escort' agencies, brothels, 'massage' parlours and 'saunas').

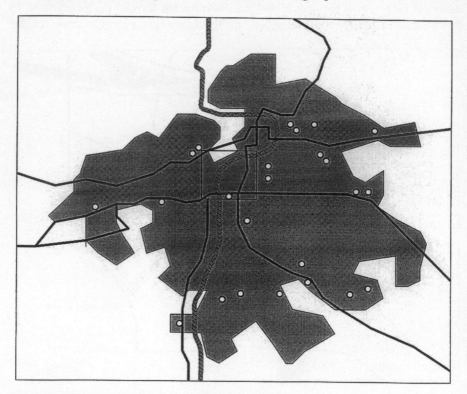

Figure 8.5 'Sex clubs' (white circles) in Greater Prague

Figure 8.6 Prague 'Erotic Street Map' and 'Prague Sex Guide'

Textual information on the cover and reverse of the map is in Czech,
German and English but is limited to a few details about opening times,
credit card acceptance and the taxi firms to use to ensure free
transportation. However, many of the advertisements feature large numbers
of small semi-pornographic photographs of women.

The second of these tourist products is the 'Prague Sex Guide', again
available from news-stands but also stocked in bookshops selling mainstream tourist guides (and often on obvious display next to the cash
register). This guide has higher production values than the 'Erotic Street
Map', being produced on glossy parchment, featuring far fewer photos and
a greater amount of text. It is aimed at the affluent tourist or business
traveller and information is available in German, English and Czech. The
guide claims to be independent and 'dedicated to quality':

> Every club and service listed in this guide has passed our stringent tests for
> attractiveness, cleanliness, and overall quality. Before setting out, it's a good
> idea to phone to inquire about rates and services. Remember, these clubs exist
> to serve you. Have fun, and stay safe.
>
> ('Prague Sex Guide', 1996:1)

The guide also contains safer-sex information and an abridged version of
the 'International Committee for Prostitutes' Rights World Charter'. The
majority of information in the guide consists, however, of 'reviews' of
selected clubs and 'escort' services. These often stress the facilities that are

available to the foreign business traveller. The following is typical:

> [this club] is especially popular with foreign business people, because all the
> girls here are required to speak at least two languages. Two top floor suites are
> fitted with whirlpool bathtub and a fax machine, and overnight guests are
> welcome. Phone the club beforehand, and they will send you a taxi.
>
> ('Prague Sex Guide', 1996, p.1)

Both the 'Erotic Street Map' and 'Prague Sex Guide' are therefore
important artefacts that enable the display stage of the prostitution
transaction to be remote from the geographically dispersed activity spaces.
The spatial operation of the 'sex clubs' themselves is similar to that found in
Amsterdam, with the premises being composed of both public bar areas and
private rooms for sexual activity. A third party (such as the proprietor), as in
the Amsterdam 'sex clubs', normally controls the negotiation and payment
stages of the transaction.

One final form of commercial sex available to tourists and travellers in
Prague is hotel lobby prostitution. Since the 'Velvet Revolution', a number
of large international and expensive hotels have opened near the city centre.
Many of these hotels have large atrium and lobby areas in which a variety
of tourism services are available (such as restaurants, casinos, shops, bars
and nightclubs). It is in these spaces that lobby prostitutes discreetly operate. These sex workers have to strike a careful balance between a display
that is restrained, while still allowing an initial negotiation to take place.
The close proximity to hotel staff also implies some degree of management
collusion or toleration of the practice.

As we have seen, the spatial organization of prostitution in Prague is
related to the health risks faced by prostitutes in their work (see Figure 8.7).
In general, those city-centre street prostitutes, while largely operating
independently, have less control over their working environment than those
who work in clubs or for 'escort' agencies. In addition, street prostitutes
earn less per contact than do other sex workers (around 1500 Kc per half-
hour compared to 3000–4000 Kc per half-hour). However, those prostitutes
working in clubs and for 'escort' agencies are liable to pay a significant
proportion of their earnings to the person who controls the transaction
(which in most cases would be the owner of the club or agency).

The spatial geography of prostitution also affects the provision of health
and outreach services to sex workers. While the more commercialized
aspects of prostitution are nominally controlled by city councils, these have
themselves undergone fundamental changes since the 'Velvet Revolution'.
Prior to 1989 Prague was centrally controlled with ten dependent city
districts; by the end of 1990 it was fragmented into 56 independent munici-
palities loosely controlled by a central city hall. This makes the provision of
some services problematic, as there 'is a range of services which must be
provided and co-ordinated city-wide and which may deteriorate if the
territorial fragmentation of competencies goes too far' (Surazska, 1996: 347).

	Prostitution (type)			
	Street	'Sex club'	Escort	Hotel lobby
Tourist clients	Opportunistic	International wealthy tourist and business travellers	International wealthy and business travellers	
Geographical/location	• Multi-functional • Space co-exists with other city uses • Concentrated • City centre	• Mono-functional (little relation to other local activities) • Venue built/adapted for purpose • Dispersed suburbs	• Workers dispersed • Workers and agencies invisible – co-exist with other city activities	• Multi-functional • Space co-exists with other lobby uses (often close to hotel casino)
Geographical/access	Foot Car	Phone Taxi	Phone	Hotel lobby
Marketing/display	Blatant Direct contact	Sex guides 'Erotic' maps	Sex guides 'Erotic' maps	Discreet
Marketing/transaction	Some distance from display (car, local hotel room)	Immediate	Dispersed Hotel room	Close to display (in same hotel)
Controls, constraint and health — Institutional	Weak (fragmented city councils) Containment	Weak (fragmented city councils) Containment	Minimal	Tolerance/collusion of hotel management
Risk, health, and safety	High risk No anonymity Possibility of violence Pressures to have unsafe sex	Anonymity Transaction controlled by owners Defensible space	Anonymity Controlled transaction	Anonymity Controlled transaction

Figure 8.7 Spatial model of Prague tourist prostitution

The fragmentation of Prague not only makes the co-ordinated control of commercial sexual services difficult, it also hinders the systematic organization of health surveillance. These difficulties are compounded by the spatial organization of prostitution in Prague. A major problem for health workers is being able to reach prostitutes – both the street workers and those working via the dispersed suburban 'sex clubs' or the 'escort' agencies. In addition, unlike Amsterdam, the geography of sexual services in the city centre does not easily allow the establishment of sustainable relationships between 'sex' and 'health' professionals. One organization that seeks to rectify this problem is the prostitute advocacy group Bliss without Risk set up in 1992 to help prostitutes with legal advice and with the obtaining of licences. It also encourages safer-sex practices and liaison with health professionals. There is also a prostitute 'drop-in' centre close to the city district where street workers operate. As well as being a place where sex workers can socialize, this centre provides free medical advice and sexual health services.

Despite these positive moves, the limited health statistics that do exist relating to sex workers in Prague present some cause for concern. The levels of HIV sero-prevalence have been low throughout the 1990s in the Czech Republic, both in the general population and among sex workers (Mikl et al., 1998). Yet there is evidence that the rates of other types of sexually transmitted illness (particularly syphilis and gonorrhoea) are elevated and rising among sex workers. In 1992, a study of street prostitutes tested a random and voluntary sample of 58 prostitutes in a single day, and of these 30 per cent tested positive for either gonorrhoea or syphilis and only two of these could be followed up for treatment (Kastankova, 1995). In 1995, health workers reported that of the women working in 'sex clubs' or for 'escort' agencies, 117 regularly attended outpatient services in Prague, and of these 15 contracted gonorrhoea or syphilis in this year (Kastankova, 1995). A more recent survey of people attending an STD referral clinic in Prague found that of the 619 female clients sampled, 74 per cent had unprotected sexual contact and 11.6 per cent were prostitutes. This survey also found that 304 of the clients sampled were aged between 11 and 19 and this group was significantly more likely to be prostitutes (8.9 per cent vs. 4.7 per cent, OR = 2.0) and to be diagnosed with gonorrhoea (21.1 per cent vs. 12.3 per cent, OR = 1.9) (Mikl et al., 1998).

Conclusions

This chapter has shown that there is a strong spatial relationship between the provision of tourism services and the provision of commercialized sexual services. In some cases, with window prostitution in Amsterdam and street prostitution in Prague, this is because sex workers occupy the same or close physical locality as other tourist activities. With other forms of prostitution, a link is established via a variety of advertising material that is explicitly aimed at the tourist and business traveller. The existence of such close ties between tourism services and urban prostitution must question the idea of 'sex tourism' as a distinct, separate and deviant activity. When examined from the perspective of tourism urbanization, the availability of commercial sexual services is just one of the many ways in which sexuality has been incorporated into the travel and tourist industries.

The study of urban tourist prostitution also shows that the spatial organization of sexual services has implications for the health and safety of sex workers. Window prostitutes in Amsterdam, because of their central-ized, discrete and permanent location could be provided with health services and education relatively easily and they were largely in control of their own working environment. On the other hand, the more fluid and amorphous street prostitution in Prague's city centre was difficult to monitor, and sex workers with no permanent activity spaces were exposed to health and safety risks. The dispersed sex workers, associated with the 'escort' agencies and clubs in both Amsterdam and Prague, worked in controllable environments that minimize physical danger and allowed anonymity. However, they were in turn subjected to working conditions that were not of their own making. The scattered location of these venues also makes health surveillance and education more costly and challenging for professional and voluntary groups alike.

As studies earlier this century showed, a further significant implication of a geographical examination of tourism prostitution is that the provision of sexual services in the city is highly dynamic – evolving in response to changes in accessibility, opportunity and constraint. The 'Velvet Revolution' produced sudden changes of access and a relaxation of constraints in Prague. Within the space of a few months, large numbers of international visitors were arriving in Prague – at a time when unemployment was rising and legal constraints on prostitution were being relaxed. It should then be no surprise that the city adapted to provide a wide range of tourism services, including the opportunity for travellers to purchase sexual services. In Europe, and world-wide, an increasing number of cities have adopted strategies to develop the economies of tourist consumption, both as a response to their own declining industries and to take advantage of increasingly cheap travel. It is highly likely that as these cities develop as tourist destinations so too will the provision of sexual services. These two case studies show that such services do not randomly appear but develop in response to local pressures and contexts. A critical examination of the relations between urban activity spaces may allow the provision of sexual services in the city to be healthier and safer for both workers and customers.

Acknowledgements

The *Großstadt-Dokumente* at the time of writing has not been translated into English (see Fritzsche, 1994, for an English review of the work). However, the works are widely cited by Park *et al.* (1967) and originals in German libraries still bear records of being consulted by members of the Chicago School in the early part of this century. I am indebted to Dietmar Jazbinsek for pointing out the existence, significance and influence of these volumes.

Note

1. The rate of exchange at the time the research was conducted was one UK pound (£) to Kc 150.

References

Amsterdam Tourist Office (1992) *Annual Reports*. Amsterdam: VVV.

Amsterdam Tourist Office (1994) *Annual Reports*. Amsterdam: VVV.

Ashworth, G. J., White, P. E and Winchester, H. P. M. (1988) The red-light district in the west European city: a neglected aspect of the urban landscape. *Geoforum* **19**, 201–12.

Burgess, E. W. (1967a) Can neighborhood work have a scientific basis? In R. E. Park, E. W. Burgess and R. D. McKenzie (eds), *The City*. Chicago: University of Chicago Press (The Heritage of Sociology).

Burgess, E. W. (1967b) The growth of the city: an introduction to a research project. In R. E. Park, E. W. Burgess and R. D. McKenzie (eds), *The City*. Chicago: University of Chicago Press (The Heritage of Sociology).

Castells, M. (1977) *The Urban Question: A Marxist Approach*. Cambridge, MA: MIT Press.

Dales, H. (1998) Redefining Amsterdam as a tourist destination. *Annals of Tourism Research* **25**, 55–69.

De Graaf, R. (1995) *Prostitutes and Their Clients: Sexual Networks and Determinants of Condom Use*. Utrecht: Ponsen and Looijen.

Dorling Kindersley (1996) *The Dorling Kindersley World Reference Atlas*. London: Dorling Kindersley, 2nd edition.

Fritzsche, P. (1994) Vagabond in the fugitive city: Hans Ostwald, Imperial Berlin and the Großstadt-Dokumente. *Journal of Contemporary History* **29**, 385–402.

Janacek, K. (1995) Unemployment and the labour market in former Czechoslovakia and the Czech Republic. In M. Jackson, J. Kolty and W. Biesbrouck (eds), *Unemployment and Evolving Labour Markets in Central and Eastern Europe*. London: Avebury.

Kastankova, V. (1995) Increasing sexually transmitted disease rates among prostitutes in the Czech Republic. *Journal of Community Health* **20**, 219–22.

Lash, S., and Urry, J. (1994) *Economies of Signs and Space*. London: Thousand Oaks; New Delhi: Sage.

Lees, A. (1991) Berlin and modern urbanity in German discourse, 1845–1945. *Journal of Modern History* **17**, 153–80.

Meethan, K. (1996) Consuming (in) the civilized city. *Annals of Tourism Research* **23**, 322–40.

Mikl, J., Sudar, Z., Smith, P. F., Bruckova, M., Jedlicka, J., Kastankova, V., Tryzna, R. and DeHovitz, J. (1998) HIV infection and high risk behavior among patients attending an STD referral clinic in Prague, Czech Republic. *Sexually Transmitted Infections* **74**, 128–30.

Mullins, P. (1991) Tourism urbanism. *International Journal of Urban and Regional Research* **15**, 326–43.

Nesporova, A. (1995) Recent labor market developments in former Czechoslovakia. In M. Jackson, J. Kolty and W. Biesbrouck (eds), *Unemployment and Evolving Labour Markets in Central and Eastern Europe*. London: Avebury.

Park, R. E., Burgess, E. W. and McKenzie, R. D. (eds) (1967) *The City*. Chicago: University of Chicago Press (The Heritage of Sociology).

Reckless, W. C. (1969) *Vice in Chicago*. Montclair, NJ: Paterson Smith (Patterson Smith Reprint Series in Criminology, Law Enforcement and Social Problems, no.84).

Sommer, M. (1994) *Living in Freedom: The New Prague*. San Francisco: Mercury House.

Surazska, W. (1996) Transition to democracy and the fragmentation of a city: four cases of Central European capitals. *Political Geography* **15**, 365–81.

Trade Links (1994) *The Czech and Slovak Republics at a Glance*. Prague: Trade Links.

World Tourism Organization (1998) *Tourism Highlights 1997*. Madrid: WTO.

Part II

Tourism, sexual activity and risk

9

Sexual risk behaviour in a sample of 5676 young, unaccompanied travellers

*Michael Bloor, Michelle Thomas, Damiano Abeni,
Catherine Goujon, Dominique Hausser, Michel Hubert,
Dieter Kleiber and Jose Antonio Nieto*

Introduction

Daniel Defoe, the author of *Robinson Crusoe*, father of modern journalism and chronicler of the Great Plague of London (Defoe, 1722), described how the country people living around London would accuse those Londoners fleeing the pestilence of deliberately and revengefully spreading the disease. Defoe was very sceptical of the reality of the phenomenon we term today 'revenge infection'. He believed that travellers were being accused groundlessly of such action as a justification for attempts to control their movements and debar them from the country parishes where they sought refuge. Defoe may have been sceptical of revenge infection, but later journalists have been more credulous, and travellers have always had a bad press when it comes to stories about the epidemiology of disease. Even Randy Shilts, in his gripping journalist's account of the early years of the HIV epidemic, *And the Band Played On* (Shilts, 1987), accused a deceased Air Canada steward of being 'Patient Zero', knowingly spreading the disease in the gay bars and bathhouses he frequented across the world's air routes.

Stories of HIV revenge infection have gone hand in hand with xenophobic discrimination against foreigners in many countries and with ineffectual attempts by a wide range of governments to restrict travel by HIV-positive persons (Gilmore *et al.*, 1989). They have *not*, however, been accompanied by a large-scale research effort to document the actual risk behaviour of representative samples of international travellers. The various national surveys of sexual behaviour conducted in the late 1980s and early 1990s (see, for example, the composite report of a number of European national studies by Hubert *et al.*, 1998) have considerable achievements to their credit, but, with one exception, they did not collect separate data on the sexual behaviour of their respondents while travelling abroad. The exception was a Swiss telephone survey of 1220 men conducted in 1990 (Hausser *et al.*, 1991). There have been a number of valuable studies of special sub-populations of travellers such as sex tourists (Kleiber and Wilke, 1995a, 1995b), lorry drivers (Carswell *et al.*, 1989) and returning expatriates (Houwelling and Coutinho, 1991). There have also been a number of studies of convenience samples of travellers attending travel clinics and STD clinics (e.g. Daniels *et al.*, 1992; Hawkes *et al.*, 1994), and two small-scale studies have been conducted on representative samples (Gillies *et al.*, 1992; Thomas *et al.*, 1997). However, the study reported here is the first large-scale example to be conducted on a representative sample of international travellers, and contains sufficient numbers of reports of sexual risk behaviour to allow some characterization of subgroups of the heterosexual travelling population most at risk of STDs, including HIV/AIDS.

Methods

This project was a feasibility study, supported by the European Commission as part of the Europe against AIDS programme, and designed to be the basis for co-ordinated, individual, national studies and intervention campaigns in the EU member states (Bloor *et al.*, 1997). As stated above, one of the objectives of the project was to gather sufficient numbers of reports of travellers' sexual risk behaviour to allow identification of subgroups of travellers suitable for the targeting of health promotion interventions. In order to gather large numbers of such reports in an economical manner, it was decided to restrict the sample to that broad section of the travelling population where it was already known from previous work (Gillies *et al.*, 1992) that most reports of sexual activity were occurring, namely younger persons travelling unaccompanied by a sexual partner. Accordingly, a two-stage sampling strategy was developed: first, the screening of representative samples to identify 18- to 34-year-olds who had travelled abroad without a partner within the past two years; and second, quota sampling (initially 500, but reduced during fieldwork to 400) of those who had screened as eligible and reported sexual intercourse with a new partner while travelling abroad, plus a control group of 568 eligible travellers who did not report such intercourse.

The screening was undertaken by a market research organization, NOP, as part of their 'Omnibus' and 'Telebus' surveys. The Omnibus survey is a weekly face-to-face survey of 2000 persons drawn from the electoral registrar, and the Telebus is a weekly telephone survey of 1000 adults, with quota controls to ensure representativeness of all adults in telephone-owning households. A composite of questions are asked based on NOP's current contracts. Data are collected on refusals and all respondents are asked if they are willing to be re-interviewed. Eligible persons were recruited from 11 Omnibus surveys and 17 Telebus surveys from March to July 1996. The refusal rates in the Omnibus surveys ranged from 32 to 38 per cent and a mean of 73 per cent agreed to be re-contacted. Men and women were equally likely to refuse to be surveyed and persons over 65 and in socio-economic grades D and E (unskilled workers and persons on state benefits) were more like to refuse re-contact. The refusal rates in the Telebus surveys ranged between 71 and 82 per cent (but quota controls are designed to ensure representativeness) and a mean rate of 85 per cent of respondents were willing to be re-interviewed. It will be appreciated that, since Omnibus surveys are a composite of many different topics, participation rates are not topic-related.

Those eligible at screening were re-contacted and surveyed by computer-assisted telephone interviews (CATI). Telephone interviewing has been used for a number of different national sexual surveys and is thought to be a particularly appropriate instrument for the posing of sensitive questions (McQueen, 1989). The CATI system entails direct data entry during interviewing and has a number of advantages over unassisted manual telephone interviewing: confidentiality is easier to protect; there will be fewer data entry errors, because invalid response codes cannot be entered; and, since question-routing is automatic, very complex routing can be handled unproblematically. Female interviewees were only interviewed by female interviewers. All data were unnamed. The interview schedule was designed and piloted specially for this study, but contained many questions common to other studies to facilitate comparative analyses. To economize on Omnibus and CATI survey costs, the study was restricted to persons living in the UK.

The second-stage (CATI) interviews took place between May and August 1996. It transpired that neither the Omnibus nor the Telebus screening interviews could generate quite enough eligible persons to fill the quotas within the study timetable and 7 per cent of the achieved sample of 968 was filled from additional telephone screening interviews using randomly generated numbers. The control quota (of eligible persons who did not report intercourse with a new partner while travelling) was filled much earlier than the target quota (of eligible travellers who did report intercourse with a new partner), but the number of contacts made with those eligible for control-group interviews continued to be logged after the quota for this group was filled, in order to provide a basis for weighting the data. The total weighted sample was 5676 individuals (400 in the 'target' group and 5276 weighted controls), giving a weighting for the completed control interviews of 9.29:1.

Some of the screened sample from the Omnibus surveys proved ineligible at the CATI interviews. Of course, this should not have occurred (all ineligible persons should have been screened out) and a special exercise was undertaken to re-contact and check a sample of these persons. It was established that the great majority of these were in fact ineligible persons incorrectly reported in the Omnibus survey, rather than 'disguised refusals'. Accordingly, our refusal rate of 35 per cent for the second-stage interviews excludes ineligible respondents; this refusal rate is comparable to the rate achieved in the UK National Survey of Sexual Attitudes and Lifestyles (NATSAL) (Wellings *et al.*, 1994).

Results

After weighting, 11 per cent (614 individuals) of persons aged 18 to 34 travelling without a partner (a total of 5676 individuals) had 'a new romantic or sexual relationship' abroad in the past two years and 7 per cent (400) had sexual intercourse with a new partner. The median number of new partners was two (who could have been met on more than one trip). Thirteen persons (0.2 per cent of the weighted sample) reported intercourse with a new partner of the same sex and 17 persons (0.3 per cent) reported a commercial sexual partner while travelling. Those reporting a new sexual partner abroad also had high rates of partner change at home: 67 per cent of those reporting a new sexual partner abroad also reported at least one 'casual' (as opposed to 'regular') partner in the UK in the previous two years, compared with just 29 per cent of the control group; 28 per cent of those reporting a new partner abroad also reported five or more casual partners in the UK in the previous two years, compared with just 5 per cent of the control group. Detailed information on the social characteristics of those reporting a new sexual partner while travelling can be found in Bloor *et al.* (1997).

Most epidemiological interest attaches to those findings concerning *unprotected* sexual intercourse among travellers. Respondents reporting a new sexual partner while travelling were asked about condom use with their most recent such partner. Condom use among travellers was high: 75 per cent of the 400 travellers reporting a new partner used condoms on all occasions they had sexual intercourse with their new partner; 10 per cent reported using condoms on some occasions; 3 per cent used condoms on just the first episode of intercourse; only 12 per cent reported never using condoms with their new partner.

Respondents were asked their reasons for not using condoms and multiple responses were allowed. Table 9.1 shows that the commonest reasons given were that condoms reduce sensitivity and that they interrupt sex. Surprisingly, female as well as male respondents gave reduced sensitivity as a reason for non-use, although this was also reported by

Table 9.1 Reasons why respondent did not use condoms with new partner abroad (n = 101)

	Count	% Responses	% Cases
Could not find condoms abroad	21	8.3	20.8
Condoms reduce sensitivity	46	18.2	45.5
Using other contraceptive	41	16.2	40.6
Think condoms are unromantic	41	16.2	40.6
Think condoms interrupt sex	46	18.2	45.5
Embarrassed to suggest condoms	4	1.6	4.0
Afraid would lose erection	13	5.1	12.9
Other reason	40	15.8	39.6
No answer	1	0.4	1.0
Total responses	253	100.0	

Holland *et al.* (1991). Only 21 per cent of those who had not used condoms with their new partner reported being unable to find condoms abroad as a reason for not using them.

A number of factors were significantly associated with unprotected sex: being female; being in socio-economic grades D/E; being married or living as married; having sexual intercourse with the new partner more than once; not carrying condoms on the journey; having previously attended an STD clinic; not having used a condom with the respondent's most recent casual partner in the UK; being on both long-term trips and being on very short trips; and travelling for purposes other than a holiday. Males were more likely to report sexual intercourse with a new partner, and among those reporting such a new sexual relationship, men and women were almost equally likely to report never using condoms. However, 78 per cent of men reported using condoms with their new partner on all occasions when they had intercourse, whereas for women the rate was only 68 per cent (χ = 7.34, df = 2, p < .05). Those in unskilled manual occupations (socio-economic grade D) and those on state benefits (E) were less likely to use condoms in all episodes of intercourse with the new partner and more likely never to use condoms with that partner (χ = 8.88, df = 4, p < .05). Those married, or living as married, were less likely to report a new partner, but if they did report a new partner, then they were significantly more likely never to use condoms with that partner (χ = 8.06, df = 2, p < .05). Of course, having sexual intercourse with a new partner more than once is bound to increase the probability of inconsistent condom use, as in this study (χ = 25.26, df = 2, p < .00001), but multiple episodes of intercourse with the same partner may also be associated with a tendency to greater intimacy and trust, and therefore with less frequent condom use.

Carrying condoms is also very strongly associated with their use with the new partner (χ = 55.42, df = 2, p < .00001): 62 per cent of those who never used condoms had not taken any condoms abroad with them. Men were more likely to carry condoms than women, but the group most likely of all to be carrying condoms (92 per cent) were older women (25 to 34 years), married or living as married, and expecting a new sexual relationship on their trip. Those who had ever attended an STD clinic were less likely to use condoms on all occasions with their new partner abroad ($\chi = 7.52$, df $= 2$, p $< .05$). Condom use abroad reflects condom use with casual partners at home ($\chi = 45.05$, df $= 4$, p $< .00001$): 85 per cent of those who reported always using condoms with their most recent casual partner at home also used condoms on all occasions with their new sexual partner abroad. Those on trips of less than a week were more likely to report never using condoms with their new partner ($\chi = 9.92$, df $= 4$, p $< .05$), but those on longer-term trips were also less likely to report condom use. Seventy-eight per cent of those whose trip was a holiday reported using condoms on all occasions, compared to 68 per cent whose trip was for another purpose, i.e. business, an overland tour, visiting family or friends, or visiting a sexual partner who lived overseas ($\chi = 6.48$, df $= 2$, p $< .05$).

A number of other factors were *not* significantly associated with unprotected sex. Age was associated with reports of a new sexual relationship, but not with condom use. Condom use or non-use was not associated with smoking or numbers of cigarettes smoked. Neither frequency of drinking nor reports of being 'very drunk' or 'a little drunk' during the trip abroad were associated with condom use or non-use. There was no association with whether or not the respondent reported receiving health advice or information before the trip. There was no association between being worried about AIDS or STDs before the trip. Respondents reporting a new sexual relationship were statistically more likely to recall seeing posters or leaflets giving advice about HIV/AIDS during their trip, but while there was an association between recalling such leaflets or posters and condom use, the association did not reach statistical significance. Similarly, respondents who had previously had an HIV test were statistically more likely to report a new sexual relationship while travelling, but the relationship between having undergone an HIV test and condom use with their new partner did not reach statistical significance.

Some STDs (such as gonorrhoea) have high rates of transmission per exposure, others (such as HIV) have a much lower mean transmissibility (de Vincenzi, 1994). In the latter cases, it may be more valuable to establish those factors which are associated with repeated exposure to possible infection, rather than just a single exposure. Twelve per cent of those reporting a new sexual partner reported four or more exposures (i.e. four or more episodes of unprotected intercourse) with their new partner, and the project also examined those factors associated with four or more exposures. Interestingly, there was only limited overlap between such factors and those associated with a single exposure (see above).

Women were significantly more likely than men to report multiple exposures ($\chi = 6.04$, df $= 2$, p $= < .05$), as were those in socio-economic groups A/B (combined), that is, professionals and senior administrative workers (χ = 9.68, df = 4, p < .05). Respondents who travelled alone were more likely to report multiple exposures than those who travelled with others (χ = 11.96, df = 2, p < .005). Once again, carrying condoms was closely associated with zero exposures (χ = 39.69, df = 2, p < .00001), and those whose trip was for a purpose other than a holiday were again more likely to report multiple exposures (χ = 9.41, df = 2, p < .05). There was a tendency for business travellers to be more likely to report four or more exposures, but this relationship did not reach statistical significance. Condom use with one's last casual partner in the UK was once again strongly inversely associated with multiple exposures (χ = 36.92, df = 4, p < .00001), but there was also an inverse association between multiple exposures and condom use with one's last UK *regular* partner (χ = 22.55, df = 4, p < .0005). Past STD clinic attenders were more likely to report multiple exposures (χ = 7.54, df = 2, p < .05), and multiple exposures were also more likely among those who reported sexual experience with both males and females (χ = 11.08, df = 4, p < .05).

Discussion

Although these data report on a large sample of new sexual relationships among travellers, the sample size is still too small to provide useful reports on the sexual behaviour of some subgroups of travellers, such as men who have sex with men (see Clift and Forrest, this volume), travel workers and injecting drug users (see Bröring, 1997). The sexual behaviour abroad of such subgroups is best addressed through special samples, rather than the representative sampling used here. The sexual risk behaviour of migrant populations should also be addressed as a separate issue from that of travellers (Haour-Knipe, 1991).

Comparison of these data with the Wellings *et al.* (1994) UK NATSAL study is not straightforward. The NATSAL study was conducted some six years before the travellers' study (with the possibility that some aspects of sexual behaviour, particularly condom use, may have changed in the interim) on a broader age-range of respondents (16- to 60-year-olds), and some of the measures used were different (no distinction was made between 'regular' and 'casual' partners, for example). However, it seems very likely that those travellers in this study reporting a new sexual partner while abroad are, as a group, reporting relatively high rates of partner change and relatively high levels of condom use, compared to a UK national sample.

Twenty-eight per cent of those reporting a new sexual partner while travelling also reported five or more casual partners in the UK in the previous two years, while only 5 per cent of the control group reported five or more casual UK partners. In the NATSAL study, by comparison, only 15 per cent of the 16- to 34-year-olds reported two or more sexual partners (regular and/or casual) in the past year, and only 1.5 per cent reported five or more partners in the past year. Those travellers reporting a new sexual partner while travelling are, on the whole, a highly sexually active group, compared with the control group and compared with similarly aged respondents in the NATSAL study. Further, those reporting a new sexual relationship while travelling are not, as a group, engaging in patterns of sexual partner change which are inconsistent with their patterns of sexual partner change in the UK. 'Sea, sun and Sangria' may indeed loosen inhibitions, but as a whole those who report a new partner abroad are also those reporting most new partners at home.

Seventy-five per cent of those reporting a new sexual partner while travelling used a condom during all episodes of intercourse with their new partner; only 12 per cent did not use condoms at all with the new partner. As reported in previous traveller studies (Gillies *et al.*, 1992; Hawkes *et al.*, 1994), these rates of condom use abroad were higher than respondents' rates of condom use with casual partners at home. Of those reporting a new partner abroad and one or more casual partners at home, 64 per cent of respondents reported condom use with their last casual UK partner during all episodes of intercourse and 18 per cent reported never using condoms with that partner. Travellers' rates of condom use are also much higher than those for new partners in the NATSAL study. Among NATSAL respondents who reported a new sexual partner within the last four weeks, those men and women who reported using condoms on all occasions with the new partner comprised only 34 per cent of the male respondents and 41 per cent of the female respondents (Wellings *et al.*, 1994).

Where condom rates are so high it may be thought that relatively little sexual risk behaviour is occurring and sexual health promotion among travellers is no longer a priority task. Such a viewpoint would be incautious for three reasons: first, sexual health promotion may still be required to sustain safer sexual practices among international travellers in the future, particularly younger travellers not previously exposed to past health promotion interventions; second, it will be clear that travellers who have a new sexual relationship abroad may be a convenient proxy group for that minority of the population with the highest rates of partner change; and third, there are some groups of travellers where condom use with new partners remains relatively low and where further health promotion efforts to reduce risk behaviour could be concentrated. This study offers a number of suggestions on appropriate targeting of interventions to achieve further risk reduction.

Targeting risk behaviour for an STD such as gonorrhoea with a high transmission rate is a rather different matter from targeting risk behaviour for HIV with a lower mean transmission rate. In the former case, one should be seeking to characterize those travellers most prone to report any 'exposure' (i.e. any episode of unprotected intercourse), whereas in the latter case, one should be identifying those most prone to multiple 'exposures'. Since persons reporting multiple exposures are a smaller group than those reporting any exposure, it is to be expected that some factors particularly associated with the latter will not show a significant association with the former. But there is also a difference between the two groups. Women, although less likely than men to report a new sexual partner while travelling, are more likely to report both any exposure and multiple exposures (see Bloor *et al.*, 1998, for a report of separate logistic regression modelling of risk factors for men and women travellers). Also, persons travelling for reasons other than a holiday and persons who had previously attended an STD clinic were both more likely to report any exposure and more likely to report multiple exposures. However, respondents in socio-economic grades D/E are more likely to report any exposure, while those in grades A/B are more likely to report multiple exposures.

It seems clear that condom use by travellers is part and parcel of broader patterns of condom use. The best predictors of zero exposures and the factors most strongly (inversely) associated with multiple exposures were those of carrying condoms on the trip and condom use with the respondent's last casual partner in the UK. Interventions which encourage broader patterns of condom use may have a spillover effect on travellers' sexual risk behaviour. Further, the reverse may also apply: interventions designed to encourage safer sex among travellers may also impact on sexual risk behaviour at home. With the exception of the 21 per cent of persons who gave being unable to find condoms abroad as a reason for not using condoms, all the main reasons given for non-use by travellers could apply with equal force to a new sexual relationship begun at home.

In addition to the characterization of travellers more prone to engage in risk behaviour, it is also possible from these data to characterize some features of the trip itself that are associated with such risk behaviour. As in Thomas *et al.*'s (1997) earlier study, longer trips of more than 15 days are associated with reports of risk behaviour, but very short trips (of less than a week) are also associated with risk behaviour if the trip results in meeting a new sexual partner. Trips for purposes other than holidaymaking are associated both with any reported exposure and multiple exposures, while trips made without any companions are associated with multiple exposures. Interventions aimed at travellers might therefore profitably be aimed towards travellers undertaking particular kinds of trips.

Finally, we would draw attention to our findings, not just on unprotected sexual mixing, but on unprotected, *concurrent*, sexual mixing. Some recent discussions on HIV spread have focused particularly on the possible epidemiological role of concurrency in the rapid spread of the virus (Hudson, 1993; Morris and Kretzschmar, 1997). Concurrent, unprotected sexual relationships facilitate more rapid HIV transmission than serial sexual relationships, both because there is less of a time-lag between different partners and because it is believed that persons are more infectious immediately after they themselves have been infected (and therefore before antibodies have developed). Those engaging in concurrent, unprotected sexual relationships in the present study are those married or living as married. These respondents are less likely to report a new sexual partner while travelling, but those married/living-as-married respondents who do meet a new sexual partner are more likely to engage in unprotected intercourse with that new partner. Further, since unprotected intercourse is more common with regular than with casual partners, these same respondents are less likely to be having protected intercourse with their married/live-in partner at home. Married and living-as-married travellers who meet a new sexual partner while travelling may therefore be a group meriting special consideration in the design of sexual health promotion interventions.

Acknowledgements

The authors are grateful for the support of Directorate-General V of the European Commission and for the assistance of Nick Moon and Gill Souter of NOP.

References

Bloor, M., Thomas, M., Abeni, D., Goujon, C., Hausser, D., Hubert, M., Kleiber, D. and Nieto, J. A. (1997) *Feasibility Study for Co-ordinated Community Action on the Improved Targeting of HIV/AIDS Prevention Campaigns among International Travellers: Final Report.* Cardiff: School of Social and Administrative Studies, University of Wales (unpublished report).

Bloor, M., Thomas, M., Hood, K., Abeni, D., Goujon, C., Hausser, D., Hubert, M., Kleiber, D. and Nieto, J. A. (1998) Differences in sexual risk behaviour between young men and women travelling abroad from the UK. *The Lancet* **352** (21), 1664–8.

Bröring, G. (1997) Prostitution, intravenous drug use and travel: European HIV/AIDS prevention initiatives. In S. Clift and P. Grabowski (eds), *Tourism and Health: Risks, Research and Responses.* London: Pinter.

Carswell, J., Lloyd, D. and Howells, J. (1989) Prevalence of HIV-1 in East African lorry drivers. *AIDS* **3**, 759–61.

Daniels, D. G., Kell, P., Nelson, M. R. and Barton, S. E. (1992) Sexual behaviour among travellers: a study of genitourinary medicine clinic attenders. *International Journal of STD and AIDS* **3**, 437–8.

Defoe, D. (1986, first published 1722) *A Journal of the Plague Year.* London: Penguin.

de Vincenzi, I. (1994) A longitudinal study of human immunodeficiency virus transmission by heterosexual partners. *New England Journal of Medicine* **331**, 341–6.

Gillies, P., Slack, R., Stoddart, N. and Conway, S. (1992) HIV-related risk behaviour in UK holidaymakers. *AIDS* **6**, 339–42.

Gilmore, N., Orkin, A., Duckett, M. and Grover, S. (1989) International travel and AIDS. *AIDS* **3**, Supplement 1, S225–30.

Haour-Knipe, M. (1991) *Migrants and Travellers Group: Final Report.* European

Community Concerted Action on Assessment of AIDS/HIV Preventive Strategies, Doc. 72. Lausanne: IUMSP.

Hausser, D., Zimmerman, E., Dubois-Arber, F. and Paccaud, F. (1991) *Evaluation of the AIDS Prevention Strategy in Switzerland: Third Assessment Report, 1989–90.* Lausanne: IUMSP.

Hawkes, S., Hart, G. J., Johnson, A. M., Shergold, C., Ross, E., Herbert, K. M., Mortimer, P., Parry, J. V. and Mabey, D. (1994) Risk behaviour and HIV prevalence in international travellers. *AIDS* 8, 247–52.

Holland, J., Ramazanoglu, C., Scott, S. and Thompson, R. (1991) Between embarrassment and trust: young women and the diversity of condom use. In P. Aggleton, P. Davies and G. Hart (eds), *AIDS Responses, Interventions and Care.* London: Taylor and Francis.

Houwelling, H. and Coutinho, R. (1991) Risk of HIV infection among Dutch ex-patriates in Sub-Saharan Africa. *International Journal of STD and AIDS* 2, 252–7.

Hubert, M., Bajos, N. and Sandfort, T. (1998) *Sexual Behaviour and HIV/AIDS in Europe.* London: UCL Press.

Hudson, C. P. (1993) Concurrent partnerships could cause AIDS epidemics. *International Journal of STD and AIDS* 4, 249–53.

Kleiber, D. and Wilke, M. (1995a) *AIDS, Sex und Tourismus: Ergebnisse einer Befragung deutscher Urlauber und Sextouriaten.* Baden-Baden: Nomos Verlagsgesellschaft.

Kleiber, D. and Wilke, M. (1995b) AIDS and sex tourism: conclusions drawn from a study of the social and psychological characteristics of German sex tourists. In D. Friedrich and W. Heckmann (eds), *AIDS in Europe: The Behavioural Aspect. Volume 2: Risk Behaviour and Its Determinants.* Berlin: Edition Sigma.

McQueen, D. (1989) Comparison of results of personal interview and telephone surveys of behavior related to risk of AIDS: advantages of telephone techniques. In F. Fowler (ed.), *Health Survey Research Methods: Conference Proceedings.* Washington, DC: National Center for Health Services Research and Health Care Technology Assessment, US Department of Health and Human Services.

Morris, M. and Kretzschmar, M. (1997) Concurrent partnerships and the spread of HIV. *AIDS* 11, 651–8.

Shilts, R. (1987) *And the Band Played On: Politics, People and the AIDS Crisis.* London: Penguin.

Thomas, M., Bloor, M. and Crosier, A. (1997) *Young People and International Travel: HIV Prevention and Health Promotion.* London: Health Education Authority.

Wellings, K., Field, J., Johnson, A. and Wadsworth, J. (1994) *Sexual Behaviour in Britain: The National Survey of Sexual Attitudes and Lifestyles.* London: Penguin.

10

International travel and the social context of sexual risk

Graham Hart and Sarah Hawkes

Introduction

Together with travel, sex is one of the world's most common forms of pleasure. Not infrequently, the two activities coincide. This chapter concentrates on the risks and consequences of unsafe sexual activity as practised by some of the UK's international travelling public. Unsafe sexual practices carry a number of risks: unplanned pregnancy and sexually transmitted infections (STIs) are probably the most important of the potential adverse outcomes (Hawkes and Hart, 1998). Like other researchers we have found that some groups are more likely than others to have sex with new partners while they are abroad. We will be describing those groups in order both to understand these behaviours and help contribute to the design of health promotion programmes to ensure that sexual activity abroad incurs as little risk as possible. It should not be forgotten, however, that sexual activity is a positive part of human existence and for many people the benefits of sexual intercourse (feelings of pleasure, closeness, excitement) far outweigh any perceived potential risks. Good sexual health is entirely compatible with the availability of pleasurable sexual relations with others, at home as well as while travelling, but this must be in the context of responsibility to oneself and others. In our view this means voluntary adult sexual relations where both partners are protected from the unwanted outcomes of sexual behaviour.

We will begin by describing the methods we used in the studies we have undertaken in this area, arguing for a methodological pluralism and a recognition of the respective contributions of a range of disciplines. Essentially, the work we have undertaken can be described as social epidemiology, combining as it does behavioural and biological measures of sexual risk exposure. We then report our results. Before concluding, we offer an alternative epistemological perspective that could be used in future research in this area.

Methodological considerations

Elsewhere in this book researchers have reported on work which has used self-completion questionnaires and interviews with large samples of respondents, through to observational data collection, in-depth interviews and focus groups. Such methodological pluralism, including policy analysis and use of secondary and unusual 'data' such as travel brochures and guides, is vital if we are to produce a more complete understanding of the relationship between sexual risk and travel (whether the risk is to travellers or to the peoples of the countries visited). In our research we focused on groups at increased risk of unwanted sexual outcomes of sexual behaviour undertaken abroad – attendees at a London travel clinic (Hawkes *et al.*, 1994), at a genito-urinary medicine clinic in London (Hawkes *et al.*, 1995) and two genito-urinary medicine clinics in Glasgow (Carter *et al.*, 1997). What makes our contribution distinctive in this field is the combined use of self-report measures of sexual risk exposure with biological markers of risk exposure, notably the HIV antibody test (Hawkes *et al.*, 1994) and tests for a range of other STIs (Hawkes *et al.*, 1995). Repeating our behavioural research with colleagues in Glasgow also served to demonstrate the reliability of the measures we used, as well as providing comparable and additional data to the London-based work.

The major criticism that is levelled at clinic-based studies of sexual risk abroad is that these populations are not 'representative' of the travelling public as a whole, and therefore the findings of such studies cannot be extrapolated to the general population (Black, 1997). This is likely to be true, although to be supported fully requires studies of the sexual behaviour of travellers by random sampling of the UK population. The recent National Survey of Sexual Attitudes and Lifestyles (NATSAL) (Johnson *et al.*, 1994) limited itself to asking a question as to whether work ever took respondents away from home overnight, and so does not refer directly to international travel, either for business or pleasure. (See Bloor *et al.*, this volume, for results from a survey of the sexual behaviour of a representative sample of young unattached travellers abroad.)

In our view it is precisely because clinic attendees are not representative of the UK population – indeed, that they are likely to be at increased risk of STIs – that it is appropriate to study this group. If we identify significant levels of risk in this section of the population, and increased morbidity associated with sexual behaviour abroad, which is then supported by other studies of non-clinic samples, then the targeting of groups for specific interventions to reduce unsafe sexual behaviour may be facilitated by the information collected.

The research we undertook was limited by the resources available to us, and therefore the primary research instrument used was a self-completion questionnaire. We would have liked to have undertaken qualitative research with our study populations, as we have recommended this approach in the past (Hawkes and Hart, 1993), but are pleased that in this collection, as elsewhere (Black, 1997), qualitative methods are being employed in the investigation of the social context of sexual risk-taking abroad.

The international travel and sexual risk behaviours of clinic attendees

Our first study took place in the outpatient department of the Hospital for Tropical Diseases, St Pancras, London, between December 1991 and May 1992 (Hawkes *et al.*, 1994). Every new patient (757 men and women: 97 per cent of those approached) was asked to complete a questionnaire on their sexual behaviour abroad and to provide a urine sample for anonymous testing for antibodies to HIV. Most (80 per cent) of these patients were from the UK, other parts of Western Europe or from North America or Australasia, and were visiting the clinic for a 'post-tropical check-up'. We found that a minority (18.6 per cent) of respondents reported a new sexual partner on their most recent trip abroad. Their mean age (29.9 years: SD = 8.1) did not differ significantly from those who did not report a new sexual partner (30.7 years: SD = 8.6). Two-thirds of those reporting new sexual partners were men.

This study generated a number of interesting results. The first was that, in terms of global sexual mixing (using WHO definitions of the patterns of HIV transmission), the majority of our respondents, who were from countries in which most HIV transmission is the result of injecting drug use or homosexual intercourse (Pattern I), primarily chose sexual partners from other Pattern I countries (56 per cent). Among our respondents from sub-Saharan Africa (a Pattern II region, in which most HIV transmission is through heterosexual intercourse), only 27 per cent of contacts were with people from Pattern I countries, suggesting even less sexual mixing in this group.

The factors which distinguished those who reported new sexual partners from those who did not do so were: going on an overland tour (21 per cent reporting new sexual partners vs. 11 per cent reporting no new partners); spending three or more months away on the most recent trip (57 per cent vs. 34 per cent); paying for sex in the last five years (21 per cent vs. 3.4 per cent); and having been treated for an STI in the last five years (24 per cent vs. 11 per cent) (all comparisons significant at chi-square $p < 0.005$). Condoms were used 'infrequently' or never by 64 per cent of those reporting new sexual partners abroad.

We found that 16 of 731 testable urine samples were anti-HIV-positive (2.2 per cent). Eleven of the 16 patients were from East, Central or Southern Africa; two men were homosexual (one UK resident, one non-UK). The remaining three heterosexual men were UK residents, two of whom reported recent sexual partners from sub-Saharan Africa, including one who had paid for sex and did not report using condoms.

This study demonstrated high levels of risk behaviour in a well-travelled group, and our findings regarding infrequent use of condoms and payment for sex, as well as HIV infection, suggested that these travellers were putting themselves and their sexual partners abroad at risk of unwanted sexual outcomes, notably STIs. We therefore decided to extend our research to another clinic population, to determine the extent to which this risk profile was distinctive, or whether other groups demonstrated comparable levels of risk exposure. Our next study was in a genito-urinary medicine clinic in central London (Hawkes *et al.*, 1995).

From March to June 1993 all patients who had travelled abroad within the previous three months who were eligible for syphilis serology (i.e. all new patients and all old patients presenting with possible new conditions) were asked to complete a questionnaire regarding their recent sexual behaviour. In this study respondents were asked not only about their behaviour while travelling but also about the period immediately prior to, and immediately after, their most recent trip. Of 462 eligible patients (18 per cent of the total attendees during the study period), 386 (83 per cent) consented to participate in the study. As with the earlier study, this was a population of young people, with a mean age of 30.2 years (SD = 8.4). Over half of the sample was female (54 per cent), and of the men, over half (57 per cent) had had homosexual intercourse at some time.

A quarter of respondents reported having one or more new sexual partners on their most recent trip abroad (as compared to 42 per cent in the three months prior to travel, and 23 per cent since returning home). Men were more likely than women to report a new sexual partner during this trip (36 per cent vs. 18 per cent), and gay men were more likely to report new partner(s) than heterosexual men (44 per cent vs. 25 per cent). Those who had a new partner on a recent trip were more likely than those not reporting a new partner to be travelling alone (62 per cent vs. 30 per cent), to have had a new sexual partner since returning (42 per cent vs. 17 per cent), to be visiting the clinic for a sexual health check-up (65 per cent vs. 46 per cent) and to have visited the clinic recently (61 per cent vs. 42 per cent). They were less likely to have a current regular sexual partner (46 per cent vs. 80 per cent) (all comparisons significant at chi-square p < 0.002). As in the previous study, over two-thirds (69 per cent) of those who reported a new partner abroad said that they either never, or only occasionally, used condoms with new partners. One in five (19 per cent) of those with a new partner abroad was diagnosed with an acute STI.

This study provided us with further evidence of the nature and consequences of sexual risk behaviour abroad. We found higher levels of reported sexual behaviour abroad compared to the Travel Clinic study (25 per cent vs. 18.6 per cent), and established that gay men were the most sexually active group. Although 19 per cent of the group who reported a recent trip abroad were diagnosed with an acute STI, this was not significantly different from the non-travellers in the clinic, 23 per cent of whom were also diagnosed with an infection. However, taking all diagnosed infections together from the same period it was possible to determine that 11.6 per cent of the total burden of disease in the clinic was associated with sexual risk exposure while abroad. If up to 12 per cent of all annual newly diagnosed STIs occur in association with travel abroad by UK residents, then this suggests that this is an area which could benefit from targeted interventions. Health gains in this area could have a major impact on the total health burden of STIs and their sequelae, which in the case of two common infections, C. trachomatis and N. gonorrhoea, include pelvic inflammatory disease and sub- or infertility in women (Hawkes and Hart, 1998).

One of the interesting findings of this study was the high level of reported sexual activity of this population, both prior and subsequent to the period of travel abroad which was the focus of our interest. Perhaps people who have sexual partners abroad are simply maintaining their usual level of sexual activity: that is, there is nothing distinctive about travel with regard to increased risk – those who have a high turnover of partners in the UK continue to do so, whether they are in Croydon, Caracas or Costa Rica. As part of our next study we sought to determine whether travel *per se* played an independent role in terms of increased sexual activity and sexual risk, this time surveying attendees at two genito-urinary medicine clinics in Glasgow (Carter *et al.*, 1997).

During a standardized pre-consultation interview attendees at the clinics were asked whether they had travelled abroad in the previous three months. If they reported that they had done so, they were asked to complete an anonymous questionnaire: of 372 eligible patients, 325 (87 per cent) produced usable questionnaires. The study took place in two three-month periods in 1993 and 1994. Most respondents were men (65 per cent) with an average age of 32.2 (range 16 to 57) compared to women, the mean age of whom was 26.4 (range 17 to 55). A larger proportion of this group reported new sexual partners abroad than in the previous studies: 91 (28 per cent) respondents reported having at least one sexual contact with someone other than their regular partner while abroad.

Examining rates of sexual contact before and during travel indicated that this group of people behaved differently when travelling. The rates of sexual contact for the three-month period before travel were compared with the time spent abroad. This showed that for the whole sample the mean number of new sexual contacts was 0.098 per week at home, but it was 0.247 per week while abroad (Wilcoxon mean ranks of 47.7 and 103.8 respectively, $p < 0.0001$). This suggests that travel may serve as an independent predictor of increased sexual activity.

However, this does not necessarily mean increased risk behaviour. Although we found that increased length of time away from home was a predictor of failure to use condoms consistently, we also found that, among those from the heterosexual population who used condoms consistently at home, most (76.9 per cent) continued to do so if they had a sexual contact abroad. Of those who were inconsistent in their condom use at home, most again (78.6 per cent) remained inconsistent in their condom use abroad ($p < 0.005$).

In summary, the studies we have undertaken have helped build a picture of the nature of sexual risk-taking by international travellers from the UK to other countries. It is, however, a complex picture. There are indeed groups who are more likely than others to report sexual partners abroad, and travel itself does appear to facilitate increased sexual activity compared to time spent at home, with length of time abroad also contributing to this, but the picture with regard to risk exposure requires further investigation. Sexual contact associated with international travel may contribute a significant amount of disease to the total health burden of STIs in the UK, but this could be occurring in people who, regardless of their sexual behaviour while travelling, would have contracted an STI because of their inconsistent condom use here and abroad.

An important issue here is sexual mixing: if unprotected sex takes place with partners in whom there are high levels of prevalent STI, then this increases the chances of infection occurring as compared to the same behaviours, and same numbers of partners, in situations where STI prevalence is low. We investigated some elements of sexual mixing, finding in the Travel Clinic patients some evidence of sexual relationships between people from global regions with different epidemiological HIV transmission patterns (Hawkes *et al.*, 1994), and we also found in the two clinics in Glasgow that gay men, and heterosexual men who were abroad for business purposes, were also more likely to report sex with local people than other travellers, whose sexual contacts abroad were with other UK residents (Carter *et al.*, 1997). The sexual mixing of this last group is therefore more likely to be with people from Gourock than from the Gambia, and the likelihood of STI depends on levels of infection in these populations.

What this section has demonstrated is that social epidemiology has a major contribution to make to delineating the nature and extent of sexual risk behaviour of international travellers. Studies of attendees at sexual health clinics are of particular value in assessing the extent to which sexual infections are associated with travel overseas. Much of the research in such contexts has been undertaken in the UK, and similar work in other countries would be of considerable interest. However, as we suggested earlier, methodological pluralism is necessary if we are to develop a more complete picture of the factors implicated in risk exposure. We would now like to suggest that this requires more than a change in the form of data collection – it calls for a change in perspective, or episteme. In the next section we adopt a very different approach to the understanding of risk behaviour, but in presenting this paradigm shift we are not suggesting this as an alternative, but as complementary to the descriptive and behavioural approach taken so far.

The social context of sexual risk behaviour abroad

Within a broader sociology of risk (Giddens, 1991; Beck, 1992; Adams, 1995) we have seen in recent years the development of a sociology of HIV risk behaviour which seeks to understand sexual (Bloor, 1995; Hart and Boulton, 1995; Hart and Flowers, 1996) and drug-related risks (Rhodes, 1995; Hart and Carter, 1998) in their social context. That is, there has been a critique of the limitations of epidemiological and psychological paradigms because they restrict attention to either the demographic or behavioural character-istics of populations (as represented by epidemiology) or their cognitive or attitudinal attributes (as represented by social psychological models). From a sociological perspective our concern has been to argue that risk behaviour can only be understood fully in its social context, and that three levels of analysis can facilitate a more complete picture than that provided by epidemiology or psychology, either alone or in combination (Hart and Flowers, 1996; Hart and Carter, 1998). The three forms of analysis are at the macro-social, the meso-social and the micro-social levels. We shall illustrate the use of this analysis by applying it to sexual risk, and particularly sex tourism, in Thailand, as this is a country which has been studied extensively from a number of perspectives.

The macro-social level is essentially concerned with the political economy of risk, in the national and supranational spheres. Risk is actively facilitated by international relations between countries, and more particularly by global markets. Thus, the availability, in a post-colonial world, of oppor-tunities for people from the North (industrialized, developed countries) to travel to the South (resource-poor countries, economies in transit, or less developed regions) depends not only upon the increasing availability of relatively cheap air travel but also on inward investment, often by international companies, in tourist sites and locations. This perspective is exemplified by the work of David Leheny (1995), who has demonstrated how Thailand's sex tourist industry was largely developed by Japanese capital and, as a result of increasing women's rights in Japan, how Japanese men sought paid sexual encounters outwith their own country, but within the South-east Asian region. Thailand has long had a history of commercial sex work, and this was reinforced and encouraged by its use by American and Australian servicemen during the Vietnam War as a place for 'rest and recreation'. Subsequently, Thailand and other Asian countries have been marketed in the West as both 'exotic' and cheap, and either direct references have been made to the sexual possibilities available there, or more coded messages about the 'welcoming' people have ensured that the region has remained a primary sex tourist destination (Carter, 1998). Leheny notes that male travellers to Thailand account for around 70 per cent of arrivals in the country which, even with a preponderance of male over female business travellers, still suggests disproportionate male interest in visiting the country.

Although the example given here is of Thailand, this macro-economic and macro-social perspective can be applied more widely, and even without the specific element of sex tourism, can be used to understand the features of a mass international tourism market which is seeing unprecedented air, sea and land travel by Western consumers, and which arguably renders tourism the largest global service industry. This is facilitated at the meso-social, or organizational, level by airlines, tour companies and local businesses serving tourists, but in addition local social structural conditions can have a significant impact on sexual risk, as exemplified by further research undertaken in Thailand by Van Griensven and colleagues (1995). They found that female prostitutes who were in debt to their employers (brothel owners) were nearly three times more likely to be HIV-infected than those not in debt, and this was just one socio-demographic factor among many that pointed to the role of meso-social conditions in potentiating risk. Young women who had started their sex work careers very early (aged 12 to 15) and who came from hill tribes in North Thailand were at particularly high risk, suggesting that a combination of socio-cultural factors are responsible for the entry into and much increased likelihood of HIV infection among commercial sex workers. Thus, at the meso-social level local social structural factors (debt and poverty in rural areas of North Thailand) can feed directly into organizational structures (brothels used by Thai and foreign men) which can have specific micro-social consequences, namely the presence of HIV infection when sexual encounters take place.

At the micro-social level, and in particular at the level of social inter-actions between individuals, the extent to which sexual risk occurs may depend strongly on perceptions of partners, and certainly supports the sociological insight of W. I. Thomas that if a situation is defined as real, it is real in its consequences (Berger and Luckmann, 1967). Researchers on male German tourists found that those who categorized the Thai women with whom they had sex as 'girlfriends' (rather than women with multiple part-ners, or prostitutes) and themselves as 'tourists' (rather than sex tourists) were more likely to spend more time during their holidays with an individual woman rather than many women, more likely to buy them gifts as well as provide them with money, but also less likely to use condoms than men who visited brothels in brief visits as clients (Wilke and Kleiber, 1991; Kleiber and Wilke, 1993). Of course, this is not entirely an issue of perception alone, and other social structural factors impact upon this situation, notably gendered relations of power (Holland *et al.*, 1992), which are also rehearsed at the micro-social level, but it is a striking example of ways in which social context is vital in explaining risk exposure.

Our choice of Thailand to exemplify the role of macro-, meso- and micro-social factors in understanding potential risk-taking abroad is primarily related to the extensive research that has been undertaken there, rather than to any other motive. Research from other locations, such as the Dominican Republic (associated with heterosexual male sex tourism) or Sri Lanka (homosexual paedophilic sex tourism), is somewhat limited (see Ireland, 1993; and O'Connell Davidson, this volume, for an account of recent research in this field). What we have tried to do in this section is to contextualize the data that we reported earlier regarding the risk-taking behaviour of international tourists, and to demonstrate the importance of a broad-ranging perspective when describing sexual activity abroad.

Conclusions

We have suggested elsewhere that risk, rather than residing within individual cognitions or epidemiological categories, is more properly understood as residing between people and, moreover, between people and the social conditions in which they find themselves (Hart and Flowers, 1996). We seek to encourage a multidisciplinary, multi-method and multi-epistemological perspective on sexual behaviour and travel. This would embrace social epidemiology and its attempts to identify more specifically who is at risk of particular sexual outcomes, and a sociological perspective on sexual risk, which takes cognizance not only of the political economy of tourism but also its organizational forms and the particular interactions between people.

It is increasingly apparent that if interventions, or what have been called 'enabling approaches' (Tawil *et al.*, 1995), are to succeed, they will require a combination of perspectives to inform their development and realization, and this can only occur if we are willing to break down disciplinary barriers. Sexual risk behaviour and travel present us with unique problems, as local and national initiatives will fail unless there is international co-operation and agreement as to how to progress. This is a challenge that warrants the expenditure not only of time, money and resources but also intellectual energy if we are to make the combination of sexual health and travel an achievable goal.

References

Adams, J. (1995) *Risk*. London: UCL Press.

Beck, U. (1992) *Risk Society: Towards a New Modernity*. London: Sage.

Berger, P. and Luckmann, T. (1967) *The Social Construction of Reality*. London: Allen Lane.

Black, P. (1997) Sexual behaviour and travel: quantitative and qualitative perspectives on the behaviour of genito-urinary medicine clinic attenders. In S. Clift and P. Grabowski (eds), *Tourism and Health: Risks, Research and Responses*. London: Pinter.

Bloor, M. (1995) *The Sociology of HIV Transmission*. London: Sage.

Carter, S. (1998) Tourists' and travellers' social construction of Africa and Asia as risky locations. *Tourism Management* **19** (4), 349–58.

Carter, S., Horn, K., Hart, G., Dunbar, M., Scoular, A. and MacIntyre, S. (1997) The sexual behaviour of international travellers at two Glasgow GUM clinics. *International Journal of STD and AIDS* **8**, 336–8.

Giddens, A. (1991) *Modernity and Self-Identity: Self and Society in the Late Modern Age*. Cambridge: Polity Press.

Hart, G. and Boulton, M. (1995) Sexual behaviour in gay men: towards a sociology of risk. In P. Aggleton, P. Davies and G. Hart (eds), *AIDS: Safety, Sexuality and Risk*. London: Taylor and Francis.

Hart, G. and Carter, S. (1998) Drug consumption and risk: developing a sociology of HIV risk behaviour. In J. Gabe, S. Williams and M. Calnan, *Theorising Medicine, Health and Society*. London: Sage.

Hart, G. and Flowers, P. (1996) Recent developments in the sociology of HIV risk behaviour. *Risk, Decision and Policy* **1**, 153–65.

Hawkes, S. J. and Hart, G. J. (1993) Travel, migration and HIV. *AIDS Care* **5**, 207–14.

Hawkes, S. and Hart, G. (1998) The sexual health of travellers. In D. Freedman (ed.), *Infectious Disease Clinics of North America: Travel Medicine*. Philadelphia: W. B. Saunders.

Hawkes, S., Hart, G. J., Bletsoe, E., Shergold, C. and Johnson, A. M. (1995) Risk behaviour and STD acquisition in genitourinary medicine clinic attenders who have travelled. *Genitourinary Medicine* **71**, 351–4.

Hawkes, S., Hart, G. J., Johnson, A. M., Shergold, C., Ross, E., Herbert, K. M., Mortimer, P., Parry, J. V. and Mabey, D. (1994) Risk behaviour and HIV prevalence in international travellers. *AIDS* **8**, 247–52.

Holland, J., Ramazanoglu, C., Scott, S., Sharpe, S. and Thompson, R. (1992) Pressure, resistance, empowerment: young women and the negotiation of safer sex. In P. Aggleton, P. Davies and G. Hart, *AIDS: Rights, Risk and Reason*. Basingstoke, Hants: Falmer.

Ireland, K. (1993) *'Wish You Weren't Here': The Sexual Exploitation of Children and the Connection with Tourism and International Travel*. Working Paper No. 7. London: Save the Children.

Johnson, A., Wadsworth, J., Wellings, K. and Field, J. (1994) *Sexual Attitudes and Lifestyles*. Oxford: Blackwell.

Kleiber, D. and Wilke, M. (1993). Sexual behaviour of German (sex-) tourists. Paper presented at IXth International Conference on AIDS, Berlin.

Leheny, D. (1995). A political economy of Asian sex tourism. *Annals of Tourism Research* **22** (2), 287–304.

Rhodes, T. (1995) Theorising and researching 'risk': notes on the social relations of risk in heroin users' lifestyles. In P. Aggleton, P. Davies and G. Hart (eds), *AIDS Safety, Sexuality and Risk*. London: Taylor and Francis.

Tawil, O., Verster, A. and O'Reilly, K. (1995) Enabling approaches for HIV/AIDS prevention: can we modify the environment and minimise the risk? *AIDS* **9**, 1299–1306.

Van Griensven, G. J. P., Limanonda, B., Chongwatana, N., Tiraswat, P. and Coutinho, R. A. (1995) Socio-economic and demographic characteristics and HIV-1 infection among female commercial sex workers in Thailand. *AIDS Care* **7**, 557–65.

Wilke, M. and Kleiber, D. (1991) AIDS and sex tourism. Paper presented at VIIth International Conference on AIDS, Florence, Italy.

11

Tourism and the sexual ecology of gay men

Stephen Clift and Simon Forrest

Introduction

In 1995, the UK Health Departments revised their HIV and AIDS health promotion strategy in the light of then current epidemiological evidence on the epidemic in the UK. The strategy document argued that the general population 'needs to be informed about the continuing potential risks from HIV', but that 'vulnerable groups need to be kept constantly aware of the more immediate risks they face'. The first three 'key groups to be targeted' identified by the strategy document were:

- gay men
- bisexual men, and other men who have sex with men
- men and women who travel to, or have family links with, high prevalence countries where the predominant mode of transmission is sex between men and women, for example in sub-Saharan Africa.

(UK Health Departments, 1995: 13)

It is notable that 'travel' particularly to sub-Saharan Africa is associated with heterosexual risks of HIV, but travel is not acknowledged as a factor which may increase risk for gay men. This is despite the fact that levels of HIV infection among populations of gay men. This is elsewhere in the world (especially in major gay cities in the United States) are considerably higher than they are among gay men in the UK (and particularly outside of London and other cities with large gay communities). The significance of different forms of population mobility for the geographic spread of HIV (and other STDs) is widely acknowledged (Hawkes and Hart, 1993; Quinn, 1994; Porter, Lea and Carroll, 1996), and international travel has been identified as an important factor in the spread of HIV infection among gay men during the early years of the epidemic (Conway *et al.*, 1990). Rotello (1997) has recently re-emphasized the potential significance of travel as one of a number of factors contributing to a distinctive 'sexual ecology' among gay men, which ensures that HIV infection continues to be a major public health threat within gay populations. There is a case, therefore, for examining the sexual behaviour of gay men in the context of tourism and, in particular, placing an examination of sex between men in tourism contexts within the broader ecological perspective put forward by Rotello.

This chapter presents findings from a recent study of tourism patterns and sexual activity among UK-resident gay men and assesses the extent to which they support the utility of the ecological perspective delineated by Rotello. Rotello's analysis and in particular his prescriptions for tackling the continued problem of HIV infection among gay men in the United States have generated vehement criticism from certain sections of the American gay community, which see them as an attack on gay men's sexual culture and rights. Whatever the merits or otherwise of the different points of view in this continuing debate, it is argued here that Rotello's presentation of a ecological perspective on gay sexual behaviour and sexual health risks is a useful framework within which to consider the significance of sexual activity among gay men in tourism contexts. Rotello elaborates his perspective and its implications in an account running to almost 300 pages, and it is difficult in the available space to do justice to his arguments and supporting evidence. Nevertheless, a brief summary of the main thesis is required before presenting empirical evidence on gay men's tourist patterns and sexual behaviour.

The sexual ecology of gay men

Rotello argues that in order to understand the nature of human diseases, their social distributions and patterns of fluctuation over time, it is necessary to adopt a broadly 'ecological' approach. Such an approach attempts to understand the complex set of environmental, biological, historical, cultural, medical and behavioural factors which account for disease patterns, rather than to explain them in terms of simplistic, mono-causal mechanisms. Sexual ecology, therefore, 'consists of the entire spectrum of causes and effects that influence the spread of sexually transmitted diseases' (Rotello, 1997: 16). These include such factors as: the microbial cause of an STD; the specific sexual behaviours by which microbes are transmitted from one person to another; biological cofactors that affect the likelihood that exposure leads to infection; human behavioural patterns which reduce or enhance risks of infection; technological developments which affect the ease of human movement; and the availability or non-availability of treatments, cures or vaccines as factors affecting transmission or the emergence of new strains of a disease.

As Rotello points out, a number of basic parameters determine whether disease incidence increases in a population, remains stable or declines (i.e.

the reproductive rate of the disease). These are: the likelihood that an infective organism will be transmitted under given circumstances; the percentage of a population that is currently infected; and the number of new sexual partners a person has in a given time. Of particular significance to the overall patterning of epidemics of sexual diseases are so-called 'core groups'. People in core groups have higher numbers of sexual partners than those not in cores; they tend to engage in forms of sex that carry greater risks, and they tend to suffer from a range of health problems which increase their susceptibility to further infection. A further concept of importance is 'bridging', that is the degree to which members of core groups are sexually active with individuals outside the core. Rotello acknowledges that the concept of 'core groups' 'is one of the most politically challenging and least understood concepts in sexual ecology', but at the same time he believes that 'No sophisticated understanding of the dynamics of the AIDS epidemic is possible without noting the crucial role played by core group dynamics' (Rotello, 1997: 48).

It is clear that during the 1960s and 1970s the sexual ecology of gay men in major urban centres in the United States developed in such a way that it fuelled epidemics of a range of STDs before and at the same time as HIV. Rotello notes, however, that HIV is relatively difficult to transmit compared with other sexual infections and that a combination of factors in respect of gay men's lifestyles was important in establishing conditions conducive to the transmission of HIV. These included: multi-partner anal sex; insertive–receptive versatility; concurrent multi-partnerism; other STDs; substance abuse and travel (bringing gay men into contact with one another internationally and within the United States).

Rotello emphasizes that this combination of factors does not have to characterize the whole of a gay community for an epidemic of HIV infection to occur; rather a small highly sexual active core group with bridging connections to the wider community is all that is needed to produce widespread infection. This pattern also has important practical implications in respect of HIV prevention, since focusing prevention efforts on members of a core group will have a greater longer-term impact on the growth of the epidemic than targeting such efforts on the population as a whole or on individuals who are not part of the core.

Much of Rotello's argument draws upon well-established concepts and findings in epidemiology which are not a matter for debate. Where Rotello does become controversial, however, is in his critique of the preventative response to the epidemic among gay men, particularly the emphasis given to the use of condoms as the central strategy for stemming the spread of HIV, and his assertion that a radical transformation of gay sexual culture is required if gay men are ever to be free from the threat of HIV.

According to Rotello, since AIDS emerged so soon after the establishment of a newly assertive gay sex-positive culture, and since the sexual practices central to a sex-positive gay identity were shown to be central to the transmission of the disease, it was inevitable that a range of possible approaches to prevention were fraught with controversy. Calls for gay men to reduce sexual partners, avoid certain sexual activities, avoid sex altogether or adopt a monogamous lifestyle were all seen as attacks on gay life and as homophobic and anti-erotic. For such reasons, the move to promote condom use as the principal means of preventing HIV transmission was preferable, as it did not appear to compromise the radical agenda of gay liberation and the central components of gay sexual lifestyle and identity – anal penetration and pleasure. Thus:

> the code of the condom became virtually the entire message of prevention. 'Condom distribution' became a rallying cry in gay bars, 'condom availability' a major goal of public education programs. The condom became a symbol of safety, prevention's magic bullet. All this was carried out, however, in knowledge of the fact that the condom code contained certain inherent risks.
> (Rotello, 1997: 102)

These risks were: condom failure rates, due to breakage, slippage and ineffective and inconsistent use; and an ignoring of the larger STD picture, which includes many diseases that can be transmitted in other ways and which may be incurable and/or serious threats to health.

In the early years following promotion of the condom code, there appeared to be considerable evidence that many gay men had changed their behaviour substantially and were using condoms, and it seemed as though the solution to the AIDS problem had been found. However, this optimism, Rotello suggests, began to be undermined during the early 1990s by reports that rates of HIV infection were beginning to increase again among gay men, especially younger men who had little experience of the trauma associated with losing a partner or friend with AIDS. During the early 1990s, too, a wide range of behavioural studies of gay men's sexual behaviour conducted around the world indicated substantial levels of unsafe sex (for recent supportive evidence, see Kalichman *et al.*, 1997 (the United States); Van de Van *et al.*, 1997 (Australia); Wang *et al.*, 1997 (Spain) and Hope and McArthur, 1998 (UK)).

More significantly, however, Rotello is sceptical that the widespread adoption of condoms was actually responsible for the declining rate of new infections which followed. He argues instead that all epidemics tend to have a natural history in which the early stages are marked by relatively slow growth in new cases, followed by a period of rapid growth and then a decline, as the number of susceptible people remaining in the population is reduced. Rotello's argument is that the condom code is predicated on a simplistic mechanical analysis of the HIV spread which focuses simply on fluid exchange – but it ignores the fact that 'a whole network of behaviours created, and continues to sustain, epidemic conditions in the gay population'.

An alternative 'deep' approach to the problem of prevention involves thinking not just about the narrow subject of fluid exchange 'but the entire triad of epidemic transmission: prevalence, infectivity, and contact rate'. In order to approach prevention in a deeper ecological way, the key message is to reduce the number of partners, and to reduce as much core group behaviour as possible.

A particular focus of Rotello's criticism are commercial sex establishments and the fact that in the short time it has taken such concerns to re-establish themselves (in the United States) the levels of risk behaviour within these environments has markedly increased. Such environments are difficult to regulate because of the commercial interests involved – but such regulation is necessary since unwillingness to intervene

> virtually guarantees that core group behaviour will continue to be encouraged by profit-minded entrepreneurs. And since the possibility exists that AIDS can be perpetuated in the gay population through such behaviour alone, failure to target such behaviour leaves open the possibility that no matter what else we do, the epidemic will rage on and on.
>
> (Rotello, 1997: 197)

Gay men, holidays and sex

It is very easy to form an impression that gay men on holiday in well-known gay destinations and resorts have ample opportunities for sex with new partners. Gay travel guides, such as *Spartacus* (Gmünder, 1997), have a very explicit and predominant focus on venues and contexts offering opportunities for sex, and gay tour companies often use sexually suggestive language in their advertisements (e.g. the gay holiday company Sensations includes the following line in a current advertisement: 'Be a clever dick. Book the UK's number one gay holiday company.'). Holiday features in the gay press underline the sexualized nature of gay culture, and the sense that this may become even more exaggerated on holiday. The most striking recent example of this is the 'holiday shag diary' which appeared in the free gay newspaper *Boyz* (13 June 1998, p. 55). The picture is also reinforced by more serious journalistic accounts of gay resorts, with their party atmosphere and hedonistic patterns of drug use and sexual behaviour. Paul Burston (1997: 4), for example, writing in the *Independent on Sunday* magazine, provides the following account of the gay scene in South Beach, Florida:

> South Beach, Florida, is a gay resort to end all gay resorts. Like London or Los Angeles, it has a highly developed commercial gay scene, built around gay men's apparently insatiable appetite for sexual adventure. Like New York or Palm Springs, it plays regular host to what are known as 'gay circuit parties' – a rapidly expanding network of large-scale themed events such as the Winter Party, held to raise money for AIDS charities, and often accused of encouraging unsafe sex through the use of disinhibiting, sexually stimulating drugs and the prevailing air of hedonistic abandon.

It is important, however, not to be misled by media representations of sexual behaviour among gay men on holiday, and to consider instead what research evidence reveals regarding levels of sexual activity and risk behaviour in the context of travel and holidays. It is remarkable, however, that until recently, little British research on travel and sexual risk among gay men has been undertaken, apart from studies of gay men in hospital clinic settings. These provide some information on the proportions of homosexual men reporting sexual activity with new partners abroad – e.g., 36 per cent (Daniels *et al.*, 1992); 44 per cent (Hawkes *et al.*, 1995) and 42 per cent (Carter *et al.*, 1997) – although only Daniels *et al.* report data on the incidence of unprotected sex (29 per cent). Such work is important but limited, given the samples studied and methodology employed. Research on the sexual activity of homosexual men in tourist resorts has also been carried out by German and American researchers in destinations such as Thailand and Bali (Wilke and Kleiber, 1992; Ford *et al.*, 1993; see also Ford and Wirawan, this volume). Such research also provides evidence of unsafe sex in tourist settings, but these findings are also of limited generalizability given the focus on sex with commercial sex workers in these destinations. The only study to date among a cross-section of gay tourists in a popular gay resort in southern Europe was undertaken by Casson and Dockrell (1996). This study found that a substantial minority of men believed they took greater sexual risks on holiday, although the incidence of unprotected sex with new partners on holiday was judged to be very low.

Given the lack of substantial research on gay tourism and sexual behaviour, it was considered valuable to undertake an exploratory survey to gather data on holiday patterns and sexual activity among a broad cross-section of gay men (see Clift and Forrest, 1998; Forrest and Clift, 1998; Clift and Forrest, 1999). The research was centred on Brighton, an important resort town on the south coast of England which has a substantial gay population.

Methodology of the Brighton survey

A large sample of gay men were surveyed by means of a self-completion questionnaire. Approximately half of the men were recruited during fieldwork in pubs and clubs in Brighton, and half through a local lesbian and gay magazine *Gscene*. The questionnaire included questions on demographic and personal characteristics (e.g. age, income, partnership status); a list of 16 destinations to assess tourist patterns (e.g. Gran Canaria, Amsterdam); 16 'motivation' items to determine what men consider to be important in planning a holiday (e.g. 'seeing well-known tourist sights', 'guaranteed sunshine'); and a set of seven statements on sexual activity in the context of holidays (e.g. 'I tend to be more sexually active on holiday than at home'). Respondents were also asked to give details of up to two holidays undertaken in 1996 prior to the survey, including sexual activity with new partners. A total of 590 men completed all sections of the questionnaire, of whom 69 per cent were resident in the Brighton area. Prior to analysis, men visiting the UK from overseas and men not identifying as either gay or bisexual were excluded, leaving a sample size of 562 (for a fuller account, see Clift and Forrest, 1998).

Four generalizations on gay tourism and sexual activity

The evidence gathered in the survey is used here to support four generalizations about tourism patterns shown by gay men and their sexual behaviours while on holiday. These will then be discussed in relation to the arguments regarding gay sexual ecology presented by Rotello.

1. Gay men engage in distinctive tourism patterns, with a large percentage of men holidaying in important gay destinations.

Men were asked to provide details of up to two holidays they had been on during 1996 prior to the survey, and details of a further holiday planned for later in the year (giving both countries and cities visited). The information was coded by region in the world (UK, Europe, North America/Australia and Rest of the World), by country and by city/region within country. City and resort destinations were classified as 'gay' if described in the gay travel guide *Spartacus* as an 'important gay city' or gay resort. For the UK, London, Brighton, Manchester and Edinburgh are given as important gay cities, and in addition Blackpool was coded as a significant gay resort. For Europe, major gay destinations included Amsterdam, Paris, Gran Canaria, Ibiza, Barcelona and Sitges. For North America/Australia, major gay destinations included New York, San Francisco, Los Angeles and resort destinations in Florida (Miami, Key West and Fort Lauderdale). Finally, for the Rest of the World, only one destination, Rio de Janeiro in Brazil, was described as an 'important gay city' in *Spartacus*, although a number of non-European, non-western destinations not described as gay cities would undoubtedly offer ready opportunities for sexual contact with men (e.g. Bangkok).

Table 11.1 reports data on the percentage of holidays undertaken in the UK, Europe, North America/Australia and the Rest of the World, giving the percentage of holidays in gay destinations as defined above.

The patterns in this table are of interest and show similarities from one holiday to the next. First, it should be noted that 167 men, or 29.7 per cent of the sample, did not provide details of a holiday up to the time of the survey, and 156 (27.8 per cent) indicated that they were not planning a holiday during the remainder of the year. Overall, approximately one-fifth of men had not holidayed at the time of the survey and had no plans to holiday for the rest of the year. Among men providing details of holidays, over half

Table 11.1 Gay men's global tourism patterns, 1996 (important gay cities and resort destinations)

	1st holiday		2nd holiday		Next holiday	
	n	%	n	%	n	%
UK and Channel Islands	63	15.8	64	27.1	51	14.3
gay destinations	37	9.4	33	14.0	31	9.2
Europe	213	54.5	124	52.5	192	58.0
gay destinations	130	33.1	72	30.5	111	33.0
North America/Australia	63	16.0	19	8.1	60	17.9
gay destinations	41	10.4	13	5.5	32	9.5
Rest of the World	54	13.7	29	12.3	33	9.8
gay destinations	0	0	1	0.4	0	0
Non-gay destinations	185	47.1	118	50.0	162	48.2
gay destinations	208	52.9	118	50.0	174	51.8
Total giving details	393		236		336	
Details missing	2		4		70	
No holiday reported	167		322		156	

holidayed in European destinations and approximately a half to three-quarters of these holidays were in important gay cities or resort destinations. Many of these cities/resorts attract very large numbers of gay tourists and provide ample and greater opportunities for sexual activity than most British men will enjoy in their home environment.

After Europe, a substantial minority of holidays were taken in the UK, and of these over half were in cities with large gay scenes. Substantial minorities of holidays were also taken in North America/Australia, with between 60 to 70 per cent of holidays in gay cities and resorts. A similar proportion of men holidayed outside of Europe and North America/ Australia, but virtually none of these destinations in the Rest of the World are characterized by *Spartacus* as 'important gay cities'.

2. Substantial minorities of gay men are motivated in their decisions about holiday destinations by opportunities for socializing and sex with other men, and have expectations of being more sexually active and taking more sexual risks on holiday than at home.

Table 11.2 summarizes findings from the survey on men's responses to holiday motivation items and statements about sex on holiday included in the questionnaire. It also reports the pattern emerging from a principal components analysis of these items. The results show that three broad dimensions of holiday motivation can be identified, together with a dimension defined by expectations of sexual activity and risk on holiday. All of the holiday sex items involved a contrast with the home environment.

It is clear that approximately one-third of men consider 'opportunities for sex' with other gay men as 'very important' when planning a holiday; just under half agree that holidays tend to offer more opportunities for sex, and
Table 11.2 Gay men's holiday motivations and expected sexual behaviours:* levels of

agreement[1] and results from a principal components analysis (n = 482)

Items	% agree	Components			
		1	2	3	4
1. Gay social life and sex					
Gay culture and gay venues	39	0.82			
Opportunities to socialize with other gay men	37	0.79			
Good nightlife	48	0.76			
Opportunities for sex	29	0.65			
Sporting facilities and opportunities for exercise	10	–			
2. Culture and sights					
Visiting art galleries, antiquities, etc.	18		0.73		
Opportunities to see local culture	38		0.70		
Dramatic or beautiful landscapes	38		0.67		
Seeing well-known tourist sights	21		0.59		
Opportunities to see wildlife and nature	13		0.58		
Getting off the beaten track	28		0.56		
3. Expected sexual behaviour					
More likely to take sexual risks on holiday*	10			0.78	
Easier to forget about safer sex on holiday*	11			0.71	
Risk from sexual infections higher on holiday*	25			0.68	
Tend to be more sexually active on holiday*	39			0.58	
More opportunities for sex on holiday*	49			0.52	
Take more precautions if I have sex on holiday*	37			–	
4. Comfort and relaxation					
Guaranteed sunshine	51				0.59
Comfort and good food	71				0.57
Opportunities for rest and relaxation	70				0.51
Getting away from other people	28				0.47
Convenient and cheap holiday package	25				–
HIV prevention on holiday is important*	94				–

[1] For motivation items: percentage of men giving ratings of 'very important' when planning a holiday. For sexual behaviour items*: percentage of men agreeing with the statement.

just under 40 per cent agree that they 'tend to be more sexually active on holiday' compared with home. Strikingly, a quarter of men agreed that a holiday setting carried greater risks of sexual infections, and 10 per cent agreed that they were 'more likely to take sexual risks on holiday'.

3. A substantial proportion of gay men, particularly those on holiday alone or with friends, report sexual activity with new partners on holiday, and higher levels of sexual activity than at home. Reported levels of unprotected penetration, however, are low.
Of the total sample of 562 men studied, 395 (70.3 per cent) had been on holiday at least once in 1996 and 393 gave details of sexual activity during the first or only holiday described (see Table 11.3). Among these men, 187 (47.8 per cent) were sexually active with a new partner(s). Numbers of partners ranged from 1 to 200, with 36.7 per cent of sexually active men

Table 11.3 Details of gay men's sexual behaviour on holiday[1]

	n	%
Sex with new partner(s)		
no	204	52.2
yes	187	47.8
Number of new partners		
1–2	90	50.8
3 or more	87	49.2
Penetrative sex		
no	74	39.6
yes	113	60.4
Unprotected penetrative sex		
no	96	85.0
yes	17	15.0

[1] Data relates to the first or only holiday.

reporting four or more new partners. Among the sexually active men, 113 (60.4 per cent) reported penetration (either insertive or receptive penetration, or both), with numbers of penetrative partners ranging from 1 to 100, and 25 per cent of men reporting 4 or more such partners.

The finding that 47.8 per cent of men were sexually active with new partners on holiday is slightly higher than the range of 36 to 44 per cent of gay men sexually active abroad reported from previous studies of gay men in clinic settings, and considerably higher than recent estimates for heterosexual men on holiday without a sexual partner (e.g. 31 per cent, Ford, 1991; 10 per cent, Bloor et al., 1997).

Despite the high levels of sexual activity reported, the incidence of unprotected sex was reassuringly low. In total 17 men reported that they did not use condoms consistently during their first/only holiday, a figure which represents 15 per cent of men reporting penetrative sex. This estimate is lower than the figure of 29 per cent (Daniels et al., 1992) for unprotected sex among gay men in the context of travel reported in a previous UK clinic study of gay men, and lower than estimates of unsafe sex among heterosexual tourists, which range from 25 per cent (Bloor et al., 1997) to 71 per cent (Conway et al., 1990). It is clear from the present study, therefore, that while gay men are considerably more likely than heterosexual men to have sex with new partners on holiday, they are also far less likely to engage in unprotected penetrative sex.

A number of factors emerged as being significantly associated with gay men's sexual activity with new partners on holiday. Factors associated with whether men were sexually active or not were modelled using logistic regression (see Clift and Forrest, 1999), and significant associations were found for: holiday companions (63 per cent of men on holiday alone or with friends sexually active vs. 26.1 per cent of men on holiday with boyfriend or family, OR = 3.87, p < 0.0001); whether condoms were taken on holiday (55.6 per cent of men taking condoms sexually active vs. 29.5 per cent of those not taking them, OR = 2.21, p < 0.05); gay social life and sex as a holiday motivation (65.6 per cent of high scorers sexually active compared with 20.7 per cent of low scorers, OR = 3.94, p < 0.001); expected sexual behaviour/risk (78 per cent of high scorers sexually active compared with 35.1 per cent of low scorers, OR = 11.88, p < 0.0001); and numbers of new sexual partners at home (78.4 per cent of men reporting 10+ sexual partners at home reporting sex on holiday compared with 17 per cent of men reporting no new partners at home, OR = 11.31, p < 0.0001).

Factors associated with penetrative sex and unprotected sex on holiday were explored using chi-square analysis. Penetrative sex was found to be significantly associated with: number of new sexual partners on holiday (31.9 per cent of men with one to two partners vs. 60.2 per cent of men with three or more partners, χ^2 = 13.49, df = 1, p < 0.0005); 'gay social life and sex' motivation (38.9 per cent low scorers vs. 68.7 per cent high scorers, χ^2 = 7.28, df = 2, p < 0.05); taking condoms (30.3 per cent of non-takers vs. 66.9 per cent of takers, χ^2 = 15.21, df = 1, p < 0.0005); and expected sexual behaviour/risk (47.8 per cent with low expectations vs. 71.8 per cent with high expectations, χ^2 = 7.29, df = 2, p < 0.05).

Three variables were significantly associated with reported unprotected penetrative sex on holiday: not taking condoms (40 per cent (4/10) of non-takers reported unprotected sex vs. 12.6 per cent (13/103) of takers, Fisher's exact test, p < 0.05); expected sexual behaviour/risk (7.1 per cent (6/84) of men scoring low to medium vs. 39.3 per cent (11/28) of men scoring high, Fisher's exact test, p < 0.0005) and HIV status (8 per cent of 'definitely' or 'probably negative' men vs. 34.4 per cent of men rating themselves from 'unsure' to 'definitely positive', χ^2 = 11.66, df − 1, p < 0.001).

4. Gay men's choice of holiday destinations reflects their motivations. Men holidaying in gay destinations are more likely to be sexually active with new partners and report more sexual partners than men in non-gay destinations.

Men holidaying in gay or non-gay destinations for the first/only holiday reported did not differ significantly in age, income, whether they were in a committed relationship, their sexual health history (an STI in the last five years or HIV status), who they went on holiday with, whether they took condoms and their expected sexual behaviour/risk. However, as Table 11.4 shows, choice of holiday destination clearly reflected general holiday motivations, with men in gay destinations more likely to have high 'gay social life and sex' scores and less likely to have high 'culture and sights' and 'comfort and relaxation' scores.

Table 11.4 Comparison of gay men holidaying in non-gay and gay destinations (first/only holiday)

Variable	Destination		χ^2	p
	Non-gay	Gay		
Sexual partners at home	n = 170	n = 192		
none	25.9	27.1		
1–3	37.1	23.4		
4–9	17.1	21.9		
10+	20.0	27.6	8.89	< 0.05
Motivation: gay social life and sex	n = 180	n = 204		
low	30.0	17.2		
medium	39.4	36.3		
high	30.6	46.6	13.34	< 0.005
Motivation: culture and sights	n = 180	n = 201		
low	18.3	29.9		
medium	52.8	48.3		
high	28.9	21.9	7.39	< 0.05
Motivation: comfort and relaxation	n = 178	n = 204		
low	1.7	5.9		
medium	36.0	42.6		
high	62.4	51.5	7.33	< 0.05
Length of holiday	n = 184	n = 209		
1–7 days	36.4	52.6		
8–14 days	38.6	32.1		
15+ days	25.0	15.3	11.53	< 0.005
Condoms easily available	n = 169	n = 202		
no	57.4	29.7		
yes	42.6	70.3	28.91	< 0.00001
Lubricant easily available	n = 168	n = 198		
no	66.7	35.4		
yes	33.3	64.6	35.65	< 0.00001
Saw safer-sex material	n = 174	n = 207		
no	63.8	32.9		
yes	36.2	67.1	36.34	< 0.00001

Men holidaying in gay destinations were more likely to have had a higher number of sexual partners at home, although it is striking that the distribution of sexual activity at home is fairly even across the range from none to 10+ for men in gay destinations. This probably reflects the fact that just under half of the men holidaying in gay destinations were in committed relationships, and just under 40 per cent were on holiday in gay destinations with their boyfriend. Interestingly, a significant difference emerged for length of holiday, with holidays in gay destinations tending to be up to a week in length, whereas visits to non-gay destinations tended to be longer. This may reflect the fact that the non-gay destinations include a higher proportion of longer-haul trips outside Europe and North America – which will tend to be longer – but also, that for many gay men, a week in a gay resort may be long enough.

Finally, a marked difference emerged between gay and non-gay destinations in whether men reported easy availability of condoms and lubricant and prominent safer-sex material targeted at gay men. These results are perhaps not surprising, but it does support the validity of the coding of destinations as gay vs. non-gay, and is consistent with the differentiation of destinations by motivation. What is noteworthy, however, are the substantial proportions of men holidaying in gay destinations who reported that condoms and lubricant were *not* easily available and who did *not* see safer-sex material. Surprisingly, this was particularly true of the major southern European gay resorts which attract large volumes of gay men throughout the summer months from all over Europe.

Table 11.5 shows that men in gay destinations were significantly more likely to report sex with new partners, and significantly more likely to report a higher number of partners, with well over half of men sexually active in gay destinations reporting three or more new partners. However, the nature of the destination appeared to have no bearing on whether men engaged in penetrative sex, and if they did, whether sex was unprotected.

Discussion

A key element of Rotello's account of sexual ecology is the argument that core group activity and multi-partner sex are facilitated by the concentration of gay men in gay places and the sexualized spaces within them, and that such activity constitutes a major collective risk factor for the continued spread of STDs including HIV. It is very clear from the survey findings that a substantial proportion of gay men holiday in destinations which can be regarded as important gay places. These have either a well-established local gay community or a large seasonal influx of gay tourists from other countries, or both, and exhibit a significant gay commercial infrastructure offering a diversity of spaces to facilitate social networking and sexual activity among gay men.

Table 11.5 Sexual behaviours reported by gay men holidaying in non-gay and gay destinations (first/only holiday)

	Destination			
Variable	Non-gay	Gay	χ^2	p
No sex vs. sex	n = 181	n = 208		
No sex with new partners	60.8	44.7		
Sex with new partners	39.2	55.3	10.01	< 0.005
Number of new partners	n = 65	n = 111		
1–2	61.5	44.1		
3 or more	38.5	55.9	4.96	< 0.05
Non-penetrative vs. penetrative sex	n = 71	n = 115		
non-penetrative	40.8	38.3		
penetrative	59.2	61.7	0.12	n.s.
Protected vs. unprotected sex	n = 42	n = 71		
protected sex	83.3	85.9		
unprotected sex	16.7	14.1	0.14	n.s.

The descriptions given in *Spartacus* of Sitges and Playa del Ingles in Gran Canaria (two of the most significant gay resorts in southern Europe) of the concentration and convenient location of gay venues, the numbers of visitors and the intense atmosphere reinforce these points:

> Despite its huge tourist industry, Sitges has managed to keep something of its old-world charm. Few places can boast such a high concentration of excellent gay hotels and apartment blocks, so many busy gay bars, and a wide range of gay beaches. From May to the beginning of October, and again in February, the gay scene in Sitges is vibrant and colourful. Gay men flock here from all over Europe, and even from North America and Australia.
>
> (Gmünder, 1997: 818)

> What can be said about some other gay holiday spots, can be said particularly about Playa del Ingles: it's on the edge. On the outer edge of Spain, of Europe. It could be said that it's part of Africa. Playa lies in the utmost south of Gran Canaria, and the gay beach is found, naturally, in the utmost corner between Playa and Maspalomas. Gay nightlife offers the other extreme. Most but not all of the gay establishments like cafes, bars, discos, saunas and sex shops are in the Yumbo Center. This is very convenient. The venues range from dusky leather-bars to buzzling [sic] discos. The distances are no problem at all.
>
> (*ibid.*: 793)

The finding that substantial proportions of gay men are motivated by opportunities to meet and have sex with gay men on holiday is entirely consistent with the findings on patterns of holiday destinations chosen by gay men. Of greater significance in understanding the sexual ecology of gay men on holiday, however, is the fact that a large proportion of men believe that opportunities for sex are greater on holiday and that they are more likely to be sexually active in a holiday environment. Comments made by a number of men in the course of interviews conducted following the questionnaire survey serve to illustrate these points very graphically, and also point to a range of factors which account for the facilitation of sexual activity in holiday contexts:

> They're abroad, they're a bit wrecked and they start doing things that they wouldn't normally do at home. Mainly because your own inhibitions go down. You're in an area which may or may not be new to you, but the men are. Because people don't know you, you certainly feel as if you can behave in a way that is different to the way you normally behave. And I know quite a few people that are at home and they're normally really uptight and prudish, you see them on holiday and you think 'that's not the same person'. I mean they're screaming round the bars, they're throwing drugs down their necks like they're going out of fashion, they're drinking like fish, they're sleeping with anything they can get.
>
> (HIV-positive respondent, age 34)

> Yes, I can understand why people do it because I'd think, I'd never dream of . . . before I actually started going abroad, over the last few years, I would have never dreamt of going into a dark room, if there was one in this country, because of being seen by somebody who knows me. But when you're abroad I

think your inhibitions drop. Whereas, you just don't care because yeah, they see you for two weeks and then you're gone. And I think a lot of people do have the same attitude, where, oh yeah, nobody knows me, I'll let myself go a bit.

(HIV-negative respondent, age 29)

Of greater significance in terms of sexual health, however, is the fact that a substantial minority perceived their risks of sexual infections as being greater while on holiday than at home. While HIV may be difficult to transmit by forms of sexual contact other than unprotected anal intercourse, and the risks of infection are substantially reduced by consistent use of condoms during penetration, other forms of sexually transmitted infections may be readily transmitted by genital–genital contact, oral–genital sex and oral–anal practices. The fact that no fewer than a quarter of men believe that their risk of sexually transmitted infections is greater on holiday points to substantial numbers engaging in such forms of sexual contact with more sexual partners on holiday than at home. In addition, however, a substantial minority agree that they are more likely to forget about 'safer sex' while on holiday (i.e. condom usage during penetrative sex), when, moreover, they may be more sexually active than at home, and with partners from outside the UK.

Just under half of the men giving details of sexual activity on a first or only holiday in 1996 reported sex with new partners, and this rose to over 60 per cent among men on holiday without a new sexual partner. Several factors were predictive of being sexually active, but from a sexual ecology perspective, the most significant of these was the relationship between numbers of new partners at home and the percentage of men reporting new sexual partners on holiday. Among 88 men reporting 10 or more new partners at home prior to the survey, no fewer that 78.4 per cent reported sex on holiday. The significance of the holiday setting in facilitating sexual activity is illustrated particularly clearly by the fact that among 94 men reporting no new partners at home during the year prior to the survey, 17 per cent reported sex with a new partner on holiday. If highly sexually active men can be regarded as a core group in Rotello's terms, then the less sexually active may be more likely to interact sexually with members of such a core group in holiday settings than at home. Numbers of new partners on holiday were also high for a substantial proportion of men who were sexually active.

From a broad ecological perspective it is important to consider sexual activity *per se*, since this is highly likely to involve activities such as genital–genital contact and oral–genital contact, which carry risks of sexually transmitted infections. Such infections may either be unpleasant and incurable in themselves (e.g. genital herpes, hepatitis B) or they may enhance susceptibility to HIV infection. Of more significance with respect to sexual health risks, however, is the incidence of penetrative sex. Just over 60 per cent of sexually active men reported penetration, and among the factors associated with reports of penetrative sex, the most important from an ecological perspective is the number of new sexual partners during the holiday itself. Even if all of these men reported consistent condom usage, and we could rely on the honesty and accuracy of their reports, there might still be cause for concern about the high levels of penetrative sex with multiple partners on holiday found in this survey, since as Rotello points out, condoms are not invariably effective, due to breakages, slippage or inappropriate use. In fact, however, the survey found that 15 per cent of men engaging in penetration reported inconsistent use of condoms. The numbers of individuals concerned is small, but nevertheless, this small number of men assumes a disproportionately great significance with respect to sexual health risks. This is underlined further by the associations which emerged from the survey between unprotected sex and HIV status, with men who describe themselves as definitely or probably negative being much less likely to report unprotected sex than those who were unsure or definite about their positive status. This later finding must be treated with some caution because of the small numbers of respondents involved, and replication is required to confirm such an association. It should be emphasized, however, that the fact that a substantial proportion of HIV-positive respondents in the survey were prepared to admit to unsafe penetrative sex with new partners while on holiday has an epidemiological significance in its own right.

It is also important to point out that the estimates for unprotected sex reported from this survey are likely to be an underestimate, since they relate to the first or only holiday reported up to the time of the survey. More accurate annual estimates need to take account of all holidays undertaken over an entire year.

Men's holiday motivations, sexual expectations, levels of sexual activity and reported risk behaviour should also be considered in relation to holiday destinations, as the social context for such activities is of substantial significance from an ecological perspective. As Rotello (1997) points out, risk of infection is not simply a function of an individual's 'risky' behaviour; it is also crucially dependent upon the current prevalence of infection within networks of sexually active individuals. The levels of HIV infection among continually reconstituted, transient and highly sexually active populations of gay men in gay resorts is simply not known, but it may well be higher than the levels of HIV infection among gay men in the local home environment of many gay tourists.

The findings from the survey show clearly that men holidaying in gay destinations are significantly more likely to report sex with new partners than those in non-gay destinations. In addition, among men sexually active on holiday, those in gay destinations are much more likely to report sex with three or more new partners. Interestingly, however, the nature of the destination had little bearing on whether men reported penetrative or unprotected penetrative sex. Such behaviours appear to be more a function of psychological factors (preferences and personality) than situational circumstances, but unprotected sex in a gay destination may well carry greater risks.

HIV prevention implications

The need to address the dimension of travel and tourism in HIV prevention work with gay men has been recognized for a number of years in the UK, and campaigns have been undertaken during the summer months by the Health Education Authority and Terrence Higgins Trust through the gay press. During 1998, the Community HIV and AIDS Prevention Strategy (CHAPS) developed a travel HIV prevention campaign aimed at gay men, consisting of three leaflets, gay press advertisements and collaborative work with gay tour operators and travel agents (Clift *et al.*, 1998).

The first of the leaflets *Some Like It Hot!* is aimed at gay men holidaying in southern European gay resorts (Terrence Higgins Trust, 1998). The text illustrates the approach to HIV prevention which Rotello is so critical of, as it aims to promote safer sex while at the same time endorsing the value placed on casual sex with new partners within contemporary gay culture:

> Why do we go on holiday? To rest, relax, get some sun, sight see . . . and of course to have some fun . . . Some like it hot and what better way to enjoy yourself than to indulge in some hot sex in some far-off sun-kissed Mediterranean resort . . . Did you know . . . that strong condoms and lube are not always available in most gay Mediterranean resorts? Pack safely! Buy before you fly!
>
> (Terrence Higgins Trust, 1998: 1)

It is difficult, however, to imagine that any alternative stance to the one adopted by the CHAPS team would be well received, either by gay men who holiday in gay resort destinations or by the commercial interests involved in all levels of gay tourism (travel agents, tour operators, hotel proprietors, etc.). For CHAPS, the priorities were to produce material which would be acceptable and meaningful for gay tourists, which they would be likely to pick up and read and which would provide a basis for positive collaboration with gay tour companies asked to distribute them to clients. In this respect, the campaign and materials appear to have been well thought through.

Such campaigns are important in order to maintain general levels of awareness among gay men of the risks associated with sex on holiday, but they do involve a blanket approach which may have limited impact on levels of risky behaviour in holiday settings. The data reported here suggest that more specific targeting is required that takes account of the factors associated with sexual activity on holiday, and that active attempts at safer-sex promotion in holiday destinations need to be strengthened. Rotello's argument that condom promotion alone will not remove the collective threat of HIV for gay men does carry considerable weight, but it is clear from the current research that more work is still needed to ensure that condoms are readily available, if needed, in gay tourist destinations.

Taking condoms on holiday emerged as a significant factor associated with the likelihood of sex *per se*, but not taking condoms was also linked with the incidence of unprotected sex. Clearly, men who anticipate penetrative sex on holiday should be encouraged to take condoms with them. In the main, however, health promoters will be 'preaching to the converted', and more specific ways of targeting men who anticipate penetration but do not take condoms need to be found. It may be that some men expect to obtain condoms while on holiday, especially if they are visiting a gay destination. This is not necessarily the case, however, since just under half of the men on holiday in southern European gay resorts reported that condoms were not easily available.

Recent ethnographic fieldwork in the gay area of Ibiza Town (Callister *et al.*, 1998) confirmed that condoms were not available in most bars and clubs despite the provision of dark rooms in these establishments. In addition, only two condom-dispensing machines were found, one of which was broken and the other providing only condoms of uncertain strength and suitability for anal sex. It is clear, therefore, that health promotion approaches other than individual exhortation are needed to ensure that gay men have condoms available in holiday settings.

Conclusions

The evidence on the sexual activity and risk behaviour of gay men on holiday presented in this chapter points to the need to regard holidays, particularly in important gay cities or resorts, as an important focus for HIV prevention initiatives, targeting men both prior to departure and, more importantly, while on holiday. More should be done, especially in major southern European gay resorts, three of which are Spanish, to ensure widespread and easy availability of condoms.

Rotello's analysis of gay sexual ecology was published after the survey described in this chapter was undertaken, but his framework has proved useful in interpreting the data gathered and considering its implications. Rotello presents his own 'deep ecological' approach to AIDS prevention, which involves transforming gay culture and challenging the value placed on casual sex and confronting the vested commercial interests involved in establishing venues which facilitate easy sexual encounters between strangers. He makes a persuasive case for thinking that such interests contribute to promoting a social and cultural pattern which places gay men collectively at continued serious risk of HIV and other sexually transmitted infections, and his analysis and prescriptions can certainly be applied to the business interests involved in tourism services for gay men. Whether the kind of cultural shift advocated by Rotello is feasible and can be realized in practice, and what such a shift might mean for future patterns of gay tourism, is clearly a matter of debate. Currently in the UK, the dominant approach to HIV prevention for gay men is well illustrated by the stance adopted by CHAPS in their recent travel campaign: seeking to work within the existing sexual culture of gay men, and building collaborative relationships with community groups and gay business interests.

Two further points should be made by way of conclusion. First, as the focus in this chapter has been on the sexual aspects of gay tourism, other dimensions of tourism among gay men have been neglected. As a counterbalance, it is important to state that only approximately one-third of men in the sample surveyed regarded opportunities for sex as 'very important' when planning a holiday, and for a substantial proportion of gay men, other tourism motivations, such as rest and relaxation and the experience of different cultures and tourist sights, were of greater importance.

Second, the emphasis has been placed on sexual health risks in the holiday context. It is recognized, however, that a substantial minority of gay men have not travelled widely overseas and that for most men, holidays take up no more that two or three weeks of the year. It certainly appears to be the case that substantial proportions of men can be more sexually active in these few weeks than they are for the rest of the year at home, but clearly most of the cases of sexually transmitted infections and HIV among gay men are not acquired on holiday.

The commercial gay scene in the UK provides ample opportunities for gay men to meet new sexual partners, and the atmosphere and patterns of behaviour seen in gay clubs in London and other large cities may differ little from that found in similar venues in cities and resorts abroad that attract gay tourists. In addition, there has been a recent, substantial increase in London of venues offering men opportunities for casual sex (back-rooms and saunas), which gay men would, only a few years ago, have had to travel to gay destinations in Europe or the United States to experience. There is currently a concern that this development in commercial sexual environments for gay men may result in an increase in sexually transmitted diseases and further fuel the HIV/AIDS epidemic. Clearly, therefore, holidays are but one setting which needs to be considered in developing HIV prevention initiatives for gay men.

References

Bloor, M., Thomas, M., Abeni, D., Goujon, C., Hausser, D., Hubert, M., Kleiber, D. and Nieto, J. A. (1997) *Feasibility Study for Co-ordinated Community Action on the Improved Targeting of HIV/AIDS Prevention Campaigns among International*

198   *Stephen Clift and Simon Forrest*

Travellers: Final Report. Cardiff: School of Social and Administrative Studies, University of Wales (unpublished report).

Burston, P. (1997) Of vice and men. *Independent on Sunday Magazine*, 12 October, pp.4–9.

Callister, C., Luongo, M. and Clift, S. (1998) *A Feasibility Study in Ibiza Town for an Ethnographic Investigation of Gay Tourism and Sexual Behaviour in Gay Resort Destinations*. Canterbury: Centre for Health Education and Research, Canterbury Christ Church University College (unpublished report).

Carter, S., Horn, K., Hart, G., Dunbar, M., Scoular, A. and MacIntyre, S. (1997) The sexual behaviour of international travellers at two Glasgow GUM clinics. *International Journal of STD and AIDS* 8, 336–8.

Clift, S. and Forrest, S. (1998) *Gay Men, Travel and HIV Risk*. Canterbury: Centre for Health Education and Research, Canterbury Christ Church University College.

Clift, S. M. and Forrest, S. P. (1999) Factors associated with gay men's sexual behaviours and risk on holiday. *AIDS Care*.

Clift, S., Forrest, S., Callister, C. and Luongo, M. (1998) *Travel-Related HIV Prevention Work with Gay and Bisexual Men*. Canterbury: Centre for Health Education and Research, Canterbury Christ Church University College (unpublished report).

Clift, S. and Wilkins, J. (1995) Travel, sexual behaviour and gay men. In P. Aggleton, P. Davies and G. Hart (eds), *AIDS: Safety, Sexuality and Risk*. London: Taylor and Francis.

Conway, S., Gillies, P. and Slack, R. (1990) *The Health of Travellers*. Nottingham: Department of Public Health Medicine and Epidemiology, University of Nottingham and Nottingham Health Authority (unpublished report).

Daniels, D. G., Kell, P., Nelson, M. R. and Barton, S. C. (1992) Sexual behaviour among travellers: a study of genito-urinary medicine clinic attendees. *International Journal of STD and AIDS* 3, 437–8.

Ford, K., Wirawan, D. N. and Fajans, P. (1993) AIDS knowledge, condoms beliefs and sexual behaviour among male sex workers and male tourist clients in Bali, Indonesia. *Health Transition Review* 3, 191–204.

Ford, N. (1991) *Sex on Holiday: The HIV-Related Sexual Interaction of Young Tourists Visiting Torbay*. Exeter: Institute of Population Studies, University of Exeter (unpublished report).

Forrest, S. and Clift, S. (1998) Gay tourist space and sexual risk behaviour. In C. Aitchinson and F. Jordan (eds), *Gender, Space and Identity: Leisure, Culture and Commerce*. Eastbourne: Leisure Studies Association.

Gmünder, B. (1997) *Spartacus International Gay Guide*. Berlin: Bruno Gmünder Verlag GMBH.

Hawkes, S. J. and Hart, G. J. (1993) Travel, migration and HIV. *AIDS Care* 5, 207–14.

Hawkes, S., Hart, G. J., Bletsoe, E., Shergold, C. and Johnson, A. M. (1995) Risk behaviour and STD acquisition in genitourinary medicine clinic attenders who have travelled. *Genitourinary Medicine* 71, 351–4.

Hope, V. D. and MacArthur, C. (1998) Safer sex and social class: findings from a study of men using the 'gay scene' in the West Midlands Region of the United Kingdom. *AIDS Care* 10 (1), 81–8.

Kalichman, S. C., Greenberg, J. and Abel, G. G. (1997) HIV-positive men who engage in high-risk sexual behaviour: psychological characteristics and implications for prevention. *AIDS Care* **9** (4), 441–50.

Kleiber, D. and Wilke, M. (1993) Sexual behaviour of German (sex-) tourists. Paper presented at IXth International Conference on AIDS, Berlin.

Porter, J. D. H., Lea, G. and Carroll, B. (1996) HIV/AIDS and international travel: a global perspective. In S. Clift and S. Page (eds), *Health and the International Tourist*. London: Routledge.

Quinn, T. C. (1994) Population migration and the spread of types 1 and 2 human immunodeficiency viruses. *Proceedings of the National Academy of Sciences USA* **91**, 2407–14.

Rotello, G. (1997) *Sexual Ecology: AIDS and the Destiny of Gay Men*. New York: Dutton.

Terrence Higgins Trust (1998) *Some Like It Hot!* London: Terrence Higgins Trust (leaflet produced by the Community HIV/AIDS Prevention Strategy – CHAPS).

UK Health Departments (1995) *HIV and AIDS Health Promotion: An Evolving Strategy*. London: Department of Health.

Van de Van, P., Campbell, D., Kippax, S., Prestage, G., Crawford, J., Baxter, D. and Cooper, D. (1997) Factors associated with unprotected anal intercourse in gay men's casual partnerships in Sydney, Australia. *AIDS Care* **9** (6), 637–49.

Wang, J., Rodés, A., Blanch, C. and Casabona, J. (1997) HIV testing history among gay/bisexual men recruited in Barcelona: evidence of high levels of risk behaviour among self-reported HIV+ men. *Social Science and Medicine* **44** (4), 469–77.

Wilke, M. and Kleiber, D. (1992) Sexual behaviour of gay German (sex-) tourists in Thailand. Paper presented at VIth International AIDS Conference/IIIrd STD World Congress, Amsterdam.

12

Exploring the contexts and meanings of women's experiences of sexual intercourse on holiday

Michelle Thomas

You definitely react different though, with drink. It's just you do things you wouldn't do. Well you would sleep with someone a lot quicker than what you would at home, and that's holidays and drink. (Jodie)

Mind you (laughs) much to do with the fact that when we actually got to bed we were so drunk (laughs) I just couldn't, if I am drunk I just go to sleep you know, probably that was a major factor [why I didn't have sex]. (Tanya)

Introduction

This chapter is based on empirical qualitative research on women holiday-travellers. Using data from focus groups and in-depth interviews it will explore those factors that facilitate, and those that impede, the occurrence of sexual intercourse with a new sexual partner abroad. Studies have been conducted that have examined the occurrence of sexual intercourse quantitatively (Conway *et al.*, 1990; Hawkes *et al.*, 1994; Bloor *et al.*, 1997; Thomas *et al.*, 1997; see also Hart and Hawkes, and Clift and Forrest, this volume) and have offered important data on the nature and extent of new sexual relationships abroad. However, a more qualitative consideration of such new relationships is vital in order to fully understand the meaning and subjective experience of such new relationships to the women involved (Hawkes and Hart, 1993; Gillies and Slack, 1996; Black, 1997). It is through such an understanding that the potential health risks associated with such new relationships may be addressed.

Sexual behaviour may vary not just between individuals but also different types of behaviour may be adopted by an individual depending on the characteristics of the partner and the context in which sexual intercourse occurs (Davies *et al.*, 1993; Buysse and Van Oost, 1997). Holidays are a very specific social setting which thus require a specific understanding of sexual behaviour within this particular context (see Shields, 1990; Bloor, 1995; Wickens, 1995; Ford and Eiser, 1996). This analysis does not attempt to provide a quantitative understanding of factors that influence decisions to have intercourse, and so does not intend to suggest a 'recipe' that will predict the likelihood of sexual intercourse occurring. Instead, women's detailed narratives have been considered in order to uncover their own understandings of the factors that relate to sexual intercourse and the meaning these have for the women involved. The importance in viewing these factors beyond the attempt to quantify variables is clearly illustrated throughout the women's accounts. Such factors do not have one unified meaning, nor do they necessarily lead to one predictable outcome. The understandings of, and meanings associated with, different factors are multifarious. Factors affecting decisions to have sexual intercourse may interact with each other in a variety of ways and, indeed, individual women may use different factors in different ways in order to justify, give meaning to and account for behaviour.

Through examining women's in-depth accounts of their sexual relationships with new sexual partners the complex and intricate nature of socio-sexual relations is highlighted. At a time when 'safer sex' or 'protected' sex is equated with condom use, these women's accounts suggest that concerns about sexual health should incorporate understanding of both the physical and emotional risks associated with sexual intercourse. Condom use will not be discussed here, as it warrants a detailed discussion beyond the confines of this chapter. (For discussion of condom use, see Maxwell and Boyle, 1995; Holland *et al.*, 1991; Moore and Rosenthal, 1992; Kitzinger, 1993; Waldby *et al.*, 1993; Buysse and Van Oost, 1997; Rosenthal *et al.*, 1998.)

This chapter begins with an outline of the study design, before briefly considering the decision to focus on sexual intercourse as the specific sexual act for analysis. It goes on to examine sexual intercourse abroad, giving particular attention to those factors which either facilitate or inhibit sexual activity and the meaning associated with these factors to the women involved. Finally, findings are discussed with reference to campaigns concerning sexual health.

Research strategy

This chapter draws on data collected over a nine-month period in 1996. Five focus groups and 19 in-depth interviews were conducted with a total of 35 women holiday-travellers. Those women who participated in the focus groups had travelled abroad on holiday without a partner in the last two years. Those women who were interviewed individually reported a new romantic or sexual relationship on a holiday taken in the last two years. A small number of women participated in both the focus groups and the interviews. The women who participated were aged between 17 and 40. One woman described herself as 'Black African', the remaining women in the study described themselves as 'white'. Holiday destinations ranged from Australia and Asia to Spain and other European destinations. However, the most commonly reported holiday was a 'package holiday' to one of several popular European holiday resorts.

Recruitment for the study took place at a regional airport. A two-stage recruitment strategy was used, where women who appeared to be travelling alone were asked to complete a short questionnaire. They were then asked whether they would be willing to participate in a focus group or an individual interview, whichever was appropriate. Names and addresses were collected and the women were contacted at a later date. Due to the low frequency of flights at the regional airport and the fact that most passengers appeared to be travelling in families or couples, ten of the women were recruited using a 'snowball' sampling method and an additional two women were recruited via an advertisement on the Internet.

Discussion in focus groups was encouraged by means of focusing exercises. These exercises involved ranking a series of statements as to why women may be more likely to have a new sexual relationship abroad, followed by a consideration of images presented in holiday brochures. In the tradition of ethnographic interviewing (Spradley, 1979) the individual interviews were unstructured and led by the respondent. This allowed opportunity for understanding the respondent's view of the world rather than privileging the preconceived ideas and perceptions of the researcher. Both interviews and focus group discussions were fully transcribed and analysed.

The impact of research on the researched, and the particular issues it may raise for the respondents, has increasingly become a cause for concern to the researcher (Finch, 1984; Maynard, 1994). With this in mind, all respondents were assured of complete confidentiality. Participants in both focus groups and in-depth interviews were offered the opportunity to see their transcripts and make any changes that they felt necessary (in the event, only one woman wished to see her transcript and the only change she requested was an amendment to the chronological order of events in her new sexual relationship abroad). While the subject was indeed a sensitive one, women were typically open and helpful. Where women experienced any problems talking about sexual behaviour it was usually because they had difficulty finding the appropriate language to describe parts of the body or specific types of sexual behaviour rather than any reluctance to talk about this aspect of their relationship with the researcher. For several, new holiday relationships were concurrent to long-term relationships with a partner. In these instances, women often expressed pleasure in having the opportunity to talk about an experience in a way that they felt they could not with friends and family members. Respondent interest in the study was reflected by those women who agreed to participate in both focus groups and in-depth interviews, and those who volunteered to contact friends eligible for participation. In addition, many women asked to be informed of the results of the study.

Talking about sexual behaviour abroad may have raised concerns about sexual health or may have led to the discussion of subjects such as sexual violence or child abuse (see Holland and Ramazanoglu, 1994). Telephone numbers for help-lines for counselling, HIV-testing and local GUM clinics were also available from the interviewer in the event that any of the participants expressed any concerns regarding their sexual health or associated issues. All participants were offered brochures produced by the Health Education Authority providing information on travel health and travel and HIV/AIDS.

Major themes emerging from the study

Social significance of sexual intercourse

For the purposes of this discussion sexual intercourse is defined as the penetration of a woman's vagina by a man's penis. There are many reasons why this specific sexual act has been chosen as a focus for analysis. The act of sexual intercourse is laden with historical meaning. It is an act which has especial significance due to the particular risks associated with its execution. Sexual intercourse may result in fears about unwanted pregnancy and sexually transmitted diseases, as well as fears related to 'reputation' and emotional damage (Wilson, 1978; Vance, 1984; Lees, 1993; Richardson, 1993). Such fears were very real for the women in this study, and sexual intercourse was much associated with both 'pleasure and danger' (Vance, 1984).

The primacy of the act of sexual intercourse was reiterated throughout the interviews. When talking to women about their sexual behaviour with a new partner many professed that they did not have sex, and it was only when probed that it was revealed that other sexual activity took place. In the event, where women had had sexual intercourse, then accounts focused on this specific act rather than instances of other sexual behaviour which may have occurred prior to or after sexual intercourse. This absence may reflect the lack of culturally acceptable terminology for sexual activity other than sexual intercourse (see Spencer *et al.*, 1988). The fact that women did not speak about oral sex or mutual masturbation may indicate that these activities are particularly difficult to verbalize rather than that they not occur. Nevertheless, the historical construction of sexuality has focused on intercourse leading to orgasm as the 'normal' and 'natural' expression of sexuality (Bland, 1987; Richardson, 1993). The designation of other sexual acts as 'foreplay' reinforces this understanding of the ultimate aim of sexual experience as penetrative sex. This association is clearly illustrated in the response to the AIDS epidemic, where strategies for protection have focused on condom use and fewer partners rather than advocating non-penetrative sex as a means of sexual expression and pleasure (see Richardson, 1993; Wellings *et al.*, 1994). It is within this dominant construction of sexual expression that behaviour is experienced and understood. Thus, it is specifically the act of sexual intercourse that will be considered in this chapter.

Holiday romances and one-night stands

In considering the situations in which sexual intercourse occurs it is useful to have some understanding of the types of relationships being described. While the notion of a 'holiday romance' is pervasive, the exact constituents of such a relationship are difficult to specify. The selection criterion for individual interviews were that women had a 'new romantic or sexual' relationship while on holiday. The type of relationships reported ranged from what may be typically described as a 'one-night stand' (sexual intercourse upon first meeting with no intention for subsequent encounters) to relationships which lasted beyond the duration of the holiday and were seen as 'special', involving a degree of emotional commitment and intensity.

In this study 11 of the 19 women who were interviewed in depth about their new relationship abroad reported having sexual intercourse with a new partner on this trip. Four of the women who did not have sexual intercourse on the trip reported engaging in some sort of sexual activity, and four reported having sexual intercourse with a partner after the holiday ended. The figures for rates of sexual intercourse in a new relationship while abroad largely reflect those of quantitative studies. The EC survey of HIV-related risk behaviour of international travellers found that approximately two-thirds of women who reported a new romantic or sexual relationship abroad indicated that this relationship included sexual intercourse (Bloor *et al.*, 1997). An earlier study based on a sample drawn from a general-practice register showed that 5 out of 12 women who reported a new romantic or sexual relationship abroad indicated that this relationship included sexual intercourse (Conway *et al.*, 1990).

Context and meaning in decision-making about sexual intercourse

There were several factors which were reported to have influenced decisions regarding whether to have intercourse. However, it also seemed apparent that for several women sexual intercourse occurred without being preceded by a conscious decision-making process. Through the women's accounts it became possible to identify key factors that influenced decision-making. It was particularly interesting to note that many of the factors which were reported to have contributed to women having sexual intercourse were also offered as explanations as to why sexual intercourse did not occur: relationships, alcohol, factors relating to space and emotional involvement were all mentioned by women in their accounts of sexual behaviour with this new partner. I shall examine these in the following sections.

Attraction and pleasure

Historically, women have been seen as passive participants in sexual relations, providing an outlet for the 'uncontrollable' and 'natural' force of the male sexual drive (Bland, 1987; Segal, 1987; Walby, 1990). In contrast to male sexuality, which is constructed as having an autonomous existence, female sexual desire, if it has been seen to exist at all, has tended to be portrayed as a response to male advances rather than something women can feel independently (Bland, 1987). Accounts from this study present evidence to suggest that women have sexual desires and feelings and may actively seek out sexual gratification. When discussing reasons why they had sexual intercourse, sexual desire and the urge for sexual fulfilment were often mentioned as motivating factors. Indeed, some relationships appeared to be based primarily on a strong physical attraction and a desire for sexual pleasure:

> I think it was because at that stage I wasn't as strong as I had been when I was in the car, it was complete lust, it was just seeing his body, his 'six-pack', his muscles and this smile that he had, it was just a complete rush of 'I want I want I want' (laughs). (Angela)

> I knew that I fancied him, I knew that I liked him. I was more interested in the sex then, I don't think I was thinking about a relationship then. I just wanted to give him some pleasure and get some pleasure back, just more of a physical thing than thinking about relationships. (Kirsty)

From the women's narratives it became clear that there existed a recognition and acceptance that women had sexual urges and desires and that 'lust' was not an exclusively male feeling. Sexual desire and physical attraction was reported by several of the women as a motivation for engaging in sexual activity. Indeed, a degree of physical attraction (not surprisingly) appeared crucial for intercourse to take place. Those women who identified the desire for sexual gratification as a motivation for sexual intercourse engaged in sexual activity at least in part because of an anticipation of the physical pleasure it would provide. However, despite this awareness of their own sexual desires, many women reported difficulties in negotiating sexual encounters in a way that resulted in pleasure for them. Nevertheless, women appeared to be comfortable expressing sexual desires and intentions (at least in the research context) without feeling this would present a threat to their reputation.

Relationships
Holidays may be demarcated as a period removed from 'everyday life'. Indeed, the very separateness of holidays was part of their very specific nature. However, decisions regarding whether to have sexual intercourse with this new partner were also influenced by certain aspects of 'everyday life' in the form of pre-existing relationships. Such relationships appeared to cross the boundaries between holidays and everyday life and acted as both a deterrent and a motivating factor in decisions regarding sexual intercourse.

A brief consideration of the history of female sexuality reveals how one of the negative effects of female sexual liberation has been the increased sexualization of women (Jeffreys, 1985; Bland, 1987; Segal, 1987; Bartky, 1993; Forbes, 1996). The importance of the reinforcement of femininity through sexual desirability was reiterated in the women's accounts of their reasons for sexual intercourse. To have sexual intercourse with an attractive and popular male was seen as a positive reflection on the woman's own desirability. This reinforcement of sexual attractiveness was perhaps particularly important for those women whose trip had been motivated by a bad or broken relationship at home. Sexual intercourse with a new partner was seen as a means of blocking out unpleasant memories and increasing self-esteem, obliterating, at least temporarily, painful or difficult emotions resulting from a previous relationship:

> I had sex with him after Brian had left as well, I was feeling down. (Kirsty)

> I thought in a way it would be a brilliant thing to do, because it would really clear my head of Alex totally and just be something really nice to do. (Alison)

> Although I was with these blokes I really wanted to be with the bloke here, I just thought maybe it would take my mind off him 'cos he might not be there when I get home. (Lauren)

While previous or existing relationships might motivate women into having sexual intercourse, they could also act as a deterrent. Despite recent changes in sexual mores, monogamy has remained an important feature of sexual relationships in Britain, both within and outside marriage. Attitudinal questions in the National Survey of Sexual Attitudes and Lifestyles found that the majority of both men and women disapproved of sexual relationships both outside a live-in relationship and a regular relationship. Women seemed to consider monogamy as a more important ideal that male respondents (Johnson *et al.*, 1994), and it apparently exerted some influence on the women in this study. The presence of a regular sexual partner at home was frequently cited by women as a reason why they were reluctant to have sexual intercourse with this new partner abroad:

> It was purely because I had a boyfriend, I've always promised him I wouldn't cheat on him and I meant it when I said, but it sort of happened, that was why I didn't want to, nothing to do with Philippe, there was nothing that, you know . . . if I hadn't have had a boyfriend it would have happened right away I'm sure as sure (laughs), 'cos there was just something there. (Hannah)

The presence of a pre-existing partner at home presented a number of problems for women regarding decisions to have sexual intercourse. Since a commitment to monogamy was reported by all those women who had a pre-existing partner, there was concern that intercourse would result in a considerable amount of unpleasant and, for some, unmanageable guilt. The fear of discovery also acted as a barrier to intercourse, as this would have threatened the continuation of the relationship at home. Finally, many women saw intercourse as resulting in an increased emotional bond with a new partner, and this was also seen as potentially threatening to the pre-existing relationship.

In addition to these relationships, several of the men with whom women reported new relationships also had pre-existing relationships, which acted as an additional disincentive: 'I think if he hadn't have had a girlfriend I would have gone further I think, yeah' (Natascha).

An existing sexual partner suggested a potential barrier to the relationship's success. This was particularly pertinent for those women who considered the possibility of a long-term relationship. If sexual intercourse was seen to result in a closer bond with this new partner, it might also increase the potential for emotional damage should the relationship end prematurely. Sexual intercourse was thus avoided to reduce the possibility of hurt and emotional pain.

Thus, concerns about engaging in sexual intercourse where either party had a pre-existing sexual partner appeared to be largely due to fears about increased emotional involvement and the corresponding potential for emotional damage. Accounts from women reinforced the ideology of monogamy and in doing so also served to illustrate the significance of the act of sexual intercourse in the current construction of heterosexual relationships: concerns about being 'unfaithful' appeared to be centred on sexual intercourse as opposed to other sexual or 'romantic' activities. However, despite reservations concerning a pre-existing partner, many of these relationships did go on to involve sexual intercourse.

Alcohol and sex
The role of alcohol in sexual relationships may be complex, and studies have been inconclusive as to the exact nature of the relationship between

alcohol and sexual behaviour. Weatherburn *et al.* (1993) in their study of gay men found no statistically significant difference between sexual behaviours that took place after consuming alcohol and those that occurred without being preceded by alcohol consumption. However, the EC survey of international travellers found a link between frequency of alcohol consumption and level of intoxication and sexual behaviour, with those reporting higher frequency of alcohol intake and more instances of being a 'little drunk' or 'very drunk' on a trip abroad being more likely to report sex with a new partner while on the trip (Bloor *et al.*, 1997). In a Health Education Authority study of young travellers' sexual behaviour abroad, respondents themselves reported alcohol as one of the major influences on why they would be more likely to have sex on holiday (Thomas *et al.*, 1997). In this study alcohol was frequently mentioned in accounts of sexual intercourse with a new partner abroad. However, the degree to which behaviour was attributed to the influence of alcohol varied both between respondents and the type of sexual relationship that was being referred to. In instances where the relationship led to a 'one-night stand', alcohol was often cited as a contributory factor to intercourse taking place:

> We just went straight out and we went clubbing, and all I remember really is being in this club and Heather saying, 'do you like anybody in here?' 'cos she had her eye on this fella. And she had this glass about that big full of tequila and she said, 'drink this', and I just don't remember anything, waking up the next morning with this bloke beside me. And Heather having a bloke next door to her, different beds obviously. I was thinking 'blinkin' heck this is the first night' (laughs). (Tanya)

Alcohol was cited as directly influential less often in relationships of a longer duration. However the role of alcohol in sexual relationships was recognized. Indeed, women often attributed their lack of clarity about the events leading to sexual intercourse to over-indulgence in alcohol.

While few women directly attributed the act of sexual intercourse to alcohol intake, most reported having been drinking when sexual intercourse occurred. Alcohol was mentioned most frequently in the context of a lessening of inhibitions regarding socio-sexual behaviour. Women talked about the increased confidence they felt when they had been drinking and how this helped to ease potentially uncomfortable situations such as the first meeting or the first instance of sexual intercourse:

> Yeah, 'cos then I'm more confident then. It's like if I haven't had a drink, you know, and I'm sitting there talking to someone I'm like really quiet, I whispers to them, and if they says something I just goes bright red. If I've had a drink like it don't register properly, it's like if I'm ashamed, you know, I don't go red, I just thinks, 'Oh my God', you know, they don't know I'm ashamed once I've had a drink. It's easier if I has a drink, I knows what I'm up to. (Naomi)

> 'Cos I'm shy, believe it or not, if I'm not under the influence of drink I am shy, I am shy. I remember sitting on the bed thinking, 'Oh yeah'. I haven't met him

since he went away you know and every night that I met him practically I was a bit drunk, and when I was here sitting with him sober thinking, 'Oh God', you know. (Tanya)

In most instances women reported that one or both parties had been drinking alcohol at the time sexual intercourse took place. However, it appeared that sexual behaviour was rarely attributed entirely to the effect of alcohol. What was important was the disinhibiting effect of drinking, which served both to enhance and ease early socio-sexual relations.

Alcohol was not seen as solely facilitating sexual intercourse but could also actually prevent it. The following excerpt from a focus group discussion illustrates not only the importance of the social situation in which alcohol is consumed and the resulting increase in confidence but also the detrimental effect that too much drink has on potential relationships:

JACKIE: You get more confident. You'll just go up and talk to anyone.
DEBBIE: Whenever you go up to a bar anyway, you always meet people by the bar.
JULIET: The majority of people drink continually on holidays, don't they?
JACKIE: And they used to get you into bars by offering you free drinks.
MT: Does that affect whether you have a relationship or not?
JULIET: Well, you meet more people in the bar than you would sitting on the beach having a bottle of water.
ABIGAIL: Unless you have that extra one and then you just want to sit with your head down the toilet.
JACKIE: It gives you more confidence to go up and talk to people, if you think 'Oh, he's quite nice'.
JULIET: It is an opportunity, because if there is someone at the bar and that you think is all right you can go up there and see him and talk.

Large quantities of drink could result in nausea, but more frequently alcohol was seen to decrease the likelihood of sexual activity because of its narcotic effect:

I was just falling asleep, 'cos I was so tired I think, 'cos I was drinking and you know when I have a drink I usually get really sleepy, but I was just falling asleep basically, so nothing had happened then. (Laura)

No, I was too sloshed to think about it [sex] really, I just wanted my bed (laughs). (Adele)

Clearly the role of alcohol in sexual behaviour is complex. The fact that alcohol consumption was frequently concurrent with sexual activity should not necessarily be taken to indicate a causal relationship. It is possible that this simply relates to the social circumstances in which alcohol is consumed. Alcohol and a good nightlife were important features of the holidays for many women. Further, the reported frequency with which alcohol was consumed, combined with the temporal boundaries surrounding new sexual relationships, suggests that in many cases it was almost inevitable that sexual intercourse would be concomitant with a period of alcohol consumption: many relationships were restricted, at least initially, to meeting in the evenings and the majority of alcohol consumption occurred in the same period.

It has been argued that certain levels of alcohol may act as a 'disinhibitor', and that a curvilinear relationship exists between alcohol intake and sexual arousal (Robertson, 1990, quoted in Plant and Plant, 1994). Indeed, for women in this study the crucial factor was the quantity of alcohol consumed. While small amounts of alcohol may have reduced inhibitions and eased sexual relations, high levels of alcohol resulted in sickness or tiredness that were unconducive to the act of intercourse. However, while small amounts of alcohol may have facilitated intercourse, the influence of alcohol alone was rarely seen as a major contributory factor. Rather, it was the entire social situation in which alcohol was consumed, combined with the general 'holiday atmosphere' and the increased confidence gained from drinking alcohol, which increased the opportunity for a new sexual relationship.

Space and privacy

In a small number of instances logistical problems relating to accommodation were given as a reason why sexual intercourse (or sexual activity) occurred. In order for sexual intercourse to take place the couple had to ensure the necessary privacy, and this often meant changing sleeping arrangements with travel companions. The pressure to provide privacy for a friend could also result in sexual intercourse:

> The last night Liz had the hotel room so I didn't really . . . I wanted to go back with him but I didn't . . . I didn't know if he wanted me there, so I said you know Liz and Vince and he said . . . there's no problem you can stay. (Judy)

> It was a combination of things, basically. I knew that Catrin and Toby were going to be together, so she would have been either in our hotel room or in his, so if she was in our hotel room I was going to have to stay somewhere else, so chances are I would have ended up going off with someone anyway, not necessarily for sex but to stay the night somewhere, but because he was attracted to me, he was coming on to me, then it was him. (Emily)

> Then the next time I slept with Simon, then I had to stay out anyway 'cos she had a bloke in the hotel, so it was a good job I did meet him. (Naomi)

A consequence of securing the necessary privacy for sexual intercourse was that the women were subsequently put in a situation where sex was available, if not always expected or desired. Needing somewhere to stay, they would often end up with males known only to the women for the duration of the holiday. While none of the women involved reported situations where men became aggressive or they felt threatened, they did refer to instances when men had indicated their expectation and desire for sexual intercourse:

> No he didn't pressure me, he just said, 'I thought that was the understanding of coming back to your room' and whatever, and I said, 'Well no, I'm not going to', and he just said, 'Well that's up to you but I think you'd enjoy it', which just made me laugh. He didn't pressure me, he just asked me to, and when I said 'No', he was OK. (Emily)

> I did go up there, and I went up there with the intention of just having a chat and stuff you know, but he kept saying come to bed with me and all this, and I wouldn't. But he wasn't like putting pressure on me, but he said, 'Oh I'd really like something to happen'. (Judy)

It is possible that while the women did not perceive men's expressions of their intent or expectation to have intercourse as a form of pressure or coercion, those women who engaged in sexual intercourse or sexual activity in these situations may have been victims of a form of male sexual violence resulting from 'ideologies of compliance' (Kelly, 1987). It has been argued that a consequence of the change in sexual mores has taken away women's right to say 'no' (Bland, 1987). Indeed, this study provided evidence to suggest that such changes have resulted in different problems for women. Women are clearly not without power and many presented accounts where they made active decisions regarding sexual behaviour. However, although sharing accommodation with unknown men was not usual, it has important implications regarding the safety of female travellers.

While limitation of space occasionally resulted in sexual intercourse, it was also one of the most frequently cited reasons for sexual intercourse not taking place. The particular type of holidays taken often involved women sharing hotel rooms or apartment bedrooms with at least one other travel companion. As a result, the opportunity for sexual intercourse could not arise simply because of the lack of space and privacy:

> Yeah, I kissed him on holiday, probably would have done something like I said if Jodie was sleeping in a different room, but yeah we slept together when we got home. (Tanya)

> And then we were together then, a couple of nights later, well we were on our own, and we could have, but I just didn't 'cos I just thought I don't want to do it here, just in case anybody comes home. It was just . . . it was the lack of privacy, 'cos if we'd have been in my apartment Ruth could have come in any second, if we'd been in his apartment all the lads could have come in. But that was that, so we just left it like that. (Jodie)

> There wasn't much of a physical side while we were on holiday, purely because we were all together, so there couldn't be in reality. (Lucy)

Concerns about being overheard, or friends or travel companions arriving unexpectedly, were often cited as disincentives to sexual intercourse. In addition, the social nature of a holiday occasionally meant that accommodation would be shared with more than just the initial travel companion(s). Parties in rooms often occurred, so there was little privacy during the night, and the daytime was rarely seen as a suitable time for sexual intercourse. In some instances, these problems were foreseen before the onset of a relationship, and complex strategies and 'rules' were devised to overcome such potential obstacles to sexual gratification (typically this involved systems of swapping beds and utilizing balconies, depending on the number of members of the group who returned to the accommodation with a new sexual partner). However, the nature of shared holiday accommodation often acted as a barrier to intercourse occurring. The EC study of international travellers found that of those respondents who had new sexual partners on a trip abroad, those who were travelling alone were more likely to report higher frequency of intercourse than those who were travelling with one or more others (Bloor *et al.*, 1997). This could be a reflection of an increased propensity for loneliness and a corresponding need for intimacy, although it may also simply reflect the difficulties of ensuring privacy in shared holiday accommodation.

Emotions and fear of vulnerability
The traditional association for women of sex with love and romance implies the existence of an emotional aspect to these sexual relationships. Indeed, given the small proportion of women who claimed to get any physical pleasure from sexual intercourse, it is possible that sexual desire may be motivated at least in part by the need for emotional fulfilment (Koedt, 1972). Duncombe and Marsden (1993) have pointed to women's need for emotional nurture, a need they have traditionally sought to be fulfilled by men. Indeed, Radway (1994), in her study of romance readers, found that a caring, nurturing and emotional hero was a key feature in women's ideal romances. For some women in this study it appeared that intimacy and not necessarily sex was a critical aspect of sexual relationships. However, in order to achieve the necessary intimacy sex often occurred:

> I wanted to have sex just to feel . . . it sounds silly . . . but just to feel that much closer to him, I wanted to feel much closer to him. (Kirsty)

> I know for me it was definitely because I was missing my boyfriend and I was feeling really down about my work and being away from home and I really was desperate for a cuddle I think, was how it started, and sort of we were both drunk and together and cuddled, and it led from there. (Hannah)

> I think what I felt, it's not so much having a partner but having the affection, the attention, that side of things, you know, that's what I miss to be honest, and that's sometimes all I'm looking for, but then men never are, are they? (Judy)

Indeed, for many women sexual intercourse signified a change in the relationship which was characterized by a greater degree of intimacy and commitment:

> It got more intense [after sexual intercourse], we obviously knew a hundred per cent then we mean a great deal, 'cos he knew, because I had been so difficult about it and I hadn't wanted to, he knew that I had decided that it meant a great deal more to me because I had actually relented, and I suppose he reacted in an equal way really, he was that much more keen, not keen but closer. (Melanie)

> Yeah, you do get a lot closer definitely. (Jodie)

> I felt closer to him actually, I felt more confident, I liked him even more really 'cos I felt a bit closer to him. (Laura)

Sexual intercourse appeared to be meaningful in that it signified a greater commitment to the relationship and to the individual. Engaging in intercourse seemed to imply a degree of trust and a depth of feeling which would not be conveyed if sexual intercourse was refused. Correspondingly, men often challenged women's commitment to the relationship if they refused to have intercourse, and this was used as a means of pressuring for sexual intercourse to take place. Holidays and travel abroad can be a time when the need for a close emotional bond with someone may be particularly acute. A strange country and culture may prove psychologically demanding, and separation from home and family can result in feelings of loneliness. In these situations the intimacy offered by a new sexual relationship may appear especially alluring.

The need for emotional closeness that may have precipitated sexual intercourse for some women, was for others, however, a disincentive. Fear of emotional involvement in a relationship that was seen to have only a very short life span was cited as a reason not to have intercourse:

> I think it is just reckless to go off on a week-long holiday, expect to sleep with someone and go home and not have any problems with that. I think emotionally and psychologically that's going to ruin you. (Natalie)

> I also thought I probably would never see him again and 'cos he was quite nice and I thought if I slept with him then I would be more upset if I thought I would never see him again. If I didn't, then it would just be a snog or a bit of fun or whatever and he'd go off and it would be fine, so it was probably that as well. (Emily)

While this study has provided evidence to suggest that for women sexual intercourse can be predominantly a function of their sexual drives and desires, for many others intercourse has important emotional implications. For several women decisions regarding intercourse were partially a function of managing emotional needs and reducing the potential for emotional damage.

Anonymity

The importance of women's sexual reputations has long been recognized (Wilson, 1978; Lees, 1993). The anonymity of a holiday abroad may offer an opportunity for women to have a short-term sexual relationship which does not threaten their reputation. Indeed, for many, anonymity had a considerable influence in decisions regarding sexual intercourse:

> I'd never do stuff like that [have sexual intercourse] at home, 'cos you'd probably find out it's your friend's cousin or something innit, and then the whole world knows then. (Naomi)

> 'Cos probably on holiday nobody's going to find out, like you said on holiday no one has to worry about what other people think, so, if you do sleep with somebody, who cares? Only you do, as long as you are careful and nobody else is going to find out about it. (Tanya)

> If you were on holiday and you did something bad, you'd never remember, if it was at home and I was sleeping 'round', I know I would get found out, and the reputation would always be there, but on holidays it don't matter. (Louise)

> VICTORIA: You wouldn't have a reputation when you were on holidays there, 'cos nobody's going to think, 'Oh, I wonder what she did last night?'
> SARAH: You haven't got people gossiping about you.
> VICTORIA: If anything you've got something to live up to (laughs).
> SARAH: Yeah (laughs).

Holidays offered some anonymity which enabled women to have sexual intercourse without worrying about their reputations. However, anonymity was not guaranteed for many women, as travel companions were able to monitor and judge behaviour and also potentially threaten their reputation on the return home. The anticipated reaction of travel companions was often of considerable importance in decisions regarding sexual intercourse:

> Oh God, yeah, you can do what you want when nobody knows you, it's marvellous! (laughs). Brilliant, nobody knows you, it's fabulous. If you go on holiday with some friends then it changes, you, you are just more reserved, you just . . . careful what you do, careful what you say. (Jodie)

> I just don't like her judgemental ways of reporting things, not that she would report to my parents, but I just don't want her to know. I just didn't want her judgements, 'Oh you slapper' sort of judgements. (Natascha)

> I just wondered what she would think of me, I think that is what it comes down to, if I did anything like that, I know she wouldn't think badly of me at all, because she's my friend and everything, but I know a little bit of me thought, 'Oh no, I wonder what she would say if I did something like that?' (Alison)

The predicted reactions of travel companions was important in influencing behaviour. Women who had met new partners on their holiday were deterred from engaging in sexual intercourse if it was felt that this would lead to judgements and possible sanctions from travel companions. Not only did women want to avoid possible confrontation and unpleasantness but travel companions also presented an important link between the world of holidays and the world of everyday life. The protection that anonymity offered to their sexual reputations was thus threatened if a degree of trust and understanding did not exist between holiday companions. Reputations at home could be threatened if behaviour on holiday was communicated.

Thus, travel companions had a considerable effect on the sexual behaviour of women holidaymakers. Co-operation was often required to facilitate the necessary privacy for sexual intercourse to occur (see above), as well as a confidence that sexual behaviour with a new partner would neither be judged negatively nor reported at home. Crossing the boundaries between holidays and everyday life, such companies potentially carried with them the norms and ideologies governing behaviour at home. In a space where such conventional norms might well be abandoned or lost, the willingness of such travel companions also to disregard these norms may exert considerable influence on behaviour. In this way travel companions could exert a degree of peer pressure which might act as a deterrent to sexual intercourse. However, companions can also influence sexual behaviour in the opposite direction. Peer pressure may force women to behave in ways which conform with the behaviour, beliefs and ideals of their peers. Thus, a sexually active travel companion may exert pressure on other companions to become engaged in sexual behaviour with a new partner.

Conclusions

In the above discussion I have attempted to highlight some of the factors that women identified as affecting their decisions regarding sexual intercourse. Clearly, such factors are multiple, but environmental considerations such as access to privacy and the necessary social situations for relaxation and the reduction of inhibitions appeared to be particularly significant. Relaxation and decreased inhibitions were seen as a function of increased alcohol intake, anonymity and the general 'holiday atmosphere'. Many women reported that they engaged in sexual intercourse significantly earlier in the relationship than they would do at home, and saw this as reflecting in part the anonymity temporal changes that they experienced while on holiday. Factors which prevented intercourse from occurring commonly included lack of privacy, over-indulgence in alcohol and fear of emotional damage.

In considering data on factors that impede and facilitate intercourse, what emerged as particularly salient was the fact that women apparently found it easier to explain why sex *didn't* happen than to offer reasons why they did decide to have sex with a new partner. There are a number of possible explanations for this. First, it may be that as sex is so often seen as an inevitable part of the relationship, women are not conscious of why they wanted sex. Second, if men do pressurize women for sex as much as we are led to believe, women may be more practised in accounting for their disinclination to have sexual intercourse than in explaining their desire to have sex. Third, there is considerable evidence to suggest that women continue to take a passive role in sexual relations, and thus a decision regarding whether to have intercourse may not have been made explicitly. Finally, the apparent difficulty in accounting for their motivations may be related to the issue of spontaneity: traditionally, for women to express sexuality in an acceptable way, it has to be associated with passion and spontaneity not premeditation (see Lees, 1993; Richardson, 1993). Thus, the difficulties in explaining motivations for sexual intercourse may also be related to the way that these 'decisions' are made (if, indeed, conscious decisions are made at all) and the processes which lead to the act.

As ideologies governing women's sexual behaviour have changed, so women have encountered new difficulties in negotiating sexual relationships and consenting to intercourse about which they feel ambivalent or undecided (Lear, 1997; see also Bland, 1987; Forbes, 1996). The decision to say 'no' to sexual intercourse and the process of negotiation within a sexual relationship may be particularly problematic in a new relationship abroad, due to the strong association between holidays and sex and the subsequent pressure this provokes (see Clift, 1994). The women's accounts suggested that for many it was not a case of whether to have intercourse but rather when and where intercourse was going to take place.

The emergence of HIV/AIDS has led to a considerable body of research on sexual health and sexual behaviour. Such research and the corresponding health education campaigns have focused on condom use as a means of promoting 'safer sex' and 'healthy sexuality'. However, the ambivalence regarding sexual intercourse and the difficulties some women felt in making the decision not to have intercourse indicate that there continue to exist other health implications regarding sexual intercourse that have recently been ignored. The right of women to say 'no' to unwanted sexual advances from all men, including their husbands, has been fought for since the beginning of the century (Bland, 1987). However, at the end of the same century, despite the changes in sexual mores and the advent of HIV, it seems the very same issues are still at stake. Many women still do not have the means to make choices regarding sexual intercourse.

The accounts from women in this study suggest that protection against the risks associated with sexual intercourse should not be limited to protection from pregnancy and STDs. 'Safer sex' may be equated with condom use but condoms cannot protect against coerced sex and the subsequent emotional damage this may entail. The pressure on women to consent to unwanted intercourse can be seen in the accounts of women sharing sleeping accommodation with males met on the holiday in order to provide the necessary privacy for friends who wish to engage in sexual intercourse with new partners. In considering incentives to promote healthy sexuality, the first step should be to ensure that sexual intercourse occurs between fully consenting individuals. This may mean efforts to empower women and move away from the focus on penetrative sex as the ultimate goal of sexual relations.

If negotiation between heterosexual couples is such that decisions to have intercourse are made in this way, then it provides little hope for successful negotiation of condom use. Health education campaigns have traditionally focused on condom use as a means of preventing HIV spread (Wellings *et al.*, 1994). This has been criticized by a number of people who argue that such a strategy ignores the power relations inherent in any heterosexual relationship (Holland *et al.*, 1991; Richardson, 1993). These power relations will define and limit communication within such heterosexual encounters (Holland *et al.*, 1991). Furthermore, health education campaigns which focus on condom use ignore the fact that the process of negotiating sexual intercourse with a new partner is frequently ambiguous and silent (Kent *et al.*, 1990). Exploring the context in which women decided to have sexual intercourse with these new sexual partners highlights the inadequacy of such campaigns. Factors which facilitate sexual intercourse may not necessarily facilitate 'safer sex'. Many women talked about the importance of alcohol in easing potentially stressful situations, in particular emphasizing its influence in the first sexual encounters with a new partner. While at certain levels they felt it helped reduce inhibitions which may have facilitated the introduction of condoms, higher levels of alcohol intake further remove the possibility of rational negotiation between new sexual partners.

Finally, it is worth drawing attention to the considerable number of women who reported that they or their new partners were involved in concurrent relationships. It has been argued that in the analysis of behavioural data relating to HIV, one must move beyond the individual as a unit of analysis and consider partnerships and wider sexual networks. In particular, recent research has drawn attention to the role of concurrent partnerships in the amplification of the HIV epidemic (Hudson, 1993; Morris and Kretzschmar, 1997), as they increase the size of the 'network' and thus the number of persons connected at any one time. In this way, the virus is not limited to a monogamous partnership but can move on to infect others who are part of this network (see Morris and Kretzschmar, 1997). When taken without a regular partner, holidays may well offer the opportunity for numerous concurrent relationships (Thomas *et al.*, 1997). Those women who are involved in sexual networks of this type may be putting themselves and their partners at particular risk.

Accounts from the women in my study appeared to challenge the idea that 'love and commitment' are necessary preconditions for the enjoyment of sexual activity. However, it also seemed that sexual intercourse was seen as an inevitable part of a relationship for many women. Thus, data from this study suggest that rather than simply focusing on condom use as a means of preventing the spread of disease, campaigns should concentrate on the empowerment of women so that they feel able to negotiate new sexual relationships in a way that protects them both physically and emotionally. STDs, unwanted pregnancy and HIV/AIDS are of course crucial health concerns, but there are other risks from sexual intercourse that cannot be avoided by using a condom, including sexual violence (in the form of emotional coercion or more physical forms) and the emotional damage associated with such sexual encounters. Health education campaigns concerned with healthy sexuality should also attempt to draw attention away from the dominant focus on sexual intercourse as the key aspect of heterosexual sexual relationships, encouraging instead other means of sexual pleasure and expression within heterosexual relationships.

References

Bartky, S. (1993) Foucault, femininity and the modernisation of patriarchal power. In S. Jackson (ed.), *Women's Studies: A Reader*. London: Harvester and Wheatsheaf.

Black, P. (1997) Sexual behaviour and travel: quantitative and qualitative perspectives on the behaviour of genito-urinary medicine clinic attenders. In S. Clift and P. Grabowski (eds), *Tourism and Health: Risks, Research and Responses*. London: Pinter.

Bland, L. (1987) Purity, motherhood, pleasure or threat? Definitions of female sexuality 1900–1970s. In C. Cartledge and J. Ryan (eds), *Sex and Love: New Thoughts on Old Contradictions*. London: The Women's Press.

Bloor, M. (1995) HIV-related risk behaviour among international travellers. In D. Fitzsimons, V. Hardy and K. Tolley (eds), *Economic and Social Impact of AIDS in Europe*. London: Cassell and National AIDS Trust.

Bloor, M., Thomas, M., Abeni, D., Goujon, C., Hausser, D., Hubert, M., Kleiber, D. and Nieto, J. A. (1997) *Feasibility Study for Co-ordinated Community Action on the Improved Targeting of HIV/AIDS Prevention Campaigns among International Travellers*. Cardiff: University of Wales (unpublished report).

Buysse, A. and Van Oost, P. (1997) 'Appropriate' male and female safer sexual behaviour in heterosexual relationships. *AIDS Care* 9 (5), 549–61.

Clift, S. (1994) *Romance and Sex on Holidays Abroad: A Study of Magazine Representations*. Travel, Lifestyles and Health Project Working Paper No. 4, Canterbury: Canterbury Christ Church College.

Conway, S., Gillies, P. and Slack, R. (1990) *The Health of Travellers*. Nottingham: Department of Public Health Medicine and Epidemiology, University of Nottingham and Nottingham Health Authority (unpublished report).

Davies, P. M., Hickson, F. C. I., Weatherburn, P. and Hunt, A. J. (1993) *AIDS: Sex and Gay Men*. London: The Falmer Press.

Duncombe, J. and Marsden, D. (1993) Love and intimacy: the gender division of emotion and 'emotion work'. *Sociology* **27** (2), 221–41.

Finch, J. (1984) 'It's great to have someone to talk to': the ethics and politics of interviewing women. In C. Bell and H. Roberts (eds), *Social Researching: Politics, Problems and Practice.* London: Routledge and Kegan Paul.

Forbes, J. S. (1996) Disciplining women in contemporary discourses of sexuality. *Journal of Gender Studies* **5** (2), 177–89.

Ford, N. and Eiser, J. R. (1996) Risk and liminality: the HIV-related socio-sexual interaction of young tourists. In S. Clift and S. Page (eds), *Health and the International Tourist.* London: Routledge.

Gillies, P. and Slack, R. (1996) Context and culture in HIV prevention: the importance of holidays? In S. Clift and S. Page (eds), *Health and the International Tourist.* London: Routledge.

Hawkes, S. J. and Hart, G. J. (1993) Travel, migration and HIV. *AIDS Care* **5**, 207–14.

Hawkes, S., Hart, G. J., Johnson, A. M., Shergold, C., Ross, E., Herbert, K. M., Mortimer, P., Parry, J. V. and Mabey, D. (1994) Risk behaviour and HIV prevalence in international travellers. *AIDS* **8**, 247–52.

Holland, J. and Ramazanoglu, C. (1994). Coming to conclusions: power and interpretation in researching young women's sexuality. In M. Maynard and J. Purvis (eds), *Researching Women's Lives from a Feminist Perspective.* London: Taylor and Francis.

Holland, J., Ramazanoglu, C., Scott, S., Sharpe, S. and Thompson, R. (1991) Between embarrassment and trust: young women and the diversity of condom use. In P. Aggleton, P. Davies and G. Hart (eds), *AIDS Responses, Interventions and Care.* London: The Falmer Press.

Hudson, C. P. (1993) Concurrent partnerships could cause AIDS epidemics. *International Journal of STD and AIDS* **4**, 249–53

Jeffreys, S. (1985) *The Spinster and Her Enemies: Feminism and Sexuality 1880–1930.* London: Pandora.

Johnson, A., Wadsworth, J., Wellings, K. and Field, J. (1994) *Sexual Attitudes and Lifestyles.* Oxford: Blackwell.

Kelly, L. (1987) The continuum of sexual violence. In J. Hamner and M. Maynard (eds), *Women, Violence and Social Control.* London: Macmillan.

Kent, V., Davies, M., Deverell, K. and Gottesman, S. (1990) Social interaction routines involved in heterosexual encounters: preludes to first intercourse. Paper presented at the Social Aspects of AIDS Conference, London.

Kitzinger, J. (1993) Safer sex and dangerous reputations: contradictions for young women negotiating condom use. Working Paper No. 47. Edinburgh: Medical Research Council, Medical Sociology Unit.

Koedt, A. (1972) The myth of the vaginal orgasm. In A. Koedt, E. Levine and A. Rapone (eds), *Radical Feminism.* New York: Quadrangle.

Lear, D. (1997) *Sex and Sexuality: Risks and Relationships in the Age of AIDS.* London: Sage.

Lees, S. (1993) *Sugar and Spice: Sexuality and Adolescent Girls.* Harmondsworth: Penguin.

Maxwell, C. and Boyle, M. (1995) Risky heterosexual practices amongst women over 30: gender, power and long term relationships. *AIDS Care* **7** (3), 277–93.

Maynard, M. (1994) Methods, practice and epistemology: the debate about feminism and research. In M. Maynard and J. Purvis (eds), *Researching Women's Lives from a Feminist Perspective*. London: Taylor and Francis.

Moore, S. and Rosenthal, D. (1992) The context of adolescent sexuality: safe sex implications. *Journal of Adolescence* **15**, 415–35.

Morris, M. and Kretzschmar, M. (1997) Concurrent partnerships and the spread of HIV. *AIDS* **11**, 651–8.

Plant, M. and Plant, M. (1994) *Risk-Takers: Alcohol, Drugs, Sex and Youth*. London: Routledge.

Radway, J. (1994) *Reading the Romance: Women, Patriarchy and Literature*. London: Verso.

Richardson, D. (1993) The challenge of AIDS. In S. Jackson (ed.), *Women's Studies: A Reader*. London: Harvester and Wheatsheaf.

Robertson, J. A. (1990) *The Role of Alcohol and Illicit Drugs in Marital Adjustment of Young People*. MPhil thesis, University of Edinburgh.

Rosenthal, D., Gifford, S. and Moore, S. (1998) Safe sex or safe love: competing discourses. *AIDS Care* **10** (1), 35–47.

Segal, L. (1987) Sensual uncertainty, or why the clitoris is not enough. In C. Cartledge and J. Ryan (eds), *Sex and Love: New Thoughts on Old Contradictions*. London: The Women's Press.

Shields, R. (1990) The 'system of pleasure': liminality and the carnivalesque at Brighton. *Theory, Culture and Society* **7**, 39–72.

Spencer, L., Faulkner, A. and Keegan, J. (1988) *Talking about Sex: Asking the Public about Sexual Behaviour and Attitudes*. London: SCPR Report for the Health Education Authority.

Spradley, J. P. (1979) *The Ethnographic Interview*. London: Rinehart and Winston.

Thomas, M., Bloor, M. and Crosier, A. (1997) *Young People and International Travel: HIV Prevention and Health Promotion*. London: Health Education Authority.

Vance, C. (1984) Pleasure and danger: towards a politics of sexuality. In C. Vance (ed.), *Pleasure and Danger: Exploring Female Sexuality*. London: Routledge and Kegan Paul.

Waldby, S. (1990) *Theorising Patriarchy*. Oxford: Blackwell.

Weatherburn, P., Davies, P., Hickson, F., Hunt, A., McManus, T. and Coxon, A. (1993) No connection between alcohol use and unsafe sex among gay and bi-sexual men. *AIDS* **7**, 115–21.

Wellings, K., Field, J., Johnson, A. and Wadsworth, J. (1994) *Sexual Behaviour in Britain: The National Survey of Sexual Attitudes and Lifestyles*. Harmondsworth: Penguin.

Wickens, E. (1995) The exodus to the sun: the tourist experience in Chalkidiki, Northern Greece. *Social Science Teacher* **25** (1), 26–31.

Wilson, D. (1978) Sexual codes and conduct: a study of teenage girls. In C. Smart and B. Smart (eds), *Women, Sexuality and Social Control*. London: Routledge and Kegan Paul.

13

EscapeEs: what sort of ecstasy do package tour ravers seek?

*Furzana Khan, Jason Ditton, Lawrence Elliott,
Emma Short, Anita Morrison, Stephen Farrall and
Laurence Gruer*

A tan doesn't mean that much to me. We didn't come here for a suntan. We came here for seven nights of hard core music. (Alan)

I came over to get drunk. (Rab)

Dancin', drink and drugs. What else is a holiday for? (Jackie)

For it was Saturday night, the best and bingiest glad-time of the week, one of the fifty-two holidays in the slow-turning Big Wheel of the year, a violent preamble to a prostrate Sabbath. Piled-up passions were exploded on Saturday night, and the effect of a week's monotonous graft in the factory was swilled out of your system in a burst of goodwill. You followed the motto of 'be drunk and be happy', kept your crafty arms around female waists, and felt the beer going beneficially down into the elastic capacity of your guts.

(Sillitoe, 1958: 9)

Introduction

Research methodologists conventionally concentrate on every aspect of the research setting bar one – its relative pleasurability. Others quiz shop-floor workers, cross-examine prisoners, question drug addicts or corner politicians. We, essentially, went on *holiday*. Armed with clip-boards, questionnaires, tape-recorders, yes; but also, and unusually for researchers, with sun cream, swimsuits and holiday money. For, in September 1995, we accompanied 203 ravers on a package holiday in a Mediterranean island resort famous for its acid-house music to see what truth there was, if any, in the regular tabloid newspaper stories of endless vacational sun, sea, sand and sex. How so?

Against a background of inordinate success in containing the spread of the HIV virus in the Greater Glasgow area, the Health Board had become increasingly concerned that trips undertaken by local inhabitants outwith the area might unwittingly open windows of infection which could later be spread locally. It was also recognized that the gradual growth of relatively cheap package holidays to hot Mediterranean resorts opened another, quite different, risk to fair-skinned Scots: sunburn today, and expensive and hard-to-treat skin cancer tomorrow.

Initial prevention campaigns had concentrated on offering advice (together with condoms and sun cream) to those departing Glasgow airport in the summer months of previous years. In 1995, however, the Health Board decided actively to research the activities of holidaymakers when they were there, rather than before they went, or after they returned.

Our main quantitative findings have been reported elsewhere (Elliott *et al.*, 1998). Some 160 of the 203 ravers departing from Glasgow airport completed a detailed questionnaire at the end of their week's holiday, in addition to a short one, focusing on their expectations, on the outward flight. This initial questionnaire collected information on the frequency with which they expected to take drugs, drink alcohol, have sex and get sunburned. The second one was designed to assess the degree to which reality matched expectations.

During the week we all spent there, the research team involved themselves in as much participant observation as decorum permitted in order to understand, as much as possible, what it meant to be a raver on holiday. Although unprotected sexual activity was an important one of several health concerns expressed by the Health Board, the whole daily round of vacational life (and not merely life when its pants were around its ankles) was the focus of observation and enquiry. Thus, the relative significance of various activities was determined by the observed, not by the observers.

Two months or so after return, this group was followed up at a reunion rave at the rave club that had been the principal source of recruitment to the original package holiday. Of the 90 who were interviewed then (using a similar questionnaire to that originally administered, but, since it was now November, deleting the questions relating to the frequency of being sun-burned the previous week), 47 had completed the first questionnaire.

In brief, it was discovered that a significantly greater number of those on holiday reported using alcohol (91 per cent) and ecstasy (77 per cent), compared with 69 per cent and 63 per cent respectively of those questioned back at home. Approximately half of those who had sex with new partners while on holiday (and at home) used condoms. Of those on holiday, 45 per cent reported sickness and diarrhoea compared with 23 per cent at home. Finally, 49 per cent reported being sunburned when on holiday.

Contrary to the stereotype, however, members of this group were *less* likely to have sex when on holiday than when at home (50 per cent did when on holiday, but 67 per cent did when at home), and also had *fewer* sexual partners on holiday than at home. Indeed, overall, although the use of alcohol and drugs was greater when on holiday than at home, the differences hardly lend weight to the much-touted media images of such vacations as endless orgies of hedonistic consumption and indulgence.

This chapter tries to put some flesh on these bare quantitative bones, specifically by using material gathered in tape-recorded qualitative interviews which were undertaken with 30 of the ravers while they were on holiday. The data contained therein reveal that respondents *wanted* even more drugs, but they were thwarted by circumstances encountered on holiday. They might have *preferred* to drink water, but sometimes switched to alcohol because of the price parity between the two. They *did* seek sexual encounters, but often failed. They *were* ill more often, but illness was not so much associated with over-indulgence as with accidents – even if 'accidents' occurred when the respondent was intoxicated.

Why did they go?

Today's tourists are sometimes described as celebrated champions of post-modern exploration. As Baudrillard has suggested, they are aware of what is on offer to them on holiday, and are fully aware of their position as a tourist. Further, they are no longer satisfied with simple sensations, but while in pursuit of the extraordinary, they disdain anything 'too contrived, planned, or obviously artificial'. 'The post-tourist is above all self-conscious, "cool" and role-distanced' (Urry, 1990: 101). Did our sample of holidaymakers fit this vision of the post-tourist?

In short, no. Simply put, the ecstasy-using holidaymaker has no wish to suspend 'ordinary' behaviour, but simply to extend a normal weekend's fun to a full week's fun. Not just a Saturday night and a Sunday morning, but a Sunday morning right through to the next Saturday night. Not only do they seek to follow the 'ordinary' but also they consciously pursue these amusements with groups of people they already know and who share the common appreciation of simple pleasures. As opposed to the 'romantic' outward-looking solitary gaze of the post-tourist (Urry, 1990: 46), these ravers collectively look inward. They were at a 'resort', not a 'destination' (Ferguson, 1992: 22). When they took photographs (which wasn't often), it was to take pictures of each other – often doing silly things. Urry (1990: 101) describes the 'mild and socially tolerated rule-breaking' of such tourists as follows:

Particularly important in tourist pleasures are those that involve the energetic breaking of the mild taboos that operate on various forms of consumption, such as eating or drinking to excess, spending money recklessly, wearing outrageous clothes, keeping wildly different time patterns, and so on.

In many separate ways, as this couple in part explained, this neatly captures the spirit in which our holidaymakers anticipated, and later enjoyed, their holiday:

> ANN: We'd been going to 'Fandangos' [fictitious name of real club] for about two years and it was just something we wanted to do . . . a lot of friends.
> STUART: It's all our pals, know what I mean? We all just came together. In fact, it's only pals we met through Fandangos, you know.
> INTERVIEWER: Why pick this holiday, though?
> STUART: It's a good crowd . . . an eccy [ecstasy] crowd.
> ANN: It is a good crowd, and we knew everybody when [the advertisement for the holiday] came up. We went on it . . . know what I mean? We hadn't planned a holiday, but when that came up we decided, 'well, we'll go to that 'cos it's what we're in to and it's wur [our] own crowd that we know well'.

Hardly the post-tourist search for new experience! One or two even interrupted already-made 'real' holiday plans to attend:

> Well, at first it was just a holiday, we were looking for a holiday for two weeks and then we thought if we get the second week of the dancing then it would be a really good laugh and that. So we decided to come across for that as well 'cos it seemed like a really good event and really well organized, 'cos we read about it in a magazine . . . It was one of my mates, he read about it and he told us about it and it seemed like a really good event, it seemed like a good idea for a holiday . . . definitely. (Alan)

For most, then, the holiday was not an attempt to explore new experiences, but rather to immerse themselves fully in particular aspects of their current lives.

What did they like and dislike?

Other holidaymakers often cite an unusual event as marking the memorability and thus validity of their travel. Our package tourists cited instead the reassurance of typicality rather than the atypicality of the unexpected. Gordon told us that he went 'to be with all the posse . . . and to get a bit of sun, and have a good time'. Stuart added, 'I think the best thing was meeting everybody and that. It was just me and him that came so we know everybody, know what I mean?' Gordon explained that for him, a good holiday meant the traditional 'no worries . . . you can get a good night, a good bounce with all your mates. You don't need to worry about things, and what's happening the next day.' He added that at home, he did have to worry about what was happening the next day – just like Alan Sillitoe's hero, Arthur Seaton:

Aye, well, I've got a fishing boat so I've got my work every Monday morning, I've got to ... Come Sunday night, I'm kind of always thinking about what's happening on Monday morning again. [On holiday] you can just relax, you've got a week to do whatever the hell you want, you don't need to worry about it.

Even in terms of safety, respondents seem to seek unstressful familiarity, as Anne explained:

ANNE: There is a lot of drunks walking around like a crowd of guys all walk about at night, and you're a lassie, by yourself late at night. So I don't think it's safe to walk about at night. I personally wouldn't do it, I wouldn't walk out myself late at night.
INTERVIEWER: Is it like that at home?
ANNE: No, I don't know why ... You know your own drunks.

Difficulties encountered with knowing how to simply fit in were also cited as negative experiences. For example, Steve described the attitude of the management at the hotel where he stayed:

The hotel manager and wee Pedro on the desk, they were getting the police to us all the time for nothing, no reason at all, no reason. Like one of the boys here, they just didn't like him, so they called the police and all that ... and chasing us about and all that. In this hotel they've been right bad, so they have. I wouldn't come here, I wouldn't recommend it to anybody.

Alex recalled how behaviour which for them was normal and expected did not appeal to 'foreign' hotel owners and police, and described how he had had his ghetto-blaster confiscated for

ALEX: Playing music! Well, I'll put mine on and I'll show you how loud it was. I had the organizer up four times, I mean, we had the guy up to us about four times last night, eh, it was just a police and, eh, he's brought the organizer, bouncer, up with him and it was sitting like that, know what I mean? We were sitting talking about it and he's like that 'if you don't turn it off we're going to take it off you again'. Know what I mean? There was nothing there, so I was like that! ... either he's standing at the door with a glass tumbler to hear that we're playing music, or he's just at it.
INTERVIEWER: So did he take it [ghetto-blaster] off you?
ALEX: Well he didn't last night, but it's been confiscated about three times in a week. They're bringing up the police with them. It's a case of you're either arguing with the police and you're going to spend the night in the gaol, or whatever. So you just gave them it and went and got someone else's. That's really what happened. Considering this hotel was supposed to know that there was a dance party coming, they weren't ready for it, there was no way they were ready for it ... There was no way they were ready for us, they didn't know what hit them when we walked in that door. They really didn't know what hit them. 'Cos like the first night we came in we've all hit the rooms and everybody was on a buzz about being here and we were all away out. Come back at 5, 6 o'clock in the morning, and we're still full of whatever, and the music went up and I'm not joking, the wee hotel guy, he went and completely freaked. He just went right overboard. He was running about like a headless chicken. He was running, chapping all the doors, going 'ahh turn

off, turn off the music'. Know what I mean? Considering he was supposed to know that there was a dance party coming. No, he just didn't know what was happening.

The notion of seeking 'the ordinary' was also expressed in terms of taste in music, as Gordon put it when asked about the worst thing that had happened on holiday so far:

> Just a bit of hassle last night with the ... a lot of the English people no' wanting to listen to our music. They didn't want to listen to it, give it a try and see what it's all about ... We've got to listen to all the music coming up from the south coast of England in London and all that. They should be entitled to listen to our music, give it a try. We've got to listen to their music. We heard folk saying, 'Oh they're all crazy, look at them jumping up and about: they're all out of their heads', and all that. But we can enjoy ourselves listening to our music the same as they can whether drunk, full of drugs or whatever. We can enjoy ourselves the same as what they can. We are willing to listen to their music, they should be willing to listen to ours. But apart from that, it's been a great holiday. I've enjoyed the first two days.

The same distaste was expressed when others behaved badly. Peter also blamed the English:

> Folk that are on holiday, like kind of English folk, that start trouble ... One night I saw them, they were just chucking bottles at lassies and that. Just neds [Glaswegian slang for working-class hooligans]. It was Saturday night when we came ... a lot of English folk were out for trouble.

For women, the security of at least being familiar with the crowd they were with was a major asset. As Mary explained when asked if she was ever harassed by males while dancing:

> Not really, everyone is just like really friendly. Everyone just wants to know what your name is and if you know such and such, and things like that. They don't really hassle you in that sense. The only time they hassle you is if folk have been drinking, but it's never like that with ravers, especially with this crowd.

What problems did they face?

Some dangerous experiences came via accidents, such as this one described by Alan:

> I saw one girl pass out with drink and she hit her head off this flower pot. She passed out and smacked her head off the thing and her head was bleeding ... and then the ambulance came up and that really really freaked me out 'cos I was on speed ... she was just outside this club before we went in to the club, and the paramedics came up ... she was just drinking and she just passed out. I don't know how she fell, and she hit her head straight off it.

Alex recalled two other 'accidents':

> ALEX: Aye, one of the guys, he just collapsed: totally blacked out. He was on

eccies and sulph and whatever, and then he dropped an acid. Then dropped himself . . . Well, nothing much happened, they kept him in hospital for two days and carried out tests. He's all right now. He left hospital this morning.
INTERVIEWER: Any other accidents?
ALEX: I had one. The Spanish don't know how to drive! He was driving along in front of me in a big truck, and he sort of swings out as if he's going to take a right, and then just slams on the brakes in the middle of the road. He's doing about, well coming along the main drive, he's doing about 40 and I don't know what speed the wee bikes do but it must be 30 mile an hour. But I'm kind of close behind him and then he slammed on the brakes in front of me! And I've just tumbled off! Jumped up, just left the bike sitting in the middle of the road and went and sat on a wall. I was all right, just a couple of minor scrapes, but I was lucky.

Sometimes, accidents intersect negatively with budgetary problems. Two men interviewed did not feel that they could spare the money to pay for medical treatment they needed for injuries they had received while on holiday. Mark (who had been taking both ecstasy and temazepam) dived carelessly into the hotel pool and cut his head badly:

> Aye, I've got epilepsy. I didn't kill myself and I'm still here, know what I mean? I needed stitches and it's a hundred and twenty pounds. But I didn't go 'cos I'm not geeing a fucking hundred and twenty pounds. No! I'm going back to [a local hospital] as soon as I get home for a brain scan.

The other male, Rab, needed treatment, but was equally reluctant to pay for it. He was interviewed six days after the incident he now describes:

> RAB: See, the first day I got stung by one of these sea porcupines, and nobody ever warned me about it. I went swimming in the sea, thinking this was a wee idyllic place. I stood on these sea porcupines, right? I know what it is when you come out of the water, you come out with them sticking out of whatever part of your body that made contact with them. They look like rose thorns, they're that length. They're really painful, my foot is going septic on me right now. Now I've had to go and buy tweezers. I've went to the chemist several times.
> INTERVIEWER: Is your foot infected?
> RAB: I'm going to need antibiotics and I'm allergic to penicillin. It happened the first day I came out here, Sunday . . . Nothing will beat me, especially a sea fucking spine.

These accidents were relatively minor, and only happened to a small minority of the group. Yet all could be classified as 'near misses'. While it is difficult to see what Scottish Health Boards can do about the problem directly, the cheap and easy availability of small motorcycles in favoured European seaside destinations (and the apparent legal freedom to ride them when drunk and without helmets) is an issue to which at least precautionary advice might be directed.

Consuming passion

The frequency of having sex on vacation with either known or unknown partners was elucidated via the main quantitative questionnaire. But this doesn't tell us what people desired. For some, for example Candera, having romance in her holiday was a key part of the experience. Asked 'Is it important to meet someone on holiday?' she replied:

> To me yeah, it is important to meet someone new and keep them for most of the holiday. I like romantic holidays, yeah. Yeah, well I was with two people and one was a mistake 'cos I was smashed, but the other one was all right . . . But I think with women, also it's . . . if you're smashed, and the guy moves on you, and you're in the mood, you very rarely knock them back, well I don't! . . . That's not all women, but that's my problem!

Others, for example Gordon (a married man who was on holiday with his wife, and was here speaking about others), thought that holiday romances assisted the future and past, rather than the fulfilment of the present:

> Well, I'm married anyway so it doesn't matter . . . but I reckon it's kind of . . . it gives a lot of folk something to remember about it. It's not important, but you're away from home and everyone is only human. So the way I see it, it gives you something to remember . . . but you know, fair enough, if something happens fair enough, you do it, but you've got the memories as well. The pictures of the memories. It's not important, but it's an extra. You can go with your mates and have a great time or you can go with your mates and meet women and have a better time, whatever you're into.

Yet for Steve, the worst thing that had happened to him on holiday was that he didn't have a sexual encounter:

> STEVE: I didn't get my balls out. That's the worst thing.
> INTERVIEWER: Would these things be as important if they happened at home?
> STEVE: Aye, I suppose, saying that though you come here everybody says, know what I mean, going on holiday.
> INTERVIEWER: Did you expect to 'get your balls out'?
> STEVE: For the money I spent, aye. But it's just one of those things, isn't it?

For Alan, the holiday experience itself, particularly his view of what sun did for women, indicated the appropriateness of sexual activity more than did the climate at home:

> INTERVIEWER: So in the past were you all out to get a 'lumber' [one-night stand]?
> ALAN: Eh, well, I was going out with the same girl last year, so I wouldn't really say I did it consciously, know what I mean?
> INTERVIEWER: But did you?
> ALAN: Yeah, like a few of us did and that was it. But it wasn't like a lumber, it was like kind of a nice wee snog and that was it, nothing else apart from that. I don't know whether it's just the sun or whatever, the weather goes to women's heads and they get horny. They can't help it, they just seem more horny in the sun, know what I mean, it's something else definitely.
> INTERVIEWER: Do guys get more horny in the sun?

ALAN: Yeah definitely, there's no doubt about it.

Couples observed the behaviour of single people on holiday, and saw the same thing:

LIZ: They're only here for the one thing, eh? Pure on the hots, and everything.
ANN: The lads and that, they're all on the go looking for women.
LIZ: Same with the girls, they're the same.
ANN: They're worse.
INTERVIEWER: How?
ROB: 'Cos they are!
ANN: 'Cos they're out looking for men, the crowd of lassies that are sitting at the back there on the pool, you see them? I don't know them, the lassie there [Ann points to another woman] that's what she says to me. I says, 'Enjoying the holiday?', she says, 'No! I've no' had a man yet!' So she's saying that's what she wants, a man. Here it was even, 'Aye you can do it on holiday, nobody will find out' and that.

For some males, like Rab, having a steady relationship at home did not seem to interfere with his anticipation of alternative sexual activity while on holiday:

I've got a bird at home as well. No I was looking for it ... but I never got it ... she's living on a totally different planet from the one I live on. She's into the planet of working part-time, single mother and that, and, eh, she's been to a few rave places and that, and, eh, it's not her cup of tea.

For Andy, also in a relationship at home, his agenda was one based on control:

INTERVIEWER: So when you're on holiday do you have sex with different people?
ANDY: No' yet I haven't.
INTERVIEWER: Would you if the chance arose?
ANDY: Oh aye, definitely. You just take every day as it comes. You never know what's round the corner.
INTERVIEWER: Do you and your girlfriend have an open relationship?
ANDY: No, she does what she's told. I'm telling you! She does what she's telt!

However, Jessie and her boyfriend were agreed about expanding on sexual experiences, as Jessie recalled:

Yeah, em, I don't know, I think, em, a holiday should be different. For example, my boyfriend, he went away on holiday a couple of months ago and he went with someone. I mean I wasn't chuffed with it, but basically if somebody asked me I'm going to go out with them if I like them, it's not going to stop me. I don't know, it's a holiday ... We spoke about it before I left, and we both agreed it was fine.

For some women like Jackie gender explained differential desires: 'The majority of men look for casual sex, and the majority of women say they look for romance, and they probably do.' Candera thought differently: 'I think it's the exact same, it's just the women wake up in the morning and think, "Oh no! What have I done", and then they do the exact same the next night!'

For Mike, his attempt at being romantic was constantly thwarted by a woman who kept on interrupting his evenings:

MIKE: She butts in every ten minutes . . . let me think, the best one I think was Thursday night, we shouted at her 'cos I got really pissed off. On Sunday night, got interrupted four times, Wednesday night got interrupted a couple of times. Thursday night just got really pissed off and just said, 'Fuck off, canna even get screwing in peace!'
INTERVIEWER: But none of it is pre-arranged?
MIKE: No, I'm just a charmer!

Indeed, having had a holiday romance seemed to be so important to some that they lied about their holiday encounters, as Gordon explained:

Aye, there's some people exaggerate a lot about it. I dare say there is, aye. 'Oh the best thing that ever happened to me!' and all that . . . and you see the same lassie with about five or six other guys throughout the course of the week, you know what they're like 'Oh she was so lovely!' and all that. A lot of folk do, aye.

And Peter added: 'Definitely. You get a lot of folk that say, eh, 'I went with so many lassies' and then when you say to the lassie, they weren't anywhere near them!' Alan went into more detail:

ALAN: Yeah, definitely. I would definitely say that, because . . . I don't know . . . came back from holiday and a few of my other friends had went to, em, Majorca last year and we were in Tenerife, and, eh, one of them was saying like stories and the other was saying like other stories. Eh, I don't know, you can't really tell the difference. You don't know what one to believe.
INTERVIEWER: Have you told lies before?
ALAN: About my holiday before? Em, I've never really had to but I think if it came down to it, I probably would. But I haven't had to so far . . . But when you come back from holiday, you feel obliged to say that you have had a holiday romance, and it really is, I don't know, you know that some folk are talking shit and that's about right but, em, unless there is any point in talking shit, it's not going to make you any better than what you are, then, eh? I don't see the point in it: fuck it!

Candera further explained the intricacies of other people's behaviour:

CANDERA: Um, well, behind the scenes it's different, because it's usually who's shagged who behind the scenes . . . but you get the usual outrageous talk as well. I hang around with a lot of guys, so you do hear a lot of stuff. Just, you know, 'I shagged her, she was fat', or, 'I shagged her and she was bogging or minging [smelly]' and things like that, you know? Like this guy here with a girlfriend, you know, 'who's really fat' and 'yeah, I can't believe he pulled that!' Only from the guys. I don't really hang around with any of the girls from the scene. I haven't got any female friends here.
INTERVIEWER: Do you reckon people tell lies about holiday romances?
CANDERA: Yeah, definitely. Em, I don't know why, I know, 'cos I heard a story about one of the club dancers, and it just wasn't true, 'cos I know that

it . . . well, it's difficult to say, 'cos maybe she's denying it, but I think she's telling the truth, 'cos I know there's a lot of crap you know? . . . that she'd been sleeping with five separate DJs in the one room, and I don't think she's like that. I mean, that's making a moral judgement on what she said. Basically she said she didn't do it and I don't believe it, it's just a story that was going round and she was crying and getting really upset. But other than that, on holidays in general I'd say you do, 'cos you're not going to find out.
INTERVIEWER: So when you go back home and you haven't had a holiday romance, are you the pits or something?
CANDERA: Well it's never happened to me. Oh! you mean what they think? Eh, no. But it's maybe different for a guy, I know a couple of guys that are getting a good slagging, but they are there to pull. I would say so, most guys are there to pull rather than have a romance, so they get slagged rotten if their score was zero.

An important quantitative finding was the relative reduction in sexual contact abroad, and that condom use with new sexual partners was the same there as it was at home. Holiday brochures, and holiday myths, aside, the empirical reality is that for most of this group, sex on holiday was much the same as sex at home.

Consuming substances

Although substance use was greater on holiday than at home, it fell short of what the holidaymakers wanted. What role did drugs play in their construction of a 'good time'? In post-modern terminology, are they 'victims' or 'explorers'? Here again, it is difficult to find a place for our holidaymakers within this simple conceptual scheme. In one sense they are victims – restricted and disapproved of by law – but on the other, they are still willing and able to use illegal drugs.

Sometimes they are neither, particularly when buying ineffective ecstasy after going to much effort to find it, an experience Rab described:

> I got ripped off last night. I bought two eccies that were bum. I've bought ten so-called micro dots that were also bum. I'm really pissed off. Drug dealers ripped me off. And they're nothing like the drugs back home – back home drugs are real. Last night I felt like humpty dumpty, I swallowed a so-called dove, and I swallowed a so-called micro dot later on when the so-called dove wasn't taking effect . . . it stopped me from enjoying myself at all!

Alan had a similar problem with some 'cannabis' he had been sold:

> I don't know, we got a really dodgy deal of hash over here, it was like green on the inside, and we were smoking it and we were tripping like anything off it. It was like taking acid or something like that, and we were getting really really paranoid off it. So I mean, like, mixing it with other drugs we were trying to come off, we stopped 'cos it was so strong, it really was . . . and 'E' at home, I haven't had a really bad 'E' apart from here when I was really gouching [in a highly sedated and relaxed state due to drugs] but then it got so much better that I forgot about the gouching.

For many, drugs were an essential part of a 'good' holiday, as Liz and Rob, a couple, explained:

> INTERVIEWER: Would it be as much fun on your holiday if you didn't have drugs?
> LIZ: It wouldn't spoil it if you couldn't get them.
> ROB: But if you can get them it helps, ken? You couldn't dance as much, you know, early bed. You just take them, you need them for the energy, you know what I mean? You need them to keep up all that fucking dancing all night.
> LIZ: No! the way you dance! (laughs)

Variable-quality drugs sometimes combined with the provision of water that was itself of dubious quality, as Jessie explained:

> Yeah, a lot of people are drinking alcohol. Even like back home, you can go into the toilets and stuff. Last night a friend went into the toilet and filled it [a bottle] up, and she says, 'I went into the toilet to fill up my water' and I was like that 'you're not supposed to drink [the] water [here]'. I think a lot of people are forgetting about that, they'll end up with typhoid or something.

Another factor was the price of bottled water. Asked, 'What about the price of water?', Candera replied:

> The price of water!? It was expensive, so I drank far less of it . . . Um, I tended not to drink much in, eh, clubs at all. I just took this miniature bottle in and I maybe bought two bottles of water all night, whereas I would be drinking a lot more than that at home, and then I would chew gum or take a mint to try and take it [the feeling of thirst] away.

Soft drinks are even more expensive, as Alex recalled:

> The weather's a lot hotter here, you know. You take more fluid to keep cool and like you're paying the same price for like Coke as what you are for a beer or a cider, so you would be as well just drinking [alcohol].

The disappointment of consumers who feel let down by a product may imply that such consumers are bargain hunters – 'explorers', where participants work within a network of associates or friends sharing experiences. However, while our group exchanged information as to who bought good 'E' and who sold them bad 'E', they do not bargain hunt in the sense of finding cheaper products. Nor do they seek novelty but rather a repetition of the feeling of well-being they are used to at home when listening and dancing to certain types of music. For example, when a small group was asked about this, they did not offer any complaints about the price of drugs they had bought, even though they were not impressed by their effects:

> INTERVIEWER: What are the drugs here like compared with home?
> DAVIE: I don't like them either . . . eccy, speed and hash . . . I don't think they were up to much at all, no. I don't know if I was too drunk when I took them to feel them, but I don't think I had much effect off them.
> INTERVIEWER: Are they cheaper?
> DAVIE: No, they're just the same price.
> ALEX: Dearer!

STUART: I hunted all day . . . just to get a bit of hash.
ANN: It's just who you know. I think the longer you're here, you get to know people, and then you'll get it.
INTERVIEWER: What's the price like?
ANN: Same.
STUART: No, no, the hash is cheaper, 75 quid an ounce, it's a hundred pounds down the road [at home].
ROB: It's no' as good here, is it? It's no' as good.
ANN: It's no' as good definitely, the hash isn't as good.

For some, drugs were not entirely unproblematic, as Peter explained:

I think someone should tell people back home about foreign drugs, like the 'Es' are so different from back home. They're so much stronger. You should just take a half if you're used to taking two back home. So many folk are coming across here and they can't handle them at all. Like if you take a half where you're taking two back home, you'll get really gouchy. Feel really ill, which you're not used to, and then suddenly feel so much better than you do back home . . . and then get paranoid for three days afterwards! They should really warn people about drugs here. 'Cos folk are . . . I'm used to going to Fandangos, and taking five or six 'E', and if you did that here you'd die, it's so heavy.

He went on to describe the ill effects from taking ecstasy he'd bought in the Mediterranean:

It was really bad gouching on an 'E', and it was really really heavy . . . and I didn't even take a full one, just three-quarters, and it was so much stronger it was unbelievable. I felt like I just came out in a total sweat and I was just . . . my arms were sweating and my legs were sweating and my whole back of my neck was all tingling . . . going up and down . . . I felt so bad, I just wanted to go and sit in a corner and die or something like that. It was really really bad. But it just changed from one [feeling] straight to another which felt so good, yeah it really was 'wow!' . . . you know.

Of course, it isn't clear whether this apparently stronger effect was a result of stronger ecstasy, or 'normal' ecstasy taken in conjunction with higher than normal temperatures, higher than normal alcohol intake and lower than normal non-alcoholic fluid intake or the change in social context. For Peter, however (and perhaps for future holidaymakers), the need for warnings exists independently of cause.

Conclusions

These holidaymakers, then, are partly simple tourists (old-fashioned in their pursuit of traditional pleasure through ordinary sensations) and partly post-modern ones, in terms of their relationship to the worshipful consumption of both types of music and types of drugs. This makes them hard to place. They are not post-modern 'hedonists' (seeking sensation 'in emotion accompanying all kinds of experiences including sad or painful ones': Campbell, 1978: 104), nor are they 'rebels' (who are thought to 'vent their anger and frustration into commodities, buying them, stealing them, disfiguring them, and investing them with meaning': Campbell, 1978: 145).

While our group complained about buying unsatisfactory ecstasy, about having to listen to music that they did not like, and that others did not appreciate their taste in music to the point where some ghetto-blasters were confiscated by hotel managers, it would be difficult to call our group rebels, since their reported intention of continued illicit drug use was not designed as a protest, or to deface society in any way, but rather to initiate feelings of warmth, co-operation, physical expression through dance and a feeling of belonging to what, for them, is in essence an extension of the 'ordinary' taken abroad. Being abroad was not in fact *the* key factor initiating uptake of the holiday package, and yet it presented conflicts of interest to them, as consumers seeking sameness, and also added risks to contend with, which they would not normally encounter at home.

In so far as this group offers lessons in health enhancement, it seems clear that no single activity is particularly hazardous. It is, instead, the various combinations of activities to which future health messages should attend: sun with alcohol; dehydrating drugs with high-temperature locales; alcohol with motorcycles; motorcycles without helmets; motorcyclists wearing very few clothes; alcohol as price-available as water, and so on.

Where do ravers in this study fit in the available taxonomies of tourism? Urry (1990: 146) suggests four types of tourist (as opposed to post-tourist) 'holidaymaking': the 'family holiday' (a couple with two or three healthy school-age children); the 'romantic holiday' (a heterosexual couple on their own 'gazing at the sunset'); the 'sex holiday' (for men, particularly, to sex tourism destinations); and the 'fun holiday' (same-sex groups each looking for other-sex partners for 'fun'). Our holidaymakers were emphatically on a fun holiday. But a fun holiday of a newish kind: to call them tourists at all stretches a point. What elements of 'touring' were there? Their experience of travelling to their resort was at best a null experience, at worst a negative one. At the best of times, travellers cannot see much out of an aeroplane window: at night, as for this group, nothing at all. When they were there, being in another place was not the desired end, neither did it much live up to expectations: the important expectations they held related to consuming passions and substances. A more appropriate term for this type of group on that type of holiday, given these conditions, would be 'trippers'.

But are they the exception or the rule? Are most holidaymakers simple tourists/trippers in this way? In this empirical sense, it is possible that 'post-tourism' analysis has concentrated rather too heavily on the aspirations of what may turn out to be a mere handful of rich middle-class young people who each week languidly turn the pages of the Sunday supplements seeking new and mentally enriching experiences, and in so doing has neglected the majority of British holidaymakers who seek simply sun, sand, sea (and, for some, sex). More actual research, and less leisurely writing, might give us the answer.

Acknowledgements

The authors gratefully acknowledge Chris Rojek's comments on an early draft.

References

Campbell, C. (1978) *The Romantic Ethic and the Spirit of Modern Consumerism*. London: Macmillan.

Elliott, L., Morrison, A., Ditton, J., Farrall, S., Short, E., Cowan, L. and Gruer, L. (1998) Alcohol, drug use, and sexual behaviour of young adults on a Mediterranean dance holiday. *Addiction Research* **6** (4), 319–40.

Ferguson, H. (1992) Watching the world go round: atrium culture psychology of shopping. In R. Shields (ed.), *Lifestyle Shopping: The Subject of Consumption*. London: Routledge.

Rojek, C. (1995) *Decentring Leisure: Rethinking Leisure Theory*. London: Sage.

Sillitoe, A. (1958) *Saturday Night and Sunday Morning*. London: W. H. Allen.

Urry, J. (1990) *The Tourist Gaze: Leisure and Travel in Contemporary Societies*. London: Sage.

14

Locality, loyalty and identity: experiences of travel and marriage among young Punjabi women in Glasgow

Hannah Bradby

Introduction

Travel plays a central role in the identities and loyalties of young women of Punjabi origin living in Britain. Travel is important both for its traditional role in the Punjabi marriage system and for its more recent role in the establishment of Punjabi communities in Britain in the 1960s. The traditional marriage system of rural Punjabis is patrilocal, which means that a bride moves from her parents' to her husband's locality. Marriage is almost universal for adult women in the Punjab and therefore womanhood implies travel. This is likely to continue to be relevant in Britain, where there are high rates of marriage among South Asians (Modood *et al.*, 1997). The British Punjabi community evidently owes its existence to migrants' travel to Britain, and this movement is characterized as labour migration because the primary motivation was the search for employment that offered better returns than were available in the sending society. The physical and cultural distance between Britain and the Indian subcontinent means that travel, both actual and imagined, informs the Punjabi minority ethnic group identity.

The current generation of young Punjabi women in Britain describe strong dual loyalties and attachments that are informed by the implications of both travel for purposes of marriage and the labour migration of the previous generation. Such dual attachments are common for Punjabi women who, unlike their brothers, always grow up in one household and move to another to bring up their own children. Honour requires that loyalty is shown to one's husband's kin, but this does not undermine devotion to one's natal family. Similarly, a sense of belonging to localities in both Britain and the Punjab is not contradictory – one loyalty does not render the other untenable. Further, loyalty to a Punjabi locality does not depend upon having actually visited it: a sense of belonging to two places and the imagined translation between them are central to women's identity, and independent of actual travel. Dual identities are likely to continue to be a feature of the Punjabi community in the face of pressures to contract transcontinental marriages.

Method

The study on which this chapter draws was conducted in Glasgow between 1992 and 1995. A sample of 47 women aged 20 to 30 with South Asian names was drawn at random from a possible 70 women of the appropriate age and ethnicity on a general-practice list in the north of Glasgow (Bradby, 1996). Of these, 32 women were interviewed twice and these interviews were tape-recorded and transcribed. Most interviews were conducted in English by the author, and five were conducted by a colleague in Punjabi or Urdu, with the author (who speaks elementary Hindi/Urdu) present to take notes and occasionally prompt the line of questioning. The same colleague helped translate the interview schedule into Punjabi and the Punjabi or Urdu transcripts into English. Interview material was complemented by an extended period of participant observation in the private and public fora of Punjabi life in Glasgow, the former involving considerable participation in the lives of four key informants, and the latter centring around one of the city's Sikh temples and one of the mosques where weekly women's meetings were held.

The interviewees reflected the population of South Asian origin in Glasgow, being Punjabi speakers who traced their origins to the east or the west Punjab; the majority was Muslim (19), with an important minority of Sikhs (10) and fewer Hindus (3). They included both married and unmarried women.

The survey data referred to come from a social survey conducted in Glasgow in 1996 of young people aged 18 to 20 (Bradby and Williams, 1998). Trained social interviewers administered a structured questionnaire. Most of the interviews were conducted in the young people's homes, and lasted between 45 minutes and three hours, with the majority lasting between one and two hours. Where the young people or their relatives were reluctant to take part, interviewers who spoke the appropriate languages were available to negotiate access. Data analysis was carried out with SPSS for Windows. Chi-squared tests and comparison of means were used to assess the significance of differences between Asian and non-Asian men and women.

Findings

Punjabi women in Britain

Bringing up a daughter is, among traditional Punjabis, like watering a tree in another man's garden, because a daughter is 'a thing to be given away' (Brown *et al.*, 1981). Brides are expected to move to their husband's locality at marriage and transfer their loyalty and labour to his family. By contrast, men are likely to remain in the same locality as their parents all their lives and will inherit their property and land holdings. For Punjabi women, but not men, the only way to become an adult woman with one's own household is to leave the natal household and often the parents' neighbourhood or region. Muslim Punjabis favour marriage to kin, usually cousins, because the reputation of the family is known and they may be resident locally, which protects daughters from moving away to live with potentially abusive strangers. But even in the case of a local move, daughters grow up in their natal home with the knowledge that they are destined to move away.

The inevitability of the move out of the parental home does not reduce the unhappiness that it can cause women. In interviews women described the loneliness of the early days of their marriages. Women who had travelled from Pakistan and India for marriage, leaving behind their natal family, described how there was 'too much loneliness' in Glasgow. So too did women who moved out of their mother's home in Glasgow to live in council accommodation only 3 miles distant. It seemed to be the necessity of moving away from the parents and siblings that caused unhappiness, rather than the actual distance of the move. However, the loneliness of separation ensuing from marriage was something that women 'were brought up to expect' and was regarded as 'just one of those things that's got to happen'.

Separation from parents was an accepted part of being a woman among the young Punjabi women interviewed, and this expectation comes from the traditional marriage system. However, the actual pattern of movement of men and women is altered in a community that has undergone migration. The nature of the migration of Punjabis to Britain was aspirant, that is the move was initially made by pioneer migrants who were mainly young men in search of labour that commanded higher wages than were available at home. These men were later joined by their families and began to establish the social institutions, such as organized religion and arranged marriage, that were familiar from home. The aim of Punjabi men's labour in Britain was to improve the lot of their families, both in Britain by facilitating their children's education and training 'to the best degree they can do' and in the Punjab by remitting money that could be invested in property and land holdings by the extended family. As one interviewee said, 'the Asians that came over . . . from India and Pakistan, all they thought about was money. They worked day and night.'

This strategy has worked, in that 'some Asians are very rich now', able to afford desirable housing, cars and provide lavish hospitality at weddings and other celebrations. The success in terms of the improvement of Punjabis' standards of living in Britain – the educational achievements of young South Asians and the considerable sums that are remitted to the Punjab – are considered by many migrants to justify the considerable sacrifices that their generation has made.

The view that migrants' travel benefits them and their families means that in marriages between British and subcontinent Punjabis there is an expectation that the couple will be based in Britain if possible. The movement of subcontinent women to Britain conforms to the expectation that women travel. But when subcontinent men leave their natal families for travel to Britain, the traditional expectations are disrupted. The young man is likely to be sponsored by his wife's parents and depend on their financial and practical support. Nonetheless, the traditional expectation that the young couple belong to the man's family means that he is still expected to offer support to his family in the subcontinent: for instance, by contributing towards building or land-acquisition costs. Given that it is the wife's parents who are providing support, this can lead to resentment from the wife and/or her parents on the grounds that the couple's children are being deprived of resources in favour of distant subcontinent kin.

Whether or not women move to their husbands' locality after marriage, travel is still implicated in the process of getting married in the transnational Punjabi community. For non-Muslims the endogamous marriage rules mean that a young woman's family must look beyond their immediate place of residence and social circle for a spouse. Among Muslims there are reasons why families favour marriage to subcontinent kin. These include the maintenance of links with extended family in the subcontinent and the knowledge of cultural and religious traditions that a young person brought up in the Punjab can bring, which will then be transmitted both to the spouse and to subsequent generations. As one woman, herself married to a subcontinent-raised cousin, explained:

> Children over here [Britain] are so bad that we can't make them understand. They do whatever they like . . . So mostly people try to get a daughter-in-law from Pakistan. And even daughters should get married from there [Pakistan], so that he [husband] can come and teach. And if both are from here, who will do the teaching?

Since most of the married women interviewed had an Indian or Pakistani husband, the women had been through the process of travelling to the subcontinent to contract their marriage. Their accounts varied very little: women would travel to the Indian subcontinent with their parents, or other close kin, ostensibly to visit relatives. Young women were not usually fully aware of the details of marriage plans, as this was considered improper, but if they were in their early twenties, then the purpose of the journey could be easily guessed. Also, delicate pre-betrothal negotiations had probably not been finalized until a face-to-face meeting in the subcontinent. Once negotiations are closed between elders, the two young people were introduced to one another and some ritual exchange of gifts undertaken. Wedding rituals are detailed in ethnographies of South Asians in Britain (Bhachu, 1985; Werbner, 1990).

Belonging to two places

Their marriage to subcontinent men and their position as the children of migrants all contribute to young women's dual loyalties and multiple attachment to place. The migrant generation did not necessarily intend long-term residency to result from their sojourn in Britain (Ballard, 1994). 'The myth of return' (Anwar, 1979) describes the generally unfulfilled aspiration of a return to the sending society to benefit from the wealth accrued while working in Britain. If the migrant generation are charac-terized as reluctant Britons (Jeffery, 1976), their offspring have been described as 'torn between two cultures' and suffering 'culture conflict'. The implication is that access to more than one linguistic and cultural code is problematic, causing confusion and the inability to function properly in either (Watson, 1977; Anwar, 1988). An alternative view is that young British Asians have shown themselves to be adept at 'code-switching' (Ballard, 1994), and their use and adaptation of the cultural resources available has been both skilful and strategic (Rampton, 1995). Young Punjabi women's sense of multiple attachment and loyalties, which differ from their parents' myth of return and from the majority ethnic group's somewhat unitary loyalties, illustrates the strength of the way that a migrant heritage can be used and combined with local British attachments.

Loyalty to Glasgow

Young women's identities are informed by their loyalty to both their South Asian and their British inheritance. The multiple influences on identity were emphasized in the following comment: 'Well, just jokingly, I sometimes say like I'm [a] British-Asian-with-Irish-born-citizen, you know.' The next quotation, from a woman who was born in East Africa of Indian-born parents before moving to Scotland as a child, mentions religion, broad ethnic group, her country of residence, continent of birth and neigh-bourhood as alternative, but not necessarily competing, sources of identity:

Well, I usually say I am a Hindu. [Do you call yourself Scottish?] Scottish Asian I suppose, yeah . . . Usually the question is, 'Where do you come from?' I say, 'I was born in Africa.' 'Africa!' You know. Then you have to go into an explanation, you know. [So when they say, 'Where are you from?' what is the first answer that you give?] Prince's Park! [Her neighbourhood in Glasgow.]

Loyalty to Glasgow was strong in young women's accounts of their own identities, but did not preclude attachment to the Indian subcontinent: 'I'm a Pakistani . . . I would say this [Glasgow] would be my home because my house is here . . . I'm Pakistani because most of my relatives are over there. I might just say the same thing if I had a lot of people living in Italy.' Glasgow was, as explained above and below, valued as the site of current daily existence:

I like living in Glasgow, I think it's the best place to be . . . There you are: speak up for Glasgow!

I think this is it, this [Glasgow] is my home here.

Furthermore, women saw Glasgow as continuing to be their home in the future:

I'm happy where I am, I've never wanted to go [to India]. For a holiday, yeah, anywhere. But I've never wanted to emigrate anywhere. I like living in Glasgow.

I think I would be homesick for here [Glasgow]. I don't think I could actually stay [in Pakistan] unless I had to, if I had a gun pointed at my head, I had to stay, sort of thing.

This sense of belonging to Glasgow on a permanent basis was reflected in survey findings of 18- to 20-year-old Asians and non-Asians. Young women of Asian origin were no more likely to report a strong likelihood of emigrating from the UK in five years time than non-Asian women (Bradby and Williams, 1998).

Women's commitment to their Glaswegian identity is illustrated by their vigorous rebuttals of verbal racist abuse which excluded women by implying that they had no claim to local attachment. When 'neds' (local term for yobs or thugs) shouted 'Paki, bastard, wog' or 'get back to where you belong' at them on the streets, women described a variety of responses. With various degrees of strength these strategies ignored, resisted or positively refuted the implication that they did not belong in Glasgow. Some women suggested that ignoring such comments undermined their effectiveness most eloquently. A more vocal response was to 'give them a mouthful', such as 'piss off you wee shite-head' in a broad Glaswegian accent. This resulted in a 'jaw-dropped, gob-smacked' expression on the part of the neds, a reaction due, the women thought, to the expectation that as 'Asian'-looking women they would be submissive and passive, and if they could speak English at all it would be with an 'Indian' accent. A strategy that demonstrated both the women's refusal of any pejorative and their expert understanding of Asian identities was used in the face of such abusive terms as 'Paki', to which women of Indian origin replied, 'I'm Indian actually'. Similarly, a woman whose young daughter was called 'a wee white Indie' by 'stupid kids' thanked them for their compliment on her daughter's fair complexion and corrected their misapprehension by making clear that she was Pakistani.

Loyalty to Punjabi localities

Women's loyalty to their South Asian heritage was as strong as their local attachment, but played a different role in their identity and was expressed in ways that did not conflict with their Glaswegian loyalty. Women made it clear that they were both Scottish and Asian and, while not foreseeing their lives anywhere other than Glasgow, were keen to maintain their links with their Punjabi culture. One woman said she wanted her children to be able to 'speak Indian' with her mother, and another explained:

> I don't like to cut myself off or be seen to [be] cutting myself off from where I originate from. I mean, I think it's OK enough for people to see Asian people mixing in, you know, going to pubs and what not, but I mean, I don't want to be perceived as totally forgetting my own culture . . . It's a very rich, it's a good religion and culture.

The commitment to their South Asian side was strongly articulated through the women's acceptance of the family responsibility to maintain land and property holdings in the Punjab. The high priority associated with maintaining family holdings was described as 'an Indian trademark' and 'a generation thing that you will have that house'. The importance of retaining ownership in the family, even if the house or land was leased out was that 'it's still carrying on their [elders'] name as long as you don't sell it, as long as it's not outside the family'.

It was expected that houses and/or farmland would be passed down through the generations of sons. For instance, one woman described a house in Pakistan that 'was actually my . . . great, great grandparents' house, my grandparents'. And then it was given to my father and my father-in-law, because they were both brothers. And they gave that house to my husband and my brother.' The strength of young women's commitment to their family name in the Punjab is illustrated by the lack of utility that such holdings afforded them in their daily lives in Glasgow. The women did not intend to live in the Punjab and many faced relative poverty in Glasgow, but nonetheless the expense, often in terms of legal fees, of maintaining the holdings would not be sacrificed.

Another articulation of the high value placed on Punjabi heritage was the idyllic description of daily life in their parents' Punjabi villages. Most, but not all, women had visited their family villages for holidays, and referred to them as 'our village', although they had never lived there permanently. The simplicity of rural Punjabi life was perceived as idyllic: 'it's an easy-going life there, you know. You seem to enjoy it more . . . You don't really have so many worries.' Specifically, there were fewer money worries: 'We'd be more secure over there [In terms of?] Money and nothing to worry about, no bills or anything, because we've got the land and whatever comes with that.' Village life offered good weather, open spaces and safety for children to play out of doors and a constant supply of good, fresh food from the family farm. The greater respect accorded to traditions meant that children experienced a 'proper Islamic upbringing' and it was easier for all religions to follow food rules and routines of worship. The dual loyalty described by Punjabi women does not imply confusion; indeed, it is a central part of British Punjabi identities. Dual loyalties feature as part of women's identity, and are likely to continue to do so for some time because of their relationship with the marriage system which is transnational.

Travel as identity and heritage

For young Punjabi women in Glasgow, travel is an inherent, unavoidable and expected part both of their identity as adult women, which effectively means married women, and of their identity as people of Punjabi origin. The system of arranged marriage, to which women are largely committed (Bradby, in press), is centrally important in maintaining the transnational networks of Punjabis by forming and maintaining alliances between branches of extended families and with non-kin. Women travel away from their natal families in order to establish their place in their husband's family where their children will be raised. When the bride's family has migrated from the Punjab and the husband is Indian or Pakistani, she will travel to his locale in order to finalize marriage arrangements and complete some or all of the associated ceremonies. So whether or not the couple eventually live in Britain, travel is crucial to marital and familial relationships.

At this point a broad contrast can be drawn. Mainstream British tourism has been analysed as a temporary withdrawal to a liminal sphere where daily obligations and norms are suspended (Shields, 1990), and as a system of visual consumption during which tourists seek, collect and record 'sights' and signs that characterize the exotic locality (Urry, 1992a and b). India is seen as a particularly good location for the collection of sights that are exotic and authentic enough to warrant the attendant risks of travel there (Carter, 1998). Young women travelling to Punjab do not so much participate in 'sightseeing', exercising the tourist gaze (Urry, 1992a and b), as become subject to the scrutiny of other Punjabis. Their relatives and elders' co-villagers view the women's conduct and consequently make judgements as to their suitability as potential brides and concerning their family's reputation. Being subjected to this scrutiny is central for participation in the honour community of Punjabi migrants.

Rather than an escape to the exotic, Punjabi women's travel to the subcontinent implies reinforcing familial bonds, the creation of marital bonds and a re-acquaintance with the culture of the sending society, which is already familiar, even for those who have never before visited. Travel is undertaken to very specific, rural locations in the Punjab, rather than the obvious tourist sights (such as the Taj Mahal or Jaipur), beach locations (Goa) or shopping centres (Delhi). The Indian Punjab has never been developed as a tourist destination due to the ongoing armed struggle between government authorities and a militant Sikh separatist movement.

Thus, the effect of Punjabi women's travel to the subcontinent, far from being escapist, is conservative, in the sense of reconfirming familial, ethnic and religious patterns. This effect is intentionally exploited when young people, and particularly young women, whose ways are considered to have become too westernized, are sent to the family village in order to experience the traditional constraints on their speech, dress and behaviour. Over a period of months it is hoped that the young women who are, for instance, 'too free going out with boys' will be modified.

One indication of the symbolic role that belonging to two places plays in British Punjabi women's identities is the fact that an ongoing commitment to maintaining family ownership of a Punjabi locality and an idyllic view of life there did not depend on it being a possible site of daily existence. It did not even depend on having ever visited the locality, as four of the women had never travelled to the Indian subcontinent. These women did not feel their understanding of, or commitment to, their Punjabi identities was compromised by the lack of first-hand experience, because the attachment was mediated through their heritage: 'It's where my parents were born . . . OK, I was born here, but I'm still Indian in a way as well. I am Indian obviously . . .' One of the four who had never visited the subcontinent said she would 'like to go' to 'see what it's like' and 'to know what it's like myself'. But the other three expressed no interest in visiting, nor harboured any plans to do so in the future. Their sense of belonging to their father's village did not depend on such experience. These women were unmarried when interviewed, but had not ruled out the possibility of contracting marriages with subcontinent men.

Transcontinental marriage

Young women's elders favoured marriage to subcontinent men both to fulfil obligations to family in the Punjab and because of the beneficial effects on their own children's behaviour, as already discussed. Thus, if considering a traditional marriage, women knew this might mean a Punjabi-raised husband and this, of course, raised the practical consideration of spending periods of time in his family's village or small town. Young women identified disadvantages associated with subcontinent husbands, the most important of which was the different expectations that a man brought up in the Punjab might hold, which could lead to misunderstanding and communication difficulties with his Scottish-raised wife:

> I find that a lot of people that have been married, one's been brought up here and one's been over there. It's been a culture clash and a lot of the marriages have been breaking up, divorce here, separation there. It's causing a lot of problems, you know. It's just a different line of thought . . . and the younger generation just can't cope. It's just causing a lot of strife.

These are the words of a woman who was herself married to her Pakistani-raised cousin, but did not think that she would contract similar marriages for her own daughters, in view of the difficulties she had experienced in managing her subcontinent in-laws' expectations. Of the women who had resisted entering an arranged marriage when interviewed, two subsequently agreed to a traditional marriage, providing the man had been brought up in Britain.

Practical assessments of the village idyll

Women's commitment to Punjabi localities came from their participation in a transcontinental marriage system, the possibility of their children's future participation and the importance of maintaining their father's family honour. The existence of young women's own and/or their husband's kin in Punjabi locations, plus their commitment to the maintenance of Punjabi family holdings, meant that they were keenly aware of the physical and social disadvantages of daily life there. Women with young children felt the risks of ill health through diarrhoea and infectious disease precluded visits to their villages within the next few years. The women generally did not wish to move to the Punjab, expressing the view that education, employment, housing and health facilities were inferior to those in Britain. There were also the constraints exerted on young women's behaviour, in terms of the elders' assessment of the suitability of contact with men outside the family, topics of conversation, dress and the labour in which women participated within and outside the home. Young women felt such restrictions would make daily life impossible: one woman said in her father's village she would live 'ten foot under' as 'a big disgrace' because of the lack of 'freedom for girls' to speak to whomever they please. Another woman said that 'I don't think I will be able to do my things', referring in particular to owning her own small business, because 'that is more for men, you know'.

The practical objections to Punjabi village life did not prevent women's commitment to the idyllic view. This idyll was used as a means of expressing discontents with daily life in Glasgow and was maintained as part of women's heritage and identity.

Changing travel locations

The goal of labour migrants' travel to Britain was to increase their family's affluence. For some South Asian groups (Modood *et al.*, 1997), including Punjabis in Glasgow (Bush *et al.*, 1995), this has been realized. The necessity of concentrating resources (including travel) on Punjabi localities by the migrant generation has become less pressing for those of the second generation who are wealthier. Those families who have succeeded in small businesses are beginning to travel to alternative tourist locations in India, such as Goa, and elsewhere, such as Disneyland in Florida, as well as visiting their Punjabi villages. As with the rejection of subcontinent husbands and the identification of the disadvantages of life in the rural Punjab, the broader choice of travel destinations does not necessarily mark a withdrawal from women's Punjabi identities, but rather a renegotiation of how they are signalled and maintained.

Strategy, travel and marriage

This chapter has been a description of some of the ways that British Punjabi women are using their position as the bicultural daughters of migrants to maintain their Punjabi identities and create British ones. The dual identities are expressed through a metaphor of belonging to two places and are closely bound up with women's ongoing commitment to the system of arranged marriages.

Punjabi women's strategic manipulation of the resources available from their dual heritage and their ability to work with the logic of British and Punjabi institutions is illustrated by accounts of the South Asians' response to the 'primary purpose rule' operated by British immigration authorities (Sachdeva, 1993). This rule, which required migrants to prove that the purpose of their removal to Britain was for marriage and not for gaining economic benefit from paid labour or from Britain's welfare provision, meant that in the 1980s it was increasingly difficult for Punjabis to gain residency rights in Britain, even if married to a Briton.

Various strategies were adopted to circumvent these difficulties. At an international level entry was sought via residency rights in other European countries that have less exclusive entry criteria, subsequently allowing Punjabis married to Britons to enter Britain as resident Europeans. Another strategy was to undertake full marriage ceremonies in the subcontinent and encourage the couple to conceive as quickly as possible in the hopes that evidence of conjugal relations and joint living arrangements would convince the authorities of the genuine nature of the union, thereby securing British residency rights. The risk of this strategy was that residency for the husband was repeatedly refused, leaving the family divided for a long period. To avoid this outcome some families adopted a strategy of hosting lavish betrothal ceremonies in Pakistan, which were recorded photographically and on video for subsequent submission as evidence of marriage. British immigration authorities are assumed to be unable to recognize the difference between a Punjabi betrothal and full wedding ceremony, so would be no more or less likely to refuse residency rights for the putative husband who is actually only a fiancé. After the betrothal ceremony, the young woman returns to Britain without her prospective spouse and the process of applying for his right of entry is initiated. Such betrothals are often undertaken at a fairly young age so that, in the eventuality that entry is repeatedly refused, the woman will be young enough to withdraw from the subcontinent betrothal and arrange a marriage with a British man. However, if the fiancé does manage to gain residency rights, then the full marriage ceremony can be undertaken. Taking this last strategy a step further, one woman described staging a farewell party when she left her father's Punjabi village, at which she wore a white costume and was photographed, as potential (although fictional) evidence of marriage at a later date. She planned to use the dated photographs as retrospective evidence of a long-standing marriage, should any of her father's friends' sons, who attended the party, wish to migrate to Britain at a later date. She felt that the white dress was important for convincing the British authorities, although the traditional colour for a Punjabi bride is bright red. At the time of writing she is legally married and living in Britain with a young man from her father's village.

Conclusion

The traditional role that travel (or at least displacement) plays in structuring Punjabi women's experience of domestic life persists in the British migrant context. Daughters of migrants from the Punjab express loyalties to both Glasgow, as the site of their daily existence, and to Punjabi land holdings and property, which represent a commitment to maintaining family honour. These two loyalties are not seen as incompatible and look likely to continue in tandem due to the migrant generation's commitment to transcontinental marriages and young women's commitment to remain within the system of arranged marriages, thereby maintaining links with the Punjab.

The maintenance of loyalty to Punjabi localities does not indicate a desire to move on a permanent basis, as young women identify the distinct drawbacks of daily life in the subcontinent. Indeed, loyalty to Punjabi places does not even depend on having visited them, as some British-born women, who saw themselves as part of a transcontinental network, with commitments in the Indian subcontinent, have never travelled beyond Britain.

Changes in patterns of marriage, travel and loyalty to place will occur with alterations to the occupations and standard of living of British

Punjabis. Greater wealth and a movement away from self-employment, which requires long working hours, makes touristic travel to a broader range of destinations possible. The commitment described among young women to participating in their elders' system of honour, including marriage and childbearing (Bradby and Williams, 1998), and the continuing low levels of out-marriage among South Asians (Modood *et al.*, 1997) make it unlikely that travel to mainstream British holiday destinations such as Florida will preclude the maintenance of subcontinent links.

References

Anwar, M. (1979) *The Myth of Return – Pakistanis in Britain*. London: Heinemann.

Anwar, M. (1988) *Between Cultures: Continuity and Change in the Lives of Young Asians*. London: Routledge.

Ballard, R. (1994) Introduction: the emergence of Desh Pardesh. In R. Ballard (ed.), *Desh Pardesh: The South Asian Presence in Britain*. London: Hurst.

Bhachu, P. (1985) *Twice Migrants – East African Settlers in Britain*. London: Tavistock.

Bradby, H. (1996) *Cultural Strategies of Young Women of South Asian Origin in Glasgow, with Special Reference to Health*. Unpublished PhD thesis. Glasgow: Glasgow University.

Bradby, H. (in press) Negotiating marriage: young Punjabi women's assessment of their individual and family interests. In R. Barot, S. Fenton and M. Boushel (eds), *The Family, Minorities and Social Change*. London: Macmillan.

Bradby, H. and Williams, R. (1998) *Health and Health Behaviour among Glasgow 18–20 Year Olds of South Asian and Non-Asian Background: A Follow Up*. MRC Medical Sociology Unit Working Paper No. 59. Glasgow: MRC Medical Sociology Unit.

Brown, P., MacIntyre, M., Morpeth, R. and Prendergast, S. (1981) A daughter: a thing to be given away. In Cambridge Women's Studies Group (eds), *Women in Society*. London: Virago.

Bush, H., Anderson, A., Williams, R., Lean, M., Bradby, H. and Abbotts, J. (1995) *Dietary Change in South Asian and Italian Women in the West of Scotland*. MRC Medical Sociology Unit Working Paper No. 54. Glasgow: MRC Medical Sociology Unit.

Carter, S. (1998) Tourists' and travellers' social construction of Africa and Asia as risky locations. *Tourism Management* **19** (4), 349–58.

Jeffery, P. (1976) *Migrants and Refugees – Muslim and Christian Pakistani Families in Bristol*. Cambridge: Cambridge University Press.

Modood, T., Berthoud, R., Lakey, J., Nazroo, J., Smith, P., Virdee, S. and Beishon, S. (1997) *Ethnic Minorities in Britain*. London: Policy Studies Institute.

Rampton, B. (1995) *Crossing Language and Ethnicity among Adolescents*. Harlow, Essex: Longman.

Sachdeva, S. (1993) *The Primary Purpose Rule in British Immigration Law*. Stoke-on-Trent, Staffs: Trentham Books.

Shields, R. (1990) The 'system of pleasure': liminality and the carnivalesque at Brighton. *Theory, Culture and Society* **7**, 39–72.

Urry, J. (1992a) The tourist gaze and the 'environment'. *Theory, Culture and Society* **9** (3), 1–26.

Urry, J. (1992b) The tourist gaze 'revisited'. *American Behavioral Scientist* **36** (2), 172–86.

Watson, J. L. (ed.) (1977) *Between Two Cultures: Migrants and Minorities in Britain.* Oxford: Blackwell.

Werbner, P. (1990) *The Migration Process: Capital, Gifts and Offerings among British Pakistanis.* New York: Berg.

15

Sex and travel: making the links

Paula Black

Introduction

Both sexuality and tourism have received increasing attention in theoretical and empirical work. An interest in sexuality has grown largely out of the feminist movement, and from Foucault's description of the explosion in discourses on sexuality since the eighteenth century (Foucault, 1990; Jackson and Scott, 1996). Interest in tourism has been fuelled by a turn to cultural factors in defining social identity at the price of a traditional emphasis on the sphere of production. Lifestyle, leisure and consumption are combined in the activity of tourism. Until recently, however, there has been a limited amount of work which attempts to draw these two areas together, although this is changing (Clift and Grabowski, 1997). Within the fields of sexuality or tourism themselves, many contradictions and silences are evident. For example, within tourist studies much work originates from a business and management perspective. Research and teaching are based upon the capital generated from tourism, or impart the practical management skills required by workers within related service industries. This area of academia has been relatively independent from the theorizing of tourism as a social and cultural phenomenon. To some extent empirical studies of tourism behaviour have bridged this gap, although they also generally draw upon one frame of reference for their research. In the sociological field, writing on tourism has been concerned with frameworks for theorizing what tourism actually is and for relating it to the structure of contemporary society (Urry, 1990; Rojek, 1993; Rojek and Urry, 1997). As such, this work potentially floats free of any empirical underpinnings. In order to develop these general theories there has been a tendency to ignore divisions within the categories of tourist over and above the debate about 'post-tourism'. Gender, ethnicity and the sexuality of travellers remain

Sex and travel 251

under-theorized, with limited attempts to integrate them into general theory. For example, Urry (1990), in *The Tourist Gaze*, devotes little more than two pages to a discussion of ethnicity.

Within the area of sexuality, too, there are gaps and contradictions. The theoretical approach to sexuality was initially informed by bio-medical and empiricist models which sought to measure and catalogue human sexual behaviour and experiences (Kinsey *et al.*, 1948, 1953). This biological reductionist explanatory framework has been challenged by constructionist theories. However, within this social constructionist approach there have been tensions, for example, between the work of Foucault and feminist critiques that emphasize his lack of materialism and an inadequate approach to power (Foucault, 1990; Ramazanoglu and Holland, 1993). Recent work has also raised the problem of the body, and a search is currently under way for theories and methodologies which allow embodied social practices to feature in sexuality without a return to essentialism (Holland *et al.*, 1994).

This overlapping and contradictory nature of research is inevitable and desirable. The possibility of accommodation and the establishment of an uncontested 'truth' of sexuality or travel is a naïve and discredited aim. However, problems do lie in the lack of exchange between differing areas of study. For example, sociologists have engaged only in a limited sense with dominant discourses of science in debates around sexuality and the body (Shakespeare, 1997). This disciplinary isolation is compounded by attempting to bring both sexuality and tourism together to form a new area of investigation. Problems arise in defining the area of study, in conceptualizing questions for investigation, in formulating appropriate methodologies, in referring to relevant existing material and in selecting a preferred framework for guiding research and analysis. Here I shall put forward arguments for the linkage of sexuality, sexual risk-taking and HIV, and tourism into an important area of study. I shall also give examples from my own research in order to discuss substantive findings and methodological approaches.

Sex, risk and travel

My research has investigated the areas of travel, sexuality and sexual risk. All of these issues are of considerable importance in contemporary British society, and in all other affluent societies. Sexuality may be seen as the key to personal identity in late modernity (Foucault, 1990). Tourism is a truly mass phenomenon, with the industry providing employment for more than 10 per cent of the global workforce and increasing numbers of people engaging in travel of some form (Clarke, 1997). Sexual risk-taking and the potential for transmission of HIV and other sexually transmitted infections are major public health concerns. HIV/AIDS also combines sexuality, risk and death, a combination which has proved fertile ground for health professionals and social scientists alike.[1]

At the beginning of the epidemic, travel was one of the 'risk factors' associated with the world-wide dissemination of the disease. This link between the travel of individuals away from their home environment and the spread of an infection which has become one of the 'moral panics' of our time is one of the factors in the linkage of sex and travel as an important area of study. However, though there is no doubt that HIV/AIDS has proved devastating for parts of the developing world, and for those engaging in specific activities in the West, the 'general population' has not been affected to the same extent. The predictions made at the start of the epidemic in the early 1980s and the accompanying public health information disseminated by governments in Western Europe can be seen to have contributed to the containment of the epidemic. There has been some evidence for heterosexual intercourse as an increasing source of infection in the UK. The fact that this has been linked to infection contracted abroad has focused attention on the role of travel.[2]

HIV/AIDS, travel and liminality

One aspect of the fascination with HIV/AIDS as a social phenomenon rather than a medical tragedy has been, at least in the West, the threat of infection from outsiders. The HIV epidemic can be seen to originate with a foreign African 'Other' (Farmer, 1992), or can be identified with 'foreign' cultures, and with the crossing of borders. HIV is associated with outsiders in terms of foreign nationals visiting the shores of home countries. It also represents entities from outside of the body crossing its protective boundaries. Once inside the body these outside forces act to promote chaos and decay. These are powerful and emotive subjects in themselves and when they are combined with homophobia, morality, sexuality and the question of the world distribution of wealth and power they become explosive.

Liminal zones are those where 'normal rules do not apply'. These may be carnival situations where everyday modes of interacting or power relationships are ceremonially overturned for a specific amount of time (Shields, 1990). They may be areas which straddle different modes of existence, for example the beach which borders both sea and earth, civilization and nature (Fiske, 1989). The removal of the person from everyday rules of behaviour at home into an unregulated and unfamiliar environment has potential liminal consequences. Liminality promotes unusual behaviour, part of which is the potential for risk-taking on a scale and in a form not commensurate with behaviour at home. Correspondingly, liminal zones are to be found in and upon the body. It is in these zones that the HIV virus obtains access to the body. The vagina, the anus and the mouth are gateways between inside and outside which allow the penetration of disease. Intravenous drug use involves traversing the boundaries of the skin, moving from the outside to the inside. The 'risk groups' associated with HIV transmission may also be described as liminal groups, occupying as they do an 'outsider' status in relation to hegemonic heterosexuality and the 'mainstream' of contemporary consumer culture. Sex workers, gay men and women, drug users and, at the end of this list, 'foreigners' have all been associated with a liminal status and with threat. The drawing of the borders of safety, normality and health are intertwined and are inextricably bound up with the borders of morality and immorality.

Methodology

The following discussion is based upon evidence drawn from in-depth interviews with attenders at genito-urinary medicine (GUM) clinics. The research was conducted in two GUM clinics in the south-east of England outside of London. All clinic attenders had travelled abroad in the previous two years and were approached to take part in the study by either myself or clinic staff.

Research methods included the face-to-face administration of 141 questionnaires covering biographical details, travel history, sexual history and history of sexually transmitted infections. The basis of the arguments made here, however, are 18 in-depth interviews conducted with clients who had originally completed a questionnaire. The interviews lasted between 30 and 100 minutes. All were tape-recorded and transcribed verbatim. These transcripts were then analysed using a grounded theory method (Strauss and Corbin, 1990). The aim of the research was to assess the implications of unsafe sexual behaviour abroad by the travellers/tourists, and to place this behaviour within its wider socio-cultural context. The concepts drawn from these testimonies were then investigated in terms of their 'fit' with current theory and the debates around tourism, risk and sexuality. For a more detailed discussion of the methodology employed in the study, see Black (1997).

The travel experience

Analysing the meaning of travel in the lives of the interviewees was important for the research in order to describe the context within which sexual encounters, if they occurred, took place. In tourism literature, tourism and leisure are proposed as existing in opposition to work and everyday life, and while this general proposition is relevant, definitions of tourism need to take into account more than this fact alone. The internal divisions within categories of tourism relate to identity. By looking at travel for women, for gay men or for those involved in sex tourism, it is possible to show that the motivation for travel varies between each group, as does the experience of travel. For example, Enloe (1989) links the structure of the tourist industry itself to gender hierarchies in employment patterns. Deem (1996) investigates Urry's concepts relating to tourism and finds that the experiences he defines as constituting tourism *per se* were either irrelevant or carried different meanings to the women in her study. These internal differentiations within the category of tourist have been inadequately addressed by theorists who are keen to develop all-encompassing theories of leisure and travel. They are, however, vital in understanding how travel plays a role in the identity formation of individuals, how their structural positioning motivates particular forms of travel and for examining in detail how specific forms of travel have effects upon behaviour, particularly sexual behaviour and risk-taking.

It is often assumed that travel *per se* is liminal and liberatory. Displacement from a familiar environment does affect behaviour, but this change is not unidirectional. The type of travel engaged in by the interviewees was dependent upon a host of influences relating to their life situation and in turn these factors shaped the experiences of travel. Sexual, or other risk-taking, was not universally or even commonly an outcome of travel abroad. Rather, the type of travel engaged in, the life situation of the individual, travelling companions, situational factors in the host destination and opportunity to engage in sexual contacts were some of the positive and negative influences on the likelihood to engage in sexual encounters abroad.

Tourism theories may also be evaluated against the concepts drawn from interviews. Separation of time and space and the reconfigurations of space are outlined as one of the defining characteristics of late modernism (Giddens, 1979, 1991; Jameson, 1984). Accompanying the spatial transformations in the operation of capitalism and forms of human relationship, social categories and individuals themselves become less defined by relations of production. Within these theoretical approaches, as consumption choices and lifestyle become indicators of social standing, leisure is moved to a more central position in social theorizing than has hitherto been the case. As leisure is organized in opposition to non-leisure activities, then its study may shed light upon social developments and the structure of contemporary society (Urry, 1990).

One particular category of tourist which appears in literature on tourism is that of the 'post-tourist' (Feifer, 1985). This is a concept which is defined in relation to the shift to a late modern society. The 'post-tourist' is said to reflect the structural changes occurring around him/her and is manifested in two forms. One type is the 'cool' and playful tourist who is aware of the inauthenticity of *all* experience and delights in the irony of gazing upon tourist spectacles. The second form of 'post-tourist' constructs him/herself in opposition to mass tourism and, despite sharing the cynicism of his/her cool compatriot, attempts to gain access to some level of authentic experience by venturing away from the mass tourist routes in the pursuit of individualistic pleasures and the exercise of the 'romantic gaze' (Urry, 1990). Changes in class structure have led to the emergence of a new and large service class, a proportion of which engages in the production and reproduction of signs through the media. It is the members of this new service class who use their travel experiences as 'cultural capital'. This cultural capital exists in the sense that Bourdieu relates class attribution not only to relationship to the means of production but also to identification through modes of consumption (Bourdieu, 1984). For the new service class who constitute the 'post-tourist', travel is a cultural asset.

The linkage of class and types of travel was evident from the testimonies of the interviewees. However, the implications concerning the compartmentalism of travel into types, and the definition of the 'post-tourist', were not supported. For the interviewees the decision to engage in travel, and the form it took, were integrated into their own biographical situation and interwoven with the lives of others. These others included relatives, lovers, dependants and employers. Four different categories of travel were evident: travel, tourism in resorts, tourism outside of resorts and work-related stays abroad. Modes of travel varied throughout the life course and were also combined at different stages of the year according to other commitments, personal choice and external restrictions. The most significant and enduring division, however, was that between traveller and tourist, both of which were defined in opposition to each other. Travel was associated with longer periods of travel in search of 'authentic' culture and was highly integrated into the biography of the individual, forming a core element of identity. Travellers generally embarked on their journeys alone and met companions as they progressed. Certain locations were popular, in particular India, the Far East and Latin America. The search for authentic experiences dominated all accounts of travelling, and influenced living conditions and activities engaged in. Tourism was seen by those who defined themselves as travellers to apply to all other forms of journeying. Tourism in this context was seen as the stereotypical 'Brits abroad' image, with holidays in resorts accounting for the majority of tourism, and also for the source of tourist mythology. The chief distinction between travel and tourism was seen to be the role of 'authenticity'. Tourists themselves, and travellers, view tourist experiences as mediated by the tourism industry, as somehow being constructed as entertainment for tourists, and as such distanced from the 'authentic' world of local inhabitants.

Such distinctions are dealt with to some extent in tourism literature, although the terms used to describe differing travel activities vary, as do the definitions of each category. Travel can perhaps be seen as a candidate for the label 'post-tourism', as it does indeed entail the espousal of an ideology which values individuality, authenticity and oppositionality. However, the notion that such travel has the capacity to form an 'oppositional tourism' which is in any significant aspects more critical than traditional forms of mass tourism has been questioned (Munt, 1994). I have drawn upon the interviewee testimonies to investigate the nature of the traveller/ tourist/post-tourist distinctions. The contradictory nature of the traveller narrations indicates that in fact the differentiation advocated between travel and tourism is spurious and based upon an ideological position rather than any qualitative differences in the value of travel over tourism. It seems that here further refinement is needed of tourism theory in order to critically evaluate the class-based distinctions between these differing categories.

Sexuality and sexual behaviour

Social constructionism defines sexuality as an area of social relations which is constructed and regulated through complex sets of social configurations and cannot be understood independently of the context within which it is experienced. Foucauldian approaches have formed the basis upon which much constructionist work is based. His unearthing of the discursive roots of sexuality and the wealth of historical material he brings to bear upon the subject have revolutionized the approach to sexuality (Foucault, 1990). For him it is not sexual acts themselves where meaning is to be sought but within the surrounding discourses which *create* the meaning of those acts. Foucault has been criticized for ignoring the systematic operations of power in constructing discourse and meaning, and the fact that though all bodies are subject to power, not all bodies feel the exercise of that power equally. An analysis of gender and the systematic concentrations of power with some groups rather than others is lacking in Foucault's work (Hartsock, 1990; Ramazanoglu and Holland, 1993). In addition, he is also anti-materialistic in his approach (Evans, 1993). I prefer what could be labelled a 'middle way' social constructionism, which seeks to avoid some of the major criticisms of Foucault by acknowledging the systematic nature of power in terms of its operation upon women, gays and ethnic minorities (Weeks, 1986, 1987). Social constructionism is consistent with the possibility that sexual behaviour will alter with a change in location, as one of the social influences on behaviour has shifted. This proposition is not so simplistic, however. Constructionism implicates a vast array of influences upon the individual, both past and present. Not all of these are altered with a change in location, and those that are may pull the person in different directions. How then does social constructionism apply in the travel situation? One methodological implication is to place an emphasis upon interpreting actions in terms of their social context.

An important part of travelling and holidaymaking is the potential for the interaction with others in a social environment. This sociability encompasses the desire to engage in the spectacles of the tourist situation or other types of activity with others who share similar interests and values.

This applies to both travellers and tourists. This form of interaction may be displaced into highly visible rituals such as sunbathing. It is here that the body becomes important for identifying group membership and for indicating the ideological commitments of the person. The tourist in a resort bar will wear different clothes, sport a different hairstyle, wear different jewellery, use different manners of speech and engage in a whole host of other cultural symbols which differentiate him/her from the traveller in a beach-side hut in a popular traveller destination. Though the symbols are different, the same purpose is served in indicating cultural identification and marking out others as potential sharers in the travel or tourist experience. This sharing of experience may lead to sexual contact but is by no means the most likely, or most desired, outcome of sociability (Hollands, 1995). Membership of a group, while offering benefits in terms of enabling interaction and increasing the potential for sexual partners, also carries with it the potential for pressure from others to conform to the standards of group behaviour. It is here that young male interviewees describing travel in single-sex groups mentioned feeling pressured into sexual conquests, or where young women felt pressured by the 'predatory' expression of sexuality by these men (Hollway, 1984; Wight, 1996). It should be noted here that not all forms of sexual contact are preceded by social interaction in an environment shared by others. Commercial sex or gay cruising do not fit this pattern. However, it holds true that such sex occurs within regulated conditions which are understood to a greater or lesser degree by the participants, and that these participants enact these expected rituals as an indication of their desire to share this type of sex with the other individual(s) concerned.

Once this initial sharing of the travel/tourist experience has led to the potential for sexual contact, then a host of other factors are brought into play over which the partners have differing levels of control. The attractiveness of the partner will already have begun to be assessed against culturally specific criteria, and this process continues throughout the period of 'pre-sexual contact'. The person's own view of sexual contact abroad plays a part in how likely it is that they will have reached this stage, and even now the mythology of the 'holiday romance' versus the 'tacky' sexual encounter is enacted in their mind. Any manoeuvres towards sexual contact at this stage are also influenced by the fact that it is (at least) a dyadic relationship which shifts as the potential encounter develops. It is interesting to note that partly because of the opacity of language and the difficulty involved in directly expressing sexual desires through language, non-verbal cues are important here. Agreement to change locations, often to a more secluded or private area is one of the actions read by partners as an indicator of consent to proceed to increased intimacy. In a holiday context this sometimes involves a move to the beach. This is one of the senses in which the beach may be described as a liminal zone, in that it is a public site during some stages of the day, but one which is used as a venue for private and intimate activities at other times (Fiske, 1989).

The relational nature of the decision-making process continues into sex itself. Safer-sex knowledge is determined by exposure to information at home, and any advice received in the location itself. Both partners must, however, be committed to safer-sex initiatives to create a situation where their implementation is likely. This is again a key point, where the range of influences upon this decision-making process become almost infinite. The first obstacle may be lack of knowledge, but even where levels of information concerning the routes of transmission of STDs and HIV are high, and the corresponding methods of preventing transmission are known, there is still a large step to be taken before safer sex is integral to the encounter. Power differences between the genders place the partners in a heterosexual encounter within a discourse which is powerful and at the same time invisible. Their negotiations are pervaded by their own discursive positioning in terms of gender, and yet neither of the participants may explicitly view these influences as affecting their behaviour. The heterosexual emphasis upon penetration of the vagina by the penis as constituting what 'sex' actually is also reduces the likelihood that alternative sexual practices will be engaged in (Wilton and Aggleton, 1991). Here the configurations of discourse and power relating to gender and sexuality are brought together powerfully.

Sexual behaviour and sexual identities may also be examined in terms of their potential to shift over time. This proposition has been advanced most strongly in post-modernist theories which criticize the notion of identity politics. The concept of the coherent and stable self has been criticized for belonging to a modernist era which is now in the process of disintegration. It was evident from the narratives of the interviewees that in the language and experiences of individuals in the clinic, sexuality and identities related to it retained some elements of classic modernist thought. For instance, activities were closely allied with identity. Sexual behaviour with a person of the same sex was seen to imply a homosexual identity not simply a 'playful' action. The configuration of identity was something unitary and comparatively stable and was predicated upon traditional dichotomies of male/female and heterosexual/homosexual. This identity was related fairly unproblematically to sexuality and gender and did not really conform in any sense to transgression in terms of gender or sexual identities. This is important if we are to evaluate the potential for sexual risk-taking away from home. By clinging to a unitary sense of sexual identity, tourists are carrying with them a set of expectations and preferences for sexual activities which are commensurate with their own sexual identity. The malleability of a fixed identity is less than that indicated by the post-modernist claims of fragmentation. It would seem that parameters of sexual behaviour remain linked to sexual identities both at home and abroad.[3]

Power relationships, particularly as discussed by women in heterosexual relationships, were also extremely evident. Hegemonic masculinity and normative definitions of what constitute heterosexual sex were prevalent. Within heterosexual sexual encounters women encountered directly the power of men to enforce their wishes in terms of sexual activity. For example, one woman interviewee described her fear of violence from a male partner when she asked about condom use. The manner of his resistance to her suggestion meant that she went ahead with unprotected sex in preference to risking further aggression from him. There was little sense that power relationships and the dichotomies associated with them were breaking down to the extent suggested, for example, by queer theory. In sexual encounters it seems that power remains a zero-sum game where power in the hands of one partner reduces the amount of power held by the other.

Risk

Risk was investigated both in terms of how various forms of risk are experienced by British visitors abroad and of how it is implicated in the formation of contemporary society. From the narrations four areas of risk were identified: health risk, cultural risk, risk of sexual infection and personal risk. Each of these types of risk carried with it strategies enacted by the interviewees in order to avoid these risks or to combat the negative outcomes of exposure to them. Health risk was not generally seen as a high priority for most interviewees and the potential for contracting illnesses or for becoming ill abroad was not a significant factor taken into account prior to travel. Cultural risks, on the other hand, did affect the evaluation of a destination. These risks related to threats of violence to the self from individuals or civil unrest in a destination, or the possibility of being stolen from or 'ripped off' while travelling. Sexual infection risks were evaluated in relation to the sexuality of the individual and their own cultural perceptions. The perceived risk from a partner was linked by the interviewees to their own images of certain locations, or to their stereotypes regarding specific types of people. The area of the world where sexual contact took place and the 'type' of person the partner was judged to be were key factors in the level of assessed risk.

The sexuality of the traveller was important in influencing the way that they viewed sexual risk. The definition of risks varied between heterosexual and gay interviewees. Heterosexual visitors saw risk in absolute terms. Penetration was seen to be the ultimate goal of heterosexual sexual encounters for both men and women, although women who differed from this expectation had limited resources for resisting a partner's insistence upon it. For heterosexuals, risk assessment related to whether a condom was used or not. For gay men risk was defined as a much more prevalent and relative concept. It was seen to be present at some level in all sexual activities, and so various activities were possible which minimized risk of infection. Finally, personal risk is a heavily gendered concept and relates to the dangers encountered by women as a result of their femaleness. The fear of violence, sexual harassment and rape is a constant and all-pervasive restriction upon the actions of women both at home and abroad. Monitoring and avoiding these risks take on a more unknown character while travelling, and this is a key experience of travel for women. To some extent, therefore, in the forms and extent of risk experienced by women, the characteristics of hegemonic masculinity can be seen as constituting a threat. This threat is experienced most severely by women, but is also of concern to men themselves, in terms of problems arising from their own behaviour and being placed at risk by the behaviour of other men.

All of the types of risk were assessed according to contextual criteria by the individual concerned. It was unsupported by the evidence from the interviews that the removal of the person to an unfamiliar environment automatically raises levels of risk assessment or risky behaviour. One key element did emerge which influenced assessment of potential risks and the corresponding avoidance strategies, and that was cultural familiarity. For all visitors a subjective sense of familiarity with the surrounding culture reduced the level of risk assessment (Black, 1998). Correspondingly, unfamiliarity may be in terms of a blanket definition of whole countries or areas as risky, or may apply to certain 'pockets' of unfamiliarity within a culture: for example, when engaging in drug-taking or the negotiation of gay sex where the person is unsure of local customs and social regulations.

Contemporary social theorists have become increasingly concerned with concepts of risk. Risk is seen to characterize the condition of late modern life, and specific forms of risk have contributed to the ontological insecurity which has come to inform the 'post-modern condition'. For Beck (1992) contemporary society contains higher levels of risk that at any time in the past. This level of risk has resulted from the disintegration of meta-narratives which provided some amount of ontological security in modern society. As the educated middle classes have grown in number so has the level of information about risks, and so too has the fear of the consequences of those risks. At the same time late modern society is unable to offer concrete guarantees or convincing explanations for the sources of risk and for the actions which are being taken to contain them. Studies of history provide evidence of wars, mass famine, widespread illness and political upheavals in earlier societies which indicate that contemporary society is not uniquely characterized by risk. It does seem, however, that late modern society is informed by a specific risk profile and that the form of these risks are contextually dependent upon the structure of Western society (Giddens, 1990, 1991).

Concepts of risk were seen by the interviewees in relation to cultural and contextual factors rather than being evaluated in terms of any 'rational' criteria. The uncertainty which Beck argues is a characteristic of the risk society was undoubtedly evident, and there was confusion over the reliability and applicability of health-related information, for example concerning HIV. This is possibly one of the reasons that a gap exists between knowledge concerning the risks of HIV transmission and corresponding avoidance behaviour. This incredulity towards medicine and confusion about advice from professionals is seen by Beck as a defining characteristic of the 'risk society'. Such scepticism has implications for the content and success of health promotion work. It suggests that information tailored towards specific groups of people, and particular risky situations would be most effective, rather than blanket statements with limited reference to context.

Though risk was experienced as a result of wider social transformations, and to some extent these risks were reliant upon perception, other sources of risk could be said to exist independently of individual perception of them. These arose from the particular structural positioning of the individual. For example, women experienced the threat of sexual attack while travelling, and two women in this study had been raped during a trip abroad. This type of risk arose from the very fact of being a woman. In this instance, the risks associated with hegemonic masculinity do not appear to be diminishing with the emergence of multiple gender identities. Power differentials in terms of economic position or gender also meant that sexual activities were not always negotiated between equal partners. The corresponding risks which arose also provide evidence for traditional forms of power structures, which remain evident despite claims of their transformation in post-modernism.

Conclusions

I have tried to show that there are inconsistencies and omissions within the areas of tourism and sexuality. However, these should not necessarily be seen as inadequacies. A multiplicity of approaches signifies intellectual vigour, and from the debates generated, more robust social theory emerges. However, there are problems where disciplines have developed without addressing relevant methodological and theoretical contributions from other sources. This difficulty is compounded when attempting to define and theorize a new area, such as that of travel health, or travel and sexuality. The writer is left with the choice of either selecting existing material to be synthesized in a new way, or with conducting original empirical work. This is precisely what has happened within the field of travel health, and the present volume attests to this.

At the same time as addressing this newly prescribed area, such work can also shed light upon contemporary debates within social theory. I have used research into the sexual experiences of British tourists abroad to question the concept of 'post-modernism' and to interrogate some of the concepts which post-modern theory has based itself upon. For example, claims about the malleability of identity and the transgressive nature of sexual actions were not supported by the interviewees in my study. For them, sexuality remained defined by a fairly fixed identity, and was accompanied by sexual activities associated with their particular identity. This, of course, has implications for sexual risk-taking and any corresponding health promotion initiatives. It seems that a masculine heterosexual identity formed a significant source of risk for heterosexual women, and was often at the root of an emphasis upon penetrative sex and a failure to use condoms. The two enterprises of contributing to knowledge in the field of travel and sexuality, and to wider social theorizing, may be achieved within the same work. The field of travel health/sexuality has much potential to offer to health promotion, sexuality, risk, tourism studies and wider theoretical debates in the social sciences. It is to be hoped that this interdisciplinarity will flourish within the area.

Notes

1. Research in this area has included investigations of the gendered nature of the epidemic (Richardson, 1996); the language of the AIDS discourse (Wilton, 1997); the language of medicine and the increasing medicalization of contemporary life (Waldby *et al.*, 1995); the 'risk society' and the impact of HIV upon ontological insecurity in late modernism (Beck, 1992); as well as empirical studies of sexual behaviour (Black, 1997; Wellings *et al.*, 1994).
2. Since reporting began in 1984, until the end of September 1998, 15,777 cases of AIDS and 32,491 cases of HIV-1 infections have been reported in the UK. Of those infected with HIV-1, 27,071 (84 per cent) are male and 5388 (16 per cent) female (CDR, 1998). Infections probably acquired through heterosexual intercourse reveal an unstable picture. In 1995, in England, Wales and Northern Ireland, they increased by 25 per cent from the previous year (635 new cases to 791). However, since then new infection figures have declined year on year (1996: 769; 1997: 738). The picture is similar for Scotland. Of this category, 80 per cent are infections considered to have occurred abroad. This figure rises to 90 per cent when infection from partners themselves considered to have been infected abroad is taken into account (PHLS AIDS Centre, 1998).
3. An interesting counterpoint to this argument are the visits made to Thai ladyboys by Western heterosexual men who do not appear to view this as a challenge to their heterosexual masculine identities, and who claim not to engage in such sexual encounters at home (Seabrooke, 1997).

References

Beck, U. (1992) *Risk Society: Towards a New Modernity*. London: Sage.

Black, P. (1997) Sexual behaviour and travel: quantitative and qualitative perspectives on the behaviour of genito-urinary medicine clinic attenders. In S. Clift and P. Grabowski (eds), *Tourism and Health: Risks, Research and Responses*. London: Pinter.

Black, P. (1998) Difference, discovery and danger: tourist perceptions of cultural difference. In F. LeSaux and N. Thomas (eds), *Unity and Difference in European Culture(s)*. Durham: University of Durham Press.

Bourdieu, P. (1984) *Distinction: A Social Critique of Taste*. London: Routledge and Kegan Paul.

CDR (1998) AIDS and HIV-1 infection in the United Kingdom: monthly report. *Communicable Disease Report* **8** (43), 385–8.

Clarke, A. (1997) *There Is More to This Than a Beach and a Bucket*. Unpublished paper. Derby: University of Derby.

Clift, S. and Grabowski, P. (1997) *Tourism and Health: Risks, Research and Responses*. London: Pinter.

Deem, R. (1996) Women, the city and holidays. *Leisure Studies* **15**, 105–19.

Enloe, C. (1989) *Bananas, Beaches and Bases: Making Feminist Sense of International Politics*. London: Pandora.

Evans, D. (1993) *Sexual Citizenship: The Material Construction of Sexualities*. London: Routledge.

Farmer, P. (1992) *AIDS and Accusation: Haiti and the Geography of Blame*. Berkeley: University of California Press.

Feifer, M. (1985) *Going Places*. London: Macmillan.

Fiske, J. (1989) *Reading the Popular*. Boston: Unwin Hyman.

Foucault, M. (1990) *The History of Sexuality: Volume 1*. London: Penguin.

Giddens, A. (1979) *Central Problems in Social Theory: Action, Structure and Contradiction in Social Analysis*. London: Macmillan.

Giddens, A. (1990) *The Consequences of Modernity*. Cambridge: Polity.

Giddens, A. (1991) *Modernity and Self-Identity: Self and Society in the Late Modern Age*. Cambridge: Polity.

Hartsock, N. (1990) Foucault on power: a theory for women? In L. Nicholson (ed.), *Feminism/Postmodernism*. London: Routledge.

Holland, J., Ramazanoglu, C., Sharpe, S. and Thomson, R. (1994) Power and desire: the embodiment of female sexuality. *Feminist Review* **46**, 21–38.

Hollands, R. (1995) *Friday Night, Saturday Night: Youth Cultural Identification in the Post-Industrial City*. Newcastle: University of Newcastle.

Hollway, W. (1984) Gender difference and the production of subjectivity. In J. Henriques, W. Hollway, C. Urwin, C. Venn and V. Walkerdine (eds), *Changing the Subject: Psychology, Social Regulation and Subjectivity*. London: Methuen.

Jackson, S. and Scott, S. (1996) *Feminism and Sexuality: A Reader*. Edinburgh: Edinburgh University Press.

Jameson, F. (1984) Postmodernism, or the cultural logic of late capitalism. *New Left Review* **146**, 53–92.

Kinsey, A., Gebhard, P., Pomeroy, W. and Martin, C. (1953) *Sexual Behavior in the Human Female*. Philadelphia: W. B. Saunders.

Kinsey, A., Pomeroy, W. and Martin, C. (1948) *Sexual Behavior in the Human Male.* Philadelphia: W. B. Saunders.

Munt, I. (1994) The 'other' postmodern tourism: culture, travel and the new middle classes. *Theory, Culture and Society* **11** (3), 101–23.

Public Health Laboratory Service AIDS Centre and Scottish Centre for Infection and Environmental Health (1998) *AIDS/HIV Quarterly Surveillance Tables: UK Data to End December 1997.* London: PHLS Communicable Disease Surveillance Centre.

Ramazanoglu, C. and Holland, J. (1993) Women's sexuality and men's appropriation of desire. In C. Ramazanoglu (ed.), *Up against Foucault: Explorations of Some Tensions between Foucault and Feminism.* London: Routledge.

Richardson, D. (1996) Contradictions in discourse: gender, sexuality and HIV/AIDS. In J. Holland and L. Adkins (eds), *Sex, Sensibility and the Gendered Body.* London: Macmillan.

Rojek, C. (1993) *Ways of Escape: Modern Transformations in Leisure and Travel.* London: Macmillan.

Rojek, C. and Urry, J. (1997) *Touring Cultures: Transformations of Travel and Theory.* London: Routledge.

Seabrooke, J. (1997) *Travels in the Skin Trade: Tourism and the Sex Industry.* London: Pluto.

Shakespeare, T. (1997) Social genetics – a polemical issue. *BSA Network*, September, p. 32.

Shields, R. (1990) The 'system of pleasure': liminality and the carnivalesque at Brighton. *Theory, Culture and Society* **7**, 39–72.

Strauss, A. and Corbin, J. (1990) *Basics of Qualitative Research: Grounded Theory Procedures and Techniques.* London: Sage.

Urry, J. (1990) *The Tourist Gaze: Leisure and Travel in Contemporary Societies.* London: Sage.

Waldby, C., Kippax, S. and Crawford, J. (1995) HIV-related discrimination in medical teaching texts. In P. Aggleton, P. Davies and G. Hart (eds), *AIDS: Safety, Sexuality and Risk.* London: Taylor and Francis.

Weeks, J. (1986) *Sexuality.* London: Routledge.

Weeks, J. (1987) Questions of identity. In P. Caplan (ed.), *The Cultural Construction of Identity.* London: Tavistock.

Wellings, K., Field, J., Johnson, A. and Wadsworth, J. (1994) *Sexual Behaviour in Britain: The National Survey of Sexual Attitudes and Lifestyles.* London: Penguin.

Wight, D. (1996) Beyond the predatory male: the diversity of young Glaswegian men's discourses to describe heterosexual relationships. In L. Adkins and V. Merchant (eds), *Sexualising the Social: Power and the Organisation of Sexuality.* London: Macmillan.

Wilton, T. (1997) *(En)Gendering AIDS: Deconstructing Sex, Text and Epidemic.* London: Sage.

Wilton, T. and Aggleton, P. (1991) Condoms, coercion and control: heterosexuality and the limits to HIV/AIDS education. In P. Aggleton, P. Davies and G. Hart (eds), *AIDS: Responses, Interventions and Care.* London: Falmer.

16

Tourism and sex: critical issues and new directions

Stephen Clift and Simon Carter

Introduction

As the chapters making up this book demonstrate, the complex intersections between international tourism and sexual behaviour and sexual health risks have generated considerable research interest in recent years. It is recognized, however, that the contributions are selective and specific in their coverage and that a comprehensive synthesis of theoretical perspectives and research evidence relevant to the links between sex and tourism and wider issues of sex and travel is lacking. This final chapter attempts to provide a basis for such an endeavour by reflecting critically on some of the major themes running through the contributions, identifying some of their limitations and pointing towards what is needed in future work, both theoretically and empirically.

A useful way of approaching these tasks is to ask six basic questions regarding the issues focused on in this volume: who and what, where and when, and how and why, being attentive to what is present in the contributions and what is missing.

Who is being studied?

Clearly, the answer to this is that 'tourists' are the main focus of study, especially tourists travelling internationally for purposes of leisure and holidaymaking. Few of the contributors explicitly address the debates commonly rehearsed in the tourism literature on how the 'tourist' is to be defined (see WTO, 1998: 24), or the complexities of proposed tourist typologies, but such work undertaken by tourism studies specialists provides a valuable contribution in thinking about sexual activity in the context of tourism and other forms of travel and mobility. Shaw and

Williams (1994), for example, suggest a typology in which the general category of 'travellers' is split into those 'within the scope of travel and tourism' and 'other travellers'. The former category is further divided into 'international' and 'domestic' tourists, and, for these, four primary purposes of travel are distinguished: business, visiting friends or relatives, personal business (e.g. shopping, medical treatment, etc.) and pleasure (e.g. recreation, sightseeing, etc.). The category of 'other travellers' includes: commuters, students, migrants, temporary workers and crews (ships and aeroplanes). Clearly, the surrounding circumstances and nature of these different forms of travel will establish differential probabilities for sexual opportunities, and it is important that research gives attention to such issues.

In the main, this book focuses on sexual activity arising in the context of international tourism pursued primarily for pleasure, and most of the studies described are concerned with travellers who fall into only one of the numerous categories in the classification presented by Shaw and Williams. In some contributions, however, sex in the context of 'domestic' business tourism is addressed (i.e. Luongo's discussion of visitors to New York from other parts of the United States), and Bloor *et al.* and Hart and Hawkes note a variety of travel purposes among the participants in their surveys. Furthermore, this book is organized around a very broad distinction between consensual and non-commercial sexual activity (between tourists themselves or between tourists and members of resident communities), and sex which involves some form of payment or transaction in goods from the tourist to a prostitute or member of the host community resident in the destination visited. As such, it neglects issues of sexual activity and risk among a diverse range of travellers other than leisure-oriented tourists, and also neglects wider questions of population mobility, sexual activity and sexual health.

The incidence and nature of sexual activity associated with work-related travel or travel-related work has been a focus of some research. In a recent investigation by Larcerda *et al.* (1996), for example, the focus of interest was on workers in the Brazilian port of Santos. This port is the largest in South America and is 'a major transportation nexus with links to all of Brazil and the rest of South America'. In this location:

> sailors from around the world and an estimated 4000 arriving truck drivers per day are served by a thriving sex industry. Seroprevalence of HIV among sex workers at the port varies by social class, with lower seroprevalance among the higher-class call girls who cater to tourists and businessmen and higher prevalence among the lower-class prostitutes who serve Santos' sailors, truck drivers and port workers.

(Larcerda, 1996: 1159)

Larcerda *et al.* gathered data on HIV status and sexual risk behaviours from a random sample of male port workers (n = 395) employed by the Santos

Port Authority. The rate of HIV infection was found to be low (four men, 1.1 per cent), but among a fifth of the men who reported sex with 'secondary partners', nearly half never used condoms and just under a fifth reported using them only sometimes with those partners. The authors conclude:

> Only time will tell whether HIV will spread widely among heterosexuals in Brazil. We believe that the main finding of this study is that we still have time to prevent a larger HIV epidemic in Santos and along the transportation corridors that emanate from that city.
>
> (*ibid.*: 1159–60)

In discussions of sex tourism in this volume, the focus has been on tourists travelling to specific destinations for sex, but it is important to acknowledge also that prostitutes themselves may be internationally mobile. This is an issue which has attracted considerable interest in recent years, and some research attention (Bröring, 1997). As the introduction to the European Project AIDS and Mobility (1996: 10) report on *Mobility, Prostitution and HIV Prevention in Central/Eastern and Western Europe* notes:

> Mobility and prostitution are two closely linked phenomena. Sex workers and clients travel in border regions as well as from continent to continent. Examples of commercial sex work in border regions can be found, for instance, along the borders of Germany, Belgium and the Netherlands, but also in other European regions. With regard to intercontinental prostitution, one might consider South American, Asian and African women working in the red light districts of Hamburg and Amsterdam, Brazilian transvestites working in Italy and European and North American clients travelling to Southeast Asia in search of sexual services.

There is some evidence that mobile prostitutes, in certain locations, may have a higher incidence of HIV infection. In a survey among prostitutes and their clients in Amsterdam, for example, van Haastrecht *et al.* (1993) found that while HIV prevalence was low (3 out of 201 prostitutes and 1 of 213 male clients were positive), all three positive prostitutes originated from AIDS-endemic countries and were recent arrivals in The Netherlands. In addition, inconsistent condom use was found to be most common among prostitutes who had migrated from Latin America and among the migrant clients of prostitutes. Of course, the social and economic circumstances of migrant women in prostitution needs to be understood in order to make sense of such findings, and alarmingly, as a recent publication by the International Organization for Migration (1995) makes clear, much of the mobility of prostituted women in Europe constitutes grossly exploitative and abusive trafficking.

In addition, there has been no discussion in this volume of the travel patterns of intravenous drug users, who are vulnerable to HIV and other infections not only in association with their drug-using practices but also through risky sexual activity with other injecting drug users. In a recent study, McCoy *et al.* (1996) examined the patterns of high-risk drug use and sexual activities engaged in by a large sample of injecting drug users in the context of travel within the United States. The purpose of the study was to explore the role of spatial and geographic factors in patterns of HIV transmission. Just under 50,000 participants were recruited from 60 sites nationwide. The results revealed that low HIV-prevalence cities were significantly more likely to have been the destinations of both men and women who engaged in high-risk drug and sexual activities. In addition, HIV-positive drug users who engaged in high-risk drug and sexual behaviours in destination cities were more likely than sero-negatives to travel to high and low sero-prevalence areas than to moderate prevalence areas. The authors conclude that their findings 'suggest a need for effective prevention educational messages about the risk of travelling and participating in high risk activities' (*ibid*.: 249). Goldberg *et al*. (1994) report a similar study of mobility and risk behaviours among injecting drug users. Just over 900 drug users were interviewed in Glasgow, Scotland, about their injecting and sexual behaviour outside the city during the previous two years. Forty-five per cent of respondents had injected outside Glasgow, 6 per cent had shared needles and 20 per cent had had sexual intercourse. Much of these activities had occurred outside of Scotland but within the UK, mainly in London. The authors conclude that 'Glasgow IDUs are a highly mobile group and although HIV prevalence remains low in this population, considerable potential for importation/exportation of HIV and other bloodborne and sexually transmitted infections exists' (*ibid*.: 387).

Larger-scale patterns of human mobility and migration also hold substantial implications for patterns of sexual behaviour and sexually transmitted diseases, and these should be acknowledged to supplement the coverage provided in this volume. A substantial contribution to an understanding of the role of different forms of population mobility in the spread of sexually transmitted infections and HIV in the contemporary global situation has been made by Quinn (1994). In the African context, for instance, major human movements have occurred over the last twenty years due to economically motivated migration from rural to urban areas, natural disasters, political instability and armed conflicts. Such large-scale population movements are heavily implicated in the development of the HIV/AIDS epidemic. More specifically, with reference to the situation in Uganda, Quinn notes that three principal hypotheses have been proposed to account for the development of the HIV/AIDS epidemic and its distinctive distribution throughout the country. First, the 'truck town' hypothesis suggests that the geographic dispersal of infection reflects the pattern of major roads in the country which 'act as principal corridors of virus spread between urban areas and other proximal settlements'. Truck drivers along these routes and commercial sex workers who offer their services to drivers at rest sites are the principal actors in this process. Second, the 'migrant labour' hypothesis suggests that HIV has moved from 'areas of labour demand in urban areas to areas of labour supply in rural districts through a process of return migration'. And a third hypothesis put forward is that the diffusion of HIV through Uganda reflected ethnic patterns of recruitment into the Ugandan National Liberation Army, after the overthrow of Idi Amin in 1979. Quinn notes that 'probably all three hypotheses together help explain the spread of HIV within Uganda'.

What is being studied?

The answer to the question of what is being studied by the contributors to this volume may appear relatively straightforward. As noted above, contributions are organized around two themes: sex in tourism and tourism for commercial sex. The major themes running through many contributions are the incidence and determinants of sexual behaviour and sexual risk in tourism contexts and the commodification of sex in tourism-receiving destinations, especially in poor countries pursuing an uncertain path of economic development via tourism. Other issues addressed include: sources of information for tourists on where sex is available in a given destination (Luongo); the spatial organization of sex industries within urban landscapes (Carter); the role of governments, international organizations and NGOs in fighting the sexual exploitation of children by tourists (Hoose *et al.*); the motivations and behaviours of young raver holidaymakers (Khan *et al.*): and travel in the search for a marriage partner (Bradby).

It should be acknowledged, however, that other connections between sexuality and tourism can be identified which are not addressed in this volume. Recent research interest has, for instance, focused on: the use of sexual imagery in the marketing of tourism products (e.g. Marshment, 1997; Oppermann and McKinley, 1997); media representations of romance and sex in the context of holidays (Clift, 1994); the role of tourism and holidays in relation to sexual identity formation and affirmation (Hughes, 1997); the extent to which tourism products and services have been developed and marketed for women travellers and sexual minorities (Jordan, 1998; Callister, 1998; Pritchard *et al.*, 1998); the organization of gay sexual spaces in urban tourist destinations (Hughes, 1998); the perceived risk of HIV infection associated with different destinations (Cossens and Gin, 1994; Carter, 1995, 1998a); travellers' intentions to be sexually active when travelling or on holiday (Mulhall *et al.*, 1993; *Barrier Protection Digest*, 1997); and the travel patterns, health precautions and health problems of HIV-positive travellers (Kemper *et al.*, 1994).

Also, while the issue of tourists and travellers as target audiences for sexual health promotion initiatives is raised in several contributions in this volume (Bloor *et al.*; Hart and Hawkes; Ford *et al.*, 1996), this area is not covered comprehensively, and a number of significant programmes of work and specific recent interventions have not been discussed (e.g. European

Project AIDS and Mobility; the Europe against AIDS Summer Campaign). Details of such initiatives are, however, readily available elsewhere (Bröring, 1996; Stears, 1996; Thomas *et al.*, 1997). In this connection, an issue which should be an important focus of research is the extent to which local initiatives in sexual health promotion have been organized within specific regions or destinations in response to a substantial seasonal influx of tourists on a seasonal basis. Brown (1995) has recently developed a critique of the dominant geographical approach to the HIV/AIDS pandemic, with its emphasis on constructing maps of the changing spatial distribution of cases of HIV infection over time, and on demonstrating the association between diffusion patterns and major routes of domestic and international traffic. Geographers, he argues, should be just as much concerned with charting the spatial characteristics of initiatives undertaken to halt transmission of the virus. In fact, very little research has examined the nature and extent of sexual health initiatives targeting tourists undertaken in tourist destinations, or orchestrated by tour operators. Examples of local initiatives are provided by work undertaken in Santorini in Greece, under the aegis of the European Project AIDS and Mobility (Bröring, 1996), and sexual health promotion work undertaken in Torbay, a popular resort in south-west England (Ford *et al.*, 1996). Further research is needed into the factors which render sexual health promotion initiatives in tourist-receiving destinations difficult to mount and maintain, despite the recognition that holiday environments can facilitate sexual mixing and risk behaviours (Ford and Eiser, 1996).

Where are studies focused on and undertaken?

A consideration of travel and tourism in relation to sexual behaviour and risk obviously involves an examination of movement from a home destination to another place for a shorter or longer period of time. The issues of 'place' and 'space', how they are defined, marked, delineated and regulated, are significant ones in these discussions. The contributors to this volume have necessarily tended to focus on travel to particular countries, and often to specific destinations within countries. Within destinations the focus may have been on very clearly delimited districts, streets within those localities and particular kinds of venues, settings or spaces within those streets. Thus, in Clift and Forrest's discussion of gay tourism and sexual behaviour, the concept of important gay cities is taken from the *Spartacus* international gay guide, and such destinations world-wide are distinguished from other destinations which are loosely characterized as 'not gay'. Because of the broad sweep of their survey, and the limited information gathered on gay men's holiday arrangements, no further specification could be given of where the sexual activity took place within the cities and resorts, but the guide itself typically provides maps indicating where the gay districts in major cities are, and where important venues can be found. A much fuller discussion of the spatial characteristics of the urban landscape in relation to sex is provided by Carter's account of the organization of sex industries in Amsterdam and Prague. Luongo goes further in discussing specific commercial sex venues where visitors to New York might find sex, and highlights the key significance of hotels as venues for sexual encounters with local male 'escorts', and Thomas identifies important spatial factors constraining and facilitating sexual activity by women tourists. It is striking, however, looking over the contributions, how varied the discussions are in their specificity with respect to locational and spatial information. Some are content to refer in the most general way to countries, without reference to specific destinations; others refer to particular cities or resorts and attempt to distinguish one type of urban/resort destination from others; and some are quite specific about the clearly delimited areas or venues within which sexual activity on the part of tourists – with other tourists or among themselves – might arise.

Country destinations considered in contributions to this volume include the Caribbean islands of Cuba, the Dominican Republic and Jamaica (Sánchez Taylor), the Pacific island of Bali, Indonesia (Ford), the Balearic island of Ibiza (Khan *et al.*) and, of course, Thailand (Hart and Hawkes). It is important to acknowledge, however, that the present volume does not, by any means, provide a comprehensive overview of those places across the globe which attract 'sex tourists', and still less those destinations and resort areas where tourist sexual activity may be particularly prevalent. There are many countries associated with particular patterns of sex tourism, for instance, which are not discussed in this volume. Information on such destinations can come from research studies, but more often is available from specialist sex guides, pornographic magazines (Clift, 1994) and the Internet (Jeffreys, 1998). Herold and van Kerkwijk (1992: 1) provide a map giving 'suggested primary routes' of global sex tourism, and 'popular' destinations for sex tourism (they suggest) are 'Thailand, the Philippines, Brazil, the Dominican Republic, Kenya, the Netherlands and more recently, countries in eastern Europe'. Kleiber and Wilke (1995) report findings from a study of German sex tourists conducted in Kenya, Brazil, Thailand and the Dominican Republic. Hall (1996), in a detailed analysis of sex tourism in South-east Asia, gives particular attention to prostitution and tourism in Korea, the Philippines, Taiwan and Thailand, but notes that prostitution serving foreign tourists (especially Japanese men) can be found throughout the region. Hall also acknowledges the well-established role of Australia as a major 'sex tourist-generating region to South-east Asia', but points out the recent development of a home-grown sex tourism industry:

> A further dimension of Australia's involvement in sex tourism has been provided by the rapid growth of inbound tourism to Australia in the 1980s, particularly from Japan. Such destinations as the Gold Coast have witnessed

ease in the amount of tourist-oriented prostitution and Asian girls have
been brought into the country to cater for both Australian and Japanese
tourists.

(ibid.: 73)

Other destinations where the use of prostitutes by tourists has been
researched or highlighted in media reports include New Zealand (Hanson,
1997), which has a surprisingly significant sex tourism industry; The
Gambia, a destination to which women from the UK and Northern Europe
reputedly travel to have sex with local men (Yamba, 1988), and Sri Lanka,
which attracts homosexual men seeking sex with boys (Ireland, 1993).

There are also countries where sex tourism has emerged very recently,
such as Estonia (especially the capital Tallinn and the southern resort of
Parnu), which, since the collapse of the Soviet Union and the opening of
borders to the West, has attracted large numbers of Finnish men seeking the
services of prostitutes (Taar and Kalikova, 1995; Kalikova *et al.*, 1998). The
recent increase in cases of syphilis in Finland are attributed to unprotected
sex in Estonia and elsewhere in the Baltic region, where syphilis levels are
much higher and have increased dramatically in the last five years
(Eurosurveillance, 1996; CDR, 1997). Other areas documented as having
local sex industries which cater to a significant degree for travellers of
various kinds and tourists include: Szczecin in Poland (European Project
AIDS and Mobility, 1996), Shenzhen in China (Abdullah, 1996), Santos in
Brazil (Larcerda *et al.*, 1996) and a large number of specific border regions in
Central Europe (Netzelmann, 1995; Steffen and Leopold, 1995).

Only relatively recently has research interest focused on the significance
of specific venues or settings for sex (whether consensual or commercial), in
relation to sexual risk, and some of this research is of significance in relation
to the study of sexual activity in tourism. For example, de Wit *et al.* (1997)
report on a study of gay men in Amsterdam which assesses the extent of
sexual activity with casual partners in a variety of different venues. Most of
the 410 men who had sex with casual partners during the previous six
months had done so in private homes (67.8 per cent), but cruising areas,
saunas and dark rooms were also frequented by between a third and half of
the sample. Unprotected anal sex with casual partners was reported by 13.3
per cent of men in private homes, 7.0 per cent in dark rooms, 6.3 per cent in
cruising areas and 5.8 per cent in saunas. The mean numbers of unprotected
sex partners reported was highest for cruising areas (1.16), followed by dark
rooms (1.10) and saunas (0.80). Given also that recent estimates suggest that
'one in every 6 homosexual or bisexual men in Amsterdam is HIV-antibody
positive' *(ibid.*: 134), the significance of de Wit *et al.*'s findings from a
tourism perspective are clear, since substantial numbers of gay tourists
travelling to Amsterdam are likely to visit saunas and dark rooms for sex.
Clift *et al.* (1999) have found in surveys of gay men attending the annual gay
and lesbian travel fair in London (1997–8) that visiting saunas and sex clubs

is a major predictor of sexual activity on holiday among gay men.

Finally, with the exception of Luongo's chapter, little attention has been given in this collection to sexual activity within the context of domestic tourism, or to travel within countries for sexual opportunities (whether consensual or commercial). The lack of attention to the former issue reflects the fact that only one major survey, undertaken by Ford in the Torbay area in south-west England, has investigated the sexual activity of domestic tourists (Ford and Eiser, 1996). With respect to the second issue, however, a number of recent studies of gay men in the UK have documented the distances which gay men are prepared to travel in order to socialize with other gay men and to meet potential sexual partners, and in some circumstances to access specialized sexual environments (Annetts *et al.*, 1996; Burnell *et al.*, 1995; Kelley *et al.*, 1996). Of course, the need for physical movement to meet new people or to have new experiences is an inherent fact of life which is hardly worthy of comment, let alone analysis. Yet in the case of sexual minorities, such as gay men, the extent of mobility reflects important social and spatial realities of contemporary gay lives (e.g. that gay social spaces are found primarily in large urban centres rather than in small towns and rural settings), and has implications for the way in which HIV prevention outreach work is planned (e.g. public sex environments which attract large groups of men from a wide geographic area are important venues for preventive work) and also for the way in which such prevention work is financed (i.e. a sexual space may be in one area, but most of the men visiting may live outside of that area, so who should be responsible for funding prevention initiatives in that location?). In this context, it is also appropriate to acknowledge that the substantial size of gay populations and the concentration of gay businesses in particular districts of 'important gay cities' are both a product of selective migration by gay men to cities and urban areas with established gay communities and the basis for such urban environments attracting short-term visitors from further afield (see Myslik, 1996 and Valentine, 1996, for discussions of sexual '(re)negotiations' of space).

When have studies been undertaken and what time periods have been studied?

It is very striking that research interest among social scientists in the interconnections between tourism and sex is relatively recent, despite the fact that the link between travel and STDs 'has been known for centuries' (Mulhall, 1993), and that epidemiological surveillance in Europe and the United States clearly established the role of travel in the global spread of penicillin-resistant strains of gonorrhoea from the mid-1970s onwards (De Schryver and Meheus, 1989). Two obvious reasons why greater attention has been given in recent years to travel and sexual behaviour are: first, the emergence of the HIV/AIDS pandemic, together with an appreciation of the role of mobility in its geographic spread; and second, recognition that mass leisure travel and tourism has assumed extraordinary proportions in a relatively short period, and that this growth is set to continue well into the next century.

All of the empirical work reported on in this volume is therefore very recent, and doubtless there is a temporal dynamism in the social and cultural issues addressed, as historical changes unfold. This is very clear with respect to the current situation in Central and Eastern Europe, with the liberalization of cross-border movement following the demise of the Soviet Union (e.g. the case of sex tourism to Estonia noted earlier). But other examples can be given of how change can occur quite rapidly in the sexual infrastructure and culture of particular cities which might impact on the sexual behaviour of tourists to that destination. The case of London is especially dramatic in this respect. Only five years ago, London had very few gay saunas and commercial sex venues, and those which did exist operated very discreetly and under constant threat of police action, closure and prosecution. Recently, however, the number of such venues has increased markedly and all openly advertise themselves in the gay press, making clear the facilities on offer. Why such a development has occurred in the mid- to late-1990s and so quickly, and why action has not been taken to close them down, given the illegality of the activity taking place within them, is not entirely clear, but recent research has clearly established that a significant minority of men engage in unprotected anal intercourse in such settings, including men who are aware of their own HIV-positive status (Keogh *et al.*, 1998). It is entirely possible that the availability of such venues will increase the rates of sexually transmitted infections seen among gay men.

These recent developments in the commercial sexual landscape available to gay men in London has obvious implications for any discussion of tourism and sex. Not only can gay men in and around London (and elsewhere in the UK) readily access venues, which only a few years ago could only be experienced abroad, but also gay men visiting London now have easy opportunities to be sexually active, which only a few years ago did not exist. It is interesting to note, too, that recently the London Tourist Board, in association with boards in Manchester and Brighton, has launched marketing campaigns in the United States and Germany to attract gay tourists, with no awareness of these changes in the sexual infrastructure for gay men in the capital.

A second aspect of time worth mentioning with respect to the present volume is that the contributions offer little in the way of a historical perspective. This is understandable given the emphasis on the contemporary situation and the fact that most contributors are social scientists. However, a historical perspective on the issues addressed here is both of considerable intrinsic interest and contemporary relevance if we are to fully understand why certain places have become significant destinations for sex tourists, or why it is that holidays are associated in the popular imagination with sexual adventure (Clift, 1994). Histories of sex within travel or on holiday, and of travel for sex, can be found in a number of different sources and no doubt there is much that could be said about these issues which remains unresearched and unwritten. Aldrich (1993), for example, provides an account of travels by homosexual men during the eighteenth and nineteenth centuries from Northern Europe to the Mediterranean, in search of homoerotic experience and self-affirmation. Hufton (1995: 312–13), in her history of women in Europe in the pre-modern period (1500–1800), discusses prostitution in a number of major centres in Europe, and points out that at different times during the seventeenth and eighteenth centuries, guides were available to 'local whores' in Amsterdam, Paris and London for visitors to these cities:

> a work, published in 1681 in Amsterdam, entitled *Amsterdamsche Hoerdom*, ... was emulated and indeed became a fashionable genre in the eighteenth century both by the *Filles du Palais Royale*, a frequently published compendium or Parisian directory which catalogued the local whores and was intended for tourists, and by Harris's *List of Covent Garden Ladies, or Men of Pleasure's Kalender*, which appeared annually updated, between 1760 and 1793 and which gives minute factual descriptions of 'fine, bouncing, crummy wenches'.

In addition, historians such as Howarth (1977) and Pemble (1987), in their studies of nineteenth- and early-twentieth-century British upper-class travellers to the Mediterranean region (especially the French Riviera), draw attention to the fact that prostitution was often an open part of 'café' or casino society, with a number of individual prostitutes gaining an international notoriety in this period.

Tourism, of course, has only recently become a predominant form of human mobility, and historical accounts of the sexual lives and activities of individuals on the move are inevitably bound up with international conflicts within Europe and Western expansionism – exploration, trade, missionary work, war, occupation and colonization – beyond European shores. Hufton (1995: 312) notes that military conflicts in Europe during the pre-modern period involved army movements of 'unprecedented scale' and military men 'were the main clientele of the prostitute in many garrison towns'.

Sexuality in the context of colonialism has also become a significant focus of historical research. Hyam (1990) provides an extraordinary account of the sexual dimensions of the British Raj in India, for example, which includes a map of the location of 'Regimental brothels' in India around 1888 and a graph of reported syphilis in the British army 'at home' and 'in India' from 1880 to 1908. The latter reveals considerably higher levels of syphilis 'in India' than 'at home' during the period 1890 to 1900 when the medical regulation of prostitution was suspended. In recent history, the most significant example of the connection between the military and organized prostitution, of course, is the role assumed by Thailand during the Vietnam War, as a 'rest and recreation' destination for American servicemen. The stimulus provided for the development of the Thai sex industry laid the foundation of the future reputation of Thailand as a sex tourism destination (Hall, 1996). Similar connections between the establishment of American military bases, the emergence of sex industries and the subsequent developments of sex tourism following the closure of bases occurred in the Philippines (Jeffreys, 1998).

How have the connections between tourism and sex been researched?

Reflecting back over the contributions to this volume, it is clear that while a range of techniques have been employed in gathering information about tourism and sex in the empirical studies reported, the methodological approaches can be broadly categorized as either 'quantitative' or 'qualitative'. Quantitative studies, using questionnaires or structured interviews, aim to gather countable data from large samples of respondents, which can then be subjected to various forms of statistical analysis and modelling, while qualitative studies are more concerned with exploring personal frameworks of meaning which social actors draw upon in making sense of events and situations and framing possibilities for action. Some studies, of course, attempt a triangulation of insights from different techniques, gathering both quantitative and qualitative data. The studies undertaken by Khan *et al.* and Clift and Forrest are good examples of such an approach in action, although in the accounts presented here, the focus is respectively on the qualitative and quantitative data gathered. The particular strengths of these two approaches and their complementary values are well illustrated by considering the large survey of travel and sexual behaviour described by Bloor *et al.* and the small-scale interview-based study undertaken by Thomas, one of the team involved in the European Commission-funded investigation. It should be noted, however, that there are some limitations to the methodologies employed in the research studies described in this volume, and equally there are techniques of data gathering and analysis which are absent from this collection of studies and which would make a useful contribution to the development of work in this field (e.g. systematic procedures for the analysis of textual data, detailed ethnographic observation and time-budget methodologies in relation to sexual behaviour).

The focus of this volume has been on the contributions made by the social science disciplines to the study of travel/tourism and sexual behaviour and risk of sexual infections, and this is reflected in the methods employed. It should be acknowledged, however, that quite different approaches to the issue of travel and sexually transmitted infections have been developed by specialists in microbiology and genetics and by epidemiologists interesting in modelling disease epidemics over time and space. Microbiologists and geneticists have developed sophisticated techniques to chart variations in the biological characteristics of particular infectious organisms in defined populations. A body of scientific research has developed from this perspective relevant to the movement of infectious organisms between and within regionally or locally defined populations. Nasioulas *et al.* (1998: 685), for instance, report a recent study which explored the genotypic variations of HIV infections in Athens. They point out that previous studies have revealed two major groups of the HIV-1 virus, M and O, and that within the major M group, ten subtypes have been identified, labelled from A to J. The distribution of HIV-1 subtypes in a given population, they suggest, points towards the degree of cross-infection within that population and between that population and others:

> The global dispersion of HIV-1 has been suggested to be due to migration of individuals and populations. Such migrations may lead to dispersion of diverse HIV-1 sub-types into regions where the vast majority of previous characterised isolates have been of one sub-type. Molecular studies have been used to document several independent introductions of different HIV strains in many regions such as eastern Europe, India, Brazil, North America and south-eastern Asia.

In their study, the HIV-1 subtype distribution in 83 positive individuals living in Greece was determined, and 71 were found to be subtype B, 5 subtype A, 4 were D, 2 were C and 1 was subtype I. Among Greek nationals studied, subtype B was most frequent (94 per cent), whereas among emigrants living in Greece, non-B types were more prevalent (57 per cent):

> Since the dispersion of diverse HIV-1 sub-types in populations experiencing a limited HIV epidemic provides new informational material on global virus propagation we attempted to determine the genotypic distribution among seropositive foreigners and travelers living in Greece. Twelve subjects were found to be infected with non-B subtypes. The majority of those (7 of 12, or 58 per cent) were found to be emigrants from Africa; 1 of them (8 per cent) was an emigrant from Portugal, 2 (17 per cent) were Greek travelers infected in Africa, and 2 (17 per cent) were Greek citizens infected in Greece.

> (*ibid.*: 688)

A further body of work of considerable relevance to this field of travel, tourism and sexual risk is the attempt to develop predictive epidemiological models of disease epidemics which include both temporal and spatial parameters. The contributions of Thomas (1996) and Wallace and his colleagues (Wallace and Wallace, 1997; Wallace *et al.*, 1997) are of especial significance here. Both address basic issues in the role of human mobility in the geographic diffusion of disease, and the general principles are clearly

278 Stephen Clift and Simon Carter

applicable to a consideration of tourist flows and their implications for the epidemiology of sexually transmitted infections. Thomas (1996: 353) explains his approach as follows:

> Geographers concerned to forecast the progress of HIV/AIDS have tended to fit space-time statistical models to recorded incidence. Their major intentions have been to reconstruct the pathways of HIV and provide short-term predictions about its expected diffusion. In contrast, many epidemiologists have engaged in more long-term ventures which apply systems models to the twin tasks of eliciting the underlying epidemic structure and estimating the consequences of preventive actions taken against the transmission of HIV.

Thomas's primary aim is to extend the second epidemiological approach by incorporating a geographic perspective in order to simulate 'transmission between populations at different risk of infection and between regions'. As he notes:

> The application of single region (community) models...have analysed national AIDS epidemics in isolation from the geographical diffusion of HIV as a pandemic infection. Multiregion modelling formats, however, provide an opportunity to study the structure of the international contact networks that support the transmission of infection from one country to another.
>
> (*ibid*.: 363)

The complexities of the models presented by Thomas and Wallace would require considerable space to elaborate and need not concern us here. The key point, however, is that their attempts to incorporate a spatial dimension into models of the HIV/AIDS pandemic are clearly of considerable relevance to any attempt to understand the interrelationships between tourism flows, tourist sexual behaviour and the spread of HIV and other sexually transmitted infections.

The only contribution in this volume which comes near to integrating epidemiological, biological and social perspectives in a discussion of travel and sex is that by Hart and Hawkes, based on their research in the context of GUM clinics in the UK, which reflects their expertise as a sociologist and a medical specialist in sexually transmitted diseases, respectively. An attempt at integrating social and ecological perspectives (*cf.* Rotello, 1997) is also found in Clift and Forrest's account of gay tourism and sexual risk. Clearly, further work is needed to promote cross-disciplinary communication and collaboration in relation to tourism and sexuality. Social scientists and tourism specialists could benefit in their work from a grasp of the principles and insights coming from epidemiological and bio-medical perspectives, and, equally, epidemiological modelling and studies of bio-medical dimensions of sexually transmitted infections could be informed by the findings from social science and tourism research. Such cross-disciplinary collaboration can only be of benefit in the planning and realization of sexual health promotion initiatives targeting travellers and tourists.

Why study the interconnections between tourism and sex?

Finally, the most basic question we can ask with respect to tourism and sex is why should it be a focus of interest and study? What justifies devoting a book to this issue? Interestingly, only a few of the contributors to this volume address this question in detail, with most taking it for granted that the issue is an important one. The question 'why' in relation to tourism and sex can be posed within a number of distinct discourses and with respect to a diverse range of specific problematics which emerge within different disciplines. At least three separate, though interconnected, discourses can be distinguished: a theoretical-empirical discourse, a public health discourse and a moral/human rights discourse.

First, the varied phenomena of sexuality within the context of travel and tourism are of theoretical-empirical interest, in diverse ways, depending upon the disciplinary perspective adopted. Many specific questions can be posed regarding tourism and sex, and answers sought in terms of an interaction between conceptual frameworks and empirical data. Principal questions include the following. Why has sex tourism arisen in certain destinations? Why is sex tourism so predominantly a male pursuit? Why have holidays and sex become so closely associated in the popular imagination? When people travel are their patterns of sexual behaviour and risk different when compared with their behaviour at home? Why do some people seek sex on holiday and others do not? What factors are associated with sexual risk-taking among travellers/tourists? What contributions have travel and tourism made to the global spread of sexually transmitted infections? Who profits from sex industries and sex tourism? Many of these questions are addressed by the contributors to this volume. As Hart and Hawkes point out, questions of interest pertaining to sociological factors and sexual behaviour/risk can be regarded as operating at a macro-, meso- and micro-social level. For Sánchez Taylor and O'Connell Davidson, historical and economic factors involving issues of race and gender are of particular importance in understanding the commodification of sexuality in tourism contexts. The significance of individual factors of motivation, attitudes, general dispositions towards risk, alcohol and drug use are also highlighted in other contributions (e.g. Bloor *et al.*, Khan *et al.* and Thomas).

A second answer to why the connections between sex and tourism attract interest draws upon an epidemiological, public health discourse. Given that travel in its diverse forms is assumed to be a significant factor in the geographic spread of sexual infections, it is important to establish the extent of sexual risk behaviour in the context of travel, and the factors associated with it, as a basis for the development of effective interventions to prevent infection. This approach is most explicitly elaborated in the contribution by Bloor *et al.*, who make it clear that until their survey, no large-scale research had been undertaken on the basis of representative samples to establish the extent of sexual activity during travel. The remarkable and important aspect of their findings is that the incidence of sexual activity among a young population of unaccompanied travellers is fairly low, and perhaps lower than one might expect in view of the kind of media coverage given to sex on holiday. Of course, such surveys provide a very broad picture on a population basis, and as other contributions make clear, such research needs to be supplemented by more detailed surveys of potentially key target groups for prevention initiatives (e.g. gay men and young people on package holidays specifically geared to a 'singles' market), who appear to engage in higher levels of sexual activity. In addition, such prevention-oriented surveys can provide valuable information on the contextual, social and psychological factors associated with sexual activity and risk during travel, which may serve to refine the planning and targeting of interventions (see also Arvidson *et al.*, 1997; Bloor *et al.*, 1998; Clift *et al.*, 1998; Clift and Forrest, 1999). Such quantitative surveys need, however, to be further supplemented by qualitative studies exploring issues of context and meaning in relation to sex during travel. As Thomas shows in her contribution to this volume, for example, aspects of behaviour such as alcohol consumption, which may emerge from quantitative studies as a factor generally facilitating sexual activity on holiday, may well in certain circumstances render such activity less likely. To date, a number of significant initiatives have been undertaken to promote sexual safety among travellers and tourists, but as Mulhall (1996) argues, 'worldwide, sexual health promotion for travellers is in its infancy' with a focus simply on providing information and advice. In future, he believes, more attention is needed to the planning of interventions which are carefully evaluated with respect to process and outcome.

The third answer to why tourism and sex attracts research and public interest draws upon a discourse of morality and human rights. As Ryan makes clear in his contribution to this volume, there are many ways in which travel/tourism and sex interact, and very distinct manifestations of this connection. Some of these manifestations, involving under-age children, for example, clearly constitute serious forms of exploitation and abuse and an assault on fundamental human rights. Some research in this field is fundamentally motivated, therefore, not by an interest in theoretical understandings of cultural values and assumptions, of social organization or the determinants of individual patterns of behaviour, but by a determination to combat and eradicate the more extreme and unacceptable manifestations of sexual behaviour in the context of travel and tourism.

As we move along the diagonal axis that Ryan proposes, however, the primary issues related to values change and become more contentious. While child sex tourism may be readily condemned, are all forms of sex tourism to be regarded as morally objectionable? Is prostitution connected to tourism, and even prostitution *per se* invariably a bad thing, as Jeffreys

(1998) so powerfully argues? To what extent is tourism directly or indirectly 'responsible' for the growth of prostitution in particular destinations, or is tourism of marginal significance in this respect in some cases (see Harrison's (1994) discussion of prostitution in Swaziland)? What impact does tourist demand for prostitution have on the social fabric of local communities, especially in Third World tourism destinations? Such questions are unavoidably value-laden and are intimately connected with more general concerns regarding the ethics of tourism, the impact of tourism on local environments and cultural traditions, and notions of longer-term 'sustainability'.

Finally, we arrive at the other end of Ryan's proposed dimension with a sense that some interconnections between travel and sex may well be positively valued, as reflections of human autonomy and a freedom to pursue uncommitted sexual encounters in novel environments, purely for pleasure and excitement. Such pursuits feed into fantasies of romance, escape into a liminal zone, and a carnivalesque liberation from the normative constraints of 'home' (Shields, 1990). Many media representations of holidays and sex, especially for young women, reinforce this perspective and serve to normalize the idea that casual sex on holiday is not only permissible but is also to be expected, planned for and viewed positively (given, of course, that one is sensible about the physical and emotional risks). As the 1997 Durex survey of 'summer sex' revealed, substantially more young people aged 16 to 17 expected to have sexual experiences on holiday than did in a similar survey undertaken in 1996 (*Barrier Protection Digest*, 1997). But are such trends as 'innocent' as they might seem? Might not the increased sexualization of the holiday experience for young people simply increase the incidence of sexual health problems in this age group? And might not the early introduction of young men, especially, to experiences of sex on holiday provide an increased supply of clients for sex tourism destinations in the future? In other words, the general 'acceptability' of the 'sun, sea and sex' equation may well be morally questionable, not necessarily in and of itself, but by its associations within the overall complex system of interconnections between tourism and sex, its sexual health implications for tourists and local communities, and broader issues of the cultural impact on tourism-receiving communities.

Conclusion

This collection aimed to present some of the recent research work undertaken by social scientists on issues connected with tourism and sex. The work spans a broad field and takes in questions of changing cultural frameworks surrounding sexuality and sexual behaviour, the commercialization of sex in tourist settings and the more extreme manifestations of sex tourism involving the coercion and exploitation of women and children. The coverage is not comprehensive. Much additional work is being pursued throughout the world on this subject, as papers presented in recent conferences (e.g. Jeffreys, 1998; Mårdh, 1998; Carter, 1998b) and the contributions to a recent collection which appeared as this volume was going to press (Oppermann, 1998) attest. The issues raised are challenging to social scientists, medical specialists and epidemiologists, and are challenging, too, to the tourism industry, national governments and international agencies concerned with health, work, women's issues and human rights. Further research on the intersections of tourism, sexuality, sexual behaviour and sexual health is needed, and more concerted efforts are needed in the field of sexual health promotion in the context of international travel and tourism. Our hope is that this volume will contribute to greater communication and stronger networking among researchers interested in this area who are currently working within different disciplines and in different parts of the world.

References

Abdullah, A. S. M. (1996) Cross-border travel and HIV/AIDS risk among travellers in Hong Kong. *Travel Medicine NewsShare*, 4th Quarter.
Aitchison, C. and Reeves, C. (1998) Gendered (bed)spaces: the culture and commerce of women only tourism. In C. Aitchison and F. Jordan (eds), *Gender, Space and Identity*. Brighton: Leisure Studies Association.
Aldrich, R. (1993) *The Seduction of the Mediterranean: Writing, Art and Homosexual Fantasy*. London: Routledge.
Annetts, J., Eisenstadt, K. and Gatter, P. (1996) *Lambeth, Southwark and Lewisham's Gay and Bisexual Men's HIV Prevention Service Review and Social Mapping* Project. London: The HIV Project.
Arvidson, M., Kallings, I., Nilsson, S., Hellberg, D. and Mårdh, P.-A. (1997) Risky behavior in women with history of casual travel sex. *Sexually Transmitted Diseases* **24** (7), 418–21.
Barrier Protection Digest (1997) More young adults regard sex as part of their holiday enjoyment. *Barrier Protection Digest* **2** (3), 8.
Bloor, M., Thomas, M., Hood, K., Abeni, D., Goujon, C., Hausser, D., Hubert, M., Kleiber, D. and Neito, J. A. (1998) Differences in sexual risk behaviour between young men and women travelling abroad from the UK. *The Lancet* **352** (21), 1664–8.
Bröring, G. (1996) International tourists: a specific target group for AIDS prevention programmes. In S. Clift and S. Page (eds), *Health and the International Tourist*. London: Routledge.
Bröring, G. (1997) Prostitution, intravenous drug use and travel: European HIV/AIDS prevention initiatives. In S. Clift and P. Grabowski (eds), *Tourism and Health: Risks, Research and Responses*. London: Pinter.
Brown, M. (1995) Ironies of distance: an ongoing critique of the geographies of AIDS. *Environment and Planning* **13**, 159–183.
Burnell, C., Dale, R., Dockrell, M., Fisher, J., Platt, M. and Rawlinson, P. (1995) *1995*

Hampstead Heath Report. London: Gay Men Fighting AIDS.

Callister, C. (1998) Holiday romance. *DIVA*, August, p. 24.

Carter, S. (1995) Places of danger and places of safety: travellers' social construction of risky locations in relation to HIV/AIDS. In D. Friedrich and W. Heckmann (eds), *Aids in Europe – The Behavioural Aspect. Volume 2: Risk Behaviour and Its Determinants*. Berlin: Edition Sigma.

Carter, S. (1998a) Tourists' and travellers' social construction of Africa and Asia as risky locations. *Tourism Management* **19** (4), 349–58.

Carter, S. (1998b) Levels of uncertainty among Europeans about 'sex tourism' involving children: an analysis of the Eurobarometer Survey. First European Meeting of the Main Protagonists in the Fight against Child Sex Tourism, Brussels Travel Fair, 24–26 November, Brussels.

CDR (1997) Sexually transmitted diseases quarterly report: syphilis in England and Wales. *Communicable Diseases Reports Weekly* **7** (22), 192–4.

Clift, S. (1994) *Romance and Sex on Holidays Abroad: A Study of Magazine Representations*. Travel, Lifestyles and Health Project Working Paper No. 4. Canterbury: Canterbury Christ Church College (unpublished report).

Clift, S., Callister, C. and Luongo, M. (1999) *Gay Men, Holidays and Sex: Findings from Surveys Conducted at the London Gay and Lesbian Travel Fairs 1997–98*. Canterbury: Centre for Health Education and Research.

Clift, S. M. and Forrest, S. P. (1999) Factors associated with gay men's sexual behaviours and risk on holiday. *AIDS Care* (in press).

Clift, S., Forrest, S., Callister, C. and Luongo, M. (1998) *Travel-Related HIV Prevention Work with Gay and Bisexual Men*. Canterbury: Centre for Health Education and Research, Canterbury Christ Church University College (unpublished report).

Cossens, J. and Gin, S. (1994) Tourism and AIDS: the perceived risk of HIV infection on destination choice. *Journal of Travel and Tourism Marketing* **3** (4), 1–20.

De Schryver, A. and Meheus, A. (1989) International travel and sexually transmitted diseases. *World Health Statistical Quarterly* **42**, 90–9.

De Wit, J. B. F., de Vroome, E. M. M., Sandfort, T. G. M. and van Griensven, G. J. P. (1997) Homosexual encounters in different venues. *International Journal of STD and AIDS* **8**, 130–4.

European Project AIDS and Mobility (1996) *Mobility, Prostitution and HIV Prevention in Central/Eastern and Western Europe: Report of the Workshop in Szczecin, 26 to 28 June 1996*. Woerden: NIGZ.

Eurosurveillance (1996) Increase in syphilis in Finland related to the Russian epidemic. *Eurosurveillance* **1** (1), 1–2.

Ford, N. and Eiser, R. (1996) Risk and liminality: the HIV-related socio-sexual interaction of young tourists. In S. Clift and S. Page (eds), *Health and the International Tourist*. London: Routledge.

Ford, N., Inman, M. and Mathie, E. (1996) Interaction to enhance mindfulness: positive strategies to increase tourists' awareness of HIV and sexual health risks on holiday. In S. Clift and S. Page (eds), *Health and the International Tourist*. London: Routledge.

Goldberg, D. J., Frishcer, M., Taylor, A., Green, S. T., McKeganey, N., Bloor, M., Reid, D. and Cossar, J. (1994) Mobility of Scottish injecting drug users and risk of HIV infection. *European Journal of Epidemiology* **10** (4), 387–92.

Hall, C. M. (1996) Sex tourism in South-east Asia. In D. Harrison (ed.), *Tourism and the Less Developed Countries*. London: Belhaven Press.

Hanson, J. (1997) Sex tourism as work in New Zealand: a discussion with Kiwi prostitutes. In M. Oppermann (ed.), *Pacific Rim Tourism*. Wallingford, CT: CAB International.

Harrison, D. (1994) Tourism and prostitution: sleeping with the enemy? *Tourism Management* **15** (6), 435–43.

Herold, E. S. and van Kerkwijk, C. (1992) AIDS and sex tourism. *AIDS and Society: International Research and Policy Bulletin* **4** (1), 1, 8–9.

Howorth, P. (1977) *When the Riviera Was Ours*. London: Routledge and Kegan Paul.

Hufton, O. (1995) *The Prospect before Her: A History of Women in Western Europe. Volume One 1500–1800*. London: HarperCollins.

Hughes, H. (1997) Holidays and homosexual identity. *Tourism Management* **18** (1), 3–7.

Hughes, H. (1998) Sexuality, tourism and space: the case of gay visitors to Amsterdam. In D. Tyler, M. Robertson and Y. Guerrier (eds), *Managing Tourism in Cities: Policy, Process and Practice*. New York: Wiley.

Hyam, R. (1990) *Empire and Sexuality: The British Experience*. Manchester: Manchester University Press.

International Organization for Migration (1995) *Trafficking and Prostitution: The Growing Exploitation of Migrant Women from Central and Eastern Europe*. Budapest: Migration Information Programme.

Ireland, K. (1993) *'Wish You Weren't Here': The Sexual Exploitation of Children and the Connection with Tourism and International Travel*. Working Paper No. 7. London: Save the Children.

Jeffreys, S. (1998) Globalising sexual exploitation: sex tourism and the traffic in women. Paper presented at The Fourth International Conference of the Leisure Studies Association, Leeds, UK, July.

Jordan, F. (1998) Shirley Valentine: where are you? In C. Aitchison and F. Jordan (eds), *Gender, Space and Identity*. Brighton: Leisure Studies Association.

Kalikova, N., Vessin, T., Melesko, L. and Kalikov, J. (1998) Prostitution in Estonia. Poster presented at the XIth International AIDS Conference, Geneva, July.

Kelley, P., Peabody, R. and Scott, P. (1996) *How Far Will You Go? A Survey of London Gay Men's Migration and Mobility*. London: Gay Men Fighting AIDS.

Kemper, C. A., Linett, A., Kane, C. and Deresinski, S. C. (1994) Frequency of travel of adults infected with HIV. *Journal of Travel Medicine* **2**, 85–8.

Keogh, P., Holland, P. and Weatherburn, P. (1998) *The Boys in the Backroom: Anonymous Sex among Gay and Bisexual Men*. London: Sigma Research.

Kleiber, D. and Wilke, M. (1995) AIDS and sex-tourism conclusions drawn from a study of the social and psychological characteristics of German sex-tourists. In D. Friedrich and W. Heckmann (eds), *Aids in Europe – the Behavioural Aspect. Volume 2: Risk Behaviour and Its Determinants*. Berlin: Edition Sigma.

Larcerda, R., Stall, R., Gravato, N., Tellini, R., Hudes, E. S. and Hearst, N. (1996) HIV infection and risk behaviours among male port workers in Santos, Brazil. *American Journal of Public Health* **86** (8), 1158–60.

Mårdh, P.-A. (1998) Changing pattern of travelling in Europe with new pathways for spread of sexually transmitted infections. Paper presented at 'Mobility and Health: From Hominid Migration to Mass Tourism', European Conference on

Travel Medicine, Venice, March.

Marshment, M. (1997) Gender takes a holiday: representations in holiday brochures. In M. T. Sinclair (ed.), *Gender, Work and Tourism*. London: Routledge.

McCoy, H. V., Correa, R. and Fritz, E. (1996) HIV diffusion patterns and mobility: gender differences among drug users. *Population Research and Policy Review* **15**, 249–64.

Mulhall, B. P. (1993) Sexually transmissible diseases and travel. *British Medical Bulletin* **49** (2), 394–411.

Mulhall, B. P. (1996) Sex and travel: studies of sexual behaviour, disease and health promotion in international travellers – a global review. *International Journal of STD and AIDS* **7** (7), 455–65.

Mulhall, B. P., Hu, M., Thompson, M., Lin, F., Lupton, D., Mills, D., Maund, M., Cass, R. and Millar, D. (1993) Planned sexual behaviour of young Australian visitors to Thailand. *Medical Journal of Australia* **158**, 530–5.

Myslik, W. D. (1996) Renegotiating the social/sexual identities of places: gay communities as safe havens or sites of resistance? In N. Duncan (ed.), *BodySpace: Destabilizing Geographies of Gender and Sexuality*. London: Routledge.

Nasioulas, G., Paraskevis, D., Paparizos, V., Lazanas, M., Karafoulidou, A. and Hatzakis, A. (1998) Genotypic characterization of human immunodeficiency virus type 1 in Greece. *AIDS Research and Human Retroviruses* **14** (8), 685–90.

Netzelmann, R. (1995) Analysis of border issues with regard to HIV/AIDS and STDs, and development of cooperative, border-crossing methods of prevention. In D. Friedrich and W. Heckmann (eds), *Aids in Europe – The Behavioural Aspect Volume 1: General Aspects*. Berlin: Edition Sigma.

Oppermann, M. (ed.) (1998) *Sex Tourism*. New York: Cognizant Press.

Oppermann, M. and McKinley, S. (1997) Sexual imagery in the marketing of Pacific tourism destinations. In M. Oppermann (ed.), *Pacific Rim Tourism*. Wallingford, CT: CAB International.

Pemble, J. (1987) *The Mediterranean Passion: Victorians and Edwardians in the South*. Oxford: Clarendon Press.

Pritchard, A., Morgan, N. J., Sedgley, D. and Jenkins, A (1998) Gay tourism destinations: identity, sponsorship and degaying. In C. Aitchison and F. Jordan (eds), *Gender, Space and Identity*. Brighton: Leisure Studies Association.

Quinn, T. C. (1994) Population migration and the spread of types 1 and 2 human immunodeficiency viruses. *Proceedings of the National Academy of Sciences USA* **91**, 2407–14.

Rotello, G. (1997) *Sexual Ecology: AIDS and the Destiny of Gay Men*. New York: Dutton.

Shaw, G. and Williams, A. M. (1994) *Critical Issues in Tourism: A Geographical Perspective*. Oxford: Blackwell.

Shields, R. (1990) The system of pleasure: liminality and the carnivalesque at Brighton. *Theory, Culture and Society* **7**, 39–72.

Stears, D. (1996) Travel health promotion: advances and alliances. In S. Clift and S. Page (eds), *Health and the International Tourist*. London: Routledge.

Steffen, E. and Leopold, B. (1995) Border-crossing area prostitution and risk of HIV. In D. Friedrich and W. Heckmann (eds), *Aids in Europe – the Behavioural Aspect. Volume 2: Risk Behaviour and Its Determinants*. Berlin: Edition Sigma.

Taar, M. and Kalikova, N. (1995) Prostitution in Estonia – a 'new' old problem. In D. Friedrich and W. Heckmann (eds), *Aids in Europe – the Behavioural Aspect*.

Volume 2: Risk Behaviour and Its Determinants. Berlin: Edition Sigma.

Thomas, L., Clift, S. and Madden, V. (1997) The Europe against AIDS – Summer Campaign 1995: an evaluation of work in the United Kingdom. In S. Clift and P. Grabowski (eds), *Tourism and Health: Risks, Research and Responses*. London: Pinter.

Thomas, R. (1996) Modelling space-time HIV/AIDS dynamics: applications to disease control. *Social Science and Medicine* **43** (3), 353–66.

Valentine, G. (1996) (Re)negotiating the 'heterosexual street': lesbian productions of space. In N. Duncan (ed.), *BodySpace: Destabilizing Geographies of Gender and Sexuality*. London: Routledge.

van Haastrecht, H. J. A., Fennema, J. S. A., Coutinho, R. A., van der Helm, T. C. M., Kint, J. A. P. C. M. and van den Hoek, J. A. R. (1993) HIV prevalence and risk behaviour among prostitutes and clients in Amsterdam: migrants at increased risk for HIV infection. *Genitourinary Medicine* **69**, 251–6.

Wallace, R. and Wallace, D. (1997) Community marginalisation and the diffusion of disease and disorder in the United States. *British Medical Journal* **314**, 1341–5.

Wallace, R., Huang, Y., Gould, P. and Wallace, D. (1997) The hierarchical diffusion of AIDS and violent crime among US metropolitan areas: inner city decay, stochastic resonance and the reversal of the mortality transition. *Social Science and Medicine* **44**, 935–47.

WTO (1998) *Tourism Highlights 1997*. Madrid: World Tourism Organization.

Yamba, C. B. (1988) Getting attached. Paper presented at the GAPP Conference on Tourism, Froebel College, Roehampton Institute, London 22–23 April.

Name index

Subject index